MW00491414

DANIEL DREW. CORNELIUS VANDERBILT.

L.W. JEROME. JACOB LITTLE.

CELEBRITIES OF WALL STREET.

TEN YEARS IN WALL STREET

TEN YEARS

IN

WALL STREET;

OR, REVELATIONS OF

Inside Life and Experience on 'Change.

INCLUDING THE

HISTORIES, MYSTERIES,
AND MEN OF THE " STREET "—THE
STOCK EXCHANGE—THE GOLD ROOM—THE SPEC-
ULATIONS IN STOCKS, GOLD, GOVERNMENTS, PORK, PETRO-
LEUM, GRAIN, ETC.—SKETCHES FROM LIFE OF THE NOTED SPECU-
LATORS AND MONEY KINGS, WITH ANECDOTES AND INCIDENTS OF THEIR
CAREERS—THE WOMEN WHO SPECULATE—THE GREAT RISES AND PANICS, AND
HOW THEY ARE PRODUCED—THE PERSONAL EXPERIENCES OF THE AU-
THOR—THE FAMOUS POOLS, RINGS, CLIQUES, AND CORNERS, AND
HOW AND BY WHOM THEY WERE FORMED—A DESCRIP-
TION OF THE BATTLES OF THE GIANTS, AND OF
THE GREAT GOLD RING OF 1869,
ETC., ETC., ETC.

" All of which I Saw, and part of which I Was," since 1857.

By WM. WORTHINGTON FOWLER.

As for the chopping of bargains, when a man buys not to hold, but to sell over again, that commonly grindeth double, both upon the seller and upon the buyer.—*Bacon's Essays.*

ILLUSTRATED BY ARTHUR LUMLEY.

PUBLISHED BY
WORTHINGTON, DUSTIN & CO., HARTFORD, CONN.;
STODDARD & PARKHURST, CHICAGO ; J. D. DENISON, NEW YORK.
G. P. HAWKES, BOSTON; H. S. INMAN, PROVIDENCE.
FRANCIS DEWING & CO., SAN FRANCISCO, CAL.
J. BIGELOW & CO., PHILADELPHIA.
1 8 7 0.

Celebrities of Wall Street.

Celebrities of Wall Street.

TO THE

Hon. SALMON P. CHASE,

WHO ORGANIZED AND CONDUCTED THE FINANCES OF THE
NATION IN WAR;

TO THE

Hon. GEORGE S. BOUTWELL,

THE TREASURER OF THE NATION AT PEACE;

AND TO

CORNELIUS VANDERBILT,

WHO HAS AIDED SO POWERFULLY TO FOSTER THE STEAM INDUSTRIES
OF THE NATION ON LAND AND WATER;

THIS WORK

IS RESPECTFULLY DEDICATED,

BY THE AUTHOR.

CONTENTS.

CHAPTER I.

WALL STREET.

CHAPTER II.

THE STOCK EXCHANGE AND GOLD ROOM.

CHAPTER III.

THE FIRST VENTURE.

CHAPTER IV.

PROFIT AND LOSS.

CHAPTER V.

CORNELIUS VANDERBILT AND DANIEL DREW.

CHAPTER VI.

JOTTINGS ON THE "STREET;" DREW ON THE WAR-PATH.

CHAPTER VII.

WAR TIMES AND GREENBACKS.

CHAPTER VIII.

BULL-LEADERS.

PAGE.

CHAPTER IX.

PACIFIC MAIL AND LEONARD W. JEROME.

CHAPTER X.

"GOLD, GOLD, GOLD, GOLD,—HOARDED, BARTERED, BOUGHT AND SOLD."

CHAPTER XI.

THE FIRST GREAT HARLEM RISE.

CHAPTER XII.

THE BRIGADE OF BEARS.

CHAPTER XIII.

ANTHONY W. MORSE AND THE CHANCELLORS-VILLE RISE.

CHAPTER XIV.

"WHAT WILL HE DO WITH IT!"

CHAPTER XV.

WHAT BECAME OF IT — HENRY KEEP AND OLD SOUTHERN.

CHAPTER XVI.

OPENING THE BALL ON ROCK ISLAND.

CHAPTER XVII.

THE GREAT RISE OF 1864.

CHAPTER XVIII.

BUBBLE COMPANIES.

CHAPTER XIX.

PANIC——FALL OF A. W. MORSE——CLEARING AWAY THE WRECK.

CHAPTER XX.

MARGINS, POOLS, CORNERS, POINTS, AND OF HOW BROKERS MAKE THEIR MONEY.

CHAPTER XXI.

THE SECOND HARLEM CORNER.

CHAPTER XXII.

IN SEARCH OF A BROKER—THE GOLD-BURST UP-WARDS—DULL TIMES.

CHAPTER XXIII.

DULL TIMES—AVERAGING ON "POINTS."

CHAPTER XXIV.

THE BREAK IN GOLD—PANIC-BIRDS.

CHAPTER XXV.

PIGS OF GOLD IN A CORNER.

CHAPTER XXVI.

THE WORSHIPERS OF THE GOLDEN CALF.

CHAPTER XXVII.

ASTRAND AND AFLOAT AGAIN.

CHAPTER XXVIII.

DREW PLAYS ON HIS ONE-STRINGED LYRE—ERIE.

2

CHAPTER XXIX.

FEMALE SPECULATORS.

CHAPTER XXX.

THE FORTUNES OF A COUNTRYMAN.

CHAPTER XXXI.

WOODWARD, FISK, JR., GOULD.

CHAPTER XXXII.

THE BATTLE OF THE GIANTS.

Ten Years in Wall Street.

CHAPTER I.

WALL STREET.

Popular Ideas of Wall Street—The Memories it Awakens—Its Annals—
The Centre of Speculation—The Money Forces—Riches with Wings
—Different Classes of Speculators—Bulls and Bears—The "Long"
and "Short" of it—Pools, Rings and Cliques—How they are
Formed—Bears in a "Corner"—The Kings and Satraps of the Mar-
ket—"Puts and Calls," what are they?—The Ghosts of the Street
—A Speculator's Life—The Close of a Misspent Career.

APITAL flows into reservoirs as naturally as
rivers flow into the ocean. These reservoirs
are in the great commercial cities. Venice
had its Rialto, where of old, high rates of usance were
taken, and ducats passed briskly from hand to hand;
London has its Lombard Street; Boston has its State
Street, and New York has its Wall Street. This last
is something more than a thoroughfare lined with
buildings, along which men and vehicles pass and
repass. It is an idea or rather a bundle of ideas
which take various shapes more or less definite in
the minds of men when they hear the name sounded.
To the merchant and banker it is a financial centre, collecting and distributing money, regulating

the exchanges of a continent and striking balances
of trade with London and Frankfort. To the outside observer and novice it is a kind of work-shop
thronged by cunning artisans who work in precious
metals, where vessels of gold and vessels of silver
are wrought or made to shine with fresh lustre, and
where old china is fire-gilt as good as new. The
moralist and philosopher look upon it as a gambling-
den,—a cage of unclean birds, an abomination where
men drive a horrible trade, fattening and battening
on the substance of their friends and neighbors,—or
perhaps as a kind of modern coliseum where gladiatorial combats are joined, and bulls, bears and other
ferocious beasts gore and tear each other for the public
amusement. The brokers regard it as a place of
business where, in mercantile parlance, they may ply
a legitimate trade, buying and selling for others on
commission. To the speculators it is a caravansera
where they may load or unload their camels and
drive them away betimes to some pleasant oasis. To
the financial commanders it is an arsenal in which
their arms and chariots are stored, the stronghold to
be defended or besieged, the field for strategy, battles
and plunder. All these ideas and a multitude of
others, more or less true, rise up at the mention of
Wall Street.

It has its memories, too. Bright as it is with glass
and gilding, and festooned with column, capital and
cornice of granite, freestone and marble, clean cut
and fresh as of yesterday, still it has a color of gray
antiquity. More than two centuries of years have
come and gone and "changed the blood and made the
frame" of seven generations of Aryan men who have

trod this street. It dates back, the antiquarians tell us, to the year 1653, for its first survey was in the palmy days of Petrus Stuyvesant when Schouts Burgomasters and Schepens lorded it over the little colony of New Amsterdam. Its name (one of the few remaining landmarks of the early Dutch possession,) was derived from the wall or *cingle* built of palisades and earth on the northern line of the street to ward off the aborigines, and also possibly the aggressive Yankee from the east. This fortified wall extended on the northerly side of the street, from Broadway to Pearl Street, which was then washed by the tides of Oost or East River. It had its dry ditches, and its embrasures; its lower end was terminated by a half circular redoubt, and through its land-gate on Broadway, and its water-gate by the river, herds of cattle were driven every night from the woods and pastures to the north, in which we are informed by the same veracious antiquarians, *bears* and other wild beasts abounded. On this same street, when the Salt-mountain or some other broad-beamed ship came in from the Scheldt—the Holland merchants drove a lively trade with the red man, bartering beads and cloth of Leyden for peltries of the beaver and otter.

But what contrasts has the light of two hundred years painted between the mimic life of New Amsterdam and this great roaring, serious, tragic Babylon of to-day. No sign now of the quaint, peaked roofs covered with Dutch tiles, the fort flying the blue lions of Holland, the old stockade and half moon embankment at its lower end. No trace now of the sturdy Netherland soldier with pike or musquetoon. But the ancient name of Wall Street still remains. That name is something more than a shadow, too, for it is in fact *Wall* Street, still lined with a succession of fortresses, behind whose bastions are garrisons well disciplined and alert, guarding the treasures, if not the lives of a nation. Within its casemates and vaults lie piles of coin, enough to excite the cupidity of ten West India companies, or to lade a hundred Spanish galleons. Here the forces of commerce silently gather and equip themselves for distant expeditions, from which they return again with the spoils of "Ormus and of Ind." In these strongholds terms are dictated to the vanquished, and treaties made. Here in niches, and on many a buttress and "coigne of vantage," the fledglings of finance make "their pendent bed and procreant cradle." Towering over all stands old Trinity, like a giant sentry, day and night, clashing out in peals and chimes of bells from his watch-tower, "all's well."

Speaking financially, the annals of Wall Street are brief; but brief though they be, they are crowded with forms and faces, full of notable incidents and varied with all the lights and shadows that flare and disappear in the passing careers of a thousand eager money-getters. As through one camera, they concentrate a picture of the material progress of the nation towards wealth, its daring enterprises, its steady industries, its wild speculations, its sharp commercial crises, and all the myriad transformations of financial life. Of its story early in the present century, only faint echoes come back to us. The names of the old merchants who went down to the sea in ships, and of the money changers and high treasurers who, in those days, were wont to come into the street to draw from or deposit in the United States Bank, the Manhattan Company, or Bank of New York, to inquire for the quotations or exchange views on the state of the market, are almost forgotten, but moving about among these phantom groups, we recognize the stateliest figure of all—that of Alexander Hamilton. Then we see new banks set up and operations slowly widening through the terms of five Presidents.

But it is only within the past thirty-five years that *Wall Street* has got to have a special significance as the centre, not only of money but of speculation. From 1835 to 1870 a series of great inflations and correspondent depressions occurring there furnish the most protracted, singular and striking chapter in the annals of finance.

The history of nations is a history of wars of conquest. The temple of Janus in old Rome was shut but twice in a thousand years. The history of finance is a history of the rise and fall of values, in other words, of speculations and panics. Wall Street is our temple of Janus. The lust of money is as strong as the lust of dominion, and avarice, like its nobler brother, ambition, "scorns delights and lives laborious days."

Other analogies exist between wars and speculation. Campaigns are planned, and strategy displayed on 'change as well as on the tented field. Wall Street has its plots and counterplots, its dashing assaults, and stout defences. He who enters that arena must be armed cap-a-pie, and cunning in all the tricks of fence. The bank account of the stock operator is his martello tower, to be defended against all kind of attacks, secret as well as open, mine, storming and escalade. He must look well to his out-works, man his parapet by day and night for the besiegers will surely press him hard. His bank account must furnish him also with weapons of offense and defense, for money is the sinews of speculation as well as of war.

The strength of Wall Street then may be said to lie in a figure three with eight ciphers after it, for this is the money balance of the banks and other depositories. Three hundred million dollars.

That massive pile of light freestone, with fluted doric columns, abutting on three streets and overlooking the Broad Street arena where the strong and nimble athletes of the Stock Exchange exercise their muscles and air their lungs, that is the Sub-Treasury so famous in the story of American Finance. It is the fly-wheel in the engine of trade accumulating and regulating the money forces. Its vaults hold ninety millions of specie and a sum in currency varying at different times from ten to thirty millions. Within rifle shot of this building are five-sixths of the banking institutions of New York City, whose daily deposits rise in flush times to one hundred and ninety millions. But these latter are overshadowed and dominated by the Sub-Treasury, the monster depository on which only the treasurer of the nation is permitted to draw. Through its gates, streams flow in and out, to deepen and broaden the river of commerce, or heighten the torrent of speculation.

In noting the prominent features of Wall Street, it will be remarked how strongly the idea of *negotiability* is there brought out. All the principal values of commerce are in this mart represented by so many paper certificates. The goods and credit of the merchant are represented by promissory notes, which are bought and sold, and pass from hand to hand, almost like bank-bills. Cotton, pork, grain, sugar, tobacco, and a thousand other bulky and gross products are represented under the form of warehouse certificates. The wealth of banks, of railway corporations, and of many other stock companies, are floating about under the guise of certificates, and to the very gold in the vaults of the Treasury, wings are given, and coin and bullion fly in notes of yellow and green.

What is the easiest mode of exchange and barter? this is the first inquiry in the operations of trade, and Wall Street has answered it. Those diaphanous slips of paper representing untold riches, pass from hand to hand, as fast as words can utter their value. The money lender can count his millions on a table three feet square, or inclose them in a bank-box not much larger than a family Bible or a Webster's Unabridged.

It is difficult to conceive of Wall Street values apart from the idea of their negotiability. Will a piece of property pass current at a market price? will it be transferred with little trouble? then is it a suitable object of purchase and sale.

The ease and swiftness with which securities change owners produce, of course, a vast volume of business, and profits or losses are duplicated with corresponding swiftness and ease.

Money and values represented on paper, are the passive forces; men who buy and sell or "operate," are the active forces of trade.

What constitutes a State ? inquires the poet:

> " Not high raised battlement or labored mound,
>   Thick wall or moated gate * * * *
>   No! *Men.*" * * *

So we might inquire what constitutes a street?—certainly Wall Street—not the granite pavements nor the long piles of masonry covering stores of uncounted wealth, but the *men* who throng this thoroughfare and keep the machinery of commerce and speculation in motion.

Wall Street, viewed as an aggregation of trading humanity, may be divided into two great classes. First, the *speculators*, or as they are pleased to term themselves, *operators*, who buy or sell stocks at their own risk of loss or expectation of profit. Second, the *brokers*, who buy and sell for others in consideration of a fixed commission. All those who deal in the street, may be said to belong to the first class; for there is hardly one of the brokers who does not speculate, directly or indirectly, but there are many of the speculators who, themselves, never buy or sell, but employ the brokers to do it for them. A broker is almost necessarily a speculator, but a speculator is not necessarily a broker. We shall at present describe only the speculators, reserving the brokers for a separate chapter.

A speculator is called a "bull" or a "bear," according to his interest in the market. A bull buys stock for a rise, and the term may be derived from his likeness to the animal of the bovine genus who tosses upwards with his horns. He is said to be "long" of stocks, because he is presumed to always hold his stock ready for their delivery on sale.

A "bear" is one who sells stocks for future delivery, which he does not own at the time of sale. In other words, he contracts to deliver stocks at a fixed price and within a fixed time. If stocks should fall during the continuance of the contract, he buys them in the market at the reduced prices, and delivers them to the party to whom he agreed to sell them at the contract price. The difference between the two prices is his profit. To illustrate this operation, suppose A agree to sell to B one hundred shares of New York Central at 180, deliverable at any time at the option of A, within thirty days, A not having the one hundred shares at the time the contract is made. If the price of the stock falls to 170, A buys it at that price in the open market, and delivers it to B, who pays him 180, the contract price, at a *profit* to A of 10 per cent. on the shares, *i. e.*, $1,000. But if the price rises to 190, and A is obliged to complete his contract, he buys it at that figure and delivers it to B, who pays him 180, entailing in this manner a *loss* of $1,000 on A.

The name "bear" is said to have been first given, at the time of the South Sea Bubble, to such persons as were operating to depress stocks, because they were acting the part of a man who would kill a bear for the sake of his skin. As a bull is said to be "long" of stocks, so a bear is said to be "short" of stocks, just as a person who has no money is said to be "short of funds." The bear has no stock when he offers to sell, but merely contracts to deliver what he does not possess, and is of course interested in depressing the market so that he may fill his contracts at lower prices, just as the bull is interested in raising stocks, so that he may profit by the increased market value of the stocks which he holds.

Two forces, it should be noted, are all the while acting in the commercial world growing out of a great variety of causes which we will not now pause to enumerate. One is a projectile force, sending values upward; the other, a kind of financial gravitation, carrying values downwards. The effect of these forces respectively, the bulls and bears, seek to heighten and turn to their own profit. A community of interest begets a community of action, and so the bulls often unite to raise the value of particular stocks, and form those combinations known in the "Street" as "cliques," "rings" or "pools,"—terms nearly synonymous,—their object being to elevate the price of stocks by owning a controlling interest and *making a market price* so that they can unload at a large advance on the price at which they bought.

These cliques, rings and pools in stocks answer to the combinations which are termed monopolies in the staple articles of commerce, such as grain, rice, sugar and tobacco. They buy up the floating supply and then satisfy the demand at the price which they choose to impose. Suppose A, B and C have contracted to deliver five thousand shares of a certain stock which they do not hold, and D, E and F hold all the stock in question, obviously, A, B and C must, in order to fulfill their contracts, buy the five thousand shares of D, E and F at whatever price they choose to sell it. In this case A, B and C, who are "bears," are "cornered" by D, E and F, who make up, we will suppose, the "bull ring."

A ring is formed thus: When money is easy, and

the financial future bright, some shrewd operator casts about for a stock, (generally railway,) which is selling at a fair, or still better, a low price in the market. The whole amount of stock issued is, we will say, fifty thousand shares of one hundred dollars each, that is, five million dollars at par. But half of this amount is held abroad or in the hands of investors at home, and will not therefore be likely to come on the market. This leaves two millions and a half, or twenty-five thousand shares of stock floating about the market, and this is the amount which must be bought by the proposed ring if it would be thoroughly successful in its results. After consultation with some other noted operator or operators, the scheme is framed and a paper drawn up which will read something like this, viz.:

We, the subscribers, in consideration of our mutual promises, hereby agree to buy the number of shares of stock of the —— Railroad Company set opposite to our names, respectively. That we authorize Martin & Son to buy said stock, and we promise to pay to Martin & Son, in order to secure them against loss which may arise in carrying said stock, ten per cent. of the market value of the shares which said firm are to buy for our account respectively, and they are authorized to sell and re-purchase the same to the best of their judgment, and to receive one eighth per cent. commission on all purchases, sales and re-purchases. We, the subscribers, agreeing to use our best efforts to aid in raising the price of said stock, and not to deal therein on our account, until said joint account is closed (or we are to be at liberty to deal in said stock at our option).

Signed	MARTIN & SON,	5,000 shares.
	W. S. WOODWORTH,	5,000 shares.
	JAMES STEWART,	5,000 shares.
	JOSEPH MILLER,	5,000 shares.
	CHARLES P. CURRIER,	5,000 shares.
	&c., &c., &c.	

The ring, or, as it is sometimes called, the *party*, having been made up, they proceed to buy the stock. Two pre-requisites are necessary to every successful ring; first, secrecy, second, simulation. The buying of the stock must be done under cover, and often occupies several months. Every possible method is taken to deceive those who are outside the ring, and prevent them from supposing that the stock is passing under the control of the party who are manipulating it. Sometimes the stock is made to assume a weakness, as though it would drop several per cent., and all sorts of reports are set afloat to depreciate its value. This is done to induce sales. As it slowly rises, more stock is brought out for sale, by holders who are tempted by the enhanced price, all of which is quietly bought by the party and laid away. The bears are meanwhile making contracts for the future delivery of the stock to the " ring." Some of these contracts are in the form of sellers' options for thirty and sixty days, during which period the bear or seller has the privilege of delivering a certain amount of stock at a fixed price. But most of these "short contracts" are made as follows, viz.: A sells a lot of stock, which he does not possess, to B, and borrows it from C, for delivery to B. A will then owe the stock to C, who can call for it at any time, and A is thus "short" of the stock to the amount which he has agreed to deliver. The ring will gladly buy the stock of the bears, and loan it to them for delivery, because in this way they create a demand for the stock, which they alone can supply. It will be readily seen that if the bears have contracted to deliver a large number of shares, so that the market is in the condition termed "over sold," a firmness is created in the price, owing to the constant demand on the part of the bears, for stock to complete their contracts.

This state of affairs is heightened as the ring goes on getting a firmer grip of the stock, and as the bears become more courageous in putting out their contracts, owing to the opportunities for making money by a fall, which the higher price of the stock naturally suggests to them.

Many devices are resorted to by the ring to induce short sales by the bears. The stock held by them is offered to the bears as a loan on easy terms, and when they sell the borrowed stock, the ring buy the very stock they have just loaned. When the stock price has risen from 20 to 40 per cent. it suddenly grows scarce. The bears find themselves troubled to make their deliveries. Now the ring prepare to "twist" their antagonists. A favorable day is selected when everything looks bright and sunny in the financial world, a plausible report, relative to the prospects of the Railroad Company, whose stock is under the control of the ring, is noised abroad, and different brokers are employed to bid up the price in the market in order to frighten the bears, and at the same time they are notified to deliver the stock which they have borrowed of the ring. Thus, the bears are compelled to "cover," that is, to close their contracts by buying and delivering the stock, which the ring alone can sell them. Sometimes, instead of buying the stock, the bears "settle" with the ring by paying them the difference between the market price and the lower price, at which they contracted to deliver it.

3

In that case, the ring find themselves saddled with a large amount of stock, for which there is little demand. And now the problem is to unload. Accordingly, they sell enough stock to "break" the market 4 or 5 per cent. downwards. The bears rush in and sell at the lowered price. When the ring have taken a sufficient number of their contracts, they bid the stock up again, and compel the bears again to cover. Every time the stock rises sharply, it has such an appearance of strength on the rising slide, that many of the outside bulls are tempted into buying, and then sell out at a loss, when the stock declines. The ring, to use a Wall Street phrase in this way, "milk the street," taking money out of the bears, who sell at a low price, and out of the bulls, who buy at a high price. This game is played for many weeks, and sometimes months, until the ring have disposed of their stock, and can reckon their profits.

The culmination in the operations of a ring, such as we have been describing, is technically called a "corner," because the bears are unable to deliver the stock they owe, and are so said to be driven into a "corner." The history of the "street," for the past thirty-five years, is one constant succession of these "corners," in which great fortunes have risen and fallen, like the waves on a stormy sea. Among the more remarkable of these corners, may be mentioned that in Canton, 1834 and 1835, when it sold up, from 60, its par value, to 300; that in Harlem, in 1864, which carried the price to 285, and that in Prairie du Chien, in 1865, which sold in three months, from 40 to 250.

Nearly all those prodigious oscillations in the stock market, which have startled the public for the past seven years, have been due to the influence of those powerful combinations, which have obtained control of certain stocks, and made them dance up in long erratic jumps, or have hurled them down still more swiftly and strangely. Hardly a week goes by without a recurrence of these singular phenomena. Sometimes it has been Pacific Mail, sometimes Erie, or Old Southern, or Pittsburg, or Reading. In these traps the bears are continually caught by the same devices, and not seldom the bulls fall into the very pits which they dig so industriously for their adversaries.

The army of speculators who form their battalions, and charge up and down the field of the stock market, is a motley crowd, and like the army of Xerxes, includes representatives from many nations,—Americans from all sections of the Republic, Englishmen, Scotchmen, Welshmen, Irishmen, Germans, Frenchmen, Spaniards, Italians, Russians, Norwegians, Danes, Hungarians, Hebrews, Greeks and Ethiopians, masquerading under the guise of bulls and bears, swell the host, and rush together in hostile combat.

The generations of professional speculators are short to a proverb, but after allowing for a floating population of occasional operators, and of those who make or lose fortunes and then disappear from the scene, there is still another portion which is a constant quantity in the estimate. These are the men whose sole business is stock speculation. When they have once entered the street, they never leave it except in a pine box or a rosewood case, according to circumstances. If they lose money, they stay ther

to regain it, and if they make money, they stay there
to make more. Constitutionally, and by temperament, they are speculators. Hear them talk, and
you would suppose they lived on hope, rather than
on those delicious ragouts and choice wines which
Delmonico, or Schedler, or some of the other famed
restaurateurs furnish them. Those saddest words of
tongue or pen, "it might have been," enter largely
into the thoughts and conversation of the thorough-
bred speculator. *If* and *but* are the most frequent con-
junctions in his vocabulary. His whole life is a series
of regrets, and strange to say, these regrets are more
often for what he might have made, but did not, than
for what he has actually lost.

According to the proverb of the race-course, everybody on the turf or under it, is equal, and the same
is true of the field of stock speculation, in which a
common interest on one side or the other, seems, for
the time being, to level all social distinctions. All
classes and grades are represented here—rich and
poor, gentle and simple, learned and illiterate. Not
unfrequently these noisy groups contain more than
one white cravat, on divines who have left their lambs
to graze at large, while they, the shepherds, wander
among a herd of another complexion, clad in bull's
or bear's clothing. A certain harmony reigns among
these discordant elements, although not quite equal
to that which prevails in the happy family of the
menagerie, in which lambs and lions, doves, eagles
and monkeys, dogs and cats, dwell together in peace
and amity. The bankrupt elbows the millionaire, and
asks of him the price of Fort Wayne, and the millionaire replies with the utmost suavity, "eighty-five,

sir, at the last quotation;" the broken operator takes whiskey "straight" with the wealthy capitalist, and the puritan and blackleg exhange a sympathetic smile, when they see the stocks advancing in which they are interested.

This social phenomenon is due not merely to the influence of a common interest, and a common hope of gain, but to a common apprehension of possible loss. Dickens, in one of his novels, has ludicrously described how polite men are to each other in the presence of a danger which all feel, but the fear of which none express. In seasons of earthquake and flood, wolves herd amicably with sheep, and the boa-constrictor twines his scaly length harmlessly beside the plumpest of does.

Besides, amid the wonderful metamorphoses of the stock market, it behooves all to be courteous to their fellows, for the Lazarus who picks up the crumbs that fall from the rich man's table to-day, may himself dispense liberal charities to-morrow; the bankrupt of yesterday may, in the circle of a single sun, become a power on change.

Notwithstanding this apparent leveling of the social conventionalities in the domain of speculation, still it is in other respects no republic, for it has its sovereigns and satraps, who often hold its tribes in captivity and subject to an iron yoke.

Charles Darwin, the English naturalist, in his great and fascinating work on the "Origin of Species," explains in part, the existence of so many different species in the animal kingdom, by the doctrine of what he terms *Natural Selection*, i. e., the weak and unfortunate becoming extinct, the strong and favored living and mating with their peers, and in this way particular species being perpetuated. There is always this struggle going on everywhere; and among men, as among animals, weak races become extinct, and the subjects of stronger races. In the battle of life, it is the few strong, determined and favored men who win the prizes. Pre-eminently is this true of Wall Street. Ever since 1862, when began the greatest era of speculation the world has ever seen, faces have been appearing and disappearing there as in a whirling stereoscope; but in all those shifting groups, certain massive faces are always seen—faces graven with the wrinkles of a purpose that never failed them. These men have "clutched the golden keys." Their names are the talismans which unveil many a dark financial secret, unlock vaults of untold treasure, and set the genii of panic at work. The world of change pays them tribute, not of applause merely, but of hard cash, with scarcely a murmur of rebellion against their sovereignty.

In the present decade among a host of lesser operators, Cornelius Vanderbilt and Daniel Drew are the central Titanic figures. These men are the Nimrods, the mighty hunters of the stock market; they are the large pike in a pond peopled by a smaller scaly tribe. They are the holders of those vast blocks of stock, the cubical contents whereof can be measured by an arithmetic peculiar to themselves; they are the makers of pools large enough to swallow up a thousand individual fortunes. Sooner or later, the money of the smaller tribe of speculators finds its way into the pockets of these financial giants.

Young men! ye "wealthy curled darlings of our nation," who are about to "put up your money in the street," let me whisper a word in your ear. Before you venture on this perilous step, go to Cornele or Uncle Daniel, and make them a free gift of all the money you are willing to risk, (for into their strong boxes it will come at last,) and thus you will be saved a world of wrong and trouble, entailed by that mysterious, protracted, and to you, painful process, which will surely end, finally, in the transfer of your money into the strong boxes aforesaid.

Next after these high princes and potentates, comes another grade of operators,—men of great financial ability and resources, hard-headed, and strong of nerve. Some of them are now, or have been, lieutenants and coadjutors of Vanderbilt and Drew. Among these may be mentioned Richard and Augustus Schell, John M. Tobin, John Morrissey and Dr. Shelton. Some have become known through their connection with the rings which have kept Wall Street in a ferment for the past seven years. Leonard W. Jerome, W. S. Woodward, H. G. Stimpson, James Fisk, Jr., and Jay Gould, belong to this class. Many of these noted organizers of rings have made war on the sovereigns of the market, and sacked some of their fortresses, in return for which they have suffered severe punishment at the hands of their liege lords.

The number of smaller operators, who do business on capitals of from ten to fifty thousand dollars, is legion, and as for those who take "flyers" in one or two hundred shares, they are a great host whom no man can describe, much less enumerate.

Many of the operators of small means, as well as the wealthier class, drive a smart trade in "puts" and "calls." These are contracts giving the holder the privilege, in consideration of a trifling sum, (rarely over one per cent. on the market value of a stock) of calling on the contracting party, or delivering to him, as the case may be, a certain amount of stock within a fixed time, at a price above the then market value in a "call," and below it in a "put."

The following is a copy of a "call:"

> *New York, February 1st,* 1870.
>
> *For Value Received, the Bearer may* CALL ON ME *for One Hundred Shares of the Preferred Stock of the* Chicago and North-Western Railroad Company, *at* 91 *per cent., any time in thirty days from date. The bearer is entitled to all the dividends or extra dividends declared during the time.*
>
> *Signed,*   DANIEL DREW.
>
> *Witness,*   DANIEL MORRELL.

The market price of the stock at the date of the call is, we will suppose, 85. Now if the price rises to 94 in the course of the thirty days during which the "call" runs, the bearer can sell one hundred shares at 94, i. e., for $9,400, and call upon Daniel Drew for one hundred shares at 91, i. e., $9,100, and deliver it to the party to whom he has just sold the same amount, netting, (after deducting the one hundred dollars which he paid for the privilege), two hundred dollars by this operation.

The following is a copy of a "put:"

> *New York, February 1st, 1870.*
>
> *For Value Received, the Bearer may* DELIVER ME *One Hundred Shares of the Preferred Stock of the* Chicago and North-Western Railroad Company, *at* 80 *per cent., any time in thirty days from date. The undersigned is entitled to all the dividends or extra dividends declared during the time.*
>
> Signed,   DANIEL DREW.
>
> *Witness,*   JAMES BOYD.

If we suppose the stock falls to 75 during the pendency of the "put," the bearer makes four hundred dollars net out of this operation.

The holder of a call, it will be seen, is a "bull," and the holder of a put is a "bear" on the market. But these contracts are often used, like so much money, to buy or sell stock, thus, viz.: Daniel Drew's call being considered "as good as wheat," it may be deposited with some broker as security for a "short sale" of one hundred shares of Chicago and North-western at 91. If the price falls to 80, the holder makes ten hundred dollars, less the brokerage. If it rises to 95, the broker is secure by the privilege of calling on Daniel Drew for a hundred shares at 91, which he delivers to the party to whom the short sale was made, and here the holder loses nothing, though he makes nothing. The "put," on the other hand, is used as security to *buy* stocks, in this manner, viz.: if the stock fall to 80, the putting price, the holder can buy one hundred shares at that price, through some broker who is fortified against loss in case the price falls, by having the privilege of delivering the one hundred shares he buys, to Daniel Drew, at 80, while if the price rises above 80, he can sell it and take for the holder of the put, a profit on this operation. In an active market, the holders of puts and calls, after making several profits in the way we have described, are sometimes able to fall back on the original contract of their puts or calls, and close them up at a handsome figure.

Daniel Drew and the late Henry Keep have been active dealers in this kind of contract, with what singular effects upon the market, will be hereafter described.

No one who has entered the precincts of the stock exchange, will have failed to notice certain nondescripts, who constantly frequent the market. They are men who have seen better days, but having dropt their money in the street, come there every day as if they hoped to find it in the same place. These characters are the ghosts of the market, fixing their lack-lustre eyes upon it, and pointing their skinny fingers at it, as if they would say "thou hast done this!" They flit about the door-ways, and haunt the vestibules of the exchange, seedy of coat, blackingless of boot, unkempt, unwashed, unshorn, wearing on their worn and haggard faces a smile more melancholy than tears. They "put up" never a penny, and yet they are perpetually asking the prices of stocks which they never buy or sell. They have their life's history—it is that of many of "Les Miserables,"—stranger than fiction, more doleful than a funeral dirge,—a spring time of hope, health, love, prosperity and the amenities of social life, then a

brief season of wild, reckless speculation, a brief revelry of smoke, splendor, champagne—then what?
penury, darkness, despair!

We have thus far only indicated a few of the different classes which make up the *genus* speculator. It
would require a volume to describe, in detail, the
numerous *species*, the strong individuality of the men
who compose them, the fortunes they roll up from
nothing, or fling to the winds in a day, the thousand
shifts to which they resort, to earn an honest or dis-
honest living, and the tricks they play which so often
make the outsiders, if not the angels, weep. The
stories to be told of some of them are worthy to be
embalmed in another "thousand and one nights,"
pointed with morals, and teaching lessons, while they
appeal to the love of the marvellous, like the tales
by which the Princess Scheherezade held the ear of
the Sultan, and redeemed her life from forfeit.

It is a popular fallacy that pronounces the life of
the Wall Street man, as anything rather than laborious. They say he dresses in purple and fine linen,
and fares sumptuously every day, though, like the
Solomon lilies of Scripture, he toils not, neither does
he spin. Let not the hard-working lawyer, the bur-
dened and anxious merchant, or the hardy sons of
manual labor, envy the gilded speculator, though he
recline on silken couches, and dally with the daintiest
of viands, and sip wines of the vintage of Waterloo,
out of Bohemian glass. True, to the casual observer,
his life seems easy enough. He produces nothing, he
drives no plough, plies no hammer, sends no "shuttle
flashing through the loom." In political economy he
would be properly classed among the strictest order

of *consumers*. His airy existence seems to be passed in chasing the flying fractions up and down the market, or in making the values which pass through his hands perspire golden drops, just as the Jews clip and sweat the coin they handle. And yet what life is more trying than his? Beneath his frontal sinuses, amid the convolutions of his brain, a silent, invisible struggle is going on, which if put into bodily shape, would startle the beholder. There the vulture passions are at work, led on by their generals, ambition and avarice. Pining envy, fear of an evil which always impends, rage over injuries inflicted by others, or by his own weakness and incapacity, jealousy and hatred of successful rivals, all hold carnival in the space of an hour, and are kept active and sleepless by hope which quickens them with her enchanted wings. Above him hovers, day and night, a vast, dark, formless shape, threatening ruin and penury. This is the spectre of panic. One day he is lifted to dizzy heights, the next, plunged into black depths. He is hurried through dark labyrinths through paths where a single step is destruction. He climbs on the edge of a sword to a fool's paradise, where he tastes joys brief as a dream, and in an hour is abased to the earth where he drinks the full cup of humiliation and want. Meanwhile nature is holding out strange signals of alarm. His lips and cheeks blanch without any assignable cause. Blacksmiths' sparks flicker before his eyes. His blood regurgitates to his heart, which seems to swell to the size of a bullock's, and beats on his ribs like a trip-hammer. Paralysis, apoplexy and aneurism are watching for their prey.

Not long since, a great man of the "street" lay

for weeks in the clutches of this last disease, and the muffled door-bell told the result of this harrowing career of a speculator. When he died, they said he left four millions. But he had paid for this colossal fortune with a life worn out in middle age by the weary burdens and sharp vicissitudes of the stock market.

The "fierce extremes" of Wall Street, may be best illustrated by the experience of W———. He came into the market, in 1862, with six hundred dollars, bought gold at 110, and sold it at 135; bought again three times as much, sold it for 160, went into Erie at 39, sold it for 80, bought Pacific Mail at 120, sold it for 165. In March, 1863, he had $49,000 at his bankers. But this was only the beginning. Something was going on, in Harlem, so he bought 2,000 Harlem; Morse was at work at Pittsburg, so he bought 2,000 Pittsburg; Erie was feverishly moving towards 90, he bought 1,000 Erie. Meanwhile, Hooker was moving on Chancellorsville, and there was silence in the stock market, for the space of a day. Now the news came, of a retrograde movement, in plain English, a repulse. The army was this side the Rappahannock, the signal was given, and the cohort of bulls moved on their enemy's works. Erie sold up to 110, Pittsburg 105 and Harlem in its proportion. He pocketed $90,000 more by this venture, and in March, 1864, he stood $250,000 ahead of the market. Then for a short space he had a charming life. A pair of spanking bays, tandem, whirled him to the Park in a tall Belmont, with a flunkey in livery, on the back seat with a bug on his hat. Over his morning repast floated the aromatic steam of

Mocha, and the flavors of exotic fruits. He lunched off partridge, stuffed with truffles, washed down by a bottle of Chateau d'Yqem or the liquid pellucid gold of the vintage of Xeres, and his dinner was nine courses of fish, flesh and fowl at Delmonico's, flanked by the most toothsome of *entremets*, and wines that would make a Mussulman foreswear his creed.

But soon W—— suffered a change— "a sea change into something (not) rich but strange." He had a friend who gave him a few "points" on Galena, then selling for 142. There was a pool in it which was going to put it up to 175; it was actually worth 200; there was an extra dividend of 40 per cent. to be declared; William B. Ogden was in the movement—these were the points. He bought 6,000 shares. Then he bought 5,000 Pittsburg at 133 and 2,000 Fort Wayne at 144. In ten days he lost $270,000. This was in the great panic of April, 1864.

We met W—— six weeks ago. He informed us that he had just breakfasted on a modest plate of hash and a cup of something called coffee, but in which the strongest imagination could not detect a drop of the infusion of the Arabian berry. His coat was foxey, his hat had a suspicious shine and he was generally run down at the heel. Such is the present condition of this individual, but the future may have great things in store for him. Let us hope it may.

Gambling in stocks, after following a legitimate business, is like quaffing brandy after sipping claret. When once a man has fairly committed himself to speculation, his imagination soon grows to lend a hideous fascination to the objects of his pursuit. An evil genius seems to hold possession of him. He takes no note of time, save as an interval between his gains and losses; the thrill of the one and the pain of the other, grow duller as the years wear away, until at length he becomes the opium eater of finance, living in a world peopled by phantoms which haunt his waking hours, and flit through his dreams. The unsubstantial pageant vanishes as the alarm bell of his ruin peals out, and he awakes to the desolation of reality.

How few of these men retire with fortunes approximate to their hopes, let the chronicles of the Stock Exchange tell. The number during the past ten years, might be almost told upon the digits. The few successful ones, are continually emerging from the intolerable repose of their retirement, and even in their dotage, coming back to the scene of their old intoxications mumbling old wives' tales of what they might have done thus and thus, and burning their fingers after a fashion, as ancient as Crœsus.

As for the rabble of the unsuccessful, they cling to their illusions, till want or decrepitude, or both, drive them into obscurity, to ruminate over a misspent life, and be laid finally in nameless graves, by the hand of charity.

CHAPTER II.

THE STOCK EXCHANGE AND GOLD ROOM.

The Focus of Speculation—The "Long Room" on a Field Day—Portraits of Operators—History of the Board of Brokers—The Public Board—Queer Characters—Volume of Business—How it is Done—Brokers' Vocabulary—Margins, Differences and Options—Machinery of Business—A Broker's Buckler—The Gold Room in New Street—Rise of the Gold Board—The Firm of We, Us & Co.—The Gold Bank, and how it Clears Gold, and Collects Differences.

THE tide of humanity that pours down Broadway, is dashed against the bulwarks of Wall Street, and whirled to the eastward, between the mighty walls of granite and sandstone, which line that renowned thoroughfare. Through two mouths, New Street and Broad Street, it is sucked into that seething, whirling, roaring maelstrom—the stock-market. Speaking in the language of the common-place, these two streets are merely avenues in the lower part of the city for the passage of men and loaded wains, and for the transaction of business; but these streets also form the environs of the Stock Exchange, which, as from the focus of a gigantic parabolic reflector, throws a light, more or less lurid, over the whole financial community. That lofty façade on Broad Street, builded as of snowy marble of Paros, " of kingliest masonry," sinks into a modest, two-story brick rear on New Street, emblematical of the stately

VIEW OF THE STOCK EXCHANGE AND BROAD STREET.

fortunes which enter that stately front, and issue diminished from that diminished rear.

This is our palace of Aladdin. Here may be found that wonderful lamp which gives speedy and fabulous wealth to him who grasps it. Here also is stabled that remarkable horse, which, on being mounted, often flies away and leaves its rider on a certain desolate island, called Ruin.

The edifice is built to defy the powers of the air and fire—massively, of stone, iron, brick and glass, with thin veneerings of wooden floorings; its ruins ages hence may for aught we know be among those which the coming New Zealander may gaze upon as he sits on a mound of dust which was once old Trinity and moralizes on the fall of nations.

A dull sound like the murmur of distant waters greets the ear as we stand before it. Let us enter between the corinthian columns through the Broad street door. A deep hall with lofty ceiling supported by fluted iron pillars, covers the length and breadth of the ground floor in the form of a letter L. Through the apertures in the thick walls in front and rear and through opaque plates of glass from above, streams in a dim, though not a religious light, by which we can hardly recognize the faces in a roaring screaming, turbulent crowd. This is the "Long Room," so-called. To the left, as we enter, is a broad stair-case with solid-set balusters leading to the upper room, where the members of this Stock Exchange hold their regular sessions. Directly in front of us is a heavy railing pierced with a gateway, where sits the Cerberus of this Hades, whose office it is to see that none pass inside of this barrier except

4

the members of the Board of Brokers and outsiders who have paid one hundred dollars for a year's privilege of being spectators of the purchases and sales, and of giving their orders to buy or sell on the spot to the Brokers whom they employ. Passing inside this railing we find ourselves on a marble-paved floor fifty by fifty, beyond which rises an elevated platform, seventy by fifty, abutting on the west, on the New Street side. The centre of this platform is scooped into an elliptical pit graded by a series of steps encircled by an iron railing, and capable of containing several hundred men, when closely packed. Within this enclosure none are allowed except the brokers. Outside the railing, stand they who have secured this privilege by paying an admission due as already described.

It is a field day on 'Change. Stocks which for weeks have been slowly rising, are now jumping upwards ten per cent. in an hour. The Long Room is like Bedlam broke loose. The pit is jammed with buyers and sellers, brandishing their arms, shrieking with every variety of tone, from the booming basso to the shrill tenore. Wall Street is fully represented this morning. The great Banking and Brokerage firms are on the ground executing their orders and reaping a golden harvest of commissions. Files of sharp-looking, smug fellows are rushing in and out, on the double-quick, holding in their hands pads of paper, on which the latest quotations are recorded; while the telegraph with ceaseless click is flashing the prices to every commercial city in the Union. The speculators both inside and outside are all here. The cunning artificers of " rings " and diggers of " pools," are moving about among the crowd watching the effect of their schemes and cheering on their journeymen. Here is the veteran Drew, the silent Shelton, the busy Woodward, and the gladiatorial Morrissey; Tobin of the opalescent eye, Stimpson of the fine Roman nose, and Dick Schell, looking like a jolly punchinello, are all here. The benevolent features of Henry Keep are missing, but the jetty beard of Gould and the blonde locks of the unterrified Fiske, are hard by; as for the "Commodore," he has a heavy hand in this game which he is playing in an office not far away, through the medium of wires.

Nearly all the outsiders have a greater or lesser interest in the course of the market. Some of them stand by the railing that surrounds the pit, others watch the battle afar off, standing between the entrance rail and the door. These outside operators have faces strongly marked by the exciting life they lead. Their features often become set into a fixed expression of anxiety. They gaze at the scale of prices with an apparent apathy, disturbed by the pain of loss or lighted up by the pleasure of gain only for an instant. Some of them seem to wear the waxen mask which grows on the faces of gamblers covering every emotion and rarely dropped except when some keener pang or more intense thrill startles them off their guard.

The combat between the bulls and bears commences with light skirmishing. As the day wears away, the solid columns move against each other, under a fire of heavy artillery. The bears begin to give ground and their banners wander in disarray. Suddenly a deafening hubbub breaks out from the pit. New York Central has risen ten per cent. in as many minutes. Some great bear is buying stock to cover his contracts, his followers rush after him and the whole army of bears are soon at work buying in or settling up. The bulls have won the day, and after counting the dead, wounded and missing, and reckoning the spoils and losses, respectively, the armies retreat to their camps, and prepare for new campaigns.

The association known as the New York Stock Exchange, was formed early in the present century. It germinated sixty years ago, in a little clique of stock dealers numbering scarcely a round dozen, who were wont to meet under a sycamore tree, which stood in Wall Street, opposite to the present banking house of Brown, Bros. & Co., and job off small lots of governments or stock in the Manhattan Company, and Bank of New York. In 1816, a permanent organization existed, consisting of twenty-eight members. The names of most of the men composing this coterie linger now only in the memory of the old New Yorkers, or are written on the "dull cold marble" which records in the conventional phrase of olden times, the virtues of these men of 'change. Two of them, A. N. Gifford and Warren Lawton, veterans of a hundred campaigns and survivors of fifty years of the sharp vicissitudes of Wall Street, are, or lately were, still wearing out a green old age.

As early as 1837, the organization had grown to be a power, but a power for evil rather than good, since it stimulated in the community a thirst for speculation. In that year, too, fell the great banking and brokerage firm of J. L. and S. Josephs, agents of the

Rothschilds, and rated at $5,000,000, involving multitudes in a wide-spread ruin. The successors and assigns of the twenty-eight brokers of 1816, have, indeed, fed on strong food, and waxed exceeding great. They number, in 1870, between ten and eleven hundred, and own, or control wealth which is counted by the ten million. The old sycamore has decayed, and fallen beneath the storm, and they meet no longer under the "greenwood tree," though there is a poetic fitness in such a place of meeting for the taurine and ursine herd; but in a marble temple dedicated to Mammon, the God of riches, the ponderous iron doors whereof turn like the Miltonic gates of the celestial city on golden hinges.

They have been always noted for their exclusiveness in admitting new men, three black-balls being sufficient to bar out any applicant. A very strong prejudice for a long time existed against Jews, and dealers of that nationality were almost always promptly black-balled, notwithstanding some of them, as for example, Seixas Nathan and Bernard Hart, had been prominent in forming the organization, and the one last named, had acted as secretary down to 1840.

They were equally remarkable for their conservative views in respect to moneyed operations. A few rich, grey headed old fogies frowned down the more enterprising, but less wealthy " Young America" element, which went in for bold, dashing moves, cliques, corners, and the like. Hence it happened that an outsider, who had distinguished himself by some brilliant coup in finance, often found the doors barred against him, when he wished to enter the legitimate circle of this close corporation, partly, perhaps, from the jealousy awakened by a skill which threatened to surpass the trained financiers in their own arena.

Of course this exclusiveness produced a reaction among the speculative public, and rival organizations were formed, according as the volume of business tempted men to share in the heavy commissions earned thereby. Prior to 1836, a new board was formed, which, after maintaining a precarious existence for a few years, became extinct. In 1862, the same causes led to the formation of another association, known first as the Public Board, and afterwards as the Open Board of Brokers. Everything was favorable to such an organization. Uncle Sam's presses were printing greenbacks by the million. A large proportion of our mercantile population were thrown out of business by the depression of 1861, and ready to embark in anything which promised the improvement of their shattered fortunes; the ebbing and flowing tide of the war itself, distorted or exaggerated by manipulations of the telegraph, also multiplied the fluctuations; these were mighty conditions precedent to such a movement. Accordingly, men of all shades and classes flocked to the "coal-hole," as the subterranean apartment in William Street was called, where this Public Board first held its sessions. Lawyers, whose tastes were speculative rather than litigious, more than one clergyman, whose pastoral labors were unremunerative, broken down operators, merchants out of business, clerks out of situations, Jews, "native, and to the manner born," as well as the greenest and most unsophisticated parties from the rural districts, swelled the motley throng.

Most of these men had some capital, more or less—

principally less. Strange stories are told of some of them. One pawned his watch, paid his hundred dollars admission dues, and had fifty cents left in his pocket. This he expended in a sumptuous lunch, and a gin cock-tail, on the strength of which, he bought ten gold, made five hundred dollars in an hour, and closed the month with five thousand six hundred and fifty dollars profits. Another mortgaged his poultry stand in one of the markets, and made, in six months, seventy-five thousand on Harlem.

The Old Board looked with great disfavor on its young rival; a bitter contest arose, in which, the former had the advantage in wealth and established position, the latter in fire, energy and numbers. The New Board offered to do business for 1-32 brokerage, *i. e.,* three dollars and twelve cents on a hundred shares; the Old Board responded by lowering their commission rates from one-quarter per cent. to one-eighth per cent., and passed a resolution of expulsion against any one of its members who had any dealings with any member of the former organization.

Meanwhile, the tide of speculation kept rising higher, and both parties had all the business they could do. The denizens of the street will recollect the singular phenomena presented by this locality in 1862 and 1863. The basements of William, Wall and Broad Streets, and of Exchange Place, seemed to have been suddenly penetrated with innumerable burrows, inhabited by new and singular animals— mostly rodents—gnawing at the vast cheese of speculation. Among these, too, were the "woodchucks" of the class, sitting in their holes, and anon appearing, frisking about, picking up a few choice bits and

disappearing like prairie dogs at stated intervals, or
upon the least alarm. Every inch of space was occupied. Queer little niches in walls were scooped
out or enlarged, so as to admit a desk, and over the
door in flaming characters was the imposing sign,
Sloper & Co., or Lunkhead & Bro., Bankers and
Brokers. It is a surprising circumstance how many
bankers were, just at this time, suddenly spawned in
the most gorgeous panoply from the head of our
financial Minerva. Some were infant prodigies, boys
of twenty summers, reared in that sharpest of schools,
a broker's office, whose financial ideas were founded
on first principles. They seemed to have resolved
society into its original elements, and gone back in
their notions respecting the sacredness of other men's
property to what ethnologists call the stone period,
when men lived in caves, and appropriated to themselves all kinds of property, irrespective of those
rights so studiously inculcated by Blackstone and
Kent. They had heads of sixty, rolling the coldest
and keenest of eyes, on shoulders in which the deltoid muscle had been hardly yet developed. Then,
too, there were in more ostentatious offices, glittering
with plate glass, and garnished with the most ara-
besque of black walnut furniture, the Oily Gammons
of a more mature age, versed in the business wiles
begotten of twenty-five years' experience. They
offered the public schemes by which wealth could be
amassed in the simplest of possible ways,—a few
hundred or thousand dollars subscribed and paid down
with the almost impossible contingency of future as-
sessments. But, mysteriously enough, most of these
schemes were founded on proper franchises, etc.,

which were situated hundreds and thousands of miles away. On Deadman's Ledge, near No Man's Peak, in Colorado, were claims yielding gold sulphurets, which assayed two thousand dollars to the ton. Near I-Euchre Lake, in Wisconsin, were ingots of virgin copper to be had for the asking. And the bituminous coal, at an easy distance from tide-water, knocked the spots out of Scotch bog and cannel. The street was fairly flooded (on paper) with flowing wells, and all these schemes were backed up by all sorts of certificates and affidavits. Swindling and imposition put on the cloak of Religion. Deacons and elders, vestrymen and church-wardens, lent their names, and too often shared in the plunder.

All these miscellaneous enterprises served to deepen and give new volume to the waves that bore upon their topmost crest, the bark which carried the Public Board and its fortunes. At the close of January, 1863, it found itself stronger in crew, better organized, with plenty of shot in the locker, and an experience won in the most perilous navigation through rough seas, and in treacherous squalls. In the spring of 1863, this organization transferred its sessions from the basement at No. 17 William Street, to which the plebeian name of the "coal-hole" had been given, and held them in a more commodious apartment on the first floor on the opposite side of the street. In 1864, they moved into their new hall, at No. 16 Broad Street, and were known thereafter as the "Open Board of Brokers." The warfare so long carried on between the rival Boards was gradually discontinued, and at last, in the spring of 1869, as consolidation seemed to be the order of the day, the two bodies joined forces, and united under the name of the New York Stock and Exchange Board, which meets in the building already described. The board organized some years ago for the purpose of buying and selling Government Bonds, was also, at the same time, incorporated with the Stock Board, forming, altogether, a monster association of men, who devote their lives, and their fortunes, if not their sacred honor, to the business of buying and selling stocks and bonds, etc., etc.

The Board of Brokers is a wheel within a wheel, an imperium in imperio—a government in itself. It makes laws and regulations which bear upon its members as strongly as the laws of the land. It has a presiding officer to compel order, to impose fines and to announce decisions and decrees; a judiciary in the shape of an arbitration committee, which passes upon disputes involving the contracts of members and its adjudications are final. It has a code in its constitution and by-laws. When a member fails to pay up he is expelled. When a bull or bear is unable to meet his contracts, the stock which he fails to deliver is "bought in" or "sold out," at the Board, "under the rule" which so provides, and the difference between the prices at which it is "bought in" or "sold out," and the contract price, is the measure of damages for the breach of contract. This expedient, by a rapid process, dispenses with the aid of the courts of law where causes drag their slow length along through weary years, in defiance of the Bill of Rights, which declares, that every man shall have justice speedily and without delay.

The room where this trading body-politic hold their regular daily sessions, is one story above the Long-

Room, and looks out on New Street. It is a lofty hall, seventy feet by sixty, with the centre of the floor beyond the rostrum, scooped out into the usual pit, for the convenience of the buyers and sellers, and surrounded on two sides by an iron railing. Its walls which are tapestried with green cloth, are adorned by the portraits of two men who made themselves noted in the annals of American finance, viz., Jacob Little and John Ward. The morning session commences at ten and a half and continues till about twelve; the afternoon session is from one till about two, during which periods, the list of the stocks and bonds, most dealt in, are called off by a sandy-haired, gentlemanly looking Vice-President, with stentorian voice, and prices are established for the moment by those who buy and sell the different stocks on *the call*, as it is termed. All business brought before the organization, such as the election of members, settlement of disputes, etc., etc., is transacted at these regular sessions, and the list of prices made is published twice a day, on slips of paper, for the use of members and for the press and the public generally.

Two things will especially strike an observer on change: first, The apparent looseness and recklessness with which business is done there. Second, The immense volume of business done. These facts may be explained by the rapidity necessitated by the shortness of business hours in the day, and by the vast range of speculation through the securities dealt in—securities representing an aggregate market value of nearly $4,000,000,000, and including Government, State and Municipal bonds, and Railway, Bank, Insurance and miscellaneous stocks.

It would seem at those seasons when speculation is rife, as if every one had a larger or smaller pecuniary interest in stocks. Not only the bankers, brokers and money-men, who are constantly in the circle, but the staid merchant, the retired capitalist, the trustee of estates, the manufacturer, mechanic, farmer, miner, the student, lawyer, doctor and clergyman, are drawn into the vortex. A large portion of these men are not seen in Wall Street, but are "operating" by telegraph and letter, putting up their margins and buying or selling with characteristic ardor and boldness, which has often been acquired in other lines of business, for there are many fields of speculation besides the Stock Exchange.

"You Americans. Ah! you are, in fact, a people reckless," says Myer, late of the Paris Bourse, "we do these things better in the beautiful France." You are wrong, Myer. More safely, perhaps, but not better. If a venture is safe, it is not a speculation. Safety is hardly an element in the calculation. It is the *risk*, after all. The greater the risk, the greater the profit seems like a paradox, but it is generally true. Boldness, shrewdness and nerve, pluck the flower fortune out of the nettle danger, and boldness, shrewdness and nerve are, at least, American traits. No doubt the volume of business on the Bourse is very great, but after all, how paltry seems the individual enterprise of the French speculator, compared to the magnificent daring of the American. Enter the Bourse from the east, on the Rue Notre Dame des Victoires, place yourself in one of those high, arched windows, which surround the interior, and beneath that vaulted and frescoed dome, you will see a tumultuous, vociferating crowd of buyers and sellers. It would seem as if the end of all things was come, and that the Frenchmen had forgotten their reliance on the Goddess of Reason and were clamoring for absolution from Saint Peter. But all this gesticulation, fuss and fury is little but "the wild hysteric of the Celt." Most of these men are buying small lots of the Rentes, or five hundred francs in the Chemin de fér du Nord, or the Crédit Mobilier. Pshaw! so the old woman in the Rue St. Honoré sell you a plate of fried potatoes—price one sou. A few francs profit gives our old ally his café and omelet, and his modest diner and vin at the Palais Royal with the inevitable eau sucré, whereof he pockets the spare lumps.

How about London? There is our friend Bullwinkle,—he of the weeping-willow whiskers and fine Saxon color, true born Briton and agent of the great English house of Bearem & Bros., who lately observed that "really you know, my dear fellow, you are a young people, do ye see, and should'nt mention old England and this blasted country, in the same breath, when you talk of money." Quite true, we reply, but those ten share lots of stock dealt in at the Royal Stock Exchange, and those fortnightly settlements seem rather small and slow affairs, compared to the vast bargains and sales made in a breath in the New York Stock Exchange.

The aggregate volume of business in an active year, has been estimated at $15,000,000,000. This does not include the principal part of the dealing in Government Bonds, (the amount of which is enormous, though difficult to be guessed, even approximately,) or the dealings in gold, which, in 1869, it is estimated, will amount to nearly $30,000,000,000, and in those famous two days, the 24th and 25th of September, 1869, ran up to $800,000,000, forty millions changing hands in five minutes. In 1863, Addison G. Jerome bid for six millions of old Southern and was ready to take it. Anthony W. Morse was in habit of bidding for five or ten millions of stock in one block; but some of these were bluff bids, you will say. True, but they were bids in open market, nevertheless, and illustrate our proposition equally well. Transfers of a million of gold or stocks from A to B, on a single bid, are of almost daily occurrence. The weekly clearings of the Gold Bank in flush times, exceed a thousand millions of dollars. The receipts and deliveries of stocks and gold by one firm, lately, were one hundred and fifty millions in a month. Lockwood & Co. have received as high as $5,000 in brokerage in one day, and this at one-eighth per cent. indicates a daily business of four millions. Morse, the great bull leader of 1864, had fifteen million dollars worth of stocks on call at one time.

Among the gigantic operations in Erie, New York Central and Gold, during the past two years, such prominent firms as Lockwood & Co., David Groesbeck & Co., William Heath & Co., Rufus Hatch & Co., Smith, Gould, Martin & Co., etc., have held blocks of stocks and gold to an almost fabulous amount. More than one leading operator may be found nearly any day who is long or short of five millions of stocks or gold, or both, *on his own account*, and these are mere flea-bites compared to the great Hudson, Harlem and Central Pool of 1869, which, it is said, hold directly or by proxy from fifty to sixty millions in these stocks, besides a controlling interest of fifteen or twenty millions more in the Lake Shore consolidated line.

How can such immense business be transacted? A large part of it is done by the payment of the *differences* between the buying and selling price, the securities bought and sold not being actually delivered. The remaining portion of the business is done by means of *certified checks*, a convenient device of the credit system. Suppose B, a broker, has bought of C, another broker, five thousand shares of Lake Shore, at 90, for which, he has to pay $450,000. B having a capital of only $50,000, but being of good standing and credit, the bank where he keeps his account will certify his check as good for $450,000, though he may then have only $10,000 on deposit. Before three o'clock, P. M., B will have obtained a loan on the five thousand shares, or have delivered the stock to other parties, who will pay him for it in certified checks, which he will deposit in his bank, and thus make good his over-draft.

These brokers' accounts are not taken by some of the banks, being founded as they are, entirely on confidence in the broker, and involving a certain amount of risk. When money is easy, and everything is bright in the financial world, all may go on well, but in times of stringency and panic, a bank is occasionally the loser by this accommodation. A notable instance occurred two years since, when a certain Wall Street bank was saddled with a loss of nearly a quarter of a million by an over-draft of a prominent broker, who failed the day after.

The business of a stock-broker may be classed among those dark trades which have a language of their own in which their mysteries are veiled. This lingo consists of a variety of single words, or concise expressions, which convey to the initiated alone, an idea of the operations of the trade, while to the uninitiated, they are almost as meaningless as the cabala of the old Jewish Rabbins.

The word *margin* is perhaps the most conspicuous in the Wall Street vocabulary. As everybody knows this word in its ordinary sense, signifies a *narrow strip of land*, an edge or border, as the margin of a lake, etc. In the stock-business it is, if we may use the phrase, a *narrow strip of money*, which *preserves* the broker from loss, and on which, the speculator may be supposed to stand before he has definitely ascertained the profit or loss of an operation. Suppose A, the speculator, gives B, the broker, one thousand dollars, and order him, B, to buy for his, A's, account, one hundred shares of Rock Island, at par; this one thousand dollars is the *margin*. Now, supposing B to have bought the stock at par, or 100; he pays $10,000 for it. $1,000 of this sum is represented by the margin, and $9,000 is paid by B. If the price falls to 93, B calls on A for more *margin*, to secure him against loss if the price should fall below 90. If A fails to respond, and the stock is sold at 93, A's loss is $700 besides the brokerage for buying and selling 100 shares, and interest on the $10,000, which the stock cost. The interest paid ranges from five to seven per cent. per annum, but when money is dear the interest rises sometimes to a fearful rate, running sometimes to 300 per cent. per annum; indeed, the rate of 1200 per cent. was paid for *carrying* stocks during the month of September, 1869.

The margin exacted for carrying stocks, is from three to twenty per cent., on the par value of the stock dealt in, and depends partly also on the kind of stock bought or sold; New York Central, a high priced security liable to wide fluctuation, called for more ample margins than others which are lower priced, and which vibrate less frequently and swiftly. Governments are dealt in on much smaller margins, which run from one to five per cent. of the par value of the bonds.

The brokerage paid is from three dollars and twelve cents, *i. e.*, one thirty-second of one per cent. to twelve dollars and fifty cents, *i. e.*, one-eighth of one per cent. on one hundred shares, which is always reckoned at par, no matter what the market value of the stock may be; one hundred shares of Mariposa, at the price of ten (10), will cost $1,000, and the brokerage on the purchase or sale of this lot will be the same as on one hundred shares of Fort Wayne at 100, or one hundred shares of Delaware and Hudson at 150.

A broker is said to *carry* stock for his customer when he has bought and is holding it for his account. This *carrying* of stock is done in various ways. Sometimes the broker pays for the stock with his own money, or with the money he has on deposit from others; sometimes he borrows money on the stock from banks or private bankers. When his capital is small, he carries his customer's stock by *turning* it.

A broker is said to *turn* stock when he sells it out for *cash*, i. e., deliverable and payable the same day, and buys it back *regular*, i. e., deliverable and payable the next day. Under certain circumstances, *cash stock* and *regular stock* bear the same price in the market. But generally there is a difference of from one thirty-second to one eighth in favor of the seller of the *regular* stock. This difference is, of course, paid by the seller of the cash stock in lieu of interest for *carrying* it. When cash stock is very scarce, a difference of from one-quarter of one per cent. to four per cent. exists in favor of the cash stock. This scarcity of stock is produced by the action of rings, (as already described), for the purpose of compelling the bears to fulfil their contracts. Thus occasionally certain stocks, e. g., Reading, &c., will sell *regular* at 94, and cash 96.

Again, when money is very dear and in seasons of panic, a stock will sell for cash, one, two or three per cent. lower than the price *regular*. On the 29th of September, 1869, certain stocks sold at a difference of four per cent. between cash and regular, reflecting thereby the great apprehension and stringency that reigned in the market.

When stocks are *carried*, by raising a loan upon them, a stock note is sometimes given to the lender, which will read as follows, viz.:

$70,000.   *New York, Nov. 26th*, 1869.

On Demand, we promise to pay to Jay Cook & Co., or Order, Seventy Thousand Dollars, for value received, with interest at the rate of 7 *per cent. per annum, having deposited with them as collateral security, with authority to sell the same at the* BROKER'S BOARD, or at public or private sale, *at their option, on the non-performance of this promise, and without notice, One Thousand Shares of* Lake Shore Railroad Company.

JOHN DOE & CO.

But loans are generally negotiated without this formality, by simply depositing with the lender the stocks as collateral security, and receiving from him a check to the amount of 80 per cent. of their market value. Nearly all these loans are payable on demand, and are termed in Wall Street, *call loans*.

When stocks are in demand by the bears to fill their contracts, they are often carried by *loaning* them to the bears, who pay the holders the market price in currency. When the borrowed stock is returned, the sum paid the holders is returned to the bear borrower.

The following statement will show the prices at which stocks are bought and sold, and the interest and commissions paid for carrying stocks, viz.:

100 shares of Rock Island, at $100 per share will cost $10,000 at par. The market price of the same being 102, (i. e., 2 per cent. above par), 100 shares bought on the 8th of November, 1869, will cost . .	$10,200 00
The brokerage for buying (⅛ per cent. on $10,000), . .	12 50
Interest 30 days, carrying same at 7 per cent., . .	57 87
Commissions, turning same (when money is tight), ¼ $25, again ¼ $25, two turns, $50, ...	50 00
Brokerage, selling same, (⅛ per cent. on $10,000), . .	12 50
	$10,332 87
Sold same December 8th, at 104. (market price) $10,400.	
Balance of profit due buyer, . . .	67 13
	$10,400 00
(Or, if the price falls to par), sold same at 100, $10,000	
Balance loss of buyer, ...	332 87
	$10,332 87

Sometimes stocks are bought and sold on buyer's

or seller's option, as already mentioned.   The following are copies of a buyer's and seller's option, viz.:

BUYER'S OPTION.

500 Shares.

New York, Nov. 24th, 1869.

I have PURCHASED of John Q. Brown, Five Hundred Shares of the Stock of the Reading Railroad Company, at 98 per cent., payable and deliverable at his option,
with interest at the rate of 6 per cent per annum.

JAMES HOWARD.

SELLER'S OPTION.

500 Shares.

New York, Nov. 24th, 1869.

I have SOLD to Solomon Stoddard, Five Hundred
Shares of the Stock of the Lake Shore Railroad Company,
at 90 per cent., payable and deliverable at my option, with
interest at the rate of 6 per cent. per annum.

HENRY E. WILSON.

Either party to one of these contracts has the privilege of calling, within a certain time, upon the other,
for a margin of ten or twenty per cent. on the
amount of the contract.   The sum, or margin so
called for, is deposited in one of the Trust Companies, to secure the party calling for it against loss
on the contract.   Parties who owe stocks on buyer's
or seller's option, or who have borrowed stocks must
be *notified* to deliver such stocks before and not after
twelve o'clock, meridian, and all stocks are required

to be delivered before quarter past two in the afternoon.

The seller, in each of these cases, is supposed to *carry* the stock, and receive interest, and the buyer to pay interest on the contract price, until the contract is closed, either by the lapse of the time named, or by the buyer at his option, in the one case, or by the seller at his option in the other. The buyer is operating for a rise, and will call upon the seller, if the stock goes up above the contract price; while the seller is operating for a fall, and if the stock goes down, will buy it at the reduced price, and deliver it to the buyer at the higher contract price, as we have described in the preceding chapter.

Most of the stocks bought in the market are carried in other ways than by these options.

A large portion of the business is transacted, as already mentioned, by paying *differences* instead of actually delivering the stock called for. Suppose A sells to B 100 shares of Chicago and Northwestern at 75, A not having the stock to deliver; if the price falls to 70, B pays A $500, and if the price rises to 80, A pays B $500 *difference* between the present market price and the contract price. This will explain how it is that so many do an immense business on a moderate capital, for if all the stocks bought and sold in Wall Street were actually delivered, it would require thrice the number of hands, and ten times the capital, to do the business.

The object of the Bankers and Brokers' Association, whose office is at No. 18, Broad Street, is to enable dealers to complete their contracts by paying differences. This is done on the Clearing House method, as in the case of the Gold Bank, which will be hereafter described ; but only a small portion of the stocks bought and sold are delivered through the Bankers and Brokers' Association.

The verdicts of juries, and the decisions of the courts, during the past ten years, have, in the litigation between brokers and their customers made the contract to carry stocks, a hard one for the brokers. Under these decisions, brokers have been held liable to carry stocks, even after the margin deposited with them has become exhausted, and notwithstanding the customer has been notified of the fact, and more margin demanded. In this way, brokers have sometimes found themselves incurring a heavy loss, after their customer's stock has been bought in or sold out in default of margin. A customer is thus enabled to fasten himself on his broker, as the old man did on the shoulders of Sinbad, the sailor, and may compel him to carry the stock held for his (the customer's) account through all manner of panics and corners, till a profit can be shown on the transaction.

To meet this difficulty, the customer is asked, by many of the brokerage houses, to sign some such memorandum as the following, to wit:—

Agreement, made this 20th day of September, 1869.
For Value Received, I hereby agree with JONES & CO., Bankers and Brokers, of the city, county and State of New York, that in case I shall be or become indebted to them at any time during the existence of this contract, for money lent or paid to me or for my account or use, or for any overdraft, or for any deficiency arising out of contracts or transactions in or relating to Stock Securities or Gold, the said

JONES & CO. may, in their discretion, sell at either of the Brokers' Boards, or wherever they deem advisable, or at public auction or private sale, with or without advertising the same, and with or without notice to me, all or any property, things in action, or collateral securities held by them belonging to me, or in which I am interested, or may hypothecate or otherwise use the same, and may apply the proceeds towards any such indebtedness and the interest thereon, and expenses of sale, or negotiation, holding me responsible and liable for payment of any deficiency existing after such application.

And in case of short sales, so called, or time contracts on my behalf, for sale or delivery of Stocks or Gold, they may protect themselves by prompt purchase in manner and place as above provided in case of sales, whenever they may deem it necessary, and without prior call on me, holding me liable in like manner, for any deficiency.

And this AGREEMENT shall never be altered or annulled by any verbal agreement, it being the intention that this contract alone shall control all business transactions for my account by said JONES & CO. from this 20th day of September until this contract is surrendered to me, and the possession of this agreement by said JONES & CO. shall be conclusive evidence that it is in full force and effect.

| Internal Revenue Stamp. | JOHN LEICESTER. |
| | In presence of WILLIAM BROWN. (Customer.) |

The speculation in gold has its focus so near that of stocks, that they seem almost one. The walls of the gold exchange rest against those of the stock exchange in a physical as well as a moral sense. A dingy room, fifty by seventy, painted in sombre fresco, on the shady side of New Street, hardly lighted by ten narrow windows, through which the golden sunlight flickers briefly of an afternoon, and then vanishes over the tall blocks of brick and mortar which line Broadway. This is the Gold Room. Its style of architecture reminds one of the shanties erected for the temporary accommodation of miners, working some auriferous vein, which may any hour be cut off

by a fault and cease to be remunerative; and should
gold drop to par, this frail building which covers the
busy bees in the honied cells of the eighths and
quarters of the gold speculation, would speedily be
levelled with the ground, and in its stead would rise
the more solid and enduring structure of staple commercial enterprise.   Inside this shell of a building,
are numerous catty-corners and nooks, fenced off by
iron railings or diaphanous pine planks.   Into these
recesses, the weary operators retire and wait for prices
to move, and then sally forth and catch the halves
and units "living as they rise."   Queer looking little
boys, whose knowing eyes belie the general vacuity
of their faces, appear and disappear through side
doors and gateways.   Voices rise and fall in discordant chorus, and in the pauses a dull burr and rapid
clicking, as of a small cotton factory, tells that the
telegraph is spinning out long rolls of paper ribbons
marked with quotations from the marts of London,
Frankfort and Paris.   The cast iron figure in the
centre of the hall, (which ought to have been, but is
not, a statue of Dame Fortune, standing by her
wheel), throws up a shower of spray which falls into
a basin, tinkling and clinking like coin of gold. 'The
operators grouped around it, hurling phantom ten
thousand dollar gold bricks, or staring at each other
through the drops, look as if they were interrogating
the fountain respecting the success of their ventures;
but like the enchanted fountain in Moore's song, it
(generally) " answers no!"   A gallery and a space
fenced off below, is lined with the anxious, haggard
faces of speculative outsiders.

What have we now, music?   Yes; and strange

music it is. Beside the president's rostrum there is a man sitting before a small piano, which communicates by electricity with an indicator on the wall, and marks the ruling price of the moment. The tunes played by this piano, enter through the eye; both the air and the words are expressed by figures which ring on a scale of prices which runs from 120 to 130 as we write. On dull days, the tune is *lento ralantando* slow and moderate, but on a rampant, or a panic-market, the strain swells to an awful diapason, through which is heard by some, the pæans of victory, by others the dirges of ruin.

The nucleus of that financial comet, the gold speculation, distinctly displayed itself first in 1862, amid the darkness of the "coal hole," No. 17 William Street, a place to which reference has already been made, in connection with the public board. It rose slowly up, drawing after it a portentous train. In two years it reached its zenith, and covered half the sky of speculation with its baleful light.

The magnitude of the operations in the precious metal, rendered a separate room necessary. In the summer of 1864, Gilpin's reading-room, on the ground floor of the southeast corner of William Street and Exchange Place, was first used as the stamping ground of the bellowing herd which made gold speculation their chief end and aim. Any subscriber to the privileges of this reading-room, (the yearly dues being twenty-five dollars), could enter and bet his pile on the oscillations.

Speculators are like jealousy, "they make the meat they feed on." The volume of business kept rolling up in a geometrical ratio, and the limits of Gilpin's

room soon became too "cabined, cribbed and con-
fined" for the expansive genius of the gold men. A
cry went up, "room for the leper! room!" (I mean
the leper of modern finance, the gold speculator.
This species of leprosy at that time seemed to have
broken out in great yellow blotches over a goodly
proportion of society here in Gotham.) Happy
thought, No. 1. Let us resolve ourselves into the
firm of We, Us & Co! Happy thought, No. 2. Let
us raise the admission dues to $100, then to $250,
then to $500, and thereby put money into our asso-
ciate purse.

These happy thoughts occurred to certain veteran
operators, and were acted upon instanter. One of
these individuals was W. G. R., late of the firm of
V. V., R. & D., a wiry, stocky little man, standing as
firm on his pins as if he could whip his weight in
wild cats, and looking as though he were constantly
rolling several hundred thousand in certificates
of his favorite metal, as a sweet morsel under his
tongue.

A long, deep, low room, (the same where the public board once held its sessions), was soon fitted up
on the southeast corner of William and Beaver
Streets, and the multitudinous firm of W. U. & Co.,
rushed in and commenced business.

In the latter part of the summer of 1865, the
members of this gold exchange moved into their present room on New Street, which we have already described. The admission dues of members were raised
to $1,000, then to $2,000, then to $5,000, and finally
to $10,000, the last sum being in the nature of a
prohibitory tariff on the vessels which desire to en-

ter the quiet haven of fortune through this stormy golden gate.

The Gold Bank was organized and went into operation in December, 1866. The object of this institution was by adopting a system of clearance on the plan of the Bank Clearing House, to simplify and facilitate the business arising out of the buying, selling, and delivering gold. The delivering and receiving from office to office of such vast sums of gold as were daily bought and sold at the Gold Room entailed not only great manual labor, but the risk of loss and theft. This trouble and expense is now saved. The Gold Bank receives and delivers the gold and collects the differences which may be due from or to the operators, or in other words, it *clears* the gold thus, viz.:

Jones & Co., a brokerage firm, buy from Brown & Co., $100,000 gold at 126¾; the gold costs $126,075 in currency. Jones & Co. sell this sum to Smith & Co. at 128, the price having risen 1¼ per cent. after the purchase. Then Jones & Co. give the Gold Bank the following notice in red ink, viz.:

---

57   *New York, Nov. 8th,* 1869.

RECEIVE GOLD.

NEW YORK GOLD EXCHANGE BANK,

To the Cashier:

> *You are advised that we shall settle through the Clearing Department to-day, with Brown & Co.,* $100,000 GOLD *for* $126,075 CURRENCY,

JONES & CO.

They also give the Gold Bank the following notice in black ink, viz.:

DELIVER GOLD.

57   *New York, Nov. 8th,* 1869.

NEW YORK GOLD EXCHANGE BANK,

To the Cashier:

> *You are advised that we shall settle through the Clearing Department to-day, with Smith & Co.,* $100,000 GOLD *for* $128,000 CURRENCY,

JONES & CO.

The next morning the Gold Bank receives $100,000 gold, from Brown & Co., for which it pays $126,075 in currency, and delivers the same to Smith & Co., who pay the Bank $128,000 in currency. The Bank thus holds the difference between these two sums, amounting to $1,025 in currency, which it pays to Jones & Co., as the profit of the operation. The following memorandum, handed by Jones & Co. to the Bank, will show the account between them, viz.:

---

57   *STATEMENT OF JONES & CO., TO*

NEW YORK GOLD EXCHANGE BANK,

Received from	Gold.	Rate.	Currency.	Deliver to	Gold.	Rate.	Currency.
Brown & Co.	$100,000	126¾	$126,075	Smith & Co.	$100,000	128	$128,000
			1,025				
			$128,000				$128,000

Currency due Jones & Co., $1,025.

The Bank receives ten cents on every ten thousand gold cleared as a compensation for so doing, a very pretty percentage on yearly clearances of $20,000,000,000.

The foregoing is only a brief and very imperfect outline of Wall street and of the Stock and Gold Exchange. Institutions can be best illustrated by their moral workings on individuals. History by tragedy, comedy, and the limner's art. Wall street, too, shows clearest by the portraits, the moving tales and comic situations, the personal aspects and experiences, of the men who have given themselves up to the chances, changes and struggles of a speculator's life.

CHAPTER III.

THE FIRST VENTURE.

A New York Boarding-house in Perspective—Wall Street Patter—Curb-
stone Brokers "At Home"—A Flyer on Old Southern—A Bird of
Omen—The Regular Brokers in Their Work-shop—Jacob Little—
His Career—The Napoleon of the Bears—A Shrewd Move—He
Scatters the Bulls—His Character and Peculiarities—Old Southern
"Firm at the Close."

N the year 1857, there stood a three story and
attic mansion in the lower part of the City
of New York, not many miles, or even yards,
from College Place. It was the last of a row of
similar domiciles which had been shoved from their
foundations, and their place occupied by a tier of
heavy built stores, which now reared themselves aloft,
and looked down like so many tall bullies with beet-
ling brows upon the solitary dwelling-house, hustled
and crowded between them.

It was easy to guess its history from its appearance.
In its first years it had been the abode of an opulent
merchant. But what had once been a private use
was now a public convenience. It was now fulfilling
the destiny to which every house in the city would
seem to be finally allotted; it was a boarding-house.

A roomy habitation cut up into chambers, windowed
or windowless and pigeon-holed like a lawyer's desk
with cells and dormitories, resonant through the

watches of the night with the stertorous breathing of hard-worked dry-goods drummers or the night-mare cries of dyspeptic law-clerks.

The dining-room was a little Babel in respect of tongues, a miniature New York in respect of callings. Square merchants, angular lawyers and rotund doctors loudly bandying the bye-words and slang of their different professions. Mysterious men, cormorants of "Queer Street," who seemed to extract a rich sustenance out of the viewless air, like the chameleon changing their color with the objects of their pursuit, haunting hall-ways and dusky basements, or on elevated perches with winking eyes and darting viscid tongues, ensnaring the tiny insects of the hour. Old buffers, narrators of the commercial legends of Pearl Street and studiously marking with intermittent glance in the columns of the Journal of Commerce, the hoistings and tumblings of cotton and the ebbings and flowings of tea. Young lads, tyros in the great school of trade, to whose ears the peals from the cupola of old St. Paul might be supposed to ring out in prophetic tones as Bow bells did to Dick Whittington: "Turn again Dick Johnson, or Jones, or Smith! Mayor of New York!"

In this dining-room in the month of June, in the year aforesaid, seated at a side table, were five persons of the masculine gender, swiftly consuming, after the fashion of their country, their six o'clock dinner. An indescribable something about their air and manner, would have subtly but surely told to the thorough-bred New Yorker what their occupation might be, though a new comer would have not so readily guessed it. All were nattily dressed, but three of them sat self-absorbed, silently attending to the important, rather than (to them) agreeable business in which they were just then engaged. The two others, however, amply made up for the taciturnity of their companions. One of these two was a gentleman moulded on the cycloidal pattern. His body, which was as nearly circular as was consistent with the vital economy, was firmly set on a pair of columnar legs. His head and face was an oblate spheroid, hair curled like a Bacchanal, eyes twin orbs, wide open and staring, eyebrows well defined and semi-circular, as if drawn by compasses, his nose the segment of a circle, and his mouth a large, red dot; in fact, the two features last named, seemed to form a perpetual interrogation point, expressive of wondering inquiry.

The other was built on precisely the opposite plan. Tall of stature, and slender of limb, a long face, with lantern-jaws, a lengthy nose and straight hair, he might be imagined to represent linear measurement as his fellow did, spherical and cubical contents. A young lady, who sat at the large table, had given this couple the sobriquet of O. and I. from their resemblance to those letters of the alphabet, and a young gentleman, fresh from the classic shades of Yale, was wont to hail their entrance with the words, Io! triumphe!

Sitting directly opposite to this couple at table, my attention was attracted by the strange jargon in which they conversed in jerky staccato tones.

"Anything doing in Nicaragua?" inquired letter O. of letter I. "Nothing said at the close," replied letter I. From which I inferred they might have some connection with the fillibustering in that country. " What's the price of Cumberland coal?" asked O. From which immediately a surmise arose that O. and I. were in the coal business.

" How is old Southern," inquired O. again. These men must be in the theatrical line, from their inquiring so familiarly after Sothern, the actor.

" Not much margin on that," said O, holding a strip of leathery steak on a fork. "A good sale," retorted letter I.

" Seller three," rejoined O, " or regular?"

" Nothing up! and buyer three."

" No commish," &c.

These observations, uttered in a jocose tone, seemed to give exquisite gratification to the whole five, and strongly excited the risibles of O.

Just then, a grave gentleman addressed him, inquiring the news from Wall Street. This cleared up the mystery. These men were dealers in the stock market. They soon rose from the table and left the room, and the grave gentleman then informed me they were Wall Street brokers. " Curb-stone brokers," said Mrs. S., correcting him. " Gutter-snipes," mamma, added the young lady.

The tribe of curb-stone brokers, which in the greenback era swarmed like locusts and filled the air with their importunate chirk, in 1857 was comparatively few in number. Their offices when they have offices are merely desk-rooms in upper lofts or murky basements. More generally the flooring of their offices is the sidewalk and its ceiling the firmament "fretted with golden fire," perhaps we should say with golden fractions—the eighths and quarters of the market

6

price which it is their business to catch. On a busy day they are all eyes and ears, scud and scamper, their fingers quivering like aspen leaves, their mouths pouring out a stream of bids and offers disencumbered of all the spare syllables, while they telegraph signals with the ten digits, and with nods and winks.

The curb-stone broker is the financial bud which if not nipped by some untimely frost, often blossoms into the flower which blooms in the garden of the regular board. He works for smaller wages than his regularly initiated brother of the Stock Exchange. In 1870 his brokerage is only 1-32, or three dollars and twelve cents for buying or selling one hundred shares, in 1857 it was 1-8, or twelve dollars and a half, and sometimes only half that amount. This brokerage is only for *buying and selling*, for the *delivering and carrying* of stocks is done mostly by the more wealthy brokers of the regular board. The curb-stone broker is the scullion in the brokerage kitchen, feasting on remnants and odds and ends, and is obliged to serve his time there before he can be admitted to the banquets and privileges of the parlor. His favorite stamping-ground in 1857, and as late as 1864, was in William Street, between Exchange Place and Beaver Street.

A few days after this, as I was passing down William Street, about ten o'clock in the morning, I ran against O. (by which name he will be designated in these pages), on the edge of a crowd of thirty or forty men who were standing on the sidewalk. He saluted me with all the familiarity of an old acquaintance, and offered with the greatest cheerfulness to show me the lions, or rather the bulls and bears of

CURBSTONE BROKERS.

the street, fairly deluging my ears with his lingo.
"How is it done? Easiest thing in the world, put up
your margin, say five hundred on a hundred shares,
then keep margined up or they'll sell you out. Buy
your stock any way you like. Buyer 30, or cash, or
regular and carry it. Don't let 'em bluff you. Never
sold short? No? Then sell on a seller thirty, put
up your margin same as before, or, if you'd rather,
sell it regular and borrow next day for delivery—interest runs in your favor on sellers' option, six per
cent. Keep your eye peeled for corners. Brokerage?
One quarter per cent. each way. I'll do your business
for an eighth. Take one of my cards (handing me
a card), good references you see. Office up three
flights."

THE CARD.

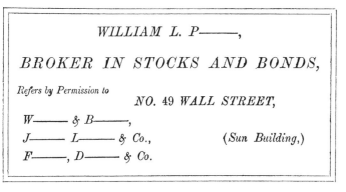

WILLIAM L. P———,

BROKER IN STOCKS AND BONDS,

Refers by Permission to

NO. 49 WALL STREET,

W——— & B———,

J——— L——— & Co.,   (Sun Building,)

F———, D——— & Co.

All this was rolled off as glibly as the patter of a
mountebank, and as he paused I detected him in the
act of winking to a short man on the other side of
the crowd, who looked very much as if he might be
the half-brother of Socrates, and who a moment after
came round and joined us. He hailed my friend O.
by the name of Little Bitters, which was the name

under which he was known among his Wall Street associates, though why he should have borne this name it is hard to say; it was certainly not from any proclivity to the beverage, and his disposition and manners were of the blandest.

Socrates was duly introduced as Mr. D. A silent man with a high forehead and a face plowed into furrows by a ten years' experience in Wall Street, where, as I afterwards learned, he had been playing a game of see-saw, making and losing alternately, and paying every year a small fortune in the shape of commissions to his brokers.

His lofty brow and general appearance of owlish wisdom, led me to expect that this man could give me the entire philosophy of speculation in a few words, and I was not deceived, for on asking him his opinion of the market, and whether it would answer to take a chance in, he uttered the following somewhat turfy apothegm: " You can't tell till you bet." Quite true, Mr. D. You never *can* tell till you put up your margin, in other words, till you *bet* in Wall Street.

But all this time, while we stood there, the knot of brokers and speculators on the side-walk were as busy as bees over a honey-pot, coming and going, brandishing their arms and vociferating, making notes in little books, now buying stock, and running back to their offices, and reporting what they had done, and anon returning with fresh orders to buy or sell.

And now a slender young man, of twenty-five summers, came bounding into the crowd. It was R. He was be-ringed and be-jewelled like a Rajah, hatted,

gloved, shod, coated and pantalooned, in all the glory
of Broadway art. He seemed to know every one,
and every one seemed to hail him with empressment,
mingled with respect, for he had gone short of Old
Southern a few weeks before, and had just bought in
at a profit of twenty-five thousand.

Michigan Southern and Northern Indiana Railroad
Stock, more familiarly known as Old Southern, or
Old Sow, for short, is one of the old historical
stocks of Wall Street. The name calls up memories
of great fortunes, won and lost in its mighty vibrations. The magic of its rings, the unfathomable
depth of its pools, are known to many a speculator,
to his joy or sorrow, and most of the great operators
of the street, for the past eighteen years, have been
mixed up with it for the weal or woe of themselves
and the public. Little, the Litchfields, Travers and
two of the Jeromes, Henry Keep, Daniel Drew and
Cornelius Vanderbilt, have thrown it up and down,
like a gigantic shuttlecock, from 8 to 140.

Old Southern was the card to-day. It had lately
been taken hold of by a ring known as the Litchfield
party, and hoisted to 55, from which point, it had
dropped, and was selling that morning for 38. Nothing was heard on the street but Old Southern, Buyer
ten, Seller ten, cash or regular. They who had gone
short of it at a higher figure, were buying in and
covering their shorts, and bagging their profits; they
who had gone long of it at a higher figure, were sell
ing it and ascertaining their losses. Some were buying for a future profit (or loss); the ring were busily
crying down the stock, and all the while quietly buying it for another twist upwards.

"I can guarantee you a handsome profit on Old Southern," remarked O; "you see the time to buy stocks is when they are down." This familiar truism, together with the fact, that R, the lucky bear above mentioned, was in the crowd, buying like smoke, decided me. An order was forthwith made out, signed, and handed to O, as follows, to wit.: "Buy for my account and risk, 100 shares of Old Southern at the market; Buyer 30." Signed, etc.

O. then elbowed his way into the crowd with the air of a man who had important business to transact, and bought in a trice the 100 shares, giving me a memorandum which read thus: "N. Y., June —, 1857, I have to-day bought of W. B. C. & Co., for your account, 100 shares of Old So. Buyer 30 at 38⅝." Signed, etc.

Having handed O. five hundred dollars as a margin on this venture, my frail bark may be considered to have been duly launched on the stormy waters of Wall Street.

It is the first venture in speculation which costs, as many a man has found to his sorrow. Lucky is he whose first flyer of one hundred shares shows a loss, for this is a lesson and a warning sufficient often to turn him from the career of a stock-operator. But when the first flyer shows a profit, ah! that first profit! The first sip of the cup, this is delight, then comes rapture, frenzy, stupor and the dreary wakening, in quick succession.

The sound of the half hour stroke after ten, from the belfry of Trinity, had hardly died away, when looking towards Wall Street, I saw approaching, a quaint figure, holding in its hand a roll of stock certificates. It disappeared down a basement office at the corner of William Street and Exchange Place, but was up again on the sidewalk in a twinkling. A tall, slight figure, with a stoop, a black alpaca coat hanging loosely about it, walking towards the crowd at a rapid pace. What a strange face! The coloring a vivid darkness, a clear-obscure, like a tropical night. The eyes dark, with a dreamy, introverted look—the eyes of a philosopher or poet, the drooping, sagacious nose of a financier, and the flexible mouth of an orator. The expression mobile, changing not only emotionally, but in the shape of the features. As he paused on the fringes of the crowd, his lips were suddenly protruded, as if the market were something to be tested by the sense of taste, and then as suddenly withdrawn to their natural position. Again they were puckered up, and protruded as if he were preparing to kiss something, perhaps a plump profit. Every motion and look spoke the Wall Street man, and something more. For during the ten seconds that he stood on the edge of the walk, balancing himself on his toes, now dropping his head on his breast, now raising it and looking over the crowd, and turning it from one side to the other with fitful glances, he seemed something uncanny—a raven or other bird of omen, hovering over the market, and preparing to croak the warning of panic. Suddenly he wheeled about, and flitted through a door opposite the crowd, on the west side of William Street. Who could he be? Gazing so intently upon him during the brief interval between his coming and going, I had till now neglected to ask O., my coryphœus, the name of this strange looking personage. "I don't know whom you mean. Let's visit the Board," replied he, " and we will find out who he is."

The Board of Brokers, in 1857, and as late as the Fall of 1865, (when they moved into their new building in Broad Street,) held their sessions in a room which overlooked Lord's Court, which formed the center of a block, bounded on the north by Exchange Place, on the east by William Street, on the south by Beaver Street, and on the west by Broad Street. "All roads lead to Rome;" the Stock Exchange Room was approached by many entrances, or rather tunnels, from different streets and quarters of the compass. These tunnels led across corridors, up stairs and down stairs, now dark, now light, and then dark again, and all converged into the central mine, echoing with the hoarse cries of the workmen in stocks as they wielded the monetary pickaxe and spade, or with words like hammers, smote the drill preparatory to some explosion which was to shake the rooted pillars of finance.

O. stuck closer to me than a brother, and by the favor of one of his broker friends, we were soon ushered into a room thronged by one or two hundred men, some moving about in circles as in a voluntary tread-mill, others in little knots, holding a discussion or retailing gossip of the market, others gathered in the pit, apparently waiting for the president to call the stock which they had orders to buy or sell. The market was at that time full of cliques and corners. Erie, New York Central, Old Southern, La Crosse, and many other stocks were under manipulation.

The call that morning had run through Governments, State Stocks and miscellaneous securities, and now ERIE rang out from the rostrum.

The whole body of dealers rushed to the front, red-faced old gentlemen, with frosty heads, left their seats, and their huge quotation books, portly men "sleek headed and such as sleep o' nights" undisturbed by dreams of panics and ruined customers, lean and hungry-looking men of sallow complexion, youths with shining morning faces, and promenade attire, all skated across the floor with a ravenous eagerness, and yelled out bids and offers, poking their quivering forefingers almost into the eyes of their competitors. In two minutes, the sharp fire of voices died away into a few dropping shots, and again the president shouted NEW YORK CENTRAL. The hubbub rose again, and swelled still louder, and then died away as before. Swiftly the call proceeded. The name of stock after stock, fell from the president's lips, caught up by the crowd, and tossed about from mouth to mouth, echoed from the lofty ceiling, but falling dead upon the cloth-lined walls.

Here was a new form of the Wall Street lingo—a mathematical form. These men spoke in figures, instead of words, and figures uttered so quickly, and poured out in such numbers, that the spectator was fairly dizzied: $36\frac{1}{4}$, $\frac{1}{8}$, $\frac{3}{8}$, $11\frac{1}{2}$, $\frac{5}{8}$, $\frac{3}{4}$, 22, 300, 500. Only the clear voice of the presiding officer, announcing the closing bids, gives any idea to an outside observer, of the real price of the stock, and as to what has been actually bought and sold by any broker, that is only known to themselves. A single word—bought or sold—lost in the din, a crook of the finger, a slight nod of the head, or a wink of the eye, all unnoticed

by the spectator, settles the business done between
the buyer and seller. This language of signs, is as
distinct and definite a part of the Wall Street lingo,
as that of words and figures. The eye is the inter-
preter here instead of the ear, while the body, and,
fingers, and features, are the speaking organs.

But all the time we had been gazing on this curious
spectacle from behind the scenes, the same strange
figure I had noticed in William Street, was moving
restlessly about, now standing on the uppermost step,
which descended into the crowded pit, and buying a
sellers' option, now sitting down in a fidgety uncertain way for a moment, and then rising and bidding
where he stood, for various stocks, as they were called.

When old Southern was reached, he moved quickly
to the centre of the room, and bought five hundred
shares, sellers' option, and sold five hundred shares,
buyers' option, while the crowd paused and turned
their eyes upon him.

"Who is that man?" inquired I. "That man,"
replied O, "that man is *Jacob Little.*"

The portrait of this noted financier, which accom-
panies these pages, is only the faithful representation
of that face in repose, the forceful will, the keen
strong intellect, the swift play of the feelings, which
lighten up that face, and shaped it into changeful successive expressions, could never have been brought
out by art. Jacob Little! A great name for twenty
years in Wall Street! Banker, broker, operator in
stocks, exchanges and cotton, he ran through the whole
scale, sounding all the heavy notes, from high to low.
He would reign the king of the market, fight a dozen
pitched battles, suffer defeat, abdicate, and then once

more ascend the throne, all in the space of six months. Master of every kind of game played in stocks, rings, corners, sleight-of-hand, beggar your neighbor, bluff, lock-up and bar-out, straddling two horses going different ways, he had the skill as well as the nerve to play them all, and for the most part came out the winner.

Born in Newburyport, Massachusetts, the son of a ship-builder in that town, he came to New York when a boy, and entered the office of Jacob Barker, another celebrated financier, and soon showed himself by his diligence and shrewdness, to be a worthy pupil of his master, from whom also he may have derived those brusque and almost rough manners, for which he was afterwards so remarkable. Circumstances decided his future career and policy, as they have that of so many other men of mark. If he had commenced his life as a stock operator in 1861, instead of 1835, he might have been a great "Bull," and have shared with Cornelius Vanderbilt, the spoils and honors of his campaigns. But soon after he started in business, the financial omens all portended the great revulsion of 1837; this fact, and the failure of several banks, organized by Jacob Barker, his former employer, inspired him with distrust as to the future value of stock-securities, and so he became a "Bear." When the severe panic of that era ensued, he was heavily short of stocks, and made enormous profits by selling short, for several years afterwards. He used to sell Vicksburg Bank Stock, and other Southern securities on sellers' options, of one, two, and three years, and as those stocks fell almost to zero, his profits were correspondingly large. From 1838, to 1845–6, he was the leading man of the street, and was rated at two millions, a great fortune in those days.

It was in 1846, if we are rightly informed, that his first failure occurred, about the time of the corner in Norwich and Worcester Railroad Stock. In this operation he was contrary to his wont, a bull, and attempted to control this stock, and entrap his old companions in arms, the bears, by compelling them to buy in the stock, and fill their contracts at 95, or thereabouts. Among his associates in this enterprise, were certain wealthy Bostonians, who, in order to secure themselves against any sales of the stock below 90, had got Mr. Little to sign a bond in the penal sum of $25,000, by which, he agreed not to sell any of the stock below that price. But after the corner had been pushed to about 90, he found that the undertaking would be impracticable, and that he would be plunged into irretrievable ruin by proceeding in it. Accordingly, he sent a large amount of the stock to Rawdon & Groesbeck, who had been old clerks of his, with directions to send it to Boston, and sell it there. The Bostonians bought the stock, in order to sustain the market, and not knowing how to account for so much stock coming on the market, wrote to Mr. Little, who replied, that he had been compelled to sell the stock, and that he was ready to settle up on the bond, and a few days after sent them a check for $25,000, which relieved him from all legal liability thereupon.

Mr. Little's losses on this Norwich and Worcester attempted corner were $1,000,000, but his foresight had prevented a worse catastrophe, and he soon paid up in full and resumed.

Of course his numerous bear operations made him fair game for a corner, and sometimes he found himself surrounded by an army of bulls, whereupon he would retreat to his last fortress, and after making terms with his besiegers would surrender, and then proceed to re-organize his shattered forces. But he was generally a hard man to corner, and occasionally, when his antagonists thought they had accomplished their purpose, he would turn on them and rout them with great slaughter. Once he sold an enormous quantity of Erie Stock on sellers' options; the bulls quietly took it, and having bought up the loose stock floating in the market, proceeded to put on the screws, bidding the stock up, and holding it for the day when Mr. Little would have to deliver the stock which he owed. No flaw could be seen in the scheme. The stock was held in a firm grip—the great bear *must* come to the conspirators and beg for mercy. The eventful day for the completion of his contracts was now come. Before twelve a notification was sent to the parties to whom the stock was due, that the stock would be delivered immediately, and a few moments after, in marched Mr. Little himself, bearing a huge bundle of *fresh certificates of Erie Railroad Stock*. The bull party were in consternation. They found themselves loaded with a burden on which they had not calculated. A panic took place, the market fell twenty per cent., and Mr. Little had won the day. How was this? It appears that the Erie Railroad Company had sometime previously issued a large number of certificates of indebtedness, *convertible into stock*, (a fact unknown to the bull party,)—these certificates had been bought up by Mr. Little, and converted into stock the morning of the day when they were delivered.

The financial star of Mr. Little had, in 1857, long ceased to be in the ascendant, but its influence was still felt on the opinions, operations and fortunes of the frequenters of the stock-market. His qualities of head, heart and character were such as had always won the respect and confidence of the stock-dealing public. Not the least remarkable among these qualities, was his intense devotion to his life-work—the buying and selling of stocks. Action to him was happiness, and in his own experience he seemed to prove the truth of the poet's lines:

> "Even when the wished end's denied,
> Yet while the busy means are plied
> They bring their own reward."

Though he were buying or selling millions, he thought no detail of business beneath his notice. He overlooked his clerks in his office, and no one could enter or leave it without his knowledge, and any day he might have been seen hurrying through the streets, diving into basements and delivering his stocks like an errand boy. Sunday brought that busy brain and hand little rest, for while the bells were pealing the hour of worship, he could often be seen wending his way to *his* sanctum in William Street. His amusement, his pleasure, his life, was business, business, still business. The story of operations so wide-embracing, close, swift and daring, is among the best-kept traditions of the street. What a record of the thousands of millions bought and sold! What a tale of marvellous diligence could be unfolded, if that huge pile of stock registers and ledgers, now amid the forgotten lumber of a garret, could be opened! To make or lose an immense fortune was, to him, what a game of chess is to others, a pastime. More than once he failed, owing a million beyond what he could pay, and in twelve months resumed business with a capital of a half million, after paying his entire indebtedness.

But saturated as he was with the spirit of Wall Street, and breathing as he had done from early youth that moral atmosphere so deadening and blighting to the noblest natures, he preserved not only an unspotted commercial reputation, but all his native kindliness and magnanimity. Beneath his blunt words and ungracious ways there was a warm and generous heart, often too proud to accept favors, but always ready to bestow them. He would compromise the claims which he held against others for what they chose to offer, but constantly insisted upon paying his own debts in full. In the latter years of his life he failed for a large amount, and, as usual in such cases, gave his notes to settle the indebtedness. Certain friends of his held some of these notes, and not expecting ever to call on Mr. Little for payment, or that he would ever be able to pay them, had cancelled them, and wiped the indebtedness from their books. But the maker of the notes one day put in an appearance for the purpose of taking them up, having just made one of his great hits. He expressed the greatest indignation on finding the notes had been cancelled, and insisted on paying their amount, which he accordingly did.

If all the claims which he had compromised during his active business life, and every other debt which was due him could have been collected, the sum it is said would have amounted to several millions. As it was, after his death, out of his old accounts, his friends collected $150,000 as a provision for his family.

For some weeks previous to the morning referred to in the fore part of this chapter, Mr. Little had been operating for a decline in Old Southern. But in what way he was operating that particular morning was not patent, at least to the eyes of a novice. The price of Old Southern was firm at 38½, and was apparently tending upwards.

CHAPTER IV.

PROFIT AND LOSS.

T was twelve o'clock, meridian. The call of stocks was over, and the brokers, with their quotation books under their arms, were hurrying out of the door through the tunnel-hall into William Street, by one exit, and into Exchange Place by another, but a goodly number descended the staircase into Beaver Street, and bent their course to lower Delmonico, which stands hard by, to refresh themselves with those dainty viands and beverages so delectable to the palate of the regular Wall Street broker, who is almost invariably a delicate feeder, and a cautious drinker, if he would be successful.

While sitting in that resounding boudoir of finance —the broker's board—O. squatted on a chair by my side, was pouring into my ear his explanations of the mysteries of the trade in stocks, retailing the gossip of the market, and pointing out the notable dealers, and recounting their profits and losses. When the

7

session broke up, he rose, remarking that he must go to his office and *report* what he had done, and asked me to accompany him thither.

A broker *reports* his purchases and sales to his office, so that they may be *compared*, in order to prevent misunderstandings and mistakes. A clerk, or office boy of the buyer, goes to the office of the seller, and announces to the stock-clerk there, that the firm or individual who employs him have bought 100 shares of Old Southern or Lake Shore, buyer 30, cash or regular, as the case may be, and the stock-clerk, if the comparison is found correct, thereupon bawls out "all right." The same form of comparison is gone through with by a clerk of the seller, who visits the office of the buyer for that purpose. Slips of paper containing memoranda of the purchases and sales, and signed by the respective brokers, are also exchanged. This report and comparison of purchases and sales clenches the bargain, and is of course a very necessary part of the business.

O. gripping my arm affectionately, trundled along through the devious passage into William Street, and so on, up to the Sun building, on the corner of Wall Street; then ascending three flights of stairs, puffing and sweating, he burst into a small room where a tall man was sitting before a solitary desk adding up columns of figures. He turned, and I recognized my table acquaintance known to the reader as letter I. His true name was Lansing. He was man-of-all-work in the office of O. his functions being those of confidential clerk, book-keeper, stock-clerk, cashier, errand-boy, and quasi-partner withal.

VIEW OF THE SUB-TREASURY.

He gave me a subdued greeting, but when O. informed him that I had just taken a flyer on 100 Old Southern, the commissions whereon redounded to the profit of their office, his face became instantly wreathed in wooden smiles, and dotted with dimples like a figure-head of curled maple. That broker's smile with which he greets a new customer, who could describe it but a Hogarth or a Dantin? How indifferent, or serious, or glum the expression of his face to the outsider, from whom he expects nothing! How cold and repellant to the customer who is "cleaned out" and marginless! But when the young operator approaches him with his pockets stuffed with greenbacks, his nerves unbruised by the shocks and thrills of the market, ready to encounter risks without a thought of the danger, and buying and selling with all the vivacity of youth, then how the face of his broker expands, brightens and warms. The corners of his mouth curve upwards, the muscles of his cheeks are hollowed into cavities in which the very sylphs of mirth seem to lurk, his eyes twinkle out of semi-circles of crows' feet, and his whole countenance appears to be under the inspiration of Momus, the God of laughter.

"Happy to see you at our office. Make it your headquarters. You've made a good a purchase this morning. Old Southern is sure to go up again; the ring are not through with it. Keep watch of it, however; don't let it run away from you, etc., etc." Under these cordial assurances of Lansing, everything looked rose-colored.

"What pleasant people these brokers are! What a charming prospect is opened to me! Let me see;

if Old Southern goes up ten per cent., I shall make a profit of $1,000. This sum I will draw out, and put $900 into a railroad bond for investment, and have $100 besides for pocket money, or I can put the $1,000 in the bank as the seed-corn for a future harvest. Suppose I add this $1,000 to my present margin and buy 300 shares in my next operation, make $3,000 out of this purchase and so on. In a year a fortune will have been piled up, etc.

These delicious reflections were interrupted by O., inquiring if I would like to accompany Lansing, his factotum, to the office of Jacob Little, to compare the 100 shares of Old Southern, (as I had seemed so much interested in his strange story,) or, as he rather disrespectfully phrased it, "stir up the Old Bear in his den."

We went. The office of Jacob Little & Co. was in the old Merchant's Exchange, and as we entered it, we saw Mr. Little vibrating between the desk where he generally stood and the desk occupied by his clerks, now snatching up a pile of stock certificates which lay before him, and fumbling them over, and now growling out something to the clerks. When he caught sight of us, he stood eyeing us with flickering and expectant glance.

"Mr. Little, we bought of your firm this morning, 100 Old Southern, at 38⅝. Buyer 30," said Lansing.

"Who's that! Who's that?"

"William L. P——," returned Lansing, giving O's. true name.

"Don't know anything about it; call again! call again! Go to Mr. P.; he will tell you all about it!"

"But, Mr. Little, I have just come from Mr. P. in order to compare this stock."

"Very well! Then go back to Mr. P. He knows all about it."

So saying, he resumed his vibrations and fumblings.

Fortunately, just then, the clerk, of whom the stock had been bought, entered the office, and the comparison was made before Mr. Little could interrupt him.

"He's a crusty, fidgetty old fellow," remarked L., as we walked up the street, "and always gives us a heap of trouble when we come to compare purchases and sales. Sometimes I slip into his office slyly, and try to compare with one of the clerks, but he generally sees me, and puts in his oar and makes a mess of it."

This peculiarity arising out of a temperament excessively nervous by nature, and made more so by the excitements of business, grew on Mr. Little, and in the last years of his life, became a source of great vexation to his brother dealers.

Old Father Time is no laggard in the stock-market. The sultry days of July flew away. Old Southern was all the while rising. During the week which followed June 28th, the day when my 100 shares were bought, it sold at 46. Why was this? The public had no confidence in the value of the stock. The financial condition of the company was known to be bad. Every morning, the New York Herald and other dailies were calling attention to the rottenness of its concerns, and yet, the stock kept rising. The speculating public had *been selling it short.* It was this that encouraged the bull party to push it up, because, sometime those who had been going short of it, would have to come into the market and buy it of them for delivery. As the whole amount of the stock was but $6,000,000, or thereabouts, of which, only a portion was floating around in the street, it would be readily handled by any party who saw fit to take hold of it. On the 28th of July, the last day of the option, the stock was sold at 53. The following account of O. will show with what result:

MR. ——— ——— IN ACCT. WITH WILLIAM L. P——,
(OTHERWISE O.)

Dr.			Cr.	
To 100 shares Old So., bought at 38⅝,	- $3,862 50	By 100 Old So., sold at 53, . .	$5,300 00	
To brokerage, Buying ⅛,	12 50	By cash, (margin,) .	500 00	
To brokerage, Selling ⅛,	12 50		$5,800 00	
To interest, 30 days, 6 per cent., . .	19 05			
	$3,906 55			
Balance due ——— ———	$1,893 45			
	$5,800 00		$5,800 00	

The balance due me then upon this operation was $1,893.45, from which, after subtracting $500, the margin which I had given O., there remained $1,393.45, as the profits of my first flyer.

If there is any feeling natural to the novice in Wall Street, it is the desire to look at the cash results of his first profitable operation, to finger and crumple up the bank-bills, whether crisp from the press, or limp with the manipulations of a hundred different possessors, to gaze with rapture on the classical features of the Goddess of Liberty stamped on ten dollar coins, and chink the golden metal in the capacious pocket.

Yielding to this desire, I found courage to ask O. to draw his check for balance due. His round face lengthened into an oval, and a cloud of disappointment passed over it, for he had been feasting his imagination on visions of prospective commissions from his new customer. Slowly he filled out and signed an elegantly engraved check which he extended towards me between his fat thumb and forefinger, then drew it back, and gazing at the figures with pride and satisfaction, exclaimed, " You should thank me for that little profit! come in and see us soon now you know who your friends are," with which remark, he handed it over to me, his thumb and fingers seeming to nurse and fondle it till it was folded up, and passed into my vest pocket.

Never fear, O.! this is not the last time that you are destined to see " that little profit." Again you will hold it as a margin, and it will drop many a commission into the " itching palm " of that plump hand.

After the scuffles and heat and noisome odors of the city, how cool and calm and sweet the air of the pine and hemlock woods. Reclining beneath some monarch of the forest, gazing at the blue sky, or at the sunlight streaming in shafts of gold between the branches, and watching the wild and beautiful things flitting through the air, or bounding along through the vistas of gray old trunks, for two weeks, I forgot that such things as stocks and quotations ever existed.

Returning to the city, on taking my seat in the

cars, on one of the great lines of travel, I heard the familiar cry, "New York papers." Hastily securing one, I opened it, when my eye fell on the money article where the price of Old Southern was quoted at 36, a fall of seventeen per cent., from 53, the price at which I had sold, and two per cent. below the price at which I had bought my first 100 shares. Here was a chance for another "little profit." It fairly "stuck out" to use the street slang. It swelled and took definite shape the longer the mind dwelt upon it. The steam-fiend which was dragging the express train at the rate of forty miles an hour was too slow for eager fancy which was already in William Street, and had bought already another 100 shares of Old Southern at 36.

It was on a close, hot evening, on the 13th of August, that I stood on the door-steps of my boarding-house, where I found O. sitting ready to receive me, clad in the lightest summer costume, his face rubicund with the heat, and radiant with good omens for the morrow. "Lively times in the street since you left," remarked he, "the ring have been unloading Old Southern, and Jake Little has been selling it right and left. If you feel like taking a turn in it be on hand to-morrow." Bright and early the next morning, I handed $1,500 margin to O., and ordered him to buy 300 shares of Old Southern. This lot cost 34½. In a week, the price went down to 30, and on the advice of O. it was sold, netting me a loss of $1,400.

The market was reported as very weak and declining. "Try a short sale," said O. I put up more margin, and *tried* a short sale of, a hundred shares, at 29,

Seller 10. Jacob Little took the contract. Three days after, the Ohio Life and Trust Company failed, and the market went down with a jump. On the 26th of August, the stock was bought in for delivery to Jacob Little, but before it could be delivered, his failure was announced. His failure had occurred in this wise. All along back there had been a difference of from three to six per cent. between a buyer's option of thirty days, and a seller's option of thirty days, in Old Southern and other leading stocks. Taking advantage of this, Mr. Little had been selling stocks on buyers' options, and buying them back on sellers' options, making a profit on the difference. When stocks fell so heavily the latter part of August, the stock on the seller's options was delivered to him at a much higher price and while the buyer's options were still open. But a few days after, these latter contracts were closed, and Mr. Little resumed business, and thus I was saved by the skin of my teeth, and bagged another profit of $900 by my first short sale.

The day was now approaching when another cycle in the history of American credit was to be finished with the crash known as the panic of 1857. The causes which led to that panic are familiar to all. It was the discovery of gold in California which mainly produced the vast expansion of the Banking system. In little more than eight years, prior to 1857, the paper money circulation had nearly doubled, and as early as 1854, five hundred new banks were issuing their bills, and stimulating trade and speculation. The basis of these banks was the *idea* of an increased supply of the precious metals. But when that supply had been diminished by exportation to Europe, to pay debts incurred by overtrading, the stimulus was withdrawn, and trade and speculation alike collapsed. American credit in that era may be likened to a vessel ill-built, badly worked, and carrying too heavy press of canvass, launched upon a spring freshet which poured through the golden sluices of Eldorado. As the waters flowed on, they broadened and grew shallower. The vessel at last broke its rudder, and went aground, and there stuck fast till a refluent tide could set it afloat.

He would have been a bold operator, who, knowing the dangers, would have dared then to buy and sell in Wall Street. During the eight weeks which succeeded the failure of the Ohio Life and Trust Company, banks and brokerage firms were breaking by the score, and the supposed profits of the lucky speculator were liable to be swept away in a moment, or actually converted into losses as the following operation, which I next engaged in, will show.

The market, towards the middle of September, began to brighten, and stocks went up for the moment. This looked like a favorable opportunity to operate for a decline, or sell short. Accordingly, I sold 100 shares Old Southern at 20, seller 10, to an operator named Slocum, who had been acting as an agent for certain western banks. A few days after, the stock was bought at 17, for delivery to Slocum, who was, by his contract, bound to pay me 20, and in this way I should have made a profit of $300. But when the stock was carried to Slocum, instead of paying for it, he announced that he was "in deep waters," "no remittances from Chicago," etc., etc., but stated that he "would be all right in a few days," and would take the stock and pay for it then. Accordingly, the stock was retained, and every day was presented to Slocum, and every day the same story was told, "come in to-morrow," while day by day the price of the stock was falling from 17 to 16, from 16 to 14, and so on, till in ten days it was selling at 10. Slocum then settled the matter, by giving his note for $1,000, that being the difference between what he agreed to pay for stock, namely, 20, and the present market price of the stock. The stock was then sold at 10, thus netting me an actual loss of $700, against which, I held the *negotiable* promissory note of Slocum for $1,000, though it would be difficult to explain why such a note should be called negotiable, since I tried in vain to negotiate it at a fifty per cent. discount.

While sitting in my office, the morning before the panic of October 13th, a tall, lathy man, with a bilious smile, walked in, and said that he had been informed that I held $1,000 of Slocum's paper. I produced the note in question, when he remarked again that Slocum was "dead broke," and would never pay a cent, but he wished to use the note as an offset, and was willing to pay something for it, perhaps as much as five per cent.

After the due amount of haggling, the bargain was struck at ten per cent., and my visitor counted down one hundred dollars in five's and ten's, looking suspiciously new, on the Bentonville Bank, Illinois. To my remonstrances against the character of the money, he produced, out of his coat pocket, a Bank Note Reporter, published the day before, in which, the notes of that bank were quoted at only one per cent. discount. As this rate took off but one dollar from the hundred which lay upon the table before me, nothing more was said, and the tall, lathy man and note vanished through the door-way.

I hastened to the office of an acquaintance, who bought Western bank bills, and on whisking my hundred dollars over, and studying the vignettes, he gave a long, doubtful whistle, and said the bills were not salable in New York, but that he would forward them to his correspondent at Chicago for redemption, though his own private opinion was, the bank was a " wild-cat," and the currency was " stump-tail and red-dog." The bills went to Chicago by express, and in due time, something like the following letter came back in reply:

CHICAGO, *October 18th*, 1857.

To ——— ———, No. —— Wall Street, New York.

My Dear Sir:—Your valued favor of date 12th inst., received, and also package of ($100) one hundred dollars, bills of the Bentonville Bank, per express. In reply, I visited Bentonville day before yesterday, and found it a small hamlet, consisting of three houses and a grocery store, situated on a prairie, about ten miles from the railroad. The back part of the grocery store was occupied by the bank, but as this institution has now suspended operations, the President and Cashier have gone to Chicago. I saw no safe or other evidences of cash, and so conclude the assets are now in the breeches pocket of the President and Cashier.

The bills have only a nominal value in our market of from 2 to 5 per cent. We cannot, to-day, pay you over 2 per cent., should you wish to sell them.

My expenses to and from Bentonville were fifteen dollars, which I have charged to you.

Yours Respectfully,

C. D. CULLENDER.

My supposed profit of $300 had thus resolved itself into thin air, and left only the residum of a little bill of expense.

On footing up the accounts of three months' operations, I found my net profits a trifle over one hundred and forty dollars. Rather a small compensation for two months' wear and tear in Wall Street, let alone the risk. And now to buy or not to buy, that's the question! The memory of that first profit was yet green and pleasing to dwell upon, but listening to financial explosions in quick succession, and gazing on tumbling banks and fortunes melting away, is not calculated to give assurance and nerve to the stock-operator, and accordingly, shutting the ear to the blandishments of hope and of O., the decision was not to buy or sell more for the present.

At this point of the narrative, the question naturally arises, why do most of the operators in Wall Street come out minus on the sum total of their operations? The answer to this question involves the whole philosophy of speculation. To the looker-on, it seems the easiest thing in the world to make money there, and so it would be if men only did the business on mercantile principles, and only took fair mercantile risks. But they rarely do. The margins on which stocks and gold are bought and sold, are too small. Any merchant doing business properly, will fortify himself with a margin of from thirty to ninety per cent. on the amount of business he does, while the ordinary stock operator buys and sells stocks on a margin of from three to twenty per cent. on stocks, and of from one to ten per cent. on gold. Add to this the fact, that most of the outside public buy stocks, when they are high and rampant, and sell short, when they are low and weak. Now suppose one thousand men, with an aggregate capital of $5,000,000, who have bought or sold stocks on the above insufficient margin, and ten men like Vanderbilt, Drew, etc., whose interest is opposed to that of the one thousand aforesaid, and whose capital is ten times as great. If these ten men wish to make stocks go down, they create a panic by locking up money or in some other way "clean out" the small holders, and then buy their stocks at low figures, make money easy, and up prices go again.

It will also be readily seen, by any one who reflects for an instant, how intimately time enters, as an element, into every stock operation. Time fights on the side of the man who buys a lot of stock at a fair price and pays for it, inasmuch as the material interests of our country are steadily advancing, *on the whole*, and the value of the stock becomes enhanced. Time, too, fights on the side of the man who speculates, when he is fortified by large margins, because he is protected by those margins from the losses incidental to the constant vibrations of the market. The man who can *keep* his position in spite of the temporary condition of prices, is the man who, in the end, wins.

The frequency of operations is another fruitful cause of losses. Of course, brokers desire their customers to buy and sell as often as possible, because they get a commission on every transaction made. But the chances are against any one who operates on margins, and therefore the oftener he operates, the more of these dangerous risks he takes. If, instead of buying and selling every day, and giving all his money to his broker in the shape of commissions, he would only buy three or four times a year, when stocks are low and after the panics which periodically occur, and then hold for a ten or fifteen per cent. rise, he would find himself ahead of the market when he came to make up his yearly accounts.

A most weighty maxim, verified by Wall Street experience, is this: "Cut short your losses and let your profits run." This has been the making of many a speculator, and yet how few have the nerve to practice it. Pat Hearne, the late noted sporting man, was wont to operate thus. He would buy 100 shares of some stock, and when it rose one per cent. he would buy another 100 shares, and so on. As soon as it fell one per cent. he sold the whole. This, everybody will say, is a sound plan of operating. In the rise of 1864, a well-known young operator made $80,000 in Reading, by operating on this principle, and lost it all by forsaking this principle and letting his *losses* run. Again, in 1865, he sold short 100 shares of Erie, on credit, having no money to use as a margin; as the price fell he kept selling. This was during the Ketchum break in August. In four days he made $12,000, but a few weeks afterwards he lost the whole by violating his principle of operation.

The practice of selling stocks short will be found, *in the end*, to be *invariably* a losing business. For while the *buying of* stocks, under fair mercantile conditions, is perfectly legitimate and regulated by rules of finance, which in the long run bring the holder out "whole" or with a profit, operations on the "*short side*" are always nearly akin to gambling, in which the "Bank" has a percentage in its favor and on the doctrine of chances is at least the winner against the gamester who bets his money on the cards. If A contracts to deliver 100 shares of a certain stock in 30 days, and if B has the whole of the stock in his hands, how can A close his contract without paying B his price ? A history of the fortunes of the leading bears of Wall Street, for the past twenty-five years, illustrates our proposition. Two examples will "point our moral" if not "adorn our tale," viz.: Daniel Drew and Jacob Little.

The losses which the former has sustained on the short side during the past seven or eight years have been estimated at near, if not quite, $5,000,000. It would not be an exaggeration to say that if he had operated on the long side with the same boldness, craft and resources, which he has used in his short operations, he would have now been possessed of a fortune approaching in amplitude to that of his great rival, Vanderbilt, who never goes short of stocks. No doubt Drew has occasionally made a great hit, as for instance in the winter of 1867 during the Erie break ; but his successes in this line have rather served to diminish the grand total of his losses than to build up a fortune on the plus-column. The traps which have been set for him would have been the death of a man of smaller means and less resolution. But Daniel always makes terms, if worsted, and uses diplomacy as skillfully as he wields that large hammer of his with which he knocks down the price of stocks.

The closing years of Jacob Little convey to all who would sell stocks short, a still more instructive lesson.

Still clinging to the objects of a pursuit which was to

him a passion, his face bearing the marks of the fierce struggles of his life, a broken weird looking old man, he haunted the Board Room like a spectre where he had once reigned as a king, offering small lots of five shares of the same stock, the whole capital whereof he had once controlled. Where then were the piled millions which that cunning hand and scheming brain had rolled up? where the prestige of his victories on 'Change? Gone, scattered, lost. Poor and unnoticed, he passed away from the scene, and left nothing behind him but the shadow of what was once a great Wall Street reputation.

Men and women of America who, making haste to be rich, and taking evil counsel would enter Wall Street and put your money on the hazard of a die, give heed to the following maxims, the fruit of a dearly bought experience:

Buy only on the amplest margins.

Be an occasional and not a constant operator.

Cut short your losses, and let your profits run.

Never sell what you have not got.

8

CHAPTER V.

CORNELIUS VANDERBILT AND DANIEL DREW.

A Panic in Stocks, and Where is the Commodore?—Driving in Central Park—Training for Wall Street—Maxims of the Vanderbilt Code, "never sell what you haven't got," etc.—Anecdotes—Vanderbilt the Bull and Drew the Bear—A Parallel between the Two—"Uncle Daniel's" Portrait and Ways—The "Merry Old Gentleman" —The Wisdom of the Serpent, but not the Harmlessness of the Dove—Daniel Drew as an Acrobat—Straddling the Market.

EDNESDAY, September 30, 1869, a day of panic. "Anguish and doubt, and fear, sorrow and pain," have possession of the hearts of the financiers. Prices of stocks, which have been sinking, for a week, are now dropping, with a heavy thump. Values have shrunk $100,000,000. These, are the losses of stockholders. The tallest column, of all—New York Central— which stands under the dome of the stock market, has broken at the top, and is crumbling off, in sections, which shake the foundation, as they fall.

Among all the crowd, which that day thronged hall and stairway, of the stock exchange, struggling vainly to arrest the panic, or, standing and gazing, upon the full extent and hopelessness, of their losses, where was he, whose stake in that perilous game, was the largest, and who was liable now to pay a forfeit of millions?

Sun and sky mock with their brightness, the gloom which hangs over the market place. It is a day for the velvet turf, and not for the stony pavement. Passing from Wall street, into Central Park, on such a day, is like going from Tartarus, into the fields of Elysium. The distorted and forbidding faces, have disappeared, the hoarse cries died away, and everything is peace and beauty. The very air seems larger here, and in the wide, smooth, winding drives, grim-visaged business, puts on a holiday smile. Standing on a slope, covered with a verdure, not yet tinged with the sober coloring, of autumn, we see approaching, a light wagon, bowling along, at an eight mile gait, drawn by two blood trotters; gazelle-eyed, and slender of limb, as if desert-born, they tread the earth daintily, and their hoofs hardly dint the ground. Behind them, holding the reins, with a light and yet firm hand, is seated an old man, with a face like a Roman senator. This is Cornelius Vanderbilt, the greatest railroad capitalist, of the age. Forgetful, apparently, of his vast interests, that day imperiled, and of great losses, actually suffered, he rides along cool, thought-free, chatting with the blooming lady, his bride of six weeks, who sits by his side. This speaks the man.

From 1817, when Thomas Gibbons, the great steamboat man of that period, recognized the promise of the youth, till 1870, when in the lusty winter of his old age he dominates with such ease the largest consolidated railway interest in the world, there has been no more remarkable figure on the horizon of commerce, than Cornelius Vanderbilt.

Steam locomotion on water and land, this has been

his specialty, the trade to which he has given the energies of an entire life. In this trade he became more than an expert—he displayed genius. The two-oared skiff plied in the bays of his native island, grew into a steamboat, the steamboat multiplied into a fleet which plowed river, inland sea and ocean, and the young water-man was graduated as a commodore of the commercial marine, a rank to which he was raised by the spontaneous voices of his countrymen, and a title as worthily earned as if won upon the gun-deck.

He was born on Staten Island in the State of New York, in the year 1794. His ancestry was of the low Dutch stock, and he himself is a worthy representative of the Holland sailors of the seventeenth century, who lashed a broom to the mast-head and boasted that they swept the seas. At the age of fourteen, he was master of a sail boat. When he was eighteen, he was captain and part owner of the largest periauger which plied in the harbor of New York. When he was twenty-three, he was captain of a steamboat, and within forty years from that time he had built and owned twenty steamships and forty steamboats.

We are, however, not to speak of him now as connected with the industrial interests of the country on the water, but as a Wall Street man, a railroad king, a stockholder and operator.

Picture to yourself, reader, a man of great natural powers of mind and body, strengthened by training in one of the roughest of commercial schools—the running of lines of steamboats—who for nearly thirty years has concentrated his faculties upon one object, viz.: the playing of games of rivalry and competition as they are played in such a business—games requiring nerve to encounter emergencies and risks and skill as against strong antagonists—and played with heavy stakes on a broad field. Then imagine that such a man in possession of vast winnings from these games, with all the ripeness of his wisdom and experience, and with even the native force of his mind and will unabated, enters Wall Street, and devotes all these various and large resources to the buying, holding and controlling of stocks, the forming of combinations and the holding of them together against all opposition, and you will have an outline sketch of what Vanderbilt has been and now is in his Wall Street operations. Intellect, resolution, foresight, the ability to measure and proportion means to ends, wealth, knowledge of men and things, all conjoined in one man, these have furnished a panoply of proof and weapons of attack to Vanderbilt, with which, like the Homeric hero, he has always defeated and scattered the opposing hosts of the market.

Like all great generals, he knows who to select as his agents and coadjutors; but he bears, "like a Turk, no brother near the throne," and when an agent or coadjutor becomes too powerful, or puffed up with a sense of his own importance, he " takes him down a peg," and then after he has humbled him sufficiently, raises him again.   Strange stories have been told of him in this respect, how he has degraded men, his associates, even those of his own family, to the ranks, when guilty of insubordination, and then promoted them again, when they had been sufficiently humbled.

His operations are always for a rise and never for a fall; he is a bull and never a bear in stocks.

Two facts appear to have led him to invest so largely in railroad stocks; first, the rapidly increasing carrying trade of the country; second, the gross mismanagement and peculation which prevailed among railroad corporations. The obvious corollary from these facts is this, viz., secure a controlling interest in a railroad stock at a reasonable price, manage it with economy, stopping all leaks and peculations, and then *hold it and wait.* This is precisely what Vanderbilt has done, first in Harlem, next in Hudson, and finally in New York Central, and with what marvelous success, is known throughout the land.

If the experience of this man could be cast into the form of maxims, what a code it would furnish for the young merchant.

" I bide my time." This is one of his maxims. Its truth every one can testify to, who has observed what strange transformations and revenges are brought about in the stock market, by the " whirligig of time."

" Never sell short," is another.

In 1864, during the memorable rise in Harlem, so the story runs, a son of the late Dean Richmond, president of the New York Central Railroad, who had been selling Harlem at low figures, found himself likely to be several thousand dollars out of pocket, in consequence of the upward movement of the stock. In his extremity, he went to Vanderbilt, introduced himself as the son of his old friend, told him his situation, and asked his advice. " Never sell what you haven't got," grimly responded the Commodore. Upon this hint young Richmond covered his short contracts, and went long, *i. e.*, bought a considerable amount of the stock, and in a few weeks recovered what he had lost.

" Never tell any one what you are going to do till you've done it," said Vanderbilt, lately, to a friend, who inquired of him what was the secret of success in business.

That he has practiced this adage, which sounds something like a Hibernianism, will be proved by the following anecdote.   In 1850, the Pacific Mail Steamship Company did the carrying trade between San Francisco and Panama, and an immensely lucrative trade it was.   To establish some other line which would tap this trade would be, of course, a great object to accomplish.   One day the Commodore was observed in his office, standing before a map of the western hemisphere, and placing his finger successively on three points.   The first of these was San Juan de Nicaragua on the Atlantic shore, the second was the Lake of Nicaragua, the third was the port of San Juan del Sur, on the Pacific.   Here was a route which, if feasible, would save nearly one thousand miles of travel, and put money in the purse of him who secured it.   He silently investigated the practicability of the route, and made all his arrangements with a view to its establishment.   A few days after, the new steamer Prometheus, owned by himself, lay at the dock, fired up, and furnished with coal and provisions for a cruise.   He went on board, and telling a friend to give his good-bye to Mrs. V., that he was off for a trip, ordered the lines to be cast off and the prow to be turned southward.   In due time he made his appearance in Nicaragua, where he lived for six weeks on toast and tea, took care of his health, and then returned to New York, and organized what was known as the Nicaragua Accessory Transit Company. In all his stock operations he seems to proceed on the basis of intrinsic values, knowing that capital from all quarters will come in to aid him on that basis. As a bull, he may be said to trade on the hopes of men; and herein he differs from Daniel Drew, his rival in the market, who as a *bear*, may be said to trade on financial fear and apprehension, for panics and general declines in stocks result from the timorousness of capital.

Cornelius Vanderbilt, and Daniel Drew—how great each in his way, how similar, and yet how different they are! Both commenced without a penny. Drew, who was born in Putnam County, in the State of New York, in the latter part of the last century, commenced life as a cattle drover, then became the rival of Vanderbilt in the steamboat business, and finally was graduated as a stock operator.

Both of these men have the mind of crystal, the heart of adamant, the hand of steel, and the will of iron. Both are unscrupulous, within the law, as to means to an end. But both have adorned their lives, by great charities, bestowed on their kind; Vanderbilt, by presenting to the Government, in its hour of need, one million of dollars, in the shape of the magnificent steamship, which bears his name, and Drew, by the gift of many hundred thousand dollars, to educational institutions.

Both, too, have identified themselves with the material progress of the country, by the great lines they have established, or held, on water and land. Put your ear to the ground, and you can hear the thunder of their trains, from Omaha to Manhattan, all day and all night long. As these words are penned, ten thousand brakemen, switchmen, firemen, and engineers, begrimed, wan, and haggard, are guiding and goading on their roaring, screaming steam-serfs, as they drag to tide water, across fat prairies, through black gorges, and over crazy trestle-work, and bridges, the treasures of our imperial valley, and gold-veined mountains, and the spices and lustrous fabrics of India.

Here the resemblance ceases. Both of these men, it is true, are playing a game on the same field, but in a very different way. Vanderbilt, is the more daring of the two. His operations, extend through years of time, and through vast arcs of circles; the table, on which he plays, covers one hundred million acres, and the dice, with which he plays, are loaded with thirty millions, of the precious metal.

Vanderbilt's intellect is the more comprehensive, Drew's the more subtle. The genius of the former, is constructive, in building up values, that of the latter, is destructive, in depressing them, for Drew is a most robust architect of panics. The one, is the greater strategist, the other, is the greater tactician, his operations, are more rapid, compact, and local.

In personal appearance, how totally dissimilar. Vanderbilt, looks like an anax-andron, a king of men. Seventy-six winters have not bowed that stately form, or quenched the light of that deep-set black eye.

Three-score years and ten, and more, have written upon the figure of his rival, more of the physical signs of decay, but through a wilderness of wrinkles, his steel-gray eyes, twinkle with all the vitality of one and twenty His face, as it appears in the market, to those, who know him, would form a study for a painter.   An odd, grotesque face, with an air of self-communion, brooding over it, and a pinched look, from the corrugated forehead, down the rect-angular jaw.   His nose, might form a separate study. It is certainly, the reverse of Roman, but to call it Grecian, would be a slur upon Praxiteles.   It may be termed *sagacious*, in every line, and swelling, a nose to snuff a stratagem in the air, or scent in the "tainted gale" a tight money-market approaching.

No one would be apt to associate with Vanderbilt anything that savored of the jocose.   We involun-tarily think of him as striding along with a grim gigantesque dignity, buying with a large lordly man-ner, thousands and tens of thousands of shares, pun-ishing his enemies with a remorseless hand, and plac-ing his adversaries *hors du combat*, or as sitting like a generalissimo in his office, issuing his orders to his battallions.   He is rarely known by any nick-name except " the Commodore," or the great consolidator, though his intimate friends sometimes speak of him as " Cornele."

But Drew appears under a variety of names, " the Old Man," " Uncle Daniel," " the Ursa Major," " the speculative director," " the Old Bear," etc.; these are a few of the designations he has received.   Well too does he deserve the title of the " Merry old gentleman " of Wall Street.   In his most earnest operations, he never seems to lose sight of " the fun of the thing."   His most serious moods are easily broken in upon by ludicrous suggestions, and then he gives vent, every now and then, to short laughs which sound like the cackle of a hen—thrown suddenly off from her propriety. He loves to rally "the boys," (as he is wont paternally to call his younger speculative acquaintance,) on their losses, or jest with them over their gains on occasions when, as he would say, they have "taken a slice out 'em." It is "as good as nuts and cheese," to him when he has succeeded in getting up a corner, or when on a high market he has put out a heavy line of shorts. He is a mighty and versatile trapper. No game is too small or too large for him. He lays his net for pigeons, sets his springe for wood-cock, digs pit-falls for bears, and lassoes the bulls. What glee in that queer old face, as he pulls the string to snare the game, and then bags them.

If a stranger were to see him driving down to his office of a morning, in his "one horse shay," he would at once pronounce him some hard headed old farmer, visiting Broad Street for the purpose of putting his savings into a small lot of government bonds. He who would learn the eccentric habits and odd ways of the man, has only to deposit a small margin with David Groesbeck, his partner, and one of his brokers, and then frequent the office and watch the old man as he goes pottering about, talking little, but that little in homely phrase, and with a strong nasal twang.

We have said his intellect was subtle. The word *subtle* does not altogether express it. It should be *vulpine*. His is the intellect of a fox of the antediluvian period, gigantic of size and portentous of brush. He is as fertile in shifts and ruses as Reynard himself. He covers his tracks, and takes to the water, the underbrush or the open country as circumstances may require. Traps innumerable have been set for him, but he generally eludes them, or if caught has broken away, though sometimes torn and bloody; from jaws that thirsted for his blood, (or what is much the same, his money). The hounds of the street, for twenty years have been following his track, now in silence and now baying in deep mouthed chorus, when they had run him to earth, but his twistings, and doublings, and countless devices have foiled them at last and he now sits in his stronghold with a grasp on his ten millions, which only the last great enemy can relax.

Not the least remarkable circumstance in his career as a speculator, is the fact that, although for so many years he has been operating for a decline in stocks, and therefore laying wagers against the material growth and progress of the country, against the increase of the precious metals and paper money, and the consequent enhancement of values; nevertheless he has not only kept his position, but grown in wealth. This proves the ability and resources of the man.

It is fair to suppose that, considering his twenty-five years' experience in Wall Street, he probably, more than any of his contemporaries, understands the science and practice of speculation, and in his time has accomplished many a feat requiring skill and strength.

Going long and short of stocks, at the same time, is what is technically called "straddling" the market. It is like riding two horses, each going a different way. This difficult feat has often been successfully performed by Daniel Drew, and that, too, with a lightness and agility, scarcely to be expected from so aged an acrobat. He holds, we will suppose, 40,000 shares of a particular stock, which has been all paid for, and locked up in his strong box. The stock is selling for par. He puts out say 20,000 shares of sellers' options, running 10, 15 and 30 days. The stock drops 20 per cent. He buys his 20,000 shares, and makes $400,000 by his little flyer. But now, supposing a bull party observe the "Old Man" as he puts out his shorts, of course they buy up the stock, sellers' options, etc., and run it up 20 or 30 per cent., expecting to corner him. Some fine day, when stocks are soaring heavenwards, they are dismayed to find themselves obliged to shoulder large blocks which come flying down upon them from some invisible quarter. They stagger under the load until they discover that they are carrying twenty or thirty thousand shares presented them (for a consideration) by their Uncle Daniel, and being a part of his 40,000 shares, long stock before mentioned. The consequence, of course, is a stampede of the bull phalanx. Daniel's cunning eye is watching them through a loophole in the Fort de Groesbeck, and he sallies forth and hurls at the flying column, great bombards of stock, which always turns the defeat into a perfect rout. Knapsacks, loaded with scrip, are thrown away, weapons dropped, and the battle-field is strewed with the dead and wounded. Then the "Old Man," with a hard metallic chuckle, calls back his myrmidons, who rifle the camp of the enemy, pick up the stocks they have dropped in their fright, and restore them to their liege lord, who retires into his stronghold, and meditates new schemes of ravin.

But we are anticipating. The filling in of the portraits of Cornelius Vanderbilt and Daniel Drew must be done by the light and shade of our succeeding chapters.

CHAPTER VI.

JOTTINGS ON THE "STREET;" DREW ON THE WAR-PATH.

More Philosophy of Wall Street—The Handwriting on the Wall—A Haunted Heart—The Panic Forgotten, and "Richard is Himself Again"—"Country Orders Executed with Promptness and Despatch!"—The Countrymen Respond to the Cry—A Rustic Bruiser on Change—My Little Commission Bill—The Devourers of Widows' Houses—What shall I buy, and How shall I buy it?—Notes on Erie —Views of the "General"—I buy One Hundred Erie, and pay for it, and what came of it—Drew the King of Erie—He Bulls Erie at 4, and sells it to "The Boys" at 40.

O the man who looks from without upon Wall Street as the field of speculation, it seems a place of deep and dangerous mystery. A region of dens and caves and labyrinths full of perils which threaten loss and perhaps ruin to him who enters there.

When mustering up courage he ventures in, and standing in the Long Room, watches the success of his first purchase, all the stories he has ever heard about men who have been reduced from affluence to beggary by speculating in stocks, flash across his memory. He sees upon the very walls inscriptions of prediction, warning and despair, like the cells where the condemned have passed their last hours. Some of these inscriptions written with a lead pencil, vigorously anathematize Vanderbilt. Some are imprecations on Drew or Fisk. Some are apothegms expressing the very philosophy of desperation. All tell the same tale: "I came here, I speculated, I lost. Beware!"

But he heeds neither counsel nor warning for *the hope of gain* is a stronger principle in human nature, than *the fear of loss*. These two active principles underlie the whole practice of stock speculation. It is the hope of gain that induces a man to buy, and the fear of loss that induces him to sell, often precipitately. These are the two strings on which the merriest as well as the most doleful tunes are played by the cunning Paganini's of the stock market. Thus a thousand brokers gain large incomes from their customers, and great capitalists accumulate immense fortunes.

Those ceaseless vibrations of the prices in the stock market, what are they owing to except it be the same causes?

To and fro, up and down, backwards and forwards, the speculator moves with the market from the moment when that first profit slides into his fingers. Not always interested pecuniarily; absent, sometimes, hundreds of miles away, in gay society or alone, studying, walking, riding, sleeping, still is he haunted by the idea of fortunes made on 'Change swiftly, easily, by a lucky hit or a quick succession of happy strokes. The five fortunate speculators of the season, glitter in a false light which never discloses the hundreds of miserable losers.

M. made $200,000 in three months on Pacific mail, commencing only with $10,000. J. & T. made a million on Old Southern. B. went into the market with a paltry thousand and left it with a hundred thousand. S., a year ago, was a clerk in a bank on a salary of $600; to-day he draws a check with five figures on a deposit in the same bank.

What has been done may be done again. Such examples fortify the doubts and misgivings which possess the mind during the first stages of a speculative career, and stimulate the hardihood and pride that goeth before a fall.

The recollection of the panic of 1857, notwithstanding its severity, and long continuance, soon faded away from the Wall Street mind. The very next day, after the final crash, (October 14th,) stocks began to rise with a bound. Railways took the lead, and bank stocks followed. In twenty-four hours, American Exchange Bank stock rose fifty per cent.

But the outsiders were still wary. The mercantile community, especially, from whom the ranks of Wall Street operators are so largely recruited, now generally kept aloof. As the winter was wearing away, however, the old familiar faces of those who had been scared and driven out by the panic, came back one after one. Wizened bank cashiers, having recovered from their fright, sallied out from their fortresses, to take a turn in the street. Merchants, weary with brooding over piles of protested notes, came down to try and repair their losses, by taking a shy at Pacific Mail. They who had retired to the country for recuperation from the fatigues of the season, now came filing in, bringing with them others who had never tried their luck in the stock-market; confiding, genial-looking fellows, their countenances rotund with long sleeps, and sleek with the rustic cheer of the nitrogenous bean and cabbage, and the carbonaceous sausage; they brought their inviolate margins

9

destined to furnish pocket money for a broker's holiday. The spring equinox found the street with very
much the same appearance it had when the narrator
first staked his modest five hundred dollars. The
curb-stone brokers were not quite so clamorous, their
brothers of the regular board not quite so bustling
and important of manner, and the general movement
of things not quite so impetuous as the year before;
but the fever of speculation was still in the blood,
and was kept alive by the fresh orders to buy and
sell, which always come in after the smoke of a great
financial conflict has cleared away.

What would become of the market if it were not
for the countrymen? "Country orders solicited and
executed with promptness and despatch!" This is
the substance of the advertisement of Brokers and
Bankers, we might almost say, the burden of their song.
The country always responds to this solicitation. The
four great monetary rivers that flow into the Wall
Street reservoir from the four quarters of the compass,
are fed by a thousand streamlets from city, town and
village. The aggregate is a vast sum, a part of which
goes into securities for a permanent investment, but
perhaps a still greater part goes, as margins, into
speculation. The countryman comes and takes a hand
in the game which is all the while going on around
the table of the stock market; he is like a young lion
who has never known either sorrow or the lack of
food. He is jovial, brave, active and sanguine. Un-
tutored in guile, he has always heard that the Wall
Street boys were a sharp set of fellows, but he cannot really understand why they are so much worse
than other folks; and then the broker who takes

charge of his pecuniary interests, is most agreeable and gentlemanly in his manners. In fact, the countryman reposes upon everything and everybody, with a confidence at once child-like and sublime.

How gallantly he enters the field, and storms the Malakoffs, where the emperors of the market lie entrenched. How incessantly he changes his position on the advice of his very dear friends, with whom he has met in the *street;* how obstinately he clings to a loss; how resentfully he "bucks" at the stock to which he owes his first or last loss, and oh! what a stream of commissions he pours into the pocket of his taciturn but absorbent broker!

From the history of one of these operators, you may learn the history of most of the others. They make money at the start, while their eyes are undazed by illusive lights, and their judgments unwarped by the influences to which they are unconsciously subjected; but in the end they almost invariably lose all their profits and their original margins besides.

Some few, very few there have been, however—hard-headed, determined men, who, after taking the first heavy knocks, have learned the art and mystery of the Wall Street trade and practiced it in a most slashing way upon the old bruisers of the market.

One of these is now in our mind's eye, a sturdy little fellow with thews and sinews like a champion of the light weights. He came from his native village into the street in 1862; was a bull, bought heavily and lost almost his all, in the fall which followed the McClellan campaign of that year. Retiring for a while into the country, he thought out the matter, replenished his exchequer, came back, beat the trained speculators with their own weapons, and retired in six months with a princely fortune.

The year 1858 passed swiftly and in the stock market, uneventfully, away. Starting February with the old margin of five hundred dollars, I found that after twelve distinct purchases and sales, in which I had been playing the ancient Wall Street game of see-saw, up and down, making and losing alternately, upon looking over the account in December, my net profits were about $200. And now first occurred to me the fact which strikes every one after operating for a time in stocks, viz: how fast the interest and brokerage items run up. Against a profit of $200 there was interest paid $210, and brokerage $300. After all my trouble and worry, only $200, while my broker received $510. Deduction from this. The broker takes the money, *i. e.*, the profit. The customer takes the risk, of *almost certain loss in the end*. If the customer buys and sells 100 shares of stock every working day in the year, he will find by calculation, that he has paid his broker nearly $8,000 in the form of commissions, at the rate of one-eighth per cent. on each transaction. During a tight money market, he will have paid a large additional sum in the shape of turns or extra commissions, for carrying his stocks, and if he is cornered and unable to borrow stock for delivery, when short of it, he will have to pay fresh commissions for the use of stock.

During 1863 and 1864, an active operator using $20,000 as a margin, discovered on perusing his accounts, that he had paid his brokers $25,000 in the form of commissions, and as his capital of $20,000 was still unimpaired, this showed that he had made a profit of $25,000, all of which had thus gone into his broker's till.

Another who started with $10,000, and for four years operated heavily, making and losing hundreds of thousands, at the end of that time had less than eight hundred left out of his original capital, but estimated the interest and commissions he had paid his brokers at the large sum of $75,000, and these are only two out of hundreds of cases.

Nothing but *great* profits will save an operator from having his substance eventually devoured in brokerage and commissions, and great profits won by the Wall Street trader, are the rare exceptions. There are two remedies for this which are certain and speedy: *First*, Never speculate. *Second*, If you must speculate, *only buy what you can pay for and hold*. These remedies naturally occurred to me, January 1st, 1859, and as the first of the year is the time generally selected to adopt good resolutions, I resolved that whereas Wall Street was a delusion and a snare, I would thereafter cease from speculation.

Alas! for the good resolutions of the one who has felt the excitements of stock-speculation. In five months I was once more in the street, looking for something "good to buy," as the operator would say. But I had made a compromise with my first resolution, and now determined to buy only so much stock as I could pay for. What should it be? The market was full of low-priced stocks. There was Cumberland at 5,—"a worthless fancy;" Old Southern at 9,—my associations with Old Southern were, on the whole, disagreeable; Harlem at 11,—the burnt child dreads the fire, for I had lost $200 on Harlem in 1858. Erie at 5½. This looks cheap. Let me think.

This stock, so famous in the annals of Wall Street, was in a bad way in 1859. The company, for six years, had been going on from bad to worse. Financiering constantly to meet its temporary wants, it had been coming on the market periodically, to negotiate a new mortgage to fund its floating debt. One of these different classes of mortgages was now overdue, the road was in default, a foreclosure had taken place, the road was advertised for sale, and a receiver had been appointed. The sale would, of course, wipe out the stock, and the public generally, looking for this to take place any day, had marked the price already down to zero. A large proportion of the old investors had long since sold out, and most of the entire capital stock was floating in the street, at the nominal market value above indicated. The very idea of investing in Erie, and holding it any length of time for a rise, was sufficient to provoke a smile from any broker who thought he understood the financial situation of things in general, and of Erie in particular.

But week after week rolled by while I was hesitating what to do, and still no sale of the road took place. In September it fell to 4, and stacks of it could be bought at that price.

It was one pleasant day in the month last mentioned, while standing in a doorway in William Street, near where the brokers used to hold their street meetings, that I saw a stout old gentleman with a white head and a merry eye, whose full name has now escaped my memory, but who in the market was

known as the "General." He lived in one of the
river towns, where it was said he had "done the State
some service" in connection with the train bands of
militia, and had the reputation of being well to do
and "awful cunning" in his speculations. He was
full of crotchets and hobbies, and was never weary of
talking upon them so long as he could find a listener.
One of these was a strong prejudice against brokers
as a class. He was in the habit of standing near the
street crowd and venting his spite against them by
calling them hard names. The brokers not being
ever very sensitive to abuse or ridicule, seemed
rather amused than otherwise by these little eccen-
tricities of the old veteran.

But his great hobby was Erie. He stood in the
center of a little knot of listeners, and was holding forth on his favorite topic, looking very red
and determined, and emphasized each sentence by
bringing his cane down with both hands upon the
pavement. "Are you buying Erie, General?" inquired one of his auditors.

"Of course I am buying Erie, and paying for it,
too. No margin business for me. You brokers would
eat a man up in twenty-four hours, with your commission, and interest, and infernal turns. I bought a
thousand shares for four thousand dollars, this morning, and here it is. [Producing the certificates.]
That stock I intend to sell at par."

"At 0, more likely," remarked a bystander.

"Why don't you sell the road out under the decree
of the court, then? you've been threatening to for six
months. Why don't you do it? What's Vanderbilt
doing now? Buying Erie. What's Drew doing?

Buying Erie, and keeping the price down till he can get all he wants. You wont hear anything more about decrees of the court, and foreclosures of chattel mortgages, or sales of the road at auction, when Drew gets all the stock he wants."

"You'd better sell the stock short, General," said a young broker, who had just entered the circle of auditors.

"Sell short!" retorted the General, "you boys would sell the shirt off your back. Look at Jake Little,—there he goes across the street,—he'll scratch a poor man's head before he dies, and you'll have to bury him by subscription."

"Isn't Drew selling it?" inquired a subdued looking operator, who had listened with a sickly smile to the whole conversation.

"Drew selling Erie at 4?" almost shrieked the General. "Daniel Drew doesn't sell stocks when they are low; he sells 'em when they are way up, and you boys are crazy to buy 'em *then*, and he sells 'em to you when you cry for 'em. That thousand shares you see in these ten certificates, I'm going to sell 'em at par, not one cent short of 100," reiterated he, "and when it sells at par you'll see me back here— not before," and he turned on his heel and walked up the street. Different opinions were now expressed by his late audience as to the soundness of these views, but the majority concurred in pronouncing the General a little "touched" on the subject of Erie.

But the more I thought about these views, the more correct they appeared. Here is a veteran in the market, who is willing to buy Erie at 4, and hold it. If it goes down to zero, a man can only lose four per cent., which he may lose any time by speculation. I invested in a few days, $400 in 100 shares of Erie at 4, laid it away in a snug place and watched for the tide to turn. Slowly it rose, but it *rose!* In thirty days it sold at 8; in sixty days it sold at 10.

Daniel Drew, in 1859, and for eight years afterwards, was chief director, high comptroller and purveyor, and head broker of the Erie Railway Company. Nothing in the conduct of the road escaped his surveillance. Every increase or diminution in the monthly earnings was known to him beforehand. He knew exactly where to place his finger on the stock circulating in the market, and how much to a share was held abroad. Every movement in the price of the stock produced by any operator or combination of operators, he watched with a jealous eye and often thwarted it. Knowledge is power. But his power over Erie was not derived simply from knowledge. The Erie Railway Company was poor, it must have money, or go into bankruptcy. Drew advanced them money. He cashed their drafts and indorsed their acceptances, *but* he always took security, sometimes in the form of bonds, convertible into stock, sometimes in the form, more useful to him, of a chattel mortgage on their rolling-stock. The borrower is the servant of the lender. Drew, during these years, held the Erie Railway Company in the hollow of his hand.

When it was for his interest that the price of the stock should decline, he closed his hand and it fell. When it was for his interest that the price should rise, he opened his hand and it rose. If the company failed to meet their obligations to him, straightway a report was spread through the market that Drew was about to foreclose the chattel mortgage, and then came a depression, but mysteriously enough, these depressions occurred when Drew was short of the stock, and the corresponding rises took place when he had bought the stock at the depressed price.

His power over the stock-price was almost unaccountable even in view of these causes. It rose and fell as if upon the waving of a wizard's wand. "Daniel says up!" and up it rose. "Daniel says down!" and down it was. "Daniel says wiggle-waggle!" and it bobbed to and fro in a small arc of two per cent.

From December, 1859, till March, 1860, Erie vibrated languidly between 8 and 10. Then it started up in good earnest. "What's going on in the stock?" was the inquiry around the board. The public ridiculed the movement. "A perfect bubble!" cried some. "Not worth the paper its written on," asserted others. "Sell it short, and you'll make your fortune!" and they did sell it short with a right good will. Panic-bitten bankers, incredulous merchants, conservative stockdealers, all took a flyer, large or small, on the short side. Month after month, the stock kept rising 15, 25, 30. Drew, and his associates, held a vast block of it, counting the number of shares, and the short contracts, and when it became generally known, that Erie's financial troubles were over, that the lawsuits were settled, and the earnings increasing, their grip tightened. Still the price kept rising, 32, 35, 38, 40, and on the 2d of October, it reached its culmination, 42⅜. The majority of the bears having covered their contracts, the corner collapsed, the price fell back to 25, and dullness resumed her "ancient melancholy reign" over the market. My 100 shares bought at 4, were sold at 40½, showing a profit of $3,600.

This buying of stocks, and paying for them, is the true policy to be pursued by an outsider, and believe me, ye novices, if you wish to elude the traps, bid defiance to the corners, and gaze serenely on the panics of Wall Street, then buy only what you can pay for, and afford to keep, and expect in due time your increase.

CHAPTER VII.

WAR TIMES AND GREENBACKS.

One Little Cloud in a Fair Sky—Business Lively, and Crops coming in
while a Thunder-storm is Brewing—The Cloud Gathers and Bursts
—Stocks Fall Down and "Take a Snooze"—New Fields for the
Speculator—The Fortune of a Chemist, and How he Transmuted
Saltpetre into Gold—The Parentage of the Greenback Currency—
Wake Up, Wall Street!—The Stimulant Begins to Work—Music
by the Whole Band!—Stocks on the Rampage—The Under-ground
Telegraph Clicking—News from the Front—The Bulls Fall Back,
but Reorganize and Prepare to Charge Again—An Army Without a
Leader.

EARLY in 1860, arose in the political sky a
cloud, at first, no larger than a man's hand.
Every one saw it, but not so many looked at
it with apprehension.

The financial prospect had never been so bright.
The country had fairly recovered from the revulsion
of '57. The banking system reorganized and strengthened, gave every facility to the expansion of legitimate enterprise. Commerce was widening, and man-
ufactures were multiplying. The largest crops ever
known before were that year gathered. Four million
bales of cotton were piled in the warehouses, and
more than fifteen hundred millions of bushels of
wheat, corn, oats, rye and other cereals had been
garnered from the harvest. All the remaining products were in similar proportions.

Here was solid wealth. Here was the means to pay our foreign debt, and the material for an immense carrying-trade on the ocean between America and other countries, and for a transportation still more immense on the *railways*.

The speculative public were looking forward to another era of inflation and of corresponding opportunities for profit in the stock market. And with reason. The amount of business done on the railways reflects the industrial activities of the country. The rises of stock which take place in Wall Street are not all the result of mere speculation. Behind all these movements lies the fact of intrinsic values always operating with a silent but mighty force. "Freight is the mother of wages." This maxim of admiralty law is as true of railroad trains as it is of sea-going vessels. The balance sheet of the earnings of railways is a mirror of the industries and products of the land. In it we can seem to see reflected, piles of cotton bales and stacks of corn and wheat, hogsheads of sugar and tobacco, herds of cattle, flocks of sheep and droves of swine, and a busy host of men working in mine and mill, for the scream of the locomotive is ever the shrillest and most frequent when the furnace, forge and factory roar the loudest.

But the hopes of the speculators were not yet to be realized. The little cloud within sixty days after the election of Abraham Lincoln was announced, had gathered blackness and swelled into a thunder-cumulus which overspread the southern sky and threw its gigantic shadow as far north as the St. Lawrence. Such a season as this had never been known before. Panics of every description had occurred, except that

growing out of a political complication so embarrass-
ing and aggravated as this. And yet, dark as the
prospect was, the stock-operators, always sanguine of
temperament, after a few weeks began to gather
courage, and many capitalists were found, particularly in New England, who, tempted by the low prices,
were bold enough to put their money in cash stock,
for permanent investment. A long continued dull
spell in Wall Street is the particular abhorrence of
the broker, and if any one who was afflicted by the
prevailing gloom, wished to derive comfort for the
future, he had only to visit the Stock Exchange and
listen to the hopeful prognostications which he would
be sure to hear on every side.

The roar of the cannonade at Fort Sumter speedily
dispelled these illusions. In three days thirteen of
the leading stocks dropped an average of twenty per
cent. Government Fives fell to 75, Sixes to 84, and
the bonds of the seceded States slumped thirty per
cent. After panic came dullness.

The few outsiders, who had for months been flut-
tering around the stock exchange, now took wing,
and the brokers were left for a time to their own devices. The market was suffering under that condition known as the "dry rot." Money was abun-
dant, but there was little "disposish," to use the
Wall Street slang, to buy or sell. Months rolled by,
and this condition seemed to have become chronic.
It was part and parcel of the condition, which affected the entire country.

The same cannonade, "that deep and dreadful
organ-pipe of war," which had reverberated through
the Stock Exchange, and stunned its inmates into a

lethargy, seemed to have lulled into a fitful slumber, a large portion of the commercial and other business enterprises of the republic.   Looms and anvils were still, wharves were silent, and vessels lay rotting at anchor, on sea, river, and lake.

But, while legitimate trade seemed almost dead, new and abnormal forms of traffic arose.   Army-uniforms, shoes, bunting, haversacks, arms, munitions, and deep-throated engines of war, were suddenly in demand.   Cotton-mills were turned into rifle-factories. The steam-derrick hoisted rifled-cannon, the triphammer forged the shaft of the war-steamer, and the peaceful foundry poured forth shot and shell in pyramids.

War had thus opened new fields for the energies of the stock-operators.   A few of them enlisted, and went to the front, to engage in struggles and stratagems, for which they had been educated, by their campaigns in Wall Street.   Some became sutlers.   Some bought old hulks, and sold them to the Government, and some haggled in army contracts.   Most of them made money, with which they returned in 1862, to ply their ancient trade, in the stock-market.

One of these speculators, in munitions of war, was B., a chemist, who had a small laboratory, in Jersey City.   He experimented in the reduction of metals, and furnished certificates of the richness of the specimens of the ores submitted to him by mining companies.   Why is it that so many chemists are found among the buyers and sellers of stocks ?   Perhaps it is because the followers of the science of chemistry are naturally given to the speculative pursuit of gold under difficulties.   Witness the old alchemists, who sought to transmute baser into precious metals; or, it may be they are brought into the stock-market, by their connection with mining companies, whose ores they assay and certify to. Certain it is, they may be frequently seen among the busy crowd in Broad Street.

B., had for many years supported himself, and earned something more by his profession; but all his surplus income went to pay his losses and commissions, in the purchase and sale of stocks. He could have been seen almost every day, from twelve to two, standing in the tunnel-entrance to the regular board, bearded like a dervish, his countenance "sicklied o'er with the pale cast of thought," or with the unwholesome fumes of his trade, waiting for the tide to turn in his favor. The tide never did turn, but kept ebbing, and finally left him high and dry on the beach.

Just before the panic which followed the bombardment and fall of Sumter, he had mortgaged his laboratory, chemicals and retorts to his broker and staked the proceeds in a margin on Border State Bonds. In less than two weeks his money was gone, and his broker's account showed him in debt $2,500, besides the mortgage of $1,000 which he owed. He therefore went back to his profession, and in six months had cleared $1,200. This sum would pay off the mortgage which fell due on the 1st of January, 1862, and save him from absolute ruin.

About the first of December he received proposals to go into the manufacture of saltpetre for making gunpowder, in partnership with a wealthy capitalist. The basis on which the expectation of great profits was founded, was the low price of nitrate of soda, which is one of the principal materials out of which saltpetre is made.   This fact was enlarged upon, and also that nearly the whole stock of nitrate of soda (four million pounds), then on hand, was held by two firms, and had been bespoken by the capitalist who furnished this information.

B. suddenly recollected that a friend in the business of manufacturing chemicals, had bought some months before, four hundred thousand pounds of nitrate of soda, with the view to make it into saltpetre, but had given up the purpose and had offered to sell it to him, B., for two and a half cents a pound.

"What is the price of nitrate of soda?" inquired B. of the capitalist with whom he was negotiating.

"Three cents a pound," replied he.

No conclusion was arrived at respecting the proposed business, but that afternoon B. called on the chemical manufacturer, who sold him the lot (400,000 pounds), at two and a half cents per pound, ten per cent. of the purchase money payable cash down, the balance in thirty days.   This operation stood thus:

400,000 lbs. nitrate of soda at two and a half cts. per lb., . $10,000
Paid cash on acc., ...   1,000

Due from B., payable in 30 days, ... $9,000

The next week was spent by B. in trying to work off his purchase at an advance over what he gave, but dealers would only buy at 2½.   B. began to feel blue.

The news now came of the seizure of Mason and Slidell.   The fear of trouble with England followed, and "villainous saltpetre," otherwise nitrate of soda, began to look up in the market.

Two or three weeks after this, while B. was sitting in his laboratory, one of the parties to whom he had offered the nitrate of soda at three cents, came in and offered three and a half cents a pound, and when his offer was refused, advanced it to four and then to five cents.

"What's got into the market?" inquired B.

"Haven't you seen Queen Victoria's proclamation just received, prohibiting the exportation of arms, saltpetre, nitrate of soda, etc.?" replied his customer. "Now then, B., talk business, at what price will you sell your nitrate of soda?"

"Six cents a pound, nothing less," returned B.

"I'll take it at six cents, and send you a check to-morrow, or as soon as we receive the stuff."

The bargain thus struck, netted B. a profit of $14,000. This sum he used as a five per cent. margin, to purchase U. S. Sixes, of which, he bought $252,000 at 90, and in six months sold them out at a net profit of $30,000. Six months after this he was at work at his old profession, with nothing left but his laboratory with which to win his bread. Such are the vicissitudes of a speculator's life.

A new cycle was soon to commence in American finance, and a new chapter to be written in the history of speculation. The people had pledged their sons to the Government, and five hundred thousand soldiers were in arms; the Government must pledge its credit to the people, to raise money to sustain that army. The money must be in the form of *promises to pay*, for hard currency was not to be had, the faith of the Government must be pledged upon the face of it, and it must have the chief attribute

VIEW OF THE GOLD ROOM.

NEVILLE & HAMMAR

WESTERN UNION TELEGRAPH

of gold, viz: the power of extinguishing debts. Thus arose the Legal Tenders.

The credit, (or as some would say, the discredit,) of originating the Legal Tender, or as it is generally called the greenback currency, is usually given to Salmon P. Chase; but the parentage of this ingenious monetary device, is also claimed by a tall man, named P., with an eye like a squab, and a pendulous nether lip, not unknown to the purlieus of the lobby. It has been asserted, that he first suggested the plan to President Lincoln, some time in the summer of 1861. However, this may be the plan was agitated in financial councils, during the last two months of 1861. In February, 1862, after due deliberation, Congress passed the Legal Tender Act, authorizing the issue by the Government, of $150,000,000, in United States notes, thus, nearly doubling at one stroke, the money circulation of the country.

Strange to relate, Wall Street failed to appreciate, with its usual quickness, the significance of this Legislative enactment. During the past twelve months, there had been, with few exceptions, no lack of money for speculative purposes in the stock-market. What was lacking then? Confidence in the future.

During all that chronic dullness on the street, whereof we have spoken, there hardly occurred one notable movement, excepting an occasional sharp rise or decline in Border State Bonds. Brokers and operators, alike, had become so habituated to this lethargic condition of things, that, for more than two months after the passage of the bill, they seemed to desire or strive after no other.

The new currency began to be seen in the Exchange brokers' offices, early in April, first in large notes of $1,000, then of $500. In a fortnight, it was coming on in sums counted by the million. The American and National Bank-Note Companies, who did the engraving and printing for the Government, in New York, sent the notes on to Washington. From Washington, they came back to the sub-treasury, in New York, by the express-wagon load, in boxes, and in bags, but generally done up in packages, the size of small bricks, in brown paper, tied with red tape, sealed with the treasury seal, and numbered and marked; at the sub-treasury, they were paid out by Mr. John J. Cisco, the sub-treasurer. Still, the stock-market was as sluggish as ever. The enormous issue of paper-money inspired alarm, instead of stimulating speculation; and large sums, instead of going into stocks, were deposited with the sub-treasurer, at five per cent interest.

Suddenly, as if by magic, on the closing days of April, the feeling changed. The stimulant, whose virtues the drowsy brokers refused to believe in, began to work most potently. The stocks which had so long lain still, now like so many puppets strung on a wire, pulled by an unseen hand, danced upwards, according to their kind. First came Government Sixes, which had stood at about 93 for many months; on the third of May they touched par, amid loud cheers in the broker's board. Bank stocks, the value of which was interlaced with that of Governments, which the banks held so largely, rose next. Then came the soundest dividend paying securities among railway bonds and stocks. After which the doubtful stocks came limping and halting upwards. But all moved up in steps, measured some by five, and others by one per cent.

In most of the great rises in Wall Street, this order is maintained. The stocks most highly esteemed lead off in the rise, and the others follow in the rank of estimation in which they are held by the brokers or the public, the worthless fancies bringing up the rear like the rag-tag and bobtail of an army. This order, however, is often varied by the artificial movements produced by combinations which take hold of these same worthless fancies and make one or more of them the most remarkable features in a general rise.

The speculation promised in 1860, and postponed till now, had commenced; and it was sustained by something more than merely the abundance of money offered at a low rate in the market place. The same mighty force of intrinsic values, of which we have already spoken, lay behind it. The new circulating notes passing through the country, seemed like the kiss of the prince on the cheek of the sleep-enchanted lady in the fairy tale, to awaken to newness of life the myriad shapes of industry. The music of rewarded labor was heard in fuller tones through the land. Spindles hummed, wheels buzzed, hammers clanged, and the giant brood of agriculture and the useful arts awoke from their slumber.

The earnings of the railways were discovered to be larger than ever before. The volume of business which they did, kept pace with the increased production, stimulated by the enhanced value of the raw material, so wonderfully do the subtle fluids which stimulate the limbs of industry, gather new force, acting and reacting on each other, like positive and negative electricity. It should not be forgotten, also, that this general increase in values, together with the stoppage of the Mississippi artery, justified higher rates of transportation.

The peninsular campaign was progressing favorably, and this gave courage to the Wall Street men. Here it should be noted that early in the war, Union *successes* were used as arguments in favor of a rise in stocks, but as the war went on, Union *defeats* were used as arguments in favor of a rise. This was correct reasoning in both cases, for up to a certain point of time the cessation of hostilities would have enabled the country to recover the old channels of business, but after that point of time the continuance of the war produced permanent devastation and derangement, and became associated with the idea of increased issues of paper money to be redeemed only at the end of the war.

While McClellan and his grand army was pushing past Yorktown and Williamsburg, and enveloping Richmond between his right and left wings, stocks kept advancing, and the speculators began to flock into the stock-market from all quarters. Rings were formed which purposed to send stocks up with a rush when the grand army should march into Richmond.

In the latter part of June, while, to the general public, everything seemed bright and promising at the front, stocks, to the astonishment of the uninitiated, suddenly dropped heavily. Why was this? We may explain it thus:

Early in May, 1862, a plan had been devised by leading brokers and operators, by which, the earliest information could be obtained from the front. Often, before it was known to the Government, a fact would be communicated to the Wall Street magnate, and acted upon. By watching the financial mercury tube on the Stock Exchange, a shrewd observer could not unfrequently predict the news of a victory or a defeat, simply by noticing the rise and fall of stocks. The system consisted in giving those at the front, who gathered and transmitted the information, a certain interest in stocks, and thus stimulating them to every exertion to forward early news. Sometimes the telegraph lines were subsidized, and the most liberal sums were paid for reliable intelligence in advance. Officers, soldiers, sutlers, politicians, lobbymen, and high officials of the Government were employed to keep the Wall Street operators thoroughly posted, as to when to buy and when to sell. This system was afterwards still more completely organized by the gold speculators, as we shall hereafter see.

News had been received through the medium above mentioned, which justified the belief that the McClellan campaign would fail to accomplish its object, then that it had fallen back, and finally that the President was about to call for three hundred thousand more men to prosecute the war. This news was interpreted to be unfavorable to the upward movement in the price of stocks, and so prices fell, and drooped for thirty days.

In July, an increase of the greenback issue was authorized to the extent of $300,000,000. The notes of this new issue soon appeared in their freshest gloss in the sub-treasury, in brokers' windows, in the merchants' petty cash-box, and in farmers' greasy old wallets. The stream taking its rise in the treasury building, flowed on, widening to a mighty river, and like the flood of Old Nile, overflowing, if not fertilizing the country.

Money could soon be had at three per cent., on call, in the market. Once more the watchful operators loaded up. In September there again occurred the same quivering, saltatory, upward movement, that had taken place early in May. "Courage, Bulls!" passed from rank to rank. "Load up! load up!" was the cry. And for the first time, those stocks which were then called the "fancies," began to move. Erie and Harlem were looking up.

Something was still wanting to the market. Stocks were cheap, money plentiful, and hope buoyant. What, then, was lacking? Some one bold enough to bid stocks up. The market demanded leaders, and straightway leaders came forth.

CHAPTER VIII.

BULL-LEADERS.

"Circumstances Make Men"—Addison G. Jerome—The Napoleon of the Public Board—His Appearance, Character and Fortunes—His Fall from Power—John M. Tobin, the Wall Street Sea-rover—Style and Policy of his Operations—Vanderbilt's Lieutenant—New School of Tactics in the Stock-market—Composition of the Public Board—Fortunes of some of its Members — A Bankrupt turns Banker—The Luck of a "Bummer and Dead Beat"—The Story of D——y—Forward Bulls!—Stocks on the March—My First Visit to the Public Board, and what came of it.

WARS bring forth generals; and revolutions, statesmen. Times of financial excitement in the stock-market develop skill and ability in that field, and bring forth what are termed *Bull-leaders*. Wall Street, considered as an aggregation of human-forces and money-forces, without bull-leaders, would be like a flock of sheep without a bell-wether, a mob without a spokesman, an army without a commander. It is the bull-leader who organizes and compacts those forces, brings them under his banner and leads them to victory or—ruin.

He must, of course, have or control large sums of money, and be distinguished for clearness of perception and promptness of decision, but above all, he must have more *nerve*, than falls to the lot of common humanity.

This word *nerve*, in Wall Street, covers and includes

much. By it is signified courage as an active quality, and fortitude as a passive quality, a firmness of bodily fibre and an equal firmness of will, a capability for enduring "punishment," as is said of some pugilists, and the strength to inflict it. It is the same quality that enables the gambler to "bluff" the table and take the "pool" of money though some of the other players may hold a better hand than he, and what, after all, is the game of speculation, but a big game of bluff in which Vanderbilt, Drew and the other heavy-weighted players take the whole pot of money staked by a hundred less skillful and nervy.

Such a man as we have described, was Addison G. Jerome, during his brief reign of nine months, as the "Napoleon of the Public Board." He was formerly of Rochester, N. Y., and previous to going into Wall Street, had been a dry goods merchant in the city of New York, and we believe successful in that vocation. Merchandising and broking, are contiguous professions; the latter being an extension and intensification of the idea of traffic, for the broker buys and sells, both much oftener and much more heavily than the merchant, of the same grade.

He was a middle-sized, quiet-loooking man, with a bluish gray eye, and a slight stoop. When he rose to bid for a stock in the Public Board, every eye was fixed upon him, and his gestures, and the expression of his face were studied, even while he was sitting down, during the call of stocks. The spring of 1863, found him master of a large personal fortune, and his prestige in the market, brought to his banking-house, immense deposits, from those who believed in his financial star. He organized, and carried through, some of the most successful corners of the year.

Mr. Jerome's associates in the Board followed his lead, with a blind confidence, that savored of infatuation, and too often with disastrous results to themselves, for he used his power most skillfully, when necessary for the success of some pet scheme, to mislead or hoodwink the uninitiated. We remember hearing him remark to a friend, "now see me fool the boys," (this was in the street after the expiration of the session.) He thereupon, offered to sell any part of fifteen thousand shares of Galena; the brokers around him thinking this only a bluff offer to depress the stock, eagerly caught him up, and in fifteen minutes he sold the whole fifteen thousand shares to different parties. Next morning the stock fell ten per cent. and he re-purchased, before night, the entire lot, bagging something like one hundred and twenty-five thousand by the operation.

Unlike many large operators, whose hearts are like the nether millstone, knowing neither "ruth nor pity," he was open to generosity, and the softer emotions. His treatment of fallen antagonists was liberal, and even magnanimous. Not unfrequently he allowed some of his outside friends to participate in the profits of some one of the numerous rings he controlled. In 1863, he called on H. L. D——, a large and successful operator, but whose painful lameness prevented him from being in the market, and told him to take a few thousand shares of a certain stock, in which he had a controlling interest. He did so, and in three days he drew out of Jerome's hands, a profit of sixty thousand dollars. Nearly every stock on the list (including gold,) first or last during his nine months reign, responded to his touch.

When he formed a ring, he was in the habit of assigning a certain interest to Mrs. Jerome, his wife, doubtless in view of the uncertainties of Wall Street. He always seems to have inspired his associates in these rings, with the same confidence which he himself felt, or seemed to feel, and if a disaster occurred, he was wont to keep up their courage, by pointing to the ease with which stocks could be manipulated, and the great profits to be earned thereby.

But nearly all our Wall Street necromancers meet, at last, some master spirit, before whom, their strongest spells become powerless, and their magic arts fail them. Mr. Jerome, with all his shrewdness and daring, formed no exception to this rule. He met his fate in Old Southern, at the hands of Henry Keep, in August, 1863, in the manner to be hereafter described. His personal losses in this stock on that occasion are said to have reached $800,000, and after that, he ceased to be a power in the street.

He died in 1864, of one of those obscure diseases of the heart, superinduced, probably, by the excitements and pressures of Wall Street life, and left no personal or real estate, unless he may be said to have had an interest in the estate of several hundred thousand dollars which he had settled upon his wife in the days of his affluence.

One of the contemporaries of A. G. Jerome, who first came out prominently as a member of the Public Board, in 1862, and as a general stock-operator, was John M. Tobin.

Tobin is an Anglo-Norman name. It is a corruption of St. Aubin. Some seven hundred years ago, St. Aubin was a Norman Baron, who accompanied Strongbow to Ireland, and assisted in the subjugation of that country. In John M. Tobin's veins doubtless runs, then, the blood of Norman Barons, and of Irish kernes. He has a spice of the old Norse Vikings about him, and has been a kind of freebooter on a large scale. He and Leonard W. Jerome have together plowed the main in Wall Street, and rifled and scuttled many a stately argosy, and taken for toll many good ducats out of Uncle Daniel Drew's strong box. All sorts of stories used to float about among the gossips of the market, respecting his antecedents. He had been a liquor dealer in Water Street; he had been employed on a ferry-boat; he was a returned Californian, etc., etc., etc. And then as to how he started in the street, some said he put up a horse and wagon as a margin, others that he came in with a capital of $500, and "bluffed the boys." The fact seems to be, that he commenced speculations some time before the war, lost heavily in the fall of stocks which followed the McClellan-Richmond-campaign, borrowed fresh capital, made heaps of money, and early in 1863, had become a power in the market. He was known to be somehow mysteriously connected with Vanderbilt. He was the principal agent of the Commodore in engineering the great rise in Harlem, during the spring and summer of 1864. This added to his prestige won in former operations. His style of operating, too, was so bold and so dashing and even reckless, and yet withal there was such method in his madness, that it quite captivated "the boys," and they were all agog when Tobin got on his pins

and commenced bidding.   Tall, lithe and straight as
an Iroquois, his eyes flaming like two opals, he would
charge up under Drew's heavy batteries and take all
the big wads of certificates the old man would fire at
him.   Unlike most of the noted operators, whose
faces are seamed and creased as if some ravenous
bird had clawed them, he has a face which, though
somewhat worn and haggard, is finely chiseled and
lit up now and then by a smile which is of the most
un-Wall Street geniality.

His policy in operations, as he, himself, lately
informed a friend, has always been to select some
stock which promised gain, find out all he could
about it, and then concentrate his energies and capital in promoting its rise.   When it had risen high
enough to insure to him a sufficiently large profit,
he would sell out, and turn his attention to some
other single stock, and treat it in the same way.

Like his associate, and sometime colleague in rings,
A. G. Jerome, his portfolio has contained at differ-
ent times, very large amounts of stocks, now of Old
Southern, now of Hudson, or Pacific Mail, or Erie, or
Rock Island.

At the close of 1864, he was rated on the street,
at three millions.   But within four months after, he
was rumored to have lost nearly two millions, chiefly
by bulling gold at 200, in the teeth of Union victories, and while the shattered hulk of the Southern
Confederacy was going down, head foremost.   Latterly, he is reported to have made and lost largely,
in New York Central.

These two men, were the bull-leaders of the Public Board, during the first few months of its existence.

They inaugurated a system of tactics in stocks, like that by which the "little corporal" defeated and scattered the Prussian and Austrian armies. This system consisted in rapid movements, and the concentration of their forces at the critical moment upon one point —a single stock. They soon found apt pupils and imitators in the market.

That energetic, but motley crowd, which composed the Public Board, in the latter part of 1862, was made up, as already remarked, of heterogeneous elements. It had more enterprise and talent than money. Many of its members had, previous to the war, carried on various lines of business extensively, but had lost their all in 1861, and owed hundreds of thousands besides. Though they had little money, they had what in Wall Street supplies its place, viz: confidence in the upward tendency of values. They had seen men almost as poor as themselves, become affluent in a few months, and the heavy operators about them were making or losing a hundred thousand in a single day. A volume might be filled with the marvelous stories of the waxing and waning fortunes of these men. One of them owed in December, 1862, one hundred and eighty thousand dollars, and in eight months after, had compromised his debts at fifty cents on the dollar, and was worth clear of the world, three hundred thousand dollars.

In 1861, I had often noticed a singular looking man standing in front of one of the billiard saloons in the upper part of Nassau Street. He bore all the marks which characterize the bar-room loafer or "bummer," seedy, bloated, he was apparently doomed to a speedy and miserable end, and a grave in the potter's field.

In one year from that time I saw him driving a pair
of ponies in Central Park, and on inquiring his name,
learned that he was C., a Wall Street man, who had
made $80,000 on gold.   He is now keeping a hotel,
and to see him looking after the comfort of his guests
in the lordly self-sacrificing way common to hotel
proprietors, no one would imagine that this was the
desolate "bummer" of Nassau Street.

Such was not the luck of D——y.   He was a
young man of New England extraction.   In 1862,
he was a salesman in a Broadway dry goods jobbing
house, on a salary of $800 per annum.   Having made
$600, by buying a few cases of cotton goods on credit,
he brought this sum to a friend who had been long
engaged in speculation, requesting him to take it and
use it as a margin to buy stock for his, D——y's,
benefit.   He received in reply, the usual good and
disinterested advice, not always, however, in such
cases given, viz: "Keep out of the street, or if you
will speculate, do it on your own hook."   He embraced the latter alternative, and joined the Public
Board.   His personal appearance and manners made
an odd impression on 'Change.   Tall, bulky and un-
gainly, his face and voice reminded one of a gigantic
bull-frog, when in one of its happiest moods of a
May evening, and the way in which he bellowed out
on the call, set the whole room in hysterics.   In an
evil hour, he caught a virulent epidemic, which prevailed extensively in the market about that time.
The name of this disease was *Harlem on the brain.*
He bought and sold nothing but Harlem; he talked
and thought of nothing but Harlem.   "It was bound
to go to two hundred, of course, and no one could stop

it. The Commodore was bulling it, Jerome was bulling it, the 'street' was all bulling it." So he always was saying and acting conformably—buying it. In four months he made, out of his $600 margin, $40,000 on his pet stock during its rise from 30 to 181. In the course of sixty days from the time when he might, by selling, have realized his profit to that amount, the stock had dropped to 90. During this decline he clung obstinately to his stock, and borrowed largely from his friends to keep his margins good, but long before the price had touched 90, he was obliged to succumb, with the loss of all he had, besides $30,000 of borrowed money. Within a week he sailed for California, and was last heard from while keeping sheep on the hills of one of the grazing counties of that State, calculating the amount of the next wool crop, as he watched his nibbling flock.

To return to the point in the preceding chapter, from which we have digressed. The eager cohort which had been waiting for orders, now commenced moving under the commands of their Generals, Jerome and Tobin. The battle of Antietam, and the retreat of Lee to the other side of the Potomac gave the bulls courage. Illinois Central opened the ball by a rise of ten per cent., Pacific Mail danced behind it almost as fast. Hudson, Old Southern, Panama, Reading, Rock Island and Pittsburg stepped blithely up, while Erie, that Rip Van Winkle of stocks, astonished the market by its nimble bounds, rising in a few weeks thirty per cent., and selling at 67. This campaign lasted about thirty days. Then stocks fell back a little and paused.

According to the traditions of the street, certain

11

seasons used to be assigned in which stocks were active, and certain others in which they were dull and depressed. December is usually set down as a dull month, while after the new year, stocks pick up and become more active. So it was in 1862. For six weeks prices remained firm, but comparatively dull.

My first visit to the Public Board was early in January 1863. The room in which they then held their sessions, it will be remembered, was the basement of No. 17 William Street. It was under the auspices of my old broker, O., that I obtained access to this grotto. The day was a nipping one. The hangers-on about the door had retreated to some of the neighboring restaurants. The winter rise had already commenced. The dense, black-coated mass of humanity swayed to and fro, while the room rang with the dissonance of bids and offers. No stock without some advance, but Hudson was the favorite that day. It opened at 77 and rose to 80 on the call, then fell back, or, as they say in Wall Street *reacted* to 78.

"Hudson is the card to-day," remarked O.

As he uttered these words, a broker came up, and asked if he was buying Hudson.

"At what price?"

"Seventy-eight and a quarter, five hundred shares, at that price?" holding up his finger, interrogatively.

"No, unless my friend," turning to me, "wishes to buy," and at the same time he nudged me and whispered: "Buy it, Buy it."

Before I knew it, the words came out from my lips, "I'll take it." "I'll take your stock," repeated O., to broker, "put it down to me." In sixty seconds by the clock, 80 was bid for the stock, and by the close of the day, it stood at 84.

Before narrating the issue of this unexpected enterprise, let us go back and follow the history of that $3,600 profit on Erie, which accrued to me in the fall of 1860.

A series of careful purchases in which the whole stock thus bought was always paid for and held till it showed a profit, had swelled the $3,600 by December 1861 to $5,000. This, and the original margin of $500 constituted all the capital that I purposed sinking in stocks.

Of this sum $5,300 was then invested in two hundred shares of Erie, at 26½. In April, 1862, 100 of these shares were sold at 37, and the proceeds, $3,700, invested in (600) six hundred shares of Harlem, at 12½. Harlem, it should be stated, is half stock, i. e., fifty dollars, instead of one hundred dollars, per share, at par; so that these six hundred shares were only equal to three hundred shares of full stock, and stood me in $3,675. (In two years and three months from the day when it was purchased, that pitiful lot of Harlem, costing only $3,675, could have been sold for $85,000. Why don't men hold on to good things when they have them? Wall Street men never do.) In November, the remaining one hundred shares of Erie, had been sold at 64. This, with the old margin of five hundred dollars, made nearly $7,000 cash on hand, besides the 300 shares of Harlem, which showed a considerable profit. *But I had broken my rule, never to operate on margins. Here was danger ahead.*

Hudson had risen fifty per cent, during the past

six or eight months. Supposing it should "break,"
and fall twenty-five per cent. Let me see; twenty-
five per cent. on five hundred shares, would be
$12,500, whew! Nearly all my profits scraped to-
gether by so much pains, swept away in an instant.
These thoughts occurred as swift as lightning, the
moment after the stock had been so rashly bought.
My reverie was interrupted by O., reminding me,
that I had no cash in his hands, and that he should
want ten per cent. margin, *i. e.*, $5,000. Having been
satisfied on this point, he parted from me, urging me
to watch the market very closely, and not let my
profit run away from me.

Hudson was passing into strong hands. A great
financial doctor was paying it daily visits. Dr. C.
Vanderbilt had it under his special care. Every day
it grew better, stronger. It jumped about like a
gymnast preparing for the prize leaps; then it
took its first leap to 94. Its second leap was to
be to the hight of 112. Its third was to carry it
to 180.

I took my profit on 400 shares at 94, and kept 100
shares out of pure curiosity, to see where the price
would finally land me.

Ten thousand dollars in cash is a very restless thing
in a speculator's hands. A little waif picked up in
the street, you can only keep it by griping it fast;
relax your fingers for an instant and it is gone to
wander among the other waifs and strays until some
one else picks it up. My ten thousand dollar waif
stayed with me until I saw something which attracted
my attention in the steamship line, as will appear
more fully in the following chapter.

CHAPTER IX.

PACIFIC MAIL AND LEONARD W. JEROME.

Creative Genius in America—The Opening of the Golden Gate—The Battles of the Steamship Kings—The Commodore Makes a Hearty Lunch off Accessary Transit Company—Features of Pacific Mail as a Wall Street Stock—It Oscillates like the Waves of the Sea—"Unstable as Water Thou *Shalt* Excel"—A Grave-yard for the Bears—A New Ring on the Changes of P. M.—L. W. Jerome's Portrait—The Sultan in Wall Street—"I Never Speculate, Sir, but I *will* Take a Little Pacific Mail"—A Secesher gives me "*Point*"—The Stock on its Upward March—Bulls Charge with Flying Artillery in Front.

HO says the American people have no creative genius? True, they have never sung of an "Achilles' wrath," or of "Archangel fallen;" they have never painted a "Transfiguration," nor composed a "Seventh Symphony," nor constructed a "Novum Organum," nor written a tragedy like that of Hamlet. They have had no Homer nor Milton, no Raphael nor Beethoven, no Bacon nor Shakspeare to fill the untenanted niches in their temple of fame with the grander shapes of Poetry, Philosophy and Art. Imagination, in this country, lives in the future rather than in the past. It is the prophet of great industrial enterprises, the framer of inventions, and subordinates itself to the spirit of the practical, everywhere. The American people, we may say, are continually groaning and in travail with such strong conceptions as were brought forth, embodied in the steamboat, sewing-machine and telegraph. To this mighty brood, also, belong the schemes like the Pacific Railroad which spans a continent with a thousand leagues of iron band, and like the Pacific Mail Steamship Company which plows the waves of the peaceful sea with keels which bear almost to our doors the tea plant and the cinnamon plant before they can shed their flowers which bloomed under the sky of Cathay.

Of American enterprises embracing the great lines of travel, steering their course by the westward star of empire, and moving with it farthest and fastest, the Pacific Mail Steamship Company was the pioneer. Its originators were three men of mark in the mercantile world—Gardner G. Howland and William H. Aspinwall, of the firm of Howland & Aspinwall, and Henry Chauncey, of the firm of Alsop & Chauncey. These men had the eyes of prophets, ranging widely over the land of promise which stretched out towards the setting sun. The accession of California to our national domain was the immediate occasion of the incorporation, in 1848, of this company. The discovery of gold in that region secured its speedy success. For twenty years it has been a modern Pactolus, through whose channel have flowed to the marts of commerce, the golden sands whirled down by the mountain torrents from the scarped cliffs of the Sierra Nevada, or crushed by the more impetuous and eager hand of man, out of quartz and the sulphurets. The yearly income which the company derived from the freights of gold were from the start, considerable, and the aggregate foots up something enormous. But its great source of revenue has always been the carriage of passengers. From 1848 to 1852, the whole world seemed to be packing its trunks, and ho! for Eldorado! Down through the Gulf, across the Isthmus, northward to the Golden Gate they hurried, and a refluent tide of the successful or disappointed, swept back again by the same route. All this swelled the profits of Pacific Mail. In 1850, it doubled its original capital of one million, and in 1853, increased its capital to four millions to meet the necessities of travel.

Meanwhile, the same three men, Howland, Aspinwall and Chauncey had, by the aid of foreign capital, carried through another great enterprise, the Panama Railroad. Though only forty-seven miles in length, from Aspinwall to Panama, the completion of this road involved difficulties and disasters which would have appalled men less rich and resolute. No white man could long breathe the miasma of those dank swamps and jungles, and live. Commerce seemed to have become a Moloch, before whose grim shrine, thousands of Irish laborers were sacrificed. But the work must go on—means were soon devised. Some one proposed our kinky-haired friends, and a few ship-loads of Jamaica negroes accordingly supplied the waste and finished the line.

But the Pacific Mail Company were not long permitted to reap the fruits of their enterprise, undisturbed. The carrying trade from New York to Aspinwall had been taken by those modern sea-kings, C. K. Garrison, Charles Morgan and Marshall O. Roberts, and above these, loomed the figure of the irrepressible " Commodore," whose march (then) "was over the mountain wave," and not as now, over the iron rail.

One of the rival enterprises in which he engaged, was the Nicaragua Accessary Transit Company, which has been heretofore mentioned.

In the history of steamship navigation, no more interesting passage could be written than that relating to the rivalries in the California trade during the first twelve years after the accession of that State to the Union. Morgan, Garrison, Roberts, Vanderbilt, the Accessary Transit Company and the Pacific Mail Company, all fighting for the largest share in that lucrative trade, and with fortunes that shifted from each to the other by turns. In some of the ancient naval battles, we read that the ships were armed with *gilded* beaks, for the purpose of running down and sinking the vessels opposed to them. In the emulous warfare of which we are speaking, the steamships may be said to have been armed with golden beaks, for the contest was to be decided by the force of hard money,—by the superior weight of the precious metal. After numerous collisions and a severe cannonade of ruinously low fares, it was found at the end of the conflict, that the eagle beak of C. K. Garrison was disfigured, Marshall O. Roberts lay crippled and helpless, and even the Commodore was not unscathed.

But, while this new edition of the old sea-rovers were fighting among themselves, the traveling public, upon whom they were wont to levy toll, were benefited. The prices of passage to California ran down to a low rate, and the hearts of the way-farers were gladdened.

In 1856, the affairs of the Nicaragua Accessary Transit Company were found to be in a bad way. C. Vanderbilt, the individual, had advanced to C. Vanderbilt, President, large sums, and was preparing to bolt without gagging the whole assets of the compai y which he held as collateral. This process was, as usual, speedily and (for C. V.) happily accomplished. The Pacific Mail Company deemed this a favorable opportunity to get rid of so formidable a competitor, paid King Cornelius an annual tribute of $480,000, per annum, for a fixed period, on condition that he would run no other competing line on the Pacific side, and once more, all was quiet on the San Juan. Out of these transactions, grew the famous suit brought by the receiver of the Nicaragua Accessary Transit Company, by John Sherwood, his attorney, vs. C. Vanderbilt, involving claims to the amount of $2,000,000, which dragged its slow length along through the courts for so many years. Pending this suit, the stock of the N. A. T. Co., oscillated for a season, between twelve and a-half cents, and nine dollars a share in the stock-market, and finally disappeared into that limbo of nothingness, to which the defunct stocks of Wall Street are consigned.

Of all the historical stocks of Wall Street, considering its vast arcs of vibration, its sudden fluctuations, its enormous dividends, the fortunes it has made and marred, its growth, and its far-reaching and accomplished aims, Pacific Mail is the most remarkable. In 1857 it sold for 50, in 1867 it sold for what was equivalent to 700, on the basis of the increased stock; in 1849 it had two second-class and frail steamships, plying between San Francisco and Panama; in 1869 it had twenty-three steamships, each one of which was a floating palace of a grandeur and beauty passing the common show of naval architecture, and plying between New York and Aspinwall, between Panama and "Frisco," and between "Frisco" and Yokohama, Nagasaki, Shanghai and Hong-Kong. He who visits the office of the company in the banking house of Brown Brothers, and in which marble, iron, plate glass, black walnut and fresco, form a pleasing combination of solidity and beauty, will be reminded that he may here shake hands with China for a small consideration.

But we are to speak of the stock as a market value, on 'Change, and of its singular fluctuations since 1861. It may be viewed as a type-stock of the street. The very fact that its value is contingent on so many circumstances arising out of the business of the Company, gives it that character. It has been associated with the water, that very unstable element; exposed to storms and marine disasters; to pirates; to the revolutions in Central America; to wars, and rumors of wars with foreign powers; to the ebbing of the tides of transmigration; to the completion of the Pacific Railroad; to competing lines on the ocean, and to mutations of business in that most speculative and ultra-enterprising of states, California. These are the variable quantities that have always entered into the calculations of the bears of Wall Street in depressing the stock. Then on the other side there are the vast assets and profits of the Company, the growth of the country in general, and of the mining interest, and latterly of the China trade in particular. These are constant quantities that have always entered into the calculations of the bulls in elevating the stock. Accordingly, long before the great speculation which commenced in 1862, it was one of the great balloons to be inflated or depressed according to the wishes of stock leaders. Jacob Little and Daniel Drew have sometimes made great sums by depressing it, but the stock has generally been a cemetery for the bears. The operator who deals in Pacific Mail, is like the mariner who embarks on a treacherous sea. He can look down through its depths and see the bleaching skeletons of bears who in their day made Wall Street resound with their growlings. Who could safely sell short a stock which rose by the hundred per cent.

More rarely this stock has proved the ruin of the bulls, not a few of whom, since 1867, have met their fate by operating in it for a rise. The recent failure of the great house of Lockwood & Co. is a noteworthy example. They owed their disasters mainly to the heavy fall in the price of stock which they had bought at a high rate.

In the year 1861, Pacific Mail was greatly depressed. The fear of complications with foreign powers kept down its market price, and at the time of the Trent affair in December of that year, it fell to 69. But the earnings of the succeeding year were enormous, and in the latter part of 1862, a "ring" of a new and singular character was formed in it. The whole stock was $4,000,000, divided into forty thousand shares. Twenty-six thousand shares of this amount were bought by a combination of such men as W. H. Aspinwall, and Brown Brothers, the Anglo-American Banking House, etc. This stock was transferred to Brown Brothers, by an irrevocable stock power, as trustees to hold it *five years* for the joint benefit of members of the ring. This left fourteen thousand shares, which was in the hands of private investors.

Who was to be the Wall Street representative of the ring—the manipulators of this stock—who would lead the upward dance of the price?

No one who has visited Central Park, will have failed to remark four bay horses, standing at least seventeen and a-half hands high, bowling along on an easy trot, and drawing after them a huge "drag." Sitting on the box, holding the reins, is a tall man, fashionably, but somewhat carelessly attired, having a slight stoop, a clear olive complexion, a tigerish moustache, and a cerulean eye. This is Leonard W. Jerome, a leader of the fashion, a prince of the turf, and lately, a potentate in the stock-market. Some men are born speculators, some achieve it, and some have speculation thrust upon them. All these conditions may be predicated of L. W. Jerome, and when he left Rochester, and came into Wall Street, he found his proper niche. The head to conceive, the daring to undertake, and the nerve to persist, are all his. Nor is his confidence and buoyancy under disaster less remarkable. Like all men of his class, he has been now and then temporarily prostrated by some one of those singular hurricanes in finance, which come and pass over as suddenly as a white squall in the Southern Pacific. But, no matter how swift or low the fall, he has always kept up good heart, and hailed his surviving comrades with the words, "I am all right, boys; I'll be with you again in a jiffy." Under such circumstances, he has always met every dollar of his obligations. Once he found himself saddled with half a million of bogus Indiana bonds. He paid up in full. Another time within the past three years, he found himself out of pocket on Pacific Mail nearly one million dollars. Then the carpers and malignants of the street were crying out—"Jerome has found his Waterloo!" but in six months he picked up half of his lost million, and made his adversaries pine with envy.

He was bred to the law, and this may account for a certain conservatism which seems to have led him to operate, for the most part, in dividend-paying securities, calling attention to the rule that intrinsic values will in the end bring profit, while the inflated "fancies" and mere market values, as surely in the long run bring loss. Like his brother Addison G. Jerome, he has generally been a bull in stocks.

A mortal feud long existed between him and Daniel Drew, in which they mutually gave and took wounds. In 1864 he took a slice out of Uncle Daniel, on Harlem, of the size of a quarter of a million. In 1865 his opponent retaliated by scooping out of him a couple of hundred thousands on Erie. There was a poetic fitness that such a man should be the bull-leader in Pacific Mail—a stock reminding us by its very name of the treasures of Eldorado, and of the "barbaric pearl and gold," which the Orient is said to "shower on its kings." In his tastes and his munificence he has been a kind of Sultan of India or Rajah of Benares. Stables rose at his bidding fit for the horses of Caligula. A race-course was laid, which bears his name, worthy of the plains of Elis, and his garlanded Apician banquets rivaled those of Lucullus. All that he did was on such a princely scale as to show that he knew how to spend as well as to make money. Under the heavy purchases which he made, Pacific Mail rose rapidly from par to one hundred and sixty.

The whole pack of Bandogs of the street sat on their haunches with mouths that watered and uttered feeble yelps of hungry excitement as they wistfully watched its upward progress, yearning to snatch at the tempting feast, but held in the leash, some by impecuniosity, and some by irresolution or prudence.

It seemed like madness to buy Pacific Mail, now that it had risen 100 per cent. in thirteen months. A few outsiders ventured in.

"What's the matter with P. M.?" inquired C., a well-known merchant, of G., a leading operator, whom he met on the street cars one morning, just as the stock had reached 145.

"Going up! Going up!" replied G., "you'd better take a little."

"I'd as soon think of opening a dress-goods store over a volcano!" rejoined C., "I never buy P. M. above 75."

"You'll never see it at 75, again," and G. whispered something in his ear, whereat C. looked astounded.

Whether C. ever bought any Pacific Mail, we cannot affirm, but this we know, that two or three weeks after, when the price was thirty per cent. higher, C. was seen emerging from G's. office, holding in his cherishing fingers, a plump check, which he regarded with a paternal smile.

In the spring of that year, and while Pacific Mail was being manipulated as above described, I became acquainted with a certain mysterious individual (a secret agent of the Southern Confederacy, as I afterwards learned), who was boarding at the same hotel, and was in the habit of taking "flyers" in the stock-market. He informed me that something very startling would soon occur in Pacific Mail, that the stock would inevitably depreciate 50 or even 100 per cent. He spoke with all the confidence of certainty; he asseverated it with as much solemnity as if he were taking his oath on the holy Evangels. On my asking for the grounds of his assertions, he replied in the soft Tuscan accent of his native State: "Dog gone it! do you doubt the word of a southern gentleman? I tell you it's dead shore." I sold short 200 shares of P. M. at 160, and 100 shares more at 162.

The stock-market in January, 1863, was like an army moving up a steep declivity. The old guard, Erie, Harlem, etc., were still skulking in the rear, but Pacific Mail was leading the van upon the double-quick. The bears sat upon different peaks of this declivity, watching the upward movement and licking their lips over the rich opportunities which would soon be offered them for attack and plunder, "for," said they, "whatever goes up much, must come down much." When the price reached 160, they began to hurl down blocks of shares to drive P. M. back. It still rose, staggering to 164, then turned and slowly fell back to 160. The bears now threw a perfect shower of missiles. It quivered a moment, and then dropped heavily to 155, rested there for one short breathing space, then darted up in a few hours to 165. In a week it sold at 178. The bears gave way with dreadful losses. Many of the oldest heads had been caught. The stock never halted till it touched 200. The rumor went round the street, that Vanderbilt was buying it. The spectacle of Tobin, bidding fiercely for the stock at 190, with the aureola of the Commodore's prestige surrounding his blonde brow, disenchanted the bears from their illusions. Some of the more deeply initiated were now warned by their friends, with dark hints of what was going on in the Jerome pool. They covered their contracts, and the stock fell back to 180.

During this rise, and after I had closed my 400 shares, short stock, at a loss of $10,000, news came that the Joseph Chapman, an armed schooner, had been seized in the harbor of San Francisco. She was a letter-of-marque of the Southern Confederacy. The plan proposed was, to capture one of the Pacific Mail Steamers, arm her, and cruise for the others. This was the secret, which my Southern acquaintance was building his hopes upon. If the Joseph Chapman programme had been carried out successfully, no doubt the stock would have fallen heavily to my individual profit, but to the damage of the Union cause. Here it might be appropriate to indulge in a little burst of patriotic enthusiasm, but oh! the memory of that $10,000!

At this point, we must take leave of Pacific Mail, for several chapters, and turn our eyes upon another form of speculation, which had, in the autumn of 1862, assumed a definite shape, and in February, 1863, first rose into huge proportions.

ADDISON G. JEROME

HENRY KEEP

JAY GOULD.

JAMES FISK, JR.,

CELEBRITIES OF WALL STREET.

CHAPTER X.

"GOLD, GOLD, GOLD, GOLD,—HOARDED, BARTERED, BOUGHT AND SOLD."

"Fresh Fields and Pastures New" for "The Boys"—The Gold Genii—The Lobbymen and Politicians Take a Turn—Where all the Gold Was—Secesh at the Front—A Petroleum Maniac—I Take a Flyer in Oil, and Find it "Oil of Joy"—I Go "Down to the Sea in a Ship," and What my Ship Brought when it Came in—New Recruits in William Street—Things are Working—Gold "Breaks" for 200 and then "Breaks" to 156—Raking in the Profits—A Sum in Algebra, $73,000 + $20,000—The Bear-leader in Distress—The Gold Dreamer, and how His Dream Came out—Men and Money in Wall Street—The Autobiography of $500.

DURING the year 1861, gold ceased, generally, to circulate, as money, throughout the Republic. Early in 1862, and soon after the passage of the Legal Tender Act, it began to be dealt in as merchandise. It was bought in the market at varying prices, and then having been bought as merchandise, it was used as money to pay Government duties on the debts due abroad. From legitimate traffic it is an easy step to *speculation* which we have already termed the abuse of trade. And now commenced the most baleful form of speculation, that which made it for the interest of the parties engaged in it that the national currency should depreciate, for as every one knows a rise in gold is nothing but another name for a fall in the value of currency.

12

Thus, when gold sells for two hundred, a dollar in currency is worth only fifty cents in gold; when gold sells for five hundred, a dollar in currency is worth only twenty cents in gold.

I will not here and now reiterate the hackneyed arguments against the morality of trafficking on the rise and fall of greenbacks, and the embarrassments caused in the commercial world, by the unsettling of the standards of value. No doubt, every one but the gold gamblers, and their friends and dependents would be better off if they were swallowed up in the ocean. I speak now as a scribe, not as a moralist. The *fact* is before us, gross and palpable and thus we are to deal with it. The precious metal prior to the year 1861, acted its part in the operations of commerce, like the beneficent Afrite, in Arabian story, obeying the behests of its master, with commendable fidelity, but the breaking out of our civil war seemed to have driven it into its casket, where it lay for a year, and then issued forth under the guise of a malevolent genié. This genié took the form of a cloud-statue, not "moulded in colossal calm," but changing its shape according to the financial weather; now looming up to a portentous size, and anon dwarfing and dwindling under all kinds of influences. Like similar malign agencies, it had its chief abiding place in Wall Street.

The daring speculators, who had by the assistance of causes already mentioned, so successfully forced up the price of stocks, now flushed with their good fortune, and comprehending the situation, turned their attention to gold. The dealings in it at the coal hole, which at first were limited, soon came to rival the transactions in stocks. In September, 1862, under the combined influence of Union disasters, and heavy purchases, it shot up to 135. Early in February following, it had risen to 150.

Now was formed the first notable combination to put up gold. The state of affairs which led to that sharp and sudden rise to 173, which was to prepare the public mind for the wild and reckless speculations, extending already through seven years, and still hardly diminished, may be described as follows, viz:

The sum total of gold and silver, estimated to be then in the country, was upwards of $250,000,000; rather a big pile to get into a "corner," you will say. But only little over one-quarter of this was in the banks, and no inconsiderable portion of that was held on special deposit. The balance was scattered throughout the country, much of it in the South. The private bankers held several millions. Several millions were in the form of plate. Much was buried in the earth and hoarded up in chimneys and garrets. How much the crusty old farmers and raven-like crones of the rural districts had hidden away in old stockings, between mattresses and in cupboards, secret drawers and hollow trees, no one can imagine, but probably enough to pay a year's interest on a $1,000,000,000 of debt. Apart from the idea of speculation, multitudes laid away sums, larger or smaller, against that very wet day, when a bushel of currency might not buy more than a peck of meal. Some of the large, but timorous capitalists, also put much of their property into exchange on London. In this way the floating supply of gold could be

readily absorbed by any strong ring which might
be organized. Bills of exchange drawn on the commercial cities of Europe, it should be here remarked,
are payable in gold, and therefore rise and fall in
price with gold.

During the preceding year, the already large army
which was "fighting the tiger" on 'Change, received
a re-inforcement. It came from the South, and having had ocular proof of the depreciation of the currency in that section, had fixed its eyes on the course
of gold in the Union States, and looked for a corresponding rise here. Most of these men had brought
with them sums, larger or smaller, principally the
latter, in bills of exchange on London, the aggregate amount whereof was great, and was deposited
as margins, in the hands of Wall Street brokers, for
the purpose of buying gold. These exiles, or rather
emigrants from the Sunny South, were a motley
crowd. Some of them tall, gentlemanly-looking men;
others swarthy, lank-haired, tobacco-ruminant individuals from the Gulf States. They haunted William
Street, birds of ill-omen, croaking all manner of disaster to the Federal arms, and predicting gold at
500. Many made fortunes by being always consistent bulls, but lost them again, by the tumble of
1865. Such was the situation, when I made my first
venture, and bagged my first profit in gold. In order
to tell the whole story, I must go back, and trace
that profit to its doubtful beginnings.

In the month of October, 1861, two gentlemen sat
in a private parlor of the Grammercy Park House.
The one was a well-known pioneer in the petroleum
enterprise, wearing a face of perennial redness and

gold-bowed spectacles; the other was the narrator of these scenes. The ruddy gentleman was holding forth with great volume and fluency upon the subject of petroleum, his favorite theme. If he was to be believed, besides the illuminating and lubricating properties of this article, it had a great variety of other uses. It was death to vermin, a capital disinfectant, and a gorgeous colorizer. As boot grease, and as hair oil, it was unequaled. The most delicious perfumes might be manufactured from it. It was a panacea for most of the "ills that flesh is heir to." It was a liniment for rheumatism, a lotion for wounds, and a "sovereign remedy for an inward bruise." In token of which last he produced a small vial from his vest pocket, and swallowed a part of its contents, declaring that he took it for an affection of the kidneys, and had derived great benefit from the medicine.

"This article," added he, "is now selling at five cents a gallon (including barrel,) at the wells, and will be a great speculation for any one who buys it."

"What will you sell me fifteen hundred barrels at?" inquired I.

"Fifteen hundred barrels, crude petroleum—I will sell at—two dollars, per barrel."

"To be paid on delivery, in New York?"

"To be paid, on delivery—at—the wharf, in New York."

This bargain was nailed by a small memorandum in writing, signed by the parties, to be charged according to the statute, so made and provided.

Six weeks after this, the barrels were duly delivered, per Camden and Amboy Railroad, and were sold on the wharf, at a net profit of $3,500, and some odd cents, petroleum having advanced largely meanwhile.

The proceeds of this lucky stroke were a few weeks subsequently, invested in refined petroleum, packed in cans and cases and shipped to Australia. The figures in this venture stood thus, viz: $9,700, of which, $6,200 was an advance on the bills of lading; the ballance, $3,500, was the actual cash embarked. The vessel which carried this merchandise, was an old tub, warranted not to make over six knots, even with "a wet sheet and a flowing sea." She reached her destination after a voyage of one hundred and twenty-five days, just after a "spirt" in the prices of the articles shipped, so that the consignees were enabled to close the shipment at a net profit of $6,500, after deducting freight, commissions, brokerage, etc., etc., etc. Several other delays now occurred, all very much to my benefit, such, for instance, as disputes over samples, references, making up the account sales, and finally, when the return bills of exchange were forwarded, the steamer which conveyed them was wrecked in the Indian Ocean. All this time, gold, and therefore exchange, was steadily rising. When the slow old ship left New York, gold was $101\frac{1}{2}$; when the gold bill on the Union Bank of London for return sales, reached New York, gold was 153. Here was a new profit. Without stopping to sell my draft, amounting to $10,000, I promptly invested it as a ten per cent. margin on $100,000 gold, bought at 153. This was late in January, 1863.

In that month, a combination had been formed, known as the "Washington party," which bought up several millions for a rise, on the grounds that Congress would authorize the issue of three or four hundred millions more currency.

This movement soon became known to the leading operators on the street. They relaxed their hold of stocks, which paused in their course upwards, and increased their line in gold.

The rise appeared so reasonable, and so inevitable, that men who had never speculated, began to make their first essay, we might say *assay*, in the precious metal. Strange faces were seen in the vicinity of the "coal-hole." Financial oracles of the rural districts, were heard on the corners uttering their predictions, as to the future price of gold. Quiet old bachelors, living on their dividends, were seen emerging from their up-town snuggeries, prepared to renew their youth, like young eagles, in the courts of the Stock Exchange. Some of the novices could be observed, hovering on the edges of the battle, or gazing with gloating eyes, on the ascending price, but hardly daring to venture in.

Meanwhile, gold kept rising. It touched 160. Now the bull machinery was put in motion. The telegraph between William Street and Washington, went click-a-ty-click. The crowd buzzed, the workmen were hard at work, lubricating the steam-presses, preparatory to another edition of greenbacks, containing all the modern emendations.

George Francis Train was seen daily leaning gracefully on the iron railing near the coal-hole, engaged in perusing telegraph literature. Beside him, stood Pepoon, looking like a Dutch Burgomaster of the olden time. George Francis said gold would sell at

200.   Pepoon repeated after him, 200; Addison G. Jerome said 200; the coal-hole echoed the words.

I bought $100,000 more at 160. In a week the price rose to 173, and looked for the moment as if it were really booked for 200. It began to sink.

The $200,000 I held, was dumped overboard, and left me with a profit of $28,000, to which add $10,000 in the gold bill, sold at 170, and making $17,000 in currency, footing up as a sum total of profit, $45,000.

But gold now commenced falling. Large amounts were forced on the market, according to rumor, by the Washington party. In a day or two, the secret came out. The Government had imposed a tax of one-quarter per cent. on all sales. I thereupon sold short, $200,000 at 169⅞ to 170½. Down it went by the run, and in three days, sold for 156. Profits on this transaction, $28,700.

In two years and upwards, with hardly more than the scratch of a pen, the fifteen hundred barrels of petroleum bought at a venture on credit, and without the ultimate expenditure of a penny, thus rolled up for the lucky buyer, $73,700!

During the rise of gold, from 130 to 173, most of the outside public, and the younger and bolder operators in the street favored a rise, and were active bulls; a few inveterate bears like Drew, etc., true to their instincts, still sold short, but were severely punished, and after the rise of gold to 170, covered their contracts and stood aloof. Drew, however, whose losses on the rise were said to have been half a million, is said to have persisted in his programme, and when it fell, recovered a good portion of his losses. The decline, which was steadily going on for the next six months, after February 26th, 1863, quite upset the calculations of those enthusiastic operators, who looked for 200, as a limit for the realization of their profits. Many of these individuals held manfully to their position, fortified by the enormous profits of their operations for a rise. Among this class were the young and inexperienced operators, who in the spring, thought themselves possessors of ample fortunes, and in the succeeding fall, found themselves either worse off, or in very much the same position, as when they commenced.

The speculation of which we have been speaking, brought out in strong relief, that which we may call the monomania of Wall Street. Men who pass all their time there, are often afflicted with this form of the speculative disease. A Wall Street monomaniac is one, who, devoting himself exclusively to some one stock, by thinking long and deeply upon it, and continually operating in it, comes at last to think and talk of little else. He clings to it, through good report and evil report, and through actual losses. The gains he makes in it, strengthen his mania. It is only by absolute ruin that he can be cured, and even then, often not permanently. He still babbles of it in the social circle, and when he revisits the street, always inquires with solicitude, the price of his old favorite, and if it has eventually risen very greatly, appeals triumphantly to that fact, in justification of his course. This was the case with H——.

He was a German-American from one of the Western cities, and came into the street with $4,500 which he had scraped together, by buying and selling the "wild-cat" currency which flooded his native

State. His personal appearance was something of the oddest. The bumps on his head, which was sparingly thatched by a "plentiful lack" of the capillary substance, would have astonished a phrenologist. His face had the color and general shape of a half-boiled Indian pudding. His eyes, large and bleary, had a dreamy look, as though they were contemplating the phantom of a million dollars which haunted his imagination; and that feature which he dignified by the name of nose, was merely an excrescence expanded into two nostrils. The facilities furnished him by his gentlemanly broker, soon taught him to appreciate the beauties of the margin system, and he was afterwards heard to express the opinion, that the time would come when he would buy up the whole of New York on a margin. By two or three lucky operations he doubled his original capital of $4,500, and commenced buying gold in the summer of 1863, at 117 or thereabouts. His first purchase was $90,000, when it rose five per cent., i. e., to 122, he bought $90,000 more. Following this programme and buying at every five per cent. advance, when gold touched 173, he found himself carrying $990,000, with a profit of nearly $300,000. During the five or six months in which he was making these purchases, he seemed to be laboring under a kind of nightmare, under the influence of which, he was unable to realize his profits, and was always compelled to buy. He thought of nothing, dreamed of nothing, and talked of nothing but gold; impalpable gold-dust seemed to float in the air he breathed, and every object to take on a yellow hue. He carried in his left breast pocket, a chunked little blank book, in which all his purchases were entered, and his time was about evenly divided between the study of this book and the perusal of the daily quotations of the price.

This delirium of speculation seemed to have somewhat shattered his nervous system, and he was wont to lie late in the morning, rarely making his appearance in the street before eleven A. M. I remember meeting him often in Broadway, making a beeline for Wall Street, on that double-quick gait, known as the negro trot; when he would suddenly halt and cry out, interrogatively, "gold?" On hearing the price he would throw up his arms, utter a little ecstatic scream and resume his trot. He used to declare he would never sell for less than a thousand. This was the limit he gave his broker every day, and every successive rise fortified him in this resolve and made him more and more callous to the arguments and ridicule of his friends, who advised him to take his profits.

But H——'s greatness was soon to be nipped by an untimely frost. In the fall of gold, which commenced on the 26th of February and continued for the next few days thereafter, his profits were abridged to the amount of $200,000, and early in June following, he was called upon by his broker, for more margin. Not being able to respond to the call, he was sold out and presented with an account which showed a balance of only five hundred dollars to his credit. This fall from such a sunlit hight to such a dead level, almost drove H—— distracted, but failed to cure him of his monomania. He still kept his dreamy eyes fixed on gold. Its tendency was plainly downwards. Gettysburg was fought, and it sank lower. Vicks-

burg fell and gold dropped to 131. When the
"swamp angel" sent its messages into Charleston,
and Fort Wagner became a Union fortress, gold at
122 looked as if it would drop to par. But now it
suddenly reversed its course and began to mount that
lofty hight which it was destined to scale before ten
months were gone. H—— jumped in and bought ten.
(Wall Street lingo for ten thousand.) He moved on
now, taking every step gingerly, and bought ten more
at each fifteen per cent. rise. In one year from September, 1863, he owned three brown-stone fronts.
He is still a flourishing operator, but only in gold,
never buying more than he can take care of, and
never letting a profit run away from him.

In Wall Street, the man is nothing; the money,
everything. The first inquiry when a new operator
enters the field, is, how much money does he carry?
Not at all what kind of a man is he, what are his
antecedents, etc. This inquiry having been answered,
he is labeled with the sum for which he is good, and
after that loses his personal identity in the money he
possesses. While a cracksman, slave-trader or pirate
might walk the street, not merely unimpeached, but
saluted with respect, if covered with the broad label
inscribed with $100,000 in front and indorsed with
it behind, an archangel would be of little account,
unless he brought with him a good store of shekels
in a golden urn, for here

"Mammon wins his way where seraphs might despair."

Thus it happens that an autobiography of experiences in Wall Street might properly be entitled the
history and growth of so much money, whatever sum

the operator may have started with. Such an autobiography as this might be presumed to commence
thus: My name is one thousand dollars, my surname
greenbacks. I was begotten in an engraver's office,
and born from a steam-press early in the year 1863.
My general appearance was pleasing, my color was
that "soft green on which the eye loves to repose."
I circulated freely in society and was much courted.
At an early age I took up my permanent abode in
Wall Street, where I thrived and grew very large.
At last, from my increased size, they called me one
hundred thousand dollars, etc., etc., etc.

In the foregoing pages, I have given the history
of $500 in Wall Street, which by April, 1863, had
after numerous trials and vicissitudes of fortune,
grown into $20,000, or was readily reducible to that
sum, standing thus:

600 Shares Harlem, (half stock, $50 per share), selling	
in the market at $56, ...	$16,800 00
100 Hudson, which showed a profit of	2,200 00
Margin on same, ...	1,000 00
	$20,000 00
Profits on gold, etc., ...	73,700 00
	$93,700 00

I stood $93,700 ahead.

The sun never shines so brightly, and fiercely,
as just before a thunder-storm, which gathers its own
force from that same brightness and heat. Metaphorically speaking, there are vast caverns in Wall
Street, where, as in the realms of Æolus, of classic
myth, the winds are accumulated and pent up. They
are let loose in panics, and panics occur when stocks

that have been over-sold, rise enormously, as well as when they fall enormously.

The king of winds, the Æolus of Wall Street, in 1863, was Cornelius Vanderbilt, for did he not carry Harlem up in a whirlwind?

CHAPTER XI.

THE FIRST GREAT HARLEM RISE.

The Tale of Three Men who met in a Doorway During a Storm—Shall We Sell Harlem Short?—The Brokers Say Yes—Investigations—What is a Broker's Opinion Good For?—The Decision is Made, and We " Sell 'em "—Vanderbilt in Search of Investments—" I Have a Few Millions Lying Idle, Sir, and I Wish to put it into Something that Will Pay "—The Patriots of the City Hall in the Field—A Large Donation to Harlem—The Commodore Gets His Dander Up—The Clown of the Stocks Plays His Antics—A Miss is as Good as a Mile—Legislative Tricks—The Stock Mounts, and the Bears are Slaughtered—Harlem the Double-edged Sword of the Stock-Market—How I Came Out—Incidents of the Rise.

HE market was taking a breathing spell. It was a complete April day. The sun had risen in an unclouded sky, and the breezes from the noble bay, blew their reveillé to the waking spring, when suddenly the heavens became overcast, the wind shifted to the north-east, and blew a gale, mixed with snow. There were three of us. We had taken refuge out of the storm, in one of the hall-ways, on William Street, near Exchange Place, and were discussing the all-absorbing topic.

"I sold out my business," said one, who was a re-tired baker, "and came into the stock-market a year ago. I've no reason to complain. I bought stocks right, and sold them right. I'm $100,000, clear of the world. I am going to get out of this business, it uses me up. Only one more operation for me, and then I shall pull up stakes, and decamp."

"And what may that 'one more operation' be?" inquired another, who was a burly railroad contractor and engineer.

"I'm only waiting for Harlem to rise to 60, and then I mean to give 'em some on the short tack." The railroad man smiled, and spoke thus: "I came into the market four months ago. They always told me I had a good eye for a country. When I came here I took my survey, and staked out my route, kept clear of steep grades, and have brought myself in on time, with one hundred and fifty thousand dollars in my baggage car. Now I am going to back train. I'm through with Wall Street, but I *do* want to make one more operation." "And what may that one more operation be?" inquired I.

"I'm bound *to sell Harlem short*, when it gets up a little higher," he replied.

"I have a little Harlem all paid for; if it wasn't for that circumstance, I should feel like selling it short," I exclaimed.

"You don't surely say that you have been buying Harlem!" exclaimed both my companions at once.

"I should as soon think of buying old newspapers," said the baker.

"Or that dust heap in the street," said the railroad man.

"I think I shall hold that Harlem just to see where it will go. But let's go round and talk with some of these brokers."

So we went out into the storm.

V——, into whose office we first entered, was a well-groomed, little man, with a bright, black eye. He sat behind a long desk, handling his papers nimbly with both hands, and looking very much as if he were playing exercises on a piano.

He saw business written on the faces of the trio, as we entered, and he stepped briskly forth from his musical exercises.

"What do you think of Harlem, V——?"

"Harlem 57½ at the close, gone up too much, must react."

"What do they say about it in the board?"

"Well! all sorts of opinions. Some say that Vanderbilt is buying it, and that it will go to par, but most of the board seem to think there's no reason in the movement. G——, B—— and L—— were selling it freely this morning."

"When it strikes 60, sell one thousand shares for my account," said the railroad man, "order good till countermanded."

Next, we went to G——'s office. He was a different type of a man from V——. Being rather heavily moulded, and still of his tongue, he had obtained the reputation of possessing great good sense.

He thought Harlem higher than it should be. A good sale undoubtedly. Its intrinsic value was about fifteen, instead of fifty-seven. "But," inquired he, "what *about the street franchise?* Hasn't Harlem got something of that kind?"

All the other brokers, whose offices we visited, were unanimous in the opinion that Harlem was a good short sale. Some said the certificates were only good for wrapping paper. Others said they would specu-

13

late in it at about 15. But all concurred in thinking its value more speculative than real.

Here let us stop a moment to remark that most men, at least novices, are wont to ask advice of their brokers, as to what stock they shall buy or sell. But is a broker's opinion worth anything? Not generally. "Never buy or sell on a broker's judgment," said a member of one of the oldest and safest firms in the street, lately to a customer, "if you do, you'll be sure to lose your money." This is a great truth. The brokers borrow their feelings from the market. If the market is depressed, they are affected accordingly; if the market is active and high, they are elated in a corresponding degree. In this way their advice to their customers is to sell when they ought to buy, and to buy when they ought to sell. Again, a broker's judgment is warped by being constantly in an atmosphere of mere market values, irrespective of real values. A broker will often laugh at a customer, who is figuring up the true value of a security by examining the condition of the railroad company which issues it. If a stock has been selling at a very low price for several years, it is consigned to the portfolio of worthless fancies by the broker, who never stops to inquire what its true value is. When one of this class of stocks goes up on its merits, he will be sure to pronounce it a good sale.

That street franchise! what could G—— mean by that? We visited a lawyer's office and called for the laws of the State of New York, hunted up the original charter of the Harlem Railroad Company, which was dated about forty years ago, but could find no street franchise granted by it. We went to the office of General S——, the counsel of the company, and inquired if he knew of any franchise granted to the Harlem Railroad Company.   He knew no more about it than he did about Numa Pompilius.

"All right," said the railroad man.   "All right," responded the other twain.   Within three days we found ourselves jointly short of eight thousand shares of Harlem, of which lot I had three thousand at different prices, from 57 to 59.   There was one man who did not share in the ephemeral opinions which prevailed in the stock-market respecting Harlem.

Vanderbilt always seems to have held faith in the ultimate value of the stock as a security, and had been for some years a director in the road.   As he was selling out his steamboats and steamships, he began to look about him upon terra firma for investments, which would make him comfortable in his old age, and, singularly enough, he pitched upon Harlem, that fag end of all the railway fancies leading apparently a precarious existence, and only tolerated by their high-mightinesses, the Regular Board of Brokers.

Did he do this with the expectation of getting control of the stock so that he could use it as the rings of Wall Street do?   Not at all.   He bought it at a low price, in order that he might put into it some of his spare cash, as a permanent investment.   In 1862, he was known to be buying a large amount of the stock.

One day a well-known retired merchant, an intimate acquaintance, met him and asked how it happened that he was buying so much Harlem.   He replied that its sale at par was only a question of time, and as he had a few millions lying idle, he was putting some of it into Harlem,—his children would reap the benefit if he himself did not live to do so.

During the winter, the price had been slowly rising, bringing up the rear of all the principal railways. In April, it had jumped in a few days, with rapid leaps to 61, and then fell back to 58. Thus it stood, when the short sales above recorded, were made. Within a week after, the price slumped to 43. The three thousand shares were bought in at a profit of $13,000, and when the price rose to 52, four thousand shares were sold short, for my account. The price hung at from 50 to 54, for a few days, then sprang up to 58, then down to 55, then up again. It seemed to have quicksilver in it, and hobbled up and down without much apparent cause, as though some strange atmosphere was at work on it. The stock was the favorite one of the whole catalogue, and was operated in, boldly, both on the long and short side, in amounts so large that the whole capital stock sometimes changed hands in a single day. Vanderbilt was known to be buying it for investment, and some of the sharp ones were chuckling at the idea of "sticking" him with big "jags" of it at 58 and 60. The idea that he was buying it for *investment*, seemed intensely funny to the brokers. They sold it right and left, in the most dashing style, amid the laughter of their associates. Still he kept buying it. He appears to have been open and above board. In these transactions, he reminded one of the tintorea shark, of the tropical seas, which announces its presence by the phosphorescent atmosphere in which it is enveloped; its prey is first stifled, and then devoured at leisure. And so it was now. The Commodore moved about through the turbid waters of the street, making no secret of his doings, and quietly absorbing into his vast financial maw, the huge slices of Harlem fed out to him, by the frolicsome and infatuated bears. The singular oscillations of the stock, set some people to thinking there was something more in it than appeared on the surface. Queer-looking boys, with pug noses, and eyes that embraced you and the opposite lamp-post at the same glance, were seen carrying notes with the most outlandish orthography, from the City Hall to the offices of prominent brokers. Men with strongly Celtic faces were seen on Wall Street, answering to the names of O'Flyn and Mac Murphy, Sixth-warders by the cut of their jib, and said to belong to the Ancient and Honorable Board of Aldermen.

The 21st of April developed the game with sufficient certainty. On the evening of that day an ordinance was rushed through the Boards of Aldermen and Councilmen, authorizing the Harlem Railroad to lay a double track through Broadway from Fourteenth Street to the Battery. This was in accordance with the terms of their amended charter of 1832, which vested in them the right to lay rails in any street in the city, subject to the consent of the Mayor, Aldermen and Commonalty of the city of New York. When we reflect that from one to two hundred millions of people pass up and down that roaring thoroughfare every year, the value of this grant may be estimated. Successive generations of speculators and lobbymen had fought to obtain it from every legislature for the preceding twenty years, but in vain; and now by the stroke of a pen, the Harlem

Railroad held it. The stock rose in an hour from 60 to 75. The bears were filled with consternation; venerable men, the grey coyotes of the Stock Exchange, who had fattened on stock depressions and panics for a quarter of a century and were now heavily short, were seen wending their way to the offices of their counsel learned in the law, to devise legal means to extricate themselves from their dilemma. The courts of justice were invoked and a shower of injunctions discharged itself forthwith on the Mayor to forbid him from ratifying the ordinance and on the company to prevent their laying rails in Broadway. The Mayor disregarded the injunction under legal advice, and signed the ordinance, while the other processes wended their sinuous way through the courts.

But the furious opposition to the grant from so many quarters, had meanwhile got the Commodore's "dander up." He and his friends held most of the stock. They made ready to twist the bears. Many of this latter class were men of large means and strong will. They believed that the franchise scheme would somehow fail, whether in the courts or in the ensuing session of the Legislature; accordingly they kept borrowing the stock and averaging themselves with commendable resolution.

The upward movement was assisted by the large purchases made by Addison G. Jerome, who drew after him a long train of imitators. Other members of the Public Board sold it short furiously.

Now commenced a dance, such as was never known before in the stock-market—the rise in stocks known as the Chancellorsville rise—which will be hereafter described. Of all the list, Harlem moved the wildest and most oddly. It pranced and capered. It had wings and flew up thirty points, then dropped like a shot partridge to its starting-place. It never would rest. Bulls and bears blessed it and cursed it in fierce chorus alternately. It ruined the bulls, and drove the bears to suicide. The Harlem operator was rich in the morning and poor at night, or vice versa.

Once when it flew up to 117, I received a call from my brokers for $40,000 more margin, but almost before I had left their offices in despair, it was down again to 105, and I was saved. During the next break, which carried it to 90, the four thousand shares, of which I was short at 52—55, was bought, and my loss was finally settled at something like $75,000. Thus ended a weary campaign of six or eight weeks.

New views of life in Wall Street!

Oh! That infernal Harlem! That terrible old Commodore!

But this is not the end of Harlem, nor of the bears. Still up and down, as the summer waxed hotter. The bears encouraged by occasional successes, became bolder; then they became bolder still, even to reck-lessness. Something was in the wind. Again, the Celtic faces, from the City Hall, were seen on the street. Again, the queer-faced boys were seen bringing notes from the Assembly Chamber of the City Fathers. These notes were all orders to sell Harlem, "at any price, only sell it." The Aldermen and Coun-cilmen of the city of New York *were selling Harlem*, the pet of the Commodore, the life of the street.

Now it sinks slowly, now drops swiftly, now it's up again, no! it has fallen to 72.   Wherefore?

The Common Council had rescinded the ordinance granting the right to lay rails in the streets of New York!   And the stock fell.

They had played Vanderbilt a trick.

This was late in June.   In three days the price stood 105.

This action on the part of the Common Council, was believed by the prominent holders of the stock to be of no effect.   But the bears undeterred by their losses, still kept selling the stock.   It vibrated heavily between 90 and 105.   But some one was always ready to buy it, particularly when the sellers wished to *go short* of it.   A great hand was always extended to receive the stock and pass it away out of sight, in a deep, broad iron chest.   The Commodore was *biding his time* to take revenge on the Legislative tricksters.

In the latter part of July, Judge Brady, of the Court of Common Pleas, dissolved the injunction, forbidding the Harlem Railroad to lay rails in Broadway. Then the price, which had been slowly heaving and collapsing for four weeks, all at once jumped to 115, amid the execrations of the whole ursine tribe.   No mercy!   Still up, 120, 125, 130, 140.   The bears loosed their hold by dozens as it rose.   At 150, most of them had covered.   Some hard heads still kept their position.   But when it touched 180, there was not a single man of them left.   As for their losses, one circumstance will show them more clearly than any array of figures; for months after the event, when any one desired to say that an operator was irretrievably ruined, he expressed it in a single phrase, "he went short of Harlem." What made the matter worse for these gentlemen, many of them when they covered at 140 and 150, bought the stock to hold for 200, and failing that point, were caught by the rebound in another trap, when Harlem fell from 180, not a few of these bulls too late, were of the City Hall clique.

The ends of the ring were now substantially and for the time being accomplished. They had sold out the bulk of their stock at prices ranging from 140 to 175; the shorts were covered. It was decided, therefore, that the stock should be dropped. Here, again, the aid of the courts and the municipal legislative bodies were invoked as hammers to smite the still erect and swelling crest of Harlem, and reduce it to its old comatose and worthless condition. A decision of Judge Hogeboom, adverse to the franchise grant, was first promulgated; this was followed by legislation of the Common Council unfavorable to the railroad company; the price dropped to 75, ruining almost as many by its fall as it had by its rise. So suddenly did this take place, that it effectually finished the enthusiastic outside holders of the stock, nor were the bears, who were sullenly waiting for their revenge, able to put out any considerable line of shorts. A few of these latter, however, when the stock was selling from 135 to 140, had still sufficient nerve to sell a few thousand shares, three weeks after which they might have been observed leaning against the various lamp-posts, gorged and happy.

I had almost forgotten to say that the 600 shares of the stock which was bought at 12, seventeen months before, and which I had held to see what would come of it, was sold at 140, with a profit of $38,400. Buy a stock low, pay for it, hold it, and finally sell it high. 'Tis well!

Many amusing anecdotes are told of the singular fortunes of some of the smaller operators during this rise. Once a broken operator asked a broker acquaintance to buy him a couple of hundred shares, as they were standing in the crowd, just after the fall to 72, which followed the rescission of the grant by the Common Council. The broker wedged his way into the crowd and bought the stock, but when he came out he could not find his impecunious customer to report the purchase and procure his margin; during this time, scarcely sixty seconds, the stock had risen five per cent. When the customer made his appearance, he promptly gave the order to sell it. Before the sale could be effected, the stock had risen five per cent. higher, and the buyer had made a thousand dollars. This sum was the foundation of a fortune of $150,000.

Another of these strange pieces of luck, was that of a butcher boy named Devoe, (no connection of Thomas D., General Scott's old caterer, in Jefferson Market), who had earned $400 driving his furious chariot at day-break, from the First avenue abattoirs to Fulton Market. Overhearing Alderman Mullowney of his ward, extolling the Commodore and his pet stock, and predicting an extraordinary rise, he became inoculated with the prevailing epidemic, and paying a visit to Wall Street, "spouted" his $400 with a broker, as margin for a hundred full shares of Harlem at 124. In five minutes it fell three and one-half per cent.; $350 of the hard earned money gone! Devoe was in despair, which he vented in the most energetic expletives known to his trade and place of residence, which was, we need not add, not far from Mackerelville. Just as the order was going forth to sell him out, a messenger from the Board brought tidings that Harlem was selling for 127. Devoe straightened himself, smiled a sheepish smile, and doubled his interest in the market, by taking another hundred shares. In two weeks he drew out $21,000 profits, of this his first and last venture among the bulls of Wall Street. He is now a flourishing broker among the bulls and other cattle who graze amid the fertile bottoms of the Illinois.

To recount the losses of individuals in this campaign, would be a dreary catalogue. Those of two, only, need be mentioned. The baker instead of retiring from Wall Street with $100,000, left in the fall with only $2,500, and returned to his old trade. The railroad man was more fortunate; he saved $40,000, but he never sold short any more.

Let us now return from the tangent on which Harlem has carried us away, and see how the general market fared during the spring and summer of 1863.

CHAPTER XII.

THE BRIGADE OF BEARS.

How Bulls are Changed into Bears—The Short Gentleman on the Anxious Seat—A Bear-garden in William Street—Office of D. Groesbeck & Co.—David Groesbeck the Pupil of Jacob Little, and the Partner of Daniel Drew—Portraits of Other Bear-operators— Dr. Shelton—C——'s Fortunes—William R. Travers, the Partner of Leonard W. Jerome—A Lucky Hit on the Bear Side—Anecdotes — The Marshalling of the Clans—The Bull-battalion—Lockwood & Co., and LeGrand Lockwood—Another Bull-leader! Who is it?

ALL STREET operators commence their career as bulls, and finish it as bears. This is a general rule, to which, of course, there are many exceptions. When a man enters the stock-market, he almost invariably operates for a rise. But when he sees how long it takes for stocks to go up, and how swiftly they sometimes fall, and moreover, when in one of those falls, he finds all the profits of months previous swept away in a day, he naturally reasons that if, instead of operating for a rise, he had waited and sold short, or operated for a fall, he would have acquired wealth with a haste commensurate with his desires. Besides this, he sees that interest always runs in favor of the bear, while it forms one of the heaviest items in the bull's account, for it will not have been forgotten that the buyer pays and the seller receives interest on all stock contracts. It is easier for a broker to sell stocks short than to carry them, and so he is prone to operate on the bear side, and is apt to encourage his customer to act on that side.

During the year ending April 1st, 1863, a numerous retinue of gentlemen with strong bear proclivities had been waiting for the tide to turn. They had had a "hard road to travel" for the twelve months then last past. One stock after another had been tried but only with ever increasing loss. The general rise had cost them money. Hudson had drawn heavily upon their purses. Gold had lowered them still more, and Pacific Mail had almost completed the drain.

Many of these gentlemen had been in the street, speculating for years, and had built up great fortunes out of the wrecks of panics, just as Christian churches in Rome have been built out of the ruins of Pagan temples. A large number of the members of the regular board of brokers, especially of the older members, were bearishly inclined, considering the enormous and unprecedent rise of stocks, and reasoning from past experience rather than from the present situation of financial affairs. Some of these brokerage houses thus affected, served as rallying points for those who thought they could make money now by selling short.

One of these rallying points was the house of D. Groesbeck & Co., of which, Daniel Drew, as already mentioned, was, and we believe now is, a partner. Here Uncle Daniel, for the past eight years, has conducted his numerous and extensive operations. Here was his head-quarters and strong-hold. Figuratively speaking, it might be supposed that it had under-

ground passages, by which mines were dug'beneath
the enemies' works, when he was preparing for an
explosion, which should hoist the bulls on some fine
day when they least expected it, or that it had para-
pets, from which, a plunging fire of blocks of stock
could be directed on the besiegers, or secret doors
which could be suddenly thrown open, so that the de-
lighted eyes of the ursine garrison could gaze on the
pleasing spectacle of a panic. On the contrary the
office of this firm, which, in 1863 and 1864, was at No.
15 William Street, was a very peaceful-looking place.
Four little rooms, all so snug and cosy. In one sat a
half dozen clerks behind a railing, figuring or drawing checks and paying for stocks, or sending them
out by two or three mealy-faced boys. In the little
room at the side, customers were wont to be consoled
when luck was against them, or congratulated when
the little joker was jumping to their satisfaction. A
short, ruddy young man (one of the firm) was stroll-
ing about, and "talking horse." In the next room,
were most of the customers of the house, some engaged in financial contemplation, others in a trance,
wherein they seemed to see panics approaching with
a beatific vision, or perhaps brooding over their losses;
on the whole they were just then (in 1863 and
1864) rather a melancholy-looking crew. On the
sofa in the rear room, seated cross-legged, was a
not very handsome, but a harmless-looking old gentleman, in close confab with some one of the lights
of the market; perhaps with Dick Schell, or it might
be Charles Gould, or one of the directors of the
Erie Railway Company. Was that Uncle Daniel the
Great Bear? Yes. Who was that tall man with a

cassimere sack coat on, who looked so saturnine and gloomy, as though he was haunted by the spectre of an adverse market? That was David Groesbeck, familiarly known among his numerous customers, as Grosy, and the head of the firm. A graduate from the office of Jacob Little, from whom he learned the art and mystery of the stock-trade, and inheriting his traditions, it was fitting that he should be the partner of the great bear of the last decade, and the head of the great bear house of 1863 and 1864. For many years, after starting in business on the street, he speculated on his own account, and like others, who, before or since, have followed his example in that respect, failed several times. But for the past eight years, he has stuck to the legitimate commission business, in which he has rolled up a large fortune. This man is probably the repository of more financial secrets, than any other man in the street. He could tell, if he chose, how it was that Jacob Little made and lost such vast sums, and by what legerdemain Daniel Drew has so often transferred to his own roomy pockets, the cash lately in the pockets of a hundred different men.

Personally, Mr. Groesbeck is a man of a kind heart and quick sympathies. He does not forget the friends of his early years, and after the death of his old principal, Jacob Little, he was one of those who aided in collecting out of the debris of a great fortune, a sufficient sum to provide for the family of the deceased financier.

We would not be understood to assert that the customers of this house were necessarily, or all of them, operators for a decline, or bears. Both sides of the market were represented, and great fortunes have been made, as well as lost, in the house of D. G. & Co., on the bull side. Nor would we say that the firm were given to the practice of advising their customers to sell short. Still there *was* an influence there all the time, working to induce short sales, not by persuasion, advice or argument, it was something more subtle than these—an atmosphere of bearishness which each one breathed, until he took on the shape and action thereof. Uncle Daniel, the bear, was the great Panjandrum of the house of D. G. & Co., and all the little Joblillies and Piccalillies patterned their operations after his.

This office was the rallying point of the bears in 1863. Some of the dealers there, afterwards became noted during the great decline and subsequent rise of 1865. One of these was Dr. S——, sometimes known as Ursa Minor, and sometimes known as the "Retired Physician," the golden sands of whose life are not yet by any means run out. He was then and still is a veteran, and a daring speculator, whose fortunes swing between zero and a million, almost in the course of one revolving moon. During 1863, and the first three months of 1864, he sat watching his pile as it dwindled away under that process of attrition peculiar to the stock-market, until it only contained $20,000. But that oaken and smileless face and still tongue told no tales of waxing or waning fortune, but in grim silence waited for the wheel to come round full circle. It came in good time. In the spring of 1865, he rose the master of three-quarters of a million.

They who loiter in the reading room of the Fifth

Avenue Hotel will have, doubtless, often remarked a
tall, atrabilious, silent man sauntering in a purposeless
way through that apartment, or conning the financial
columns of the various papers strewed about. This
is C——, a man who has tasted the "fierce extremes"
of Wall Street life between a plump million and
hungry impecuniosity. He is and always was a bear
by his very constitution and habit of body. His
biliary system causes him to look at stocks through
the most cerulean of spectacles. Who can tell how
much that useful, but exceedingly troublesome organ,
the liver, has had to do with success in anything?
Napoleon lost the battle of Waterloo through a fit of
indigestion, and C—— lost the battle in Wall Street
because his liver is chronically deranged. He is a
Pennsylvanian, and came into the street with a half
million or so, which a few successful operations on
the short side in the early part of the war swelled to
twice the amount. But selling stocks short between
1863 and 1864 proved a losing business, and April of
the latter year found our friend among the small figures. When Fort Wayne sold from 153 to 90, however,
he forgot his programme and bought largely of that
stock, selling it again at 125 and pocketing a quarter
of a million, it is said. Encouraged by this success,
he went back on himself and his bear proclivities,
became unconscious that he had a liver, and for a few
months was a rampant bull; too late! too late! The
spring of 1865 found him high and dry on the beach.
But it was deemed by some of the magnates of Wall
Street that so valuable a customer ought to be kept
in the market, and so Daniel Drew's bowels warmed
with compassion; he sent for our friend and told him

14

in his peculiar vernacular, that a "few sheers of Eyrie wouldn't hurt him." "But," said C——, "I have no money to buy them." "Never mind that," replied Daniel, "send in five thousand shares to me, I'll take care of them." C—— was, in a few days on his legs again, with $50,000 in his pocket.

Joseph G. M——s, a tall, burly man, with a small, unwinking eye, early connected with the Public Board, was another bold bear in 1863, though he occasionally went in strong as a bull. He, too, retrieved his fortunes during the gold panic of 1865, and has since been a prominent operator of the Open Board, oftener on the bear side.

Up to the passage of the Legal Tender Act, William R. Travers, another leading operator, known among his friends as Bill Travers, was to be counted among the bear brigade. He was formerly one of the firm of Jerome & Travers, Leonard W. Jerome, who has already been described, being his partner, and a likely span of bold, shrewd financiers they made.

Some years before the commencement of the war, this firm made a great hit in Old Southern, at the time when it was selling at from 120 to 140. It was done in this wise: The stock was a favorite one then, and was viewed as safe as a government bond. Nearly everybody in the street had a little, and the outside public speculators, as well as investors, were long of it. This created a favorable condition for the formation of a ring to depress the stock. Just now, Jerome & Travers discovered, either by their native shrewdness or by accident, that there had been a considerable over-issue, fraudulently, or at least irregularly. Acting on this, with the utmost secrecy and dispatch, they put out all the short contracts they could arrange for, and then sprung the mine. When the news of the over-issue had been communicated to the street, the stock fell heavily, from fifty to sixty per cent., and the profits of the sharp operators were enormous—rated by some as high as a million and a half.

The portrait of Travers is familiar to the stock-dealing public. A tall, slender man, with a rubicund face and a jolly nose, never smiles, and speaks with a pronounced stutter. Long since, I saw him while standing on the curb-stone, buying some stock of a dealer whose countenance bespoke his descent from Shem. "What is your n-n-name?" inquired T., of the Hebrew. "Jacobs," replied the seller. "But what is your c-c-christian name?" asked T., whereat the crowd was convulsed. But T's head is as clear as a quill. He is constantly figuring. His lips move as he walks the streets. When he sits down in the circle of his family he is still figuring, $\frac{1}{8}$, $\frac{1}{4}$, 187, Central consolidated 96. He bears the reputation of an honorable business man, a kind friend. His judgment is called in often to decide bets, and on the turf he rates A. 1, being President of the American Jockey Club. His rate on 'Change is from two to three millions.

Previous to his entrance into the street, he resided and did business in Baltimore, where he married a daughter of Reverdy Johnson. His Southern affiliations, as well as his own judgment, taught him that the war between the sections was to be long and bloody, and he was among the first to understand its effect in Wall Street. At least, as early as the first months of 1862, he predicted the future course of the market, and a vast enhancement of values. About that time he met an acquaintance, on a ferry-boat, and the conversation turning on stocks, then very much depressed, asked what he was doing, and how much money he had to speculate with. He replied that he had about six thousand dollars unemployed, but dared not invest it, in those uncertain times. "Then," said Travers, "buy Governments, Erie, or anything else you please. When they advance, sell them, and buy as much more as you can, and don't, above all things, go short of a share." Acting on this advice, he bought and is now a rich and flourishing broker.

Occasionally, however, during the rises of 1863 and 1864, Travers would take a turn on the bear side, and often showed great judgment and skill in these operations, running against the general upward tide.

The ranks of the bears were, in the spring of 1863, recruited from those who, during the past year, had been operating for a rise and had made great fortunes by so doing. They had gone with the current upwards, and now deeming that its force had been "discounted," and remembering their old bearish habits, hoped to swell their already bloated purses by descending on the same current when it culminated and began to flow downward. The next great rise, said they, and we will turn about and resume our old practice of selling short. But their time was not yet come. The years 1863 and 1864 were, in Wall Street, a disastrous period for all those who operated for a decline in stocks. The strength of the street in money, numbers, talent and enthusiasm was in great majority on the side of the bulls.

No one who has operated in Wall Street, will have failed to remark how wonderfully the spirits and force of the market are stimulated by the rise of one or two leading stocks, when the rest of the market is halting and uncertain in its movements. So it was in the early part of 1863, when Pacific Mail jumped sixty per cent. upwards; the courage of the bulls was fortified by this to an amazing extent. The bears, however, in April, stood sulky and obstinate, rather strengthened in their resolution, by what to them, savored of insanity. This was only the beginning. They were soon to "blench and grow pale" at the very name of Harlem, and a new general rise was already being engineered, before which all former rises in Wall Street should sink into insignificance.

Outside of the two rival boards of brokers, stood Commodore Vanderbilt, Henry Keep, Leonard W. Jerome, etc., and backed up by a long file of capitalists who followed their lead, and believed in their policy. The Public Board led on by A. G. Jerome and John M. Tobin, focalized into one burning center the scattered rays of speculation from every quarter. While in the more conservative regular board, there were enterprising and sagacious firms who were considered the exponents of the bull feeling, as strongly as the house of D. Groesbeck & Co., were of the bear feeling, in the market.

Among these was the firm of Lockwood & Co., which, from its wealth, its long and high standing, and its business affiliations, stood out in 1863 and 1864, not only as the rival of D. Groesbeck & Co., in competing for the business of the street, but as being almost as pronounced in its bull proclivity as the latter was in its bearish policy. Its business, of course, was large and various on both sides, but more on the bull side.

Le Grand Lockwood, the head and founder of the house, is in personal appearance the antipodes of D. Groesbeck. A short, rather stout gentleman, with a face unworn and almost youthful, after twenty-five or thirty years of that wearing, tearing, terrible Wall Street life. He is a native of Connecticut, and brings into his business all the thrift and keenness of that most thrifty and shrewd of States. His financial views are generally large and sound. How much confidence the community reposed in him, is proved by the quickness with which he was enabled to settle up his affairs, and resume after his recent most disastrous failure; a failure which occurred, it will be remembered, in consequence of too heavy ventures on the bull side, made prior to the crash of September, 1869. The commission business done by his firm, during the war, was something unprecedented in the annals of the street.

But it was reserved for another man to earn the title of the bull-leader in the regular board, during 1863 and part of 1864.

His operations constitute a distinct and memorable chapter in the stock speculation of those two years.

CHAPTER XIII.

ANTHONY W. MORSE AND THE CHANCELLORSVILLE RISE.

The First Game of "Brag" in the Village of Hanover—"The Boy's the Father of the Man"—First Appearance of Morse—Wall Street Men's Wives—Getting Ready for a Twist—The Ursine Vocabulary —A Vindictive Bear Going Short of Pittsburg—Waiting for News from the Front—Chasing a Telegram—The Hook-nosed Man Nursing the Market—Sounding the Charge Along the Whole Line—The Second Game of "Brag"—Raking in the Profits—$113,500 in My Right Boot-leg, and No Money to Pay for My Dinner.

NE summer's day, about twenty-five years since, in the pleasant village of Hanover, in the old Granite State, celebrated for its seat of learning—Dartmouth College—and for its placid scenery of mountain, vale and river, four boys in their teens, were squatted on the green sward behind a tree in the outskirts, playing a game of cards. It was the game of "brag," so called, which some graceless collegian from the West had taught them in an hour of idleness. The young scape-graces had each contributed a copper penny, and thus made up a "pool," the stake they were playing for. One of these boys had a face somewhat besmirched by recent fistic combats, but his eyes and nose were like those of a hawk. He far surpassed his companions in that boldness and address requisite to a successful playing of the game. He won the stake every time. "The boy's the father of the man." Fifteen years later, that boy, then a man, made his appearance in Wall Street, where the game of "brag" is played all the time on a great scale and around a crowded table. His name was Anthony W. Morse. He came into the market as an adventurer, like so many of his fellows. He had little money or credit, but (which was as good as either), he was a member of the board of brokers in 1862, when the inflation began to take place. The name of the firm which he represented, was Morse & Co. Who were the separate members of this firm? What were their names? It appeared, on investigation, that the only person composing the firm, bore the Christian name of a woman instead of a man. It was the wife of A. W. Morse, who was buying and selling stocks; her husband was her agent and broker. This drew forth severe criticism from his associates. The making of a financial convenience of a wife is an old device of the stock-market. The Wall Street man's wife is often a lady of substance. She carries bags of gold coin under her crinoline; certified checks are quilted into her skirts. She hides notes of hand and stock certificates in her bosom, and sails down Fifth Avenue with gems worthy of a duchess, entangled in her hair, while her husband, panic-smitten and moneyless, limps up and down Wall Street.

Who would have picked out from among the brawny shoulder-hitters of the market, that slight, boyish figure, as the bull-leader of the regular board? This man, the casual observer would say, is an English Jew, who has gone into the business of a note broker. He always reminded us of a man who was playing a part, and rather a farcical part at that, as he came jauntily out into the crowd to take a survey of the market. But he had not forgotten the game of brag which he had played when a boy, and he was making ready to play it with a vengeance.

A few bold operations on the bull side had put two hundred and fifty thousand dollars into his pocket, and in the spring of 1863 he cast about him for something to make a good stroke in, after the Wall Street cornering fashion. Nothing offered better than Pittsburg. It was a small stock, only $4,000,000, and could be readily handled; its earnings were such as to justify the expectation of a speedy dividend, and less than half of the stock was floating about the street. The market price ranged from 65 to 70. He commenced to buy it. The act to increase the legal tenders, by a new issue of four hundred millions, passed. He bought more. Money grew easier, first 6, then 5, then 4 per cent. He borrowed money on the stock he had already bought, and with this money bought more largely. Stocks moved languidly upwards.

Suddenly the money rate tightened to 7 per cent. and stocks dropped to their old place. General Hooker had been lying for months, with the "finest army on the planet," watching the heights of Fredericksburg, the slaughter-ground of the December preceding. A dark rumor, hardly yet breathed, but believed in, told every one that another great military movement would soon be made. Capital grew timorous, and called in its forces. Money was scarce, but only for a brief season.

The greenbacks, which poured by the hundred million into the sub-treasury, were poured out again, to pay the government creditors. Money flowed into the stock-market, in a full steady stream. The interest rate fell once more. Stocks moved upwards in earnest.

Wall Street had already decided in its mind, that the spring campaign on the Rappahannock, would be disastrous. The sequence to this would be a great rise in values.

Stocks were moving up, one by one, after their ancient custom, but slowly as yet when I met J. F—— It was about the middle of April, on the brink of the coal-hole, while the market was lagging, and the doubtful condition of things looked just then doubly uncertain. J. F—— was the most plantigrade of bears. The panic of 1857, had changed him from an operator for a rise, into an operator for a fall. For six years he had kept his eyes fixed on the rises and falls of stocks, and now they haunted him. He presented a singular psychological phenomenon—a distinct phase of the mania for speculation. He had got to look upon the market as a live thing—a fantastic monster. He spoke of it as of the feminine gender. "She rises." "She falls." He seemed to think of it as a debter which owed him money. It was a question of revenge, however, with him, more than money. He hungered for revenge for his losses. His operations were undertaken in a spirit of vindictiveness against every stock in which he had lost. When he made a lucky hit, he would flourish certified checks, and boast like an Indian brave over the scalps which he had taken from an enemy.

For nearly a year he had hardly kept himself from ruin, but when gold lurched and went down in March,

"Has Daniel Drew made any money lately, selling short?" asked the old gentleman, banteringly.

"Never mind Daniel Drew," retorted F——, "he'll eat you all up yet."

"Now you've been talking about this Pittsburg stock, I'll take a thousand shares at 75, buyer thirty," quietly remarked the old gentleman.

F——'s face writhed and curled like a dog about to nip the leg of a beggar. "I'll sell it to you," snarled he.

"Sell me a thousand shares, buyer thirty, F——?" inquired I.

He wheeled around, and shaking his fist in my face as if he had some special grudge against me, which he wished to indulge by selling me a thousand Pittsburg, thundered "yes!"

"Thirty per cent. up, in the Trust Company?"

"Thirty per cent. up in the Trust Company, by both parties," he screamed, "and right away, too."

The buyer and the seller have the right to demand from each other a sum ranging from ten per cent. upwards, to secure the bargain. This sum or margin is generally deposited in the hands of some corporation or responsible firm, who thus become the stakeholders and pay over the money to the party who wins.

Two thousand shares of Pittsburg at 75, is $75,000, for this stock is like Harlem, only $50 per share at par.

We went together to the Trust Company. J. F—— put up in the Trust Company, $30,000. The old gentleman put up $15,000, and I put up $15,000, all in certified checks. Then we parted. The old gen-

"Has Daniel Drew made any money lately, selling short?" asked the old gentleman, banteringly.

"Never mind Daniel Drew," retorted F——, "he'll eat you all up yet."

"Now you've been talking about this Pittsburg stock, I'll take a thousand shares at 75, buyer thirty," quietly remarked the old gentleman.

F——'s face writhed and curled like a dog about to nip the leg of a beggar. "I'll sell it to you," snarled he.

"Sell me a thousand shares, buyer thirty, F——?" inquired I.

He wheeled around, and shaking his fist in my face as if he had some special grudge against me, which he wished to indulge by selling me a thousand Pittsburg, thundered "yes!"

"Thirty per cent. up, in the Trust Company?"

"Thirty per cent. up in the Trust Company, by both parties," he screamed, "and right away, too."

The buyer and the seller have the right to demand from each other a sum ranging from ten per cent. upwards, to secure the bargain. This sum or margin is generally deposited in the hands of some corporation or responsible firm, who thus become the stakeholders and pay over the money to the party who wins.

Two thousand shares of Pittsburg at 75, is $75,000, for this stock is like Harlem, only $50 per share at par.

We went together to the Trust Company. J. F—— put up in the Trust Company, $30,000. The old gentleman put up $15,000, and I put up $15,000, all in certified checks. Then we parted. The old gentleman took an omnibus up town, with a serene smile playing on his venerable features at the thought of his Pittsburg. J. F—— passed down William Street with the air of a man who had inflicted, or was about to inflict, a terrible revenge on his old enemy Pittsburg, and joined a group of sad but determined looking men, who belonged to the bear brigade and used to stand in front of the office of D. Groesbeck & Co.

During the two weeks then next ensuing, it was amusing to watch the goings, comings and general looks of the bear brigade. Every pleasant morning they could be seen roosting on the iron railings in William Street, and sunning themselves, or standing like lay figures around the inside entrance to the regular board. First they were loud-mouthed in their predictions that the market was just on the eve of panic. Then, as the prices rose, they grew stiller, and finally subsided into a sulky silence.

May was now come. Hooker and the grand army were across the Rappahannock. Stocks were up ten per cent., but were just then halting, as if waiting for something. What was it? News from the front.

Passing down Wall Street, about noon, one day, I saw a well-known operator named L——, rush out of the telegraph office, holding a paper ribbon which he gathered up into a wad as he ran. I plucked him by the sleeve as he flew past me, and asked what's the row? He mumbled something, broke away from me, jumped down into a broker's office in the basement corner of William Street, reappeared in an instant, and darted off the street into the tunnel which led to the regular board.

What news could he have?

I followed him closely and came up with him as he was giving an order to his broker, whom he had called out from the board which was then in session.

"What's up, L——?"

He drummed against the wall with his boot-heel and looked knowing, but kept his mouth shut.

His broker shortly made his appearance and handed L—— a memorandum, telling him that he had bought for his account, one thousand Erie and five hundred Hudson.

L—— now informed me that he had news from the front. Hooker was this side the Rappahannock. The campaign was over. Stocks must go up. "If you buy anything," added he, "let it be Erie and Hudson."

"How about Pittsburg?"

"Good! You can't help making money, only buy, buy! buy! go it blind. Pitch in your greenbacks and pick up gold."

I bought straightway three hundred Erie and five hundred Hudson.

The news from the front was already known to others, and they were acting on it. The market hummed like a bee-hive. Erie rumbled along up the declivity. Hudson flew up. Harlem tumbled up. Pittsburg skipped up gaily. My profits were rolling up at the rate of $1,000 an hour. But my losses on Harlem, of which I was short, as already told, swallowed up my profits. I kept buying Erie, Pittsburg, Hudson.

The neglected stocks which had lain lifeless at the foot of the list, now began to show life and dance

HALL OF THE BROKERS' BOARD.

about like Fantocinni in a showman's box.   Terre Haute "was a good thing to buy, cheap as dirt!" so said my broker.   I bought four hundred shares, and before night it danced up ten points.

Meanwhile, one hooked-nosed man was observed to be very busy.   In his office, he was packing away certificates of Pittsburg stock in a little black box, or inclosing them in portly brown envelopes.   He was closeted with attenuated cashiers in bank parlors looking after his loans.   He was nursing the general market, hovering over it broodingly, inquiring with solicitude after its welfare.   But Pittsburg was his pet, and he had gathered it under his wing.   When it was weak, he stimulated it.   When it was halting and hesitating he coaxed it and drove it alternately.

Many of those who had bought stocks at a lower figure, now sold out, and realized their profits.   The market yielded gracefully to this pressure; paused for a day ready to absorb anything in the way of a short sale or any small favors from those who thought of taking their profits.   Then its ranks were re-formed; the hook-nosed man waved his baton, and sounded the charge.   The whole line moved up in a twinkling to the top of the declivity.   Erie from 70, had touched 110.   Hudson from 105, had touched 142; and Pittsburg from 68, had touched 108.

It is one thing to "get stocks up," as they say, but quite another to sell them at the high price.

"Now, who is going to buy your high-priced stocks?" shouted the bear brigade.

This inquiry seemed very pertinent.   Upon that hint I acted, giving orders to sell everything I held at the market price, and notifying J. F—— that I was about to sell the Pittsburg (I had bought of him at 75), and thus transfer $12,000 of his money into my pocket.

But how did the hooked-nosed man, alias A. W. Morse, succeed in working off his Pittsburg? He played the old game of brag. Everything assisted him in this. Money easy as an old shoe, the bears tremblingly eager to cover, the men who had sold out at a lower figure now crazy to buy back their stocks at a higher figure, the whole market looking as if it never would break again.

The prices which had been galloping up for ten days now closed the heat with a rush. When Pittsburg was struck on the morning call, Morse jumped into the center of the crowd and yelled at the top of his voice, "I'll give 105 for the whole capital stock (about $4,000,000), or any part. I'll give 100, seller one year, for the whole capital stock or any part." He bluffed the whole board. No one took him up on his liberal offers. But while he was holding up the market price by making these magnanimous propositions, his agents were busily at work selling Pittsburg quietly on every side. The bears bought it to cover their contracts, the bulls bought it for a new profit; in twenty-four hours the bulk of what he held had been worked off at from 97 to 105. He had raked in as his winnings about half a million.

The movement having culminated, and the heavy holders having sold out, the market, as usual, took a turn now in the other direction. There are always pretexts offered, for any course which stocks may take. They had just *risen*, because Hooker's campaign had been a failure, just as they had *fallen* when the McClellan campaign, the year before, had been a failure. Now they fell again, on the news that Grant had achieved some successes on the Mississippi. Such are the sapient reasonings of Wall Street. The bankers called in their loans, money became scarce, the weak holders were weeded out, and everybody was figuring up the column of profit and loss.

This was our pecuniary situation, in round numbers, on the 15th of June, 1863, after deducting all losses on Pacific Mail, Harlem, etc.

Profits on Hudson, including the 100 shares bought
   at 78, ... $38,000
Terre Haute, ... 3,500
Pittsburg, bought at 75, of J. F., ... 12,000
Erie, ... 11,000
Sundries, including Harlem, bought at 12, ... 49,000
                                   ————
                                 $113,500

This sum came into my hands in the form of checks, all elegantly lithographed, signed by different brokers with whom I had kept accounts, and duly certified as good by the banks on which they were drawn. These pleasing evidences of property were forthwith rolled into a wad, and consigned to an inner pocket.

I stood in a delicious reverie on the steps of the Bank of America.

"Have a hack?" said an insinuating voice at my elbow.

"I *will* have a hack."

The hackman held open the door of a dilapidated looking vehicle. I stepped in and lay back on the cushions.

15

"Where to?" said the Jehu, touching his hat in military style.

"Drive me —— up town."

Taking the checks out of my pocket, I contemplated them first sideways, then front, then upside down. Was it a dream? $113,500! there it was, in real green and black letters and figures! It ought to have been $200,000, and would have been but for those confounded losses on Harlem and Pacific Mail. Still, here was wealth, and what was better, freedom; freedom from the life of a speculator—freedom to do what I pleased, and to go where I pleased. Ah! there is ——.

These contemplations were rudely broken in upon by my Jehu, who had stopped in front of Delmonico, corner of Fourteenth Street and Fifth Avenue.

"Beg pardon; but I thought as you'd been making some money off 'em, you'd like to stop here, sir." How did he know I'd been "making some money off 'em?" He must have seen me handling my checks. Hide your money, said caution. I took it out and tucked it in my right boot-leg. It began to worry me, already. Not that I had the sum of $113,500 on my person, because it was in unendorsed checks, which if lost or stolen, would do nobody any good but myself. No, it was the mere fact that I possessed so much money, that began now to oppress me like a burden which a man has suddenly shouldered.

I entered Delmonico's, and sat down at a table. The walls seemed to be all written over with figures, 113,500! 113,500! on every side. I thought I saw a label before me with 113,500 written on it. It was the paper placed before me by the waiter on which to write my dinner order. I muttered "113,500." I looked up; the waiter was smiling as hard as is consistent with the gravity of a servitor of Delmonico.

I recollected myself and put my hand in my pocket to present him with fifty cents, as a *pour boire,* when it flashed across me that I hadn't a cent of money— nothing but certified checks! No money to pay my hack-hire or buy my dinner, or even to fee the waiter. Nothing but $113,500 in certified checks. I had to get the hack-man to trust me, and "ran my face" for a dinner that day; but this is not very difficult in New York at any time, especially when a man is backed by that peculiar moral force produced by the proud consciousness that he has carefully tucked away the sum of $113,500 in certified checks in his right boot-leg.

CHAPTER XIV.

"WHAT WILL HE DO WITH IT?"

The Life of an Operator; Excitement and Repose—In Pursuit of Happiness Furiously—The Terrestrial Paradise of a Money Winner—The Delights of the Eye and the Pride of Life—Two Comrades in Luck—"Is this Happiness?"—Birds of Passage on the Wing to Long Branch—Wall Street at the Watering Places—Dowagers, Damsels and Dunderheads—Saratoga the "Sweet Boon" to the Broker—The Congress and Court of Vanderbilt, and the Other Money Kings—They Spell S-t-o-c-k-s, and then They Buy Them—A Good Resolution in Danger of Being Broken—Operating by Telegraph—"Once More Upon the Waters, yet Once More and the *Stocks* Bound Beneath us like a Steed that Knows its Rider"—Grasp the Substance ere the Shadow Fade.

HE life of the Wall Street man is like that of savage races—a life of fierce extremes. One day he is in the hottest and busiest of all market-places—the stock-market-place—agitated by all the hopes and fears, and torn by all the emotions and passions, engendered by the thirst for speedy riches; the next day the struggle is over, and he is plunged, at once, into the opposite extreme of stillness and repose. This stillness and repose is bred sometimes of utter and irretrievable ruin, it is then the calmness of despair; sometimes it is derived from that serene sense of satisfaction, which the successful speculator feels when he has made a hit. This feeling is a negative one. He has *not* lost his money, he has *not* failed in his pursuit of money. The fact that he has great riches won against so much odds, gives him little pleasure. He undervalues it. It seems of little account, until he thinks what it will procure. It will buy such pleasures as money can buy—*material pleasures.*

The Wall Street operator is a materialist logically, and in the strictest consistence with his earnest pursuits. After his toils and anxieties he craves enjoyments. He would repay with prodigality these toils and anxieties to which he has been subjected in the pursuit of his gains. The captors of a fortress which has been obstinately defended, sometimes put the garrison to the sword. The hunter joyfully spears the wild animal which has led him a long chase. The successful Wall Street man takes *his* revenge on the money which has cost him dearly—he spends it on himself and his friends—he pours it out as though it were common and cheap as the water he drinks or the air he breathes.

He proposes to himself a terrestrial paradise, not like that of the Mahometan, however, who prescribes wine. He would "suck the subtle blood of the grape till the high fever seethe his blood to froth." Retinues of lackeys, studs of horses, banquetings, garlands, singing men and singing women, spectacles in the theatre shall be his, amid which, he shall walk as a literal cloud-compeller, while the partaga or the miraculously carved roseate foam-tinted meerschaum distills its fragrance under the quiet pressure of his lips.

The paths in this paradise are all circuitous; one eternal round of enjoyments which become at last tasteless. Then comes restlessness, a craving for change of scene. He becomes first a perambulator, then a pedestrian, then a tourist—the nomad of the watering places.

E—— was a "red check man," in other words he had made $100,000 in stocks.

Two men of about the same age, temperament and tastes may see each other every day for twenty-five years, and yet they may never come together; though their paths be ever so near, they are in parallel lines, which never meet. Now magnetize them by giving them a hundred thousand dollars apiece, and they fly together like the iron and the lodestone. This means conviviality, fraternity, sympathy.

E—— and I were Damon and Pythias, over again, like Juno's swans, we went always "coupled and inseparable." We had made our money in the same stocks and now we spent it in company—a partnership in the business of pleasure-seeking. We dined together, rode together, slept together. When we quarreled with each other we had never "let the sun in Capricorn go down on our anger."

We were both engaged in pondering the same important question: what shall we do with *it?* the $100,000. The answer to the question was partly contained in what we had just been doing, viz., dining at Delmonico's—innocent, but expensive amusement. We were spending it as fast as horses, banquets, and the etceteras would permit.

One thing, however, had been resolved upon, we would never, no, never, any more speculate in Wall Street, at least by buying and selling upon a margin, *except*, (ah! that unfortunate word) except in Government Bonds, of which we severally held $175,000 worth bought on a margin of $8,000, and paid for by loans obtained from Savings Banks.

Two men in their golden prime, both worthy to receive a first-class diploma from a Life Insurance Company, with $100,000 at their bankers, sitting before an open window, at Delmonico's, in the twilight of a glorious July evening, after a sumptuous dinner, would, in the popular use of the term, be called *happy*. We tried to believe ourselves so. But there was something wanting. Somehow, that day, the soup *a la reine* was a trifle worse flavored than it was a month before. The filet of sole was not done to the proper turn, the game-bird was a "little too high." The Roederer champagne was flat, and suggested sugar of lead, to the already squeamish palate.

Restlessness again! Where can we go? not to ride, for our horses have the ring-bone, or quarter-crack, or some one of the other ills that horse-flesh is heir to. Ah! a happy thought—a watering-place.

"Garçon."

The waiter stood by us, looking fractional currency out of his eyes. "Bring us a Herald." "Oui, oui!" The newspaper was handed to us, and carefully conned, in search of new places of summer resort. We found nothing new that was tempting, so we made a trip to Long Branch; two days was enough for us there. Sachem's Head, then; after this, the Pequot House, from which we hurried to Newport.

One of these watering-places was a type of all the others. Of course, the beauty and fashion was there! it always is. There were the Smitthes, and the Taylourres, the De Bylkes, the Van Ohnehosens,

and other lights of the gay world. Scandal and
flirtation hunted in couples. Argus-eyed dowagers
watched Hesperidean damsels, and at the same time
tore reputations to tatters. Damsels made dangerous
play of eyes, fans and handkerchiefs. Fat babies
stared very hard at the ocean. Stout, single old
gentlemen sported like dolphins in the surf, or rolled
ten-pins, and imagined they were young again. Of
course, everybody was bound to consider himself
happy, or act as if he did.

But Wall Street cropped out everywhere. The
husbands of the matrons, the fathers of the damsels,
the brothers of the dowagers and the single old gentlemen, all appeared to have made money in stocks,
or if they had lost it no one heard anything about it
there. The operators and brokers were on hand in
force. It was stocks on the piazzas, stocks in the
parlor, stocks at breakfast, dinner, tea. The bevy of
dames in the drawing-rooms would listen with breathless interest to tales of hair-breadth escapes in the
Harlem fight, or fortunes won "in the imminent
deadly breach" in Pacific Mail or Hudson, all which
tales were broken in upon after the usual style by
such hen-words as "Oh, that's so nice," "perfectly
splendid," "heavenly," etc., "to make a hundred
thousand in a month, just think of it!" "Well I
never," "no, I *never* did see," etc., etc., etc.

After this we went to Saratoga. If there is any
one place for which the Wall Street man has a pre-
dilection in his days of relaxation, that place is Saratoga. King Cornelius holds his court there. The
other monarchs of the stock-market make royal pro-
gresses thither. Their lieutenants go there. The

rank and file go there. The gay Spa, to borrow a phrase from Artemus, is a "sweet boon" to the whole tribe of stock-jobbers and operators, as a head-clearer, blood-cooler and general renovator of a biliary system too often disordered by deep potations of the Delmonico brand—"the foaming grape of eastern France," or of that tutelar alcoholic genius of bibulous Columbia—corn juice.

Of course, E—— and I made the rounds at Saratoga after the usual fashion, drinking bilge-water in the morning, driving to the lake and eating the celebrated potatoes prepared there with the deftest manipulation of culinary fingers. Then we plied the cranks of the hand-cars on the circular railway, always selecting the stoutest young ladies for our companions with a sharp eye to the development of biceps, pectoral and deltoid muscles. The stout young ladies sat up very straight in the hand-cars, and smiled very sweetly upon E—— and me, while we toiled at the winch, and made the vehicle spin round the iron groove. We also didn't forget the bowling-alley, or the pistol gallery, or the Indian encampment. We made ten-strikes, and blazed away at the bull's-eye, and after we had made the rounds we came back and smoked very large and full-flavored regalias.

At other watering places, they *talked* stocks; at Saratoga they *bought* and *sold* them. Little knots of dealers stood in the piazzas of the United States Hotel, the Union and the Congress, and traded in Erie and Harlem. The great pulsations of the heart-financial, one hundred and eighty miles away, throbbed here through the telegraphic wires.

Another great rise in stocks began to be predicted.

Speculation is a contagious disease. In Saratoga it is generally more or less an epidemic.

E—— and I found ourselves discussing the point whether we might not reconsider our resolution and make just one more operation on a margin. Everything looked bright. It could do us no harm to buy a thousand shares or so of some good dividend paying stock.

Even deliberation is dangerous upon such points. The woman who hesitates is lost. The retired Wall Street man, who asks himself whether he may not buy stocks on a margin, just once more, is as good as committed again to his old vice—speculation.

One evening, early in August, just as the male animals were about to prance in the parlors of Union, at the bidding of the queens of society, E—— and I retired to a seat in the rear-grounds, for a quiet smoke, when looking towards the back piazza, we saw emerge from one of the parlor doors, somebody we had seen before. It was a tall man, all shaven and shorn, in a spotless evening costume, brisk and debonair, who seemed as if he were looking for some "party," he didn't know exactly whom.

We recognized him quickly, as L—— the operator, who had given me telegraphic news of the retreat of Hooker, the week before the Chancellorsville rise, and who had just arrived by the evening train.

L—— belonged to the unnoted branch of the Q—— family, which had established a kind of title by adverse possession to certain government offices, which they had held from Washington's administration, down to Lincoln's. At present, he had a brother in the treasury department, an uncle in the war

office, a cousin was a brigadier-general, and his
brother's wife's father was mixed up with telegraph
companies.   Hence, it was that L—— had organized
a system of early telegraphic information, and had
thereby, got admitted into some of the "rings" in
the street.   In this way he had made $300,000, and
having sweltered in the stock-market all summer,
now that he was in Saratoga, he was naturally in
fine spirits.

He saw us, moulded his hands into the telescopic
shape and took a squint at us.   Then advanced towards us, pointing with his dexter forefinger as if to
some planet then faintly twinkling in the zenith, put
his left hand to one side of his mouth and whispered
something as though he expected it to be conveyed
to us by some unseen medium; all of which panto-
mime we interpreted to mean that he had sold his
stocks at a high figure.

First, salutations, then "how are stocks, L——?"
Stocks were firm with an upward tendency.   He had
sold everything he had, except Erie.   That he was
going to hold for 125.   The pool in Hudson had
carried the price to 180.   He did not think they
would be able to unload.   He had sold his Hudson at
175, etc., etc.   Did he know of anything good to
buy?   Yes.   Erie was good.   Daniel Drew had been
going short of it, but he would lose money by it.
There's another stock that's going up, sure.   Old
Southern; A. G. Jerome had taken hold of it, it was
good for 120.   Lots of shorts.   Had left word with
his broker to buy a thousand shares any where under
94.   Thus L—— talked.   He further added that he
was going to stay at the Springs the rest of the

month, and thought he could make more money by *keeping away from the market and operating by telegraph.*

That night E—— and I each telegraphed to our brokers thus: " Buy 500 Old Southern and 500 Erie at the market price. Have mailed $10,000, margin."

The following afternoon came the answer. " Have bought 500 Old Southern, 92 ; 500 Erie, 103." We had broken our resolution to buy no more stocks. We had once more embarked on the stormy sea, out of our haven of rest.

After this, our walks lay between Union Hall and the telegraph office, where we received the stock quotations two or three times daily, from our respective brokers in Wall Street. The telegraph commenced to prick off as the price of old Southern, 92 ; next day 88 ; then 96. Again the message was sent down : " Buy 1000 Old Southern, market price." Before that lot was bought, the price had risen to 104. Then whish! it went to 111. Old Southern was doing well. Erie rose more gradually. Heavy bodies move slowly. When Old Southern darted to 111, a rise of 19 per cent., Erie stood at 110. " Buy 1,000 more Erie," said greed. " Don't," whispered caution. Greed was stronger than caution. I telegraphed " Buy 1,000 Erie, market price." That lot cost 114. The regret that I had not bought sooner and before the price was lower, began to work in the mind. Its fruit was anger, rashness. I bought 1,000 more Erie at 115½. Then I sat down and figured up first what my profits would be on the supposition that I sold at the ruling prices, viz., Erie, 120, and Old

Southern at 108½; for Erie had risen, and Old South‹ ern had fallen meanwhile.

Thirty-one thousand, six hundred and twenty-five dollars! Now, I had put my selling price at 125 for Erie, and 120 for Old Southern. If the 2,500 Erie, and the 1,500 Old Southern were disposed of at those prices, the profits would foot up fifty-nine thousand eight hundred and seventy-two dollars! I decided to hold for the higher price. Greed of gain like the horse-leeches daughters, which cry give, give! Was I grasping at the *shadow*, while I let the substance fade? Was I to furnish another example to point the moral of the fable of the dog, who dropped the bone to catch at the image reflected in the water? Time will show. Of this one thing be assured, reader, the Wall Street man lives in the midst of shadows.

Phantasies of what might be, memories of what has been, regrets for what might have been. His mind feeds upon these figments of the brain. They become to him the same as a living active reality, which soothes and pains alternately.

> "For like the bat of Indian brakes,
>   Its pinions fan the wound it makes,
>   And soothing thus the victim's pains,
>   It drinks the life-blood from his veins."

CHAPTER XV.

WHAT BECAME OF IT. HENRY KEEP AND OLD SOUTHERN.

Our Financial Oracle gives us General Views on Stocks—News of Panic in the Woods—The Nightmare Ride in Sleeping-Cars—I Learn my Fate—The History of the Mystery—The P—— Pool in Erie—Cornering Uncle Daniel with $300,000—A. G. Jerome Playing with Old Southern, and Working the Bears—The Final Grip—A Gray-eyed Man Reading a Telegram at Saratoga, "Come on to New York Without Delay, the Fruit is Ripe"—Henry Keep, His Antecedents, Character and Operations—A Pauper's Son Dies Worth $4,000,000—The Plot—Money Tightens, and the Trap is Sprung—Jerome Laid Out Cold—A Meditated Scolding Terminates in a Dinner at Delmonico's—What Came of the Dinner—A Flyer in Harlem—The Last Resort—Almost Cleaned Out—An Operation in Seven-thirties—I Play my Last Card; Is it a Trump?

—— was the oracle of our particular coterie at Saratoga. All knotty questions, having reference to finance and the mysteries of stocks, were referred to him, and his answers were received without demurrer. Any one who had snatched $300,000 out of the ravenous jaws of Hudson and Harlem, deserved to be called an oracle. Moreover, this oracle was somewhat given to voluntary expositions of the all-absorbing topic.

L—— had "views" of stocks and speculation in general. "Nothing can be easier than to make money in Wall Street," said he.

This, spoken in the tone of one having authority, caught our attentive ear.

"First, buy your stocks *low*. *Low* is of course a relative term, but any man who can tell B from a bull's foot can decide when stocks are *low*."

"Aye, aye," say we.

"Second, put up a large margin; by the term large I mean at least twenty per cent."

"Very well, what next?"

"Third, get out of the "street," leave the city, go away from hotels, railroads, telegraphs, out of the ken of brokers, into the woods, where the word *stocks* is never sounded."

"But why go away after you have bought stocks?"

"Because a man is befooled, bewitched and be-deviled by what he hears in the market. He is sure to sell out just when he ought to hold on, or do some other foolish thing."

"Now," continued he, "I'm off to the woods for a couple of weeks or so, and if you'll go along you'll make more money than you will here, listening to that buzzing telegraph."

That afternoon we bought rifles, fishing tackle, etc., etc., and in sixty hours were lying under a big hemlock, forty miles from a railroad or telegraph, smoking and laying out for a murderous campaign against the trout.

Two weeks sped away before we saw a daily paper —the New York Tribune. We laid it out on the grass and three heads bumped against each other, while three pair of eyes riveted on the financial column, saw the following announcement, viz.:

"Thursday, September 4th. *The panic which commenced in stocks yesterday, has been of greater magnitude and of a more excited character to-day!*" etc.

"Old Southern, 88!"

"Erie, 104½!"

"I'm out $80,000," said L——.

"I'm out $40,000," said E——.

"And I $40,000,"——

That ride, forty miles in a country wagon over a rough road, was a little the slowest and longest ever taken by Wall Street men. When we struck the railroad we made a general rush for the telegraph office. L—— wrote three separate telegrams to our three several brokers, "Don't sell our stocks. Have sent more margin." Then three separate checks were drawn and mailed. L——'s check was for sixty thousand dollars; E——'s and mine for thirty thousand, each. We reached Troy in time to take the ten o'clock night train.

"Sleeping cars!" "Ha! ha!" said E——, "a queer idea that. They are called sleeping cars, I suppose, because people never sleep in them." We certainly never slept a wink of genuine sleep that night. True, now and then, we sunk into a kind of doze, crowded with dreams—nightmares, in which we seemed to be falling from vast heights, amid screamings and the roaring of many waters. Men with lanterns came and shook us, when the train stopped, and said we were making too much noise, moaning and muttering, and disturbing the other passengers.

When the train started, we commenced falling again down the heights, amid the same unearthly noises, and the roar of the wheels sufficed again to drown our gurgling cries. Three pallid, hollow-eyed men, we rose betimes, as the cars thundered past Manhattanville, and watched for the first newspaper boy. It was in the gray of the dawn, that we read the gratifying announcement, that "there was an active speculative demand for stocks, etc."

Old Southern closed at 95.

Erie stood at 107.

We were saved! When we reached the station, we got into a hack, and drove down town. Breakfast at lower Delmonico's. While discussing our *dejeuner a la fourchette*, of which we stood greatly in need, after our nightmare journey, a dapper little man, with eyes that resembled black glass beads, fixed firmly in his head, entered the lower room where we were sitting, and proceeded to imbibe something which had a greenish hue, suspiciously reminding us of that demoniac drink absinthe, with which it seems he was in the habit of refreshing himself before his daily toil. This dapper little man did the outside buying and selling for my broker. He saluted us with a sedate smile, judiciously tinged with suggestions of panic, and a deprecating look withal, which augured ill as it appeared to my apprehensive sense.

"Did you get my telegram, and the margin I sent you?"

"Oh, yes. But too late."

"Too late! What do you mean?"

"Why, too late to apply on your stocks. We had to sell them."

"You had to sell them?"

"Yes. You see the market was panicky. There was only one per cent. of your margin left. You were away; we had to look out for ourselves. If you'll go to our office you can find out all about it. I'm in a hurry, the market is brisk to-day. Bye, bye."

16

On going to my broker's office, the account of my stock transactions for the past month was duly rendered.

The Erie had been sold at 100.

The Old Southern, at 82.

I had lost $60,000, my original margin, and found myself indebted to my broker in the sum of $1,000 and more! This is the custom of Wall Street. When an operator's margin runs low he is promptly sold out, if on notice he fails to furnish more margin.

At the time these sales were made, I had $40,000 in the bank to my credit. The thirty thousand dollar check, fresh margin, which I had forwarded after coming out of the woods, reached my broker three or four days after the stock had been sold. Of course I could not complain, it was my misfortune.

How happened it that it should come up to blow so quickly out of a sky, which looked as though it promised every one a long season of bright sunshine?

Hardly any two stocks could have been selected, which would have inflicted more serious damage upon a buyer than Erie and Old Southern. Erie and Old Southern had both been in the hands of cliques. The movement in the former stock commenced late in July. The leader in this movement was P——, a young operator who had, or controlled about $300,000. He is said to have been a Californian, and now came down like a lusty bullock from the Sierra, prepared to attack the king of all the Bears in his fortress. He and his coadjutors proposed to themselves the Herculean feat of cornering Daniel Drew! Corner Uncle Daniel with $300,000! " Canst thou draw out leviathan with a hook? Canst thou put a hook into his nose, or bore his jaw through with a thorn?" Quixotic as the enterprise appeared, it is said to have been very nearly successful.

Drew commenced selling Erie for future delivery, when it was in the neighborhood of 100. The stock amounted then to about $11,000,000. At least half this amount was on the street. The rest was held abroad, or in the hands of permanent investors at home, outside of Wall Street. As the price rose, Drew kept selling, and the clique kept buying. Everything seemed to assist them. Erie was earning dividends. The money market was easy at five per cent. Large blocks of the stock were taken by various outside bull operators, who vowed to hold it for 150. The borrowing demand created by the heavy short sales of Drew and his brother bears, helped to keep the price firm at 120. The stock rose to 123, and now the bulls were rampant. Bets were offered that Drew would have to settle within a week. Such was the situation of Erie during the latter part of August, 1863. The party which had the control of Old Southern then, was a much stronger one.

A. G. Jerome, the Napoleon of the Public Board in 1863, was then in the height of his power. A long series of dashing operations on the bull side had brought him a million or two in money on his own account, but what was more, had raised his prestige to such a point that he could command an almost unlimited credit, while a crowd of depositors brought money to his banking-house, bidding him use as he thought best. A dangerous point for a financier to reach, especially if he accepts the trusts thus forced upon him. His position in August seemed impregnable. The stocks in which he was most deeply interested showed him an enormous profit. One of these stocks was Harlem, so famed in financial story. Its wonderful vibrations for three months were due largely to him.

But Old Southern was his pet.

He commenced paying it attention early in July. He played with it, fondled it, tossed its bulk up and down, tantalizing the bears and bulls alternately. All the while he was apparently playing in this way, serious business was going on. He was weeding out the weak holders when he dropped the price, and quietly taking every short contract. Then he gripped it fast and pushed it steadily up, dropping it now and then, however, to encourage the short-sellers.

Torrid August came, but brought no rest or vacation for those who held Old Southern. Jerome had promised his customers and the street that he would make Old Southern a second Harlem. His grip tightened. On the 14th Old Southern jumped 16 per cent., from 92 to 108. The next day it rose to 113, *but fell suddenly back to 108*. Some undaunted bear was selling it. It was dropped from 113 to 107, in order to take these sales. The stock came on the market by the ten thousand shares. The greater part of these sales were made in the public board. The market was staggered, but only for a moment. Jerome, armed with a twenty per cent. profit, which the price of the stock then showed him, stepped into the breach, and held up the market price on his Atlantean shoulders. The stock at last was no longer offered, except in hundred share lots. Now he had the bears in his power.

We shall see.

Who was the undaunted bear who sold thirty thous-
and shares of Old Southern in August, 1863, and so
would place his head between the upper and lower
jaw of the lion of the Public Board?

Three weeks before the panic, by which we suffered
as already described, and while we were still at Saratoga, feasting our imaginations with the prospect of
the profits which we were going to finger when Old
Southern should touch 120, something occurred, which,
could we have guessed its full significance, would
have made us fly to New York instead of going to
the woods.

A middle-aged, thick-set man, with a round, smooth
face, and a deep gray eye, stood on the piazza of
Congress Hall, reading a telegram, the very morning
we started on our sylvan excursion. We saw him
fold it up and consign it to his pocket, just as we entered the 'bus which was to take us to the cars.

That telegram of a dozen words cost us an aggregate loss of $79,000. The middle-aged, thick-set
man was Henry Keep. This noted operator and
money king, was about to do several things, when he
stood on the piazza of Congress Hall that morning.
He was about to break the Old Southern corner, and
ruin Jerome. He was about to make a million dollars for himself, and in doing this, he was about to
take away from L——, E—— and myself, the sum
of $79,000, as already stated.

For the past twelve years, Henry Keep had slowly,
but surely been advancing his fortunes in the stock-
market. Like most other very wealthy and successful Wall Street men, he commenced without a penny,
and although he died when hardly past the meridian of

life; he was then worth $4,000,000! He used to boast that he graduated at the poor-house, where he finished his academical education, and this was literally true, for it is said his father was a town-pauper somewhere in the interior of the State of New York. He learned lessons in that iron school of poverty, which stood him in good stead. An open countenance, but thoughts concealed, a still tongue, but a busy brain and quick hand. He once told a gentleman, after his fortune was counted by the million, that the idea of money haunted him day and night, during all his boyhood. It stood before him as a visible presence, during his maturer years. His first operations were in money. He bought paper money at a discount, made a few thousand dollars by these operations, and then, about twenty years ago, came to the money seat —Wall Street.

Here he soon linked his fortunes with the stock market. Old Southern Railroad Company became his favorite stock. No clause in its charter, no railroad law having relation to it, no by-law of the Company, that he did not know by heart. In 1862, and in the early part of 1863, he had made large sums by buying it. I remember, in the spring of 1863, seeing him stand behind his broker in the street-crowd and pull his coat-tail, as a signal to buy. His broker after buying one thousand shares of Old Southern stopped, when he felt his coat-tail jerked again, violently, and he commenced buying until after seven successive jerks he had bought eight thousand shares, all for the account of the quiet man in the rear, who thereupon relaxed his grasp, and retired to his office without saying a word. He believed in the proverb,

LOOKING FOR DIVIDENDS.

BUBBLE COMPANIES.

FIGHTING FOR STOCK.

"Speech is silver; silence is golden." His reticence about everything relating to stocks was one of the strong points in his character as a financier, for certainly if there is one thing needful in stock operations, it is reticence, first, last and always.

This trait became, in his later years, somewhat less marked at least in matters relating to himself. I recollect seeing him show to a prominent broker, whom he met in the office of Lockwood & Co., a certificate for ten thousand shares of North Western stock, then selling for 60, which he held as an investment, and remarking that he should never sell that stock till it brought him one million dollars. A few months after, the price rose to par, and he could then have realized his profit. Whether he did so, I cannot say.

In 1863, Henry Keep was a director of the Michigan Southern and Northern Indiana Railroad Company, commonly nicknamed Old Southern.

The telegram before mentioned, was from another high official of the company, informing him that the stock was selling for 107, and requesting him to come to New York without delay!

Why was this message sent to him?

The next morning, he was seen in the office of the company. He was generally a bull; now he was preparing to play the part of a bear.

"The best laid schemes o' *mice* an' *men* gang aft agleg."

In the iron links of the Jerome ring there was one flaw which had escaped the eyes of the shrewd leader. The charter, or the by-laws of the Old Southern Company *permitted an increase in the amount of the capital stock by vote of the directors.*

Within a few hours after the return of Keep from Saratoga, a further issue of fourteen thousand shares was authorized by the directors in secret session. The new stock certificates were made out and everything was ready. But it would never answer to send out these *new* stock certificates without disguise. In that case the market would know of it too soon. The price would fall and the Old Southern Company would fail to derive the full benefit which they hoped would accrue from the selling the new stock at so high a price, and the great bear movement of Keep would be a failure. Accordingly the necessary amount of stock was borrowed from the ring and sold. This created the impression that a heavy short interest was being developed and completely blinded the ring. In addition to the shares of the new issue, Keep went short of the stock on his own account to an enormous amount, and then stood and watched the market. Not long, however.

September drew near and a delicate pressure began to be felt in the money market. Many of the heavy holders began to talk about realizing their profits, but as the prices began to yield they waited for them to rise aga'n.

Such is the custom of operators who cannot bear to face a loss, however small. They waited too long, for stocks, instead of regaining the summit price, sagged down lower. To Secretary Chase has been attributed two great panics, that of September, 1863, and that of April, 1864. Whether or not with reason, we will not say. But certain it is, that he came into the market in Wall Street in August, 1863, for a loan, and early in September he secured from the banks a loan of $35,000,000, and now the Old Southern trap was sprung. The entire lot of fourteen thousand shares, was used to repay the borrowed stocks. The money-lenders tightened their hold of their cash-boxes; the interest ran up three per cent. In one day, stocks fell from ten to twenty per cent. The next day they fell ten per cent. lower. Harlem and Hudson came toppling down from Alpine heights. Erie fell down with a rush, and struck 99. But Old Southern came down like an avalanche. Jerome's personal losses were said to have been nearly one million dollars, his prestige was destroyed and after that his power ceased to be felt in the market. As for the P—— Pool which hoped to swallow Uncle Daniel and his strong box, it was utterly annihilated. Some of the members of that combination still haunt the market, mere shadows of operators, without money, or credit or even decent habiliments. Daniel Drew covered his shorts with an immense profit.

The first thing a loser in Wall Street does, after a heavy stroke of bad luck is, to find fault with his broker. The second thing he does is, to curse his luck. The third thing he does is, to gather together the wreck, and get ready for another venture on the treacherous waves.

In accordance with this programme, I held a conference with my broker, in his private room, out of ear-shot of his clerks, for I wished to spare his feelings, so far as a broker may be said to have feelings. He was a big man. His personal presence was overpowering. He was seated in a large chair. The province of big men like him seems to be to sit in large chairs, and take change, as one of the editors of a New York newspaper once remarked to me. His face was that of a globose Jupiter Tonans. Every wrinkle seemed large enough to form the grave of a small margin, all in the way of legitimate commission business. His principal occupation appeared to be smoking monstrous regalias, and signing checks.

When a broker reaches the dignity of a daily check signer for a million dollars, he may be said to have drunk the full cup of such bliss as Wall Street life can give. The mere fact that a man is daily signing his name to twenty or thirty bits of paper, all of which are certified as good by his bank, and each one of which can, on presentment at the counter, be exchanged for forty thousand dollars in crisp greenbacks, conveys to an observer's mind, an idea of mysterious power. My broker sat in his private room that day, signing checks for untold amounts, as coolly as though he were scribbling his name in pure chirographical wantonness. I waited for him to finish his task before I opened my broadside. Just as he was putting the final flourish on the last check, he opened his lips and let drop one word, "well!" This was to let me know that he had the floor, and was about to speak. Then he laid the pen down, removed the huge cigar from between his lips, blew an immense volume of smoke from his mouth, looked at me through it as it circled to the ceiling, rose from his seat and continued:

"I am going out to get something to eat, come along."

This "getting something to eat," after the heavy

labors of the day, means in Wall Street parlance, an elaborate dinner with all the etceteras, or at least an elaborate lunch.

My guns were spiked by this hospitable invitation, but were still loaded and threatening. I held my peace, and without more ado we wended our way to the neighboring chateau of Delmonico. My heavy-set broker had probed my wound, and now proceeded to apply healing lotions. Twice I began a sentence, half expostulatory, half indignant; and twice I was interrupted by his stopping business acquaintances and addressing them in a jocular strain.

We reached Delmonico's, and elbowing our way through a group of florid, coraline-nosed individuals, whose principal occupation between the hours of ten A. M. and four P. M., seems to be standing very erect in the lower room of that far famed restaurant, looking very jolly, and taking brandy straight at regular intervals. We sat down at one of the little tables. A waiter flew to us, as waiters always do at Delmonico's, when well known heavy feeders and sippers make their appearance. He chattered like a monkey in a southern forest, seized our plates and polished them with his napkin till they shone again, then fairly bewildered our ears with the names of a host of dishes, all smoking hot, and waiting the pleasure of Messieurs, beneath as many smoking tins.

"We will take soup a la Julien."

"Oui! oui!"

"Then a little fish—Spanish mackerel."

"Oui! oui!"

"A bottle of *haut sauterne* with the fish. After that we will take a filet of beef with mushrooms; then game, the half of a grouse. Vegetables, of course; potatoes lyonaise, French peas, and a bottle of Cliquot, with the meats. Then ice-cream meringues. *Café noir and petit verre.*"

In three minutes we were under full headway. The soup silenced me with its trickling juices. The *sauterne* mollified me. The filet and game equilibrized me, and when the Cliquot had diffused its genial glow, I took new views of Wall Street life. The broker had done nothing but what was right in selling my stock, after my margin had run down so low. The loss could easily be made up. I had $40,000 to do it with; it should be done! We lay back in our chairs and puffed at our cigars. We exchanged views. We both concurred in thinking that stocks were cheap, particularly *Harlem.* This last named stock had fallen sixty per cent. from 181. The Commodore had not got through with it, that was plain. He was an all-day man, and he would send Harlem up kiting yet.

We talked so long about it, and fortified each other with such potential reasons for believing that this stock must rise, that at last we considered it a foregone conclusion. Then we rose from the table, and passed out into the street. The Boards had both adjourned. The crowd was buzzing as usual on the sidewalk. Stocks were quoted firm, with an upward tendency. The votaries of Harlem began to recover faith in their Magnus, Apollo—the Commodore, and once more filled the street with rumors of another great rise in the stock.

"You see," remarked one enthusiast, "A. G. Jerome had to pitch overboard all the Harlem he was carrying, when Old Southern broke. The Commodore hasn't sold any stock. They (the ring,) are picking up all the loose stock. There is one of Vanderbilt's brokers now buying everything offered under 120. The next hitch will be 200."

A part of these remarks were whispered in the ear of my broker, who immediately bought two thousand shares, on his own account. This amount he generously offered to share with me, and his offer was accepted promptly.

One thousand shares of Harlem at 120, cost sixty thousand dollars, for as already noted, this stock is only fifty dollars per share, at par. This amount of stock was placed to my account on the broker's books.

"This Harlem," said my broker, "I shall consider as a kind of permanent investment, at all events, I shall not sell it for less than 198."

One thousand shares of Harlem, bought at 120, and sold at 198, (for it is never best to wait for the highest point, which was agreed to be 200) would show a profit of $39,000. This would go towards wiping out that loss of $61,000.

The position of this notorious stock was, in the fall of 1863, very peculiar. It had been, the past six months, the double-edged sword of the market, held in the hands of the Commodore. The bears had first been cut down like grass, then the legs of the bulls were hewn in two. What was singular, the men who had gone short of the stock during the spring and summer were now buying it for a rise while many of those, who, during the same period, had operated in it for a rise, were selling it now in expectation of a fur-

ther decline. Its future depended on two things, viz.:
a decision of one of the judges of the Supreme Court
and the action of the Common Council of the city of
New York, respecting the street franchise grant. After a few rapid vibrations, it fell to 110. The stock
looked weak. I wished I was out of it. But I dared
not face a loss of $5,000 which had already accrued.
One desperate expedient remained. I could buy one
thousand shares more at 110 and then as soon as it
rose to 115, sell out the two thousand shares without
any loss except two or three hundred dollars brokerage and interest, for carrying the stock.

I bought one thousand shares more at 110!

The price sunk lower and lower.

One morning, soon after this, a stout red-haired
man, a stranger to every one, made his appearance
on the street, and offered five hundred shares of Harlem at the ruling price. No one took him up, but
some one on the other side of the crowd, bid one per
cent. below the market price, and the red-haired man
cried out, "sold," and gave up the name of a well-
known broker. In a moment, every eye in the crowd
was fastened on the stranger.

It might be laid down as a general proposition that
in certain conditions of the market, any stout, red-
haired man, (who is a stranger to the crowd of operators), appearing on the street and offering to sell
five hundred shares of a certain stock one per cent.
below the market, would occasion a panic.

The stranger in this case proved to be a lawyer
from one of the river counties, who was believed to
have obtained early information in some way, that
the decision of Judge Hogeboom was adverse to Har-

lem. As soon as this fact became known to the
street, Harlem dropped like lead, to 90. On the heels
of this decision, came adverse legislation by the Common Council, and before my two thousand shares
could be disposed of, the price had reached 81. Out
of $113,500, I had remaining, five thousand and some
odd in cash on hand, and the $9,000 invested on a
margin in the 7 3-10 bonds, bought as mentioned in
the last chapter. Should I sell the bonds and put the
proceeds into stock margins? No! This eight thousand dollars was turning out to be one of the snug-
gest financial snow-balls that was ever rolled, as will
appear to the reader, if he will examine the following
account, the figures being approximate, and made up
from memory:

175,000 worth of $7\frac{3}{10}$ per cent. Government Bonds, at 104, bought July, 1863, ...	$182,000
Interest accrued on same, at $7\frac{3}{10}$ per cent., (say three months,) in currency, ...	2,235
	$184,235
Which Bonds were paid for by a loan from Savings' Banks, at par, ...	$175,000
Margin, ...	9,235
	$184,235

Interest on loan, for four months, at $5\frac{1}{2}$ per cent., in currency, on $175,000,. . .	$5,616	
Interest on bonds, $7\frac{3}{10}$ in gold, for four months, ...	$8,036	
Premium on $8,036 gold, sold at 140 , . .	3,214	
	$11,250	
Add 2 per cent., rise in bonds, ...	3,500	
	$14,750	

My net profits was the difference between $14,750

and the sum of $5,616 interest paid the savings banks which showed the sum of $9,134 in which, however, was included the entire interest paid in gold, viz.: $2,235. Now, if gold rose to 200, my interest on this operation which I regarded in the light of a permanent investment would be nearly 150 per cent. on my margin, to say nothing of any rise which might take place in the price of the bonds. On looking at these figures my resolution was confirmed to keep my bonds. But what should be done to retrieve my losses? I would make one last venture. In what? Did the fickle goddess relent and whisper something in my ear when one day after taking a survey of the market, I gave an order to buy five hundred shares of Rock Island, at par. However this may be, the stock was bought and $5,000 margin delivered to my broker, with instructions to sell the stock if it fell to 91, but if it went up, to let my profit run. Then I took a week's rest, expecting every day the worst, and hardly daring to hope for the better.

CHAPTER XVI.

OPENING THE BALL ON ROCK ISLAND.

Bulls, Bears and Changelings—How Bears Make Stocks go Up—Dull Seasons, Rises and Panics—Dark Times for Bulls—A Rocket Shoots Up in the Darkness—More about A. W. Morse—How He Came to be a Broker—The Rock Island Pool Taking in the Shorts—Undercurrents—The Financial Outlook; Is it to be Up or Down with Stocks?—Loans and Taxation *vs.* Fresh Currency—Two Bears try to Cover their Shorts but Can't—A Tantalizing Stock—The Story of My Five Hundred Shares—A Bone-boiler's Opinion about Rock Island—" Boiling Down the Gristle of the Bears "—The Final Twist—A Big Profit, and a Smile all Round.

HE operators in Wall Street may be divided into three grand classes. First, those who are by constitution and temperament, opertors for a rise, *i. e.*, bulls. Second, those who are by constitution, temperament and education, operators for a fall, *i. e.* bears. Third, those who are bulls or bears by turns. This last class is by far the largest.

As we have before remarked, they who commence by operating for a rise often end by operating for a fall.

A. G. Jerome was an example of these converts. The Napoleon of the Public Board, after a career of unparalleled success, found his Waterloo in Old Southern. Henry Keep was the Iron Duke who defeated him as we have already shown. When Old Southern

17

fell to 77, Jerome, who had been operating for a rise with such success up to the time of that disaster, now became a bold operator for a fall. He and his associates in the clique, turned about and sold Old Southern short. Their losses on both these operations were rated at $2,500,000. But Jerome was only one of a host of men who, having lost heavily on the bull side, by the panic of September 3d and 4th, now changed their policy, and prepared hereafter to act as bears. It should be remembered, that *bears play an important part in assisting every great rise,* by creating a demand for the stocks which they have sold for future delivery. This fact should be noted in connection with what we have to describe hereafter.

In accordance with the traditions of Wall Street, the fall of the year is the dull season in stocks. The reason for this may be stated thus : the money which flows into the banks of New York City, from all parts of the country, at other seasons of the year, is withdrawn largely in the fall by its owners, for the purpose of using it in different ways. One of these ways is the moving to market of the crops of the West and South. In a few weeks, or at most, months, the money begins to flow back, and seek employment and investment in New York. The banks and other money-lending institutions, also call in their loans late in the fall or early in the winter, preparatory to making their January dividends. Hence it is, that operators generally shorten sail in the autumn, during which season the stock market is dull. These dull seasons are the breathing spells of the market between its great rises and corresponding falls, which might be illustrated by a diagram as follows, viz. :

From September 4th till December 16th, nothing occurred that was noteworthy in the course of prices, except the break in Harlem. But Harlem was looked upon now as a specialty quite unconnected with the general market. During all this period, the bear party were daily growing stronger and more clamorous. Everything seemed to work in their favor. The banks, alarmed by the wild speculations in stocks and gold, and noting the periodical panics which had occurred, were all this time contracting their loans and discouraging stock operations. The financial movements of the government in the direction of fresh loans to be negotiated in New York, were held in dread by the operators. The press thundered forth in its money articles, denunciations of the *stock bubble* and its engineers, accompanied with words of prediction of and warning against the speedy collapse. Under these circumstances, the bulls found it difficult to lift prices. In November, and early in December, they made a feeble effort which failed, and left them in a worse condition. The confidence of the public in the upward tendency of values was more than impaired.

The five hundred shares of Rock Island, mentioned in the last chapter, was bought on its intrinsic *merits,* after a break in the market, on the 9th of December. How dark and cheerless everything looked that day ! The sun hardly shone through the leaden sky upon the stagnant market. For a week, Wall Street speculation looked like a dead sea, and the financial air grew closer and darker. Suddenly, out of this level waste, something shot up like a rocket with a bengal light fastened to its tail! The bull carnival had been ushered in by the rise of Rock Island! This movement startled men by its brilliancy, but inspired fresh confidence. It was the harbinger of another great rise. Its leader was hailed by the bulls with acclamation. The name of A. W. Morse rang through the street.

After an interregnum of seven months, he again took the throne, as king of the Regular Board, and of the street, to maintain his blazing reign till the following April. Now the outside public began to inquire who he was. It appears that in 1860, he was a clerk in a mercantile house, and was employed by them to go down into Wall Street, to negotiate their paper, and look after their money matters there.

One day a gentleman connected with a large firm in the street, noticing the rapidity with which he ran up columns of figures, and the general sharpness and accuracy of his mental operations, views on stock, etc., asked him why he did not come into Wall Street, and commence business on his own account. Morse replied that he had no capital. The gentleman told him, that with talents like his, he could go on without capital, and that most of the successful brokers commenced with little or no money. "Money," said he, "will flow into the hands of the Wall Street man, who has the qualities of shrewdness, activity, and boldness. Don't wait another day, but take a little office near the Stock Exchange, and get admitted into the board as soon as you can." On this advice, Morse acted without delay. In three years he had

HOW A FORTUNATE OPERATOR SPENDS HIS MONEY.

risen to be the leader of the board, during the Chancellorsville rise, and he was now the fugleman, who formed the bulls into one compact and obedient phalanx, moving up the heights of the market in 1864.

He was the most dashing operator ever known in Wall Street. In buying stocks he rarely seemed to cover his hand. The heavy dealers held him at first in low estimation. His bodily appearance was so slight and frail, his air so jaunty and holiday-like, his money resources seemed so inadequate to what he undertook, that when after buying quietly as much Rock Island as he could pick up, he came out boldly, bid for heavy blocks of the stock at 107–109, the old money kings of the board sold him all he bid for, laughing in their sleeves at the "blind confidence" of this wild speculator, and when the price fell back to 105, cries of derision were heard all through the street. From this point it rushed to 114, with enormous transactions. The whole capital stock, $6,000,000, is said to have been bought and sold twice over in a week. Neither buyers nor sellers abated their confidence, the former in the continued upward movement, the latter in the ultimate downcome, coupled with a firm belief in the insanity of their rivals. Morse kept buying it by the thousand shares, buyer thirty, seller thirty, cash, regular or in any way he could get it best. The more conservative members of the board prognosticated his speedy downfall.

"Morse will get bit;" "Morse will be saddled with the whole capital stock;" "Morse will break;" "Morse is crazy;" these remarks passed around the bear conclave.

But the pool in Rock Island was stronger than these confident and prophetic gentlemen dreamed. It comprised, besides the brave leader and manipulator, a Washington banker, an eminent railroad capitalist and financier, and a wealthy retired California merchant, besides ten or twelve other operators. There was money enough pledged to carry the entire stock on a twenty per cent. margin, *i. e.*, $1,200,000. When the price struck 116, the pool is said to have held, in actual stock or contracts, thirty-nine thousand shares. These contracts were buyers' and sellers' options, for three, five, ten, fifteen, thirty and sixty days. As fast as they fell due they were renewed by the still confident bears.

A little lull now took place in the price, which languidly moved between 114 and 118. But though Morse no longer bid personally for the stock, he was not idle. In the nobbiest of sack-coats, his face a little thinner, and his nose a little more hooked than usual, he could have been seen flying from bank to bank, or standing behind his desk, adding up figures like the lightning calculator, or making playful bids for one or two hundred shares of Rock Island, or offering to sell ten thousand shares in one lot, at two per cent. below the market. All this time his agents were at work, taking every new contract offered, now bidding up the price, and now dropping it to entice more shorts.

The members of the Pool began to find fault with Morse, and ask why he did not put up the price. "Leave that to me," he would reply, "and I will make all your fortunes." When they importuned him to know what he was doing, he would laugh and tell them to be patient, and ask them what they thought of 175 for Rock Island. Here it should be noted that in the Rock Island Pool, nick-named by the bears, the "Blind Confidence Pool," Morse was the sole manager. All his associates did was to sign the Pool contract and pay the money which represented their interest. After that they knew little or nothing of what was going on in the stock. This was a shrewd policy for the Pool manager, for it deterred his associates from operating on the stock outside, to the prejudice of the combination. They dared not buy the stock, for fear of a break, and still less dared they to go short of it.

The money-market, during the month of December, had been by fits and starts, cheap and dear; capitalists were timorous. But when January came, there was for a while a *steady* stringency, and still stocks stood firm.

It was Morse standing on the "perilous edge" of the battle in December, that held the market up, by the moral effort of his thus far successful move.

One fear hung over the bears like a thunder-cloud. It was the fear of the new issue of $400,000,000 legal tenders, authorized in March, but a small part of which had yet been set afloat. The Government had shrunk from doing this as long as possible. Now it looked as if it must be done. The currency of the country would in that case be $1,000,000,000. This, to the Wall Street man, would signify a new and unparalleled era in speculation.

The panic of the preceding September had been precipitated by a loan made by the banks to the government on $50,000,000 of the new legal tender five per cent. notes, and as the policy which had been pursued by Secretary Chase for the past four months was that which contemplated the raising of money by loans and taxation, rather than by the issue of fresh currency, the bears had been flattering themselves on the prospect of a continued tightness in the money market from the absorption of the floating currency in the five-twenties and other government loans. The result of this state of affairs would finally be, lower prices in the stock market. Such were the grounds on which a host of bears had been resting ever since September.

But a new loan at a lower rate of interest (the ten forties) would have to be soon placed upon the market. Would the public subscribe to it if money were not made easier, *i. e.*, if new currency were not issued? The financial policy of the Secretary may be best described by a simile. The government loans may be likened to so many different vessels, large and small. The legal tenders may be likened to the waters in which those vessels were to be floated. The lower the interest of the bonds the more difficult to get them taken by the people, just as the lower the vessel's keel sinks the more depth of water required to float her.

This was the question about which the bulls and bears differed. The bulls had decided already that $1,000,000,000 millions of notes would soon be afloat. Morse foresaw it clearly when he made his apparently desperate venture in Rock Island. The shrewdest of those men, who had been selling stocks, began to take the same views and would have acted upon them by turning right about face and buying for a rise, but for one little circumstance. *If they bought in their shorts they would have to do so at a heavy loss.* They dared not look their losses boldly in the face; they dared not confess they were in the wrong. Avarice and vanity made cowards of them.

Here let us note, that as long as his contracts remain open, the Wall Street man is buoyed up by what is so often his evil genius, viz.: Hope—hope, either that his gains will be greater, or his losses less. He cannot bear to fix his eyes on those terrible accounts, rendered to him by his broker, with the long columns of interest, commissions and margins, all swallowed up in that voracious stock-market. When his account is handed to him, if it shows a loss, he will fold it, and thrust it into his most secret pocket, without even looking at the "demnition total." Successive accounts, each showing losses, are like successive blows of some demon-hammer, upon his sensitive nervous system. Even the iron nerves of Daniel Drew quiver under it. It appears that he keeps several different accounts at his brokers, entitled thus, viz.: "Erie account," "North-west account," etc., etc. When he makes a loss on one account, he is wont to put it down on some one of the other accounts, which shows a profit, as if he would juggle himself out of the idea that he has made any loss.

On the 5th of January, 1864, the long pending question between the bulls and bears, was decided in favor of the former. $20,000,000 of the new interest bearing, five per cent. legal tender notes, were received by the banks of Philadelphia, New York and Boston.

Two days before this, and while Rock Island was selling at 123, two prominent bears, who were short of the stock fifteen per cent. below that figure, received a telegram from Washington, informing them that several millions of the new notes were to be sent to New York on the next day. They promptly gave orders to their brokers, to cover at 123¼. This was their limit, and but for an unfortunate accident, their order might have been executed. *The message was intercepted by the enemy.* It had been carried by a small boy, one of those rattle-pated little urchins, too often entrusted with important messages in Wall Street. While on his way to the brokers, he was seen by an agent of Morse, scuffling with one of his mates. A moment after, he dropped a slip of paper, which Morse's agent picked up, read, and handed it back to the boy, who thereupon, scuttled away to do his errand. In sixty seconds from that moment, Morse knew that two prominent bears had given an order to cover several thousand shares of Rock Island at 123¼. In sixty seconds more, two brief notes had been dispatched; one to his agent who bought and sold for him in the street, the other to his agent representing him in the Public Board. The purport of these notes was, not to let Rock Island go below 124, and if any one came in to buy at the market price, to bid the price up all the time, and buy everything that was offered. He himself attended to matters in the Regular Board. The two bears finding themselves unable to cover, kept giving fresh orders, one quarter per cent. above the market, 124¼, 125¼, 126¼. But just as they were going to lay their hands on the stock as they fondly hoped, it danced away from them, till it reached 129. These orders in accordance with a Wall Street custom, were

only in force during the particular session of the
board, held immediately after they were given.
When they ceased giving orders, the stock price
remained quiet, or fell off a trifle.

Let us leave, for a while, these brothers in misfor-
tune, cutting their financial throats by the penny-
wise and pound-foolish policy, of limiting their broker
in the price at which he was to buy, blissfully unconscious of the hawk-eyes which watched their every
motion, and return to the story of the five hundred
shares of Rock Island, bought by me on the 9th of
December, at 101.

Morse's office in 1864, was in William Street, nearly
opposite to one of the entrances to the Regular Board.
It was a small room, more like a niche in the wall
than a banking office, in which operations were soon
to be carried on, the results whereof were destined
to shake the stock market to its very center. As
there was little space inside to accommodate the numerous customers which began to flock thither, attracted by the fame of the bull leader, and hoping to
build their fortunes upon it, these gentry were wont
to stand outside upon the flag-stones which descended
into the street, and a singular looking group they
were. Among them I had often noticed a man with
a carbuncular nose who was continually standing sentry at that particular spot, and seemed to act as if
he knew something about what was going on.

One morning after Rock Island had risen to 129,
and deeming now that my profits had been let run
so long that this was the hour to embrace them, by
fingering a check for $14,000 or thereabouts, I was
on my way to my brokers, to give the necessary order

to sell, when a friend introduced me to the carbuncular nose, as it glowed like a beacon in front of Morse's office. The owner of the nose, it appears, was also the proprietor of a small, but extremely vigorous bone-boiling establishment, somewhere up town. In this legitimate, but disagreeably odoriferous business, he had amassed the sum of five thousand dollars, which as luck would have it, had been recently staked as a ten per cent. margin, on five hundred shares of Rock Island. The first question I put to him involved his opinion of Rock Island. As this was his first appearance in the street as an operator, and not having yet acquired the Wall Street habit of reticence, he was free to say that he thought well of it, he had made a little money on it and was going to make more.

"Will she go up? She hasn't *begun* to bile yet. When she *does* bile, she won't leave a gristle or a jynt of them air bears. Morse is agoing to pile on the fire and melt 'em all into soup."

This forcible expression of his opinion, savoring so strongly of the bone-boiling trade, had its due effect.

I decided to let my profits run.

She *did* "begin to bile." The following Saturday, Rock Island sold at 133. The two bears thought of the matter over Sunday. *Their* decision was made. Early Monday morning they gave the order which they ought to have given two weeks before. "Buy our Rock Island at the *market price!*"

That was a blue Monday for the ursine tribe. It was "twisting day." The pass-word was "excelsior." At half-past nine o'clock, I saw Morse standing on his office steps, a strange smile distorting his face as he looked at the curb-stone crowd, yelling for Rock Island at 140. Before night it touched 149. The two bears settled up their shorts at 145. The bone-boiler took his profits at 145. The writer, the next day, was perusing a deeply interesting volume of stock literature, by which it appeared he had to his credit on the books of his broker, a net profit of $21,546.45, derived from the sale of five hundred shares of Rock Island at 145.

Never sell stocks short!

Always be a bull! *Verb. Sap.*

Twenty-one thousand, five hundred and forty-six dollars and forty-five cents!

Here were the pin-feathers of a rich plumage for a bird so lately plucked! Everybody smiled in my broker's office that morning. The little errand boy grinned and winked as he darted past me. The clerks beamed with smiles. The book-keeper simpered, as he graciously allowed me to feast my eyes on my account in his ledger, which expanded before me. I thought I could perceive a slight contortion on the stony face of the cashier, as he passed me a check for $500 pocket money. And when I handed to my broker a series of orders to buy three hundred Michigan Central, five hundred Illinois Central, four hundred Old Southern, all at the market price, his countenance was one conglomeration of smiles as he looked down the vista of my future commissions. He punched me in the ribs, joked me about Old Southern and Harlem, vowed that I would have revenge on them yet, and finished by inviting me to go with him to Delmonico's at four P. M. sharp, to take soup and wet my profit with bumpers of Roederer.

CHAPTER XVII.

THE GREAT RISE OF 1864.

THE general market, awakened from its long lethargy in December, by Morse's Rock Island pyrotechnics, began in January to throb and stir with a strange, feverish life.

The next stage was to be frenzy.

The three hundred shares of Michigan Central, cost me 132½. The five hundred shares of Illinois Central, cost me 125. The four hundred shares of Old Southern, cost me 87½. In one week, the first named of these stocks was selling at 139, the second, at 132 and, the third, at 90. I could, by selling, have realized a profit of $6,450; instead of which, I bought twice the amount of my first purchase. All at once, money tightened up to ten per cent., and in a few hours Michigan Central had fallen to 126, Illinois Central to 124, and Old Southern to 86. If I sold my stocks now, my loss would be $20,900, besides interest and brokerage.

When a heavy loss stares him in the face, a man is apt to seek advice and sympathy from his broker. Seeking advice and sympathy from brokers, when margins are diminishing, is like gathering grapes from thorns, and figs from thistles. Instead of smiles, I now saw only dark looks in my broker's office. The market was panicky; a further decline of $4\frac{1}{2}$ per cent., and I should be laid on my back once more.

That globose face, which, ten days before, was radiant with smiles, was now overcast and lowering.

Why do brokers' faces look black when their customers' margins have nearly run out?

Tricks of the trade!

When stocks begin to break, they often quietly sell their customers' stocks. Then, after prices have declined so far as to leave little *apparent* margin on the account, the customer, quite unconscious that his stocks have been sold at a much higher price, finds himself subjected to various influences to induce him to give the order to sell. His broker looks glum, and talks of tight money, and the dangerous condition of the market. If the customer gives the order to sell, of course the broker puts into his own pocket, the difference between the higher price at which he sold his customer's stock, and the order to sell, given under the pressure of those glum looks and bear talk. This trick may be better illustrated by the following little account:

Customer buys one hundred Erie at 120, ... $12,000
Market begins to fall, and broker sells the stock (without
    telling customer) at 119.
Stock price falls to 105, ... 10,500

Then come the black looks and talk of bad market. The customer gets frightened and says sell. The stock has already been sold at 119, but the broker returns on the account, 100 Erie sold at 105, and pockets the difference between 119 and 105, i. e., $1,400, which sum comes out of his customer's margin. We do not allege that *all* brokers are in the habit of doing this, but it is certainly one of the ways by which the public are fleeced.

I was unable to stand the pressure of that lowering face, and the doleful tale he told, respecting the market ; I lightened ship by throwing overboard the nine hundred shares of Michigan Central at a loss of over $9,000, but still kept fifteen hundred shares of Illinois Central, and the twelve hundred shares of Old Southern though under the greatest trepidation lest the market, by a further decline, might clear away my remaining margin. Of course this sale was made at the lowest cash price, and as usual, in ten minutes afterwards, stocks began to rise again.

Two weeks passed away—two busy fervid weeks. Money was pouring into Wall Street now like the cataract of the great lakes. One after one, stocks had risen higher than the bulls would have dared to hope in bleak December. Even the colossal bulk of Erie was moving upwards with slow elephantine strides. Then stocks paused. Many holders thinking that prices had culminated, sold out. The market took all their stocks without budging, and still it did not advance much. Why ? Pools were forming ; powerful combinations on the pattern of the Rock Island pool. They were keeping down the prices till they had loaded up. Morse and his associates still kept their

grip of Rock Island and were taking hold of Pittsburg, of Erie and of Fort Wayne. A pool in Old
Southern made its head-quarters in the office of L——
& Co. The Commodore and his friends had Harlem
and Hudson in hand. Illinois Central, Galena, in fact
nearly every stock on the catalogue was passing into
the hands of pools. The market was agitated for the
moment by a great downward movement in Rock Island. In three days, Morse sold the bulk of his Rock
Island between 140 and 118. He wished to break
down the entire market, so that he could buy other
stocks. He was preparing to concentrate his best energies on Fort Wayne and Erie. The chasm made
by Rock Island closed up, and everything grew
smooth again. Fort Wayne looked heavy for the
moment. Its leader was taking a flyer on Erie!
This movement in Erie, had, under the quiet purchase of Morse, advanced the price to 112. Then
he tried to break the market down by hurling huge
blocks of Rock Island and Erie upon it. But Erie
stood firm.

It was time now to play the bold game. The first
move in this game commenced at the *Evening Exchange.*

The Evening Exchange was one of the institutions
of the stock market during the years 1864 and 1865.
Some enterprising dealer hired a room in the basement of the Fifth Avenue Hotel. Any one could
have access to it by paying fifty cents. In February
of the former year, this room was jammed with buyers and sellers, from seven till nine P. M., after which
hour they adjourned to the halls and bar-room above,
and plied their vocation till midnight.

18

Morse jumped on a bench in this basement one night, dressed in a light blue beaver overcoat, and gracefully waving his potent hand, bid for ten thousand shares of Erie, or any part. No one "took him up." While he stood there, still holding open his bid, a slim young man with dark eyes, darted up the steep staircase, rushed into the hotel, and whispered to Daniel Drew's broker, who stood in the hall apparently waiting for something. " Sell him the ten thousand shares," said he " and give up my name."

The young man darted down into the basement, rushed up and shook his finger in the face of Morse, yelling out, " I'll sell you that ten thousand Erie."

Morse nodded his head, and then stretching out his hand, bid for twenty thousand shares more. The crowd knew that Daniel Drew was selling the stock, and shrunk back at the boldness of the man who dared to meet the old man "on his native heath," Erie.

In two days the whole capital stock of $11,000,-000 changed hands. The price ran up ten per cent. Morse had hoisted the huge load to 122, and the "Old Man's" account on that little operation was out $100,000.

Men began to count on their fingers, the successful operations of Morse. Pittsburg, Rock Island, Erie; and to enquire what stock this bold leader would take hold of next. I had not yet sold the fifteen hundred Illinois Central, nor the twelve hundred Old Southern, which at present prices, showed me a profit of something like $14,800. I bought one thousand more shares of Old Southern at 95, and five hundred Illinois Central at 134.

Then I was joined by allies. The Saratoga trio came together again. E——, who had retired from the market in disgust after his losses in September, now came into the market again, rejuvenated by his long rest, and bellowed like a bull of Bashan. L——, after being hit heavily on his long stocks, had been converted to the bear creed, and having covered his shorts at a further loss of $75,000, had determined hereafter never to go short, but always operate for a rise.

Our little coterie received an accession in the person of W. B. C——, a Westerner, with a heart as big as a bullock. Poor fellow! he sleeps now the sleep that knell of panic will never disturb. We laid out our campaign on the following plan : Each one was to keep an account in the office of a prominent broker, but no two in the same office. Each one was to get admitted to a different pool, and then we were mutually pledged to furnish each other with all the information we could obtain from these different sources. L—— opened an account with Morse, E—— with L—— & Co., W. B. C—— with M—— & B——. I kept one account with my old broker, and opened another with B—— & Co. L—— joined the Fort Wayne ring. E—— cast his bread upon the Old Southern Pool. W. B. C—— entered the Galena combination, and I took five hundred shares in the Canton pool at 38. Then we exchanged "views," the result of which was that each one made outside purchases of the different pool-stocks, inside of which his mates had embarked. I sold my two thousand Illinois Central at 135 and bought one thousand Fort Wayne, five hundred Galena, and five hundred Old Southern.

Then our quartette lay back, and went "up in a balloon."

What a tremendous moral engine, is the New York press. Every day this engine spreads before a million readers, and a thousand minor journals, a record of facts. To say that the money articles of the Daily Journal of Traffic, the Daily Harbinger, the Daily Rostrum, the Daily Age, the Daily Orb, the Daily Letter, the Daily Messenger, etc., etc., are written with great ability, would be but simple justice. If they sometimes make mistakes in their views of money matters, still, it cannot be denied, that they see as far into the financial grindstone as any one. Every day, during the great rise of 1864, this moral engine was laying before the people these facts, viz.: A thousand millions of currency will soon be circulating through the country; railroads are earning enormous sums; an unprecedented inflation is taking place in values; a certain daring speculator, named Morse, is setting Wall Street in a blaze; speculation is rampant, and no one can predict when this speculation will cease. The whole country was startled by this record of facts. The large ear of the confiding public was caught. The speculative element rushed into Wall Street, in one compact body. Countrymen rarely go short of stocks; they are generally bulls. Buy! buy! anything, no matter what! put in your greenbacks, and and pick up gold!

The whole street was lined with rustics. They marched in files, stood in groups, discussed matters and then formed in battalions and gave their orders to buy. Lank, sun-burned men, stout men, with husky voices, tall short and middle-sized men, with country-cut coats, entered the city in the morning, with nothing but a paper collar and a comb in their carpet bag and a small check on some city bank, and left town the next day with a bundle of greenbacks larger than a small sized encyclopedia! These were the lucky ones. Others staid there for three months and then left with very large fleas in their ears. Morse's office was besieged. Strangers came to him and thrust portly wallets into his hand. Shrewd financiers almost went down on their knees, begging him to tell them what to buy, and forcing upon him checks for hundreds of thousands of dollars. He was watched as closely as if he were some great criminal under the surveillance of detectives. In the board or on the curbstone, every shade of expression in his face was scrutinized by hundreds of sharp eyes.

The other bull leaders were ably seconding the great upward movement. Tobin had Harlem in hand for the Commodore. Every brokerage firm that had charge of any particular stock for a pool, became a General, urging on the bull movement. L. W. Jerome, though little seen in the street, was operating enormously for a rise and making millions. A well-known clergyman laid down a check for three thousand dollars on the desk of this noted financier. He didn't tell him to buy stocks, oh! no! That would be gambling. But mysteriously enough, in the course of a couple months after, the same clergyman was seen to deposit in his bank, a check for $80,000, signed by L. W. Jerome.

During the two months from the 18th of February till the 18th of April, there was no form of humanity, no profession, age, sex or condition, that might not have been seen in Wall Street. Even decrepitude and disease seemed for the time being, to have lost their power. The corridors of the Stock Exchange and the cushioned sofas of the brokers' offices looked like the wards of a hospital, filled with limbs palsied and swollen, and eyes purblind, while the hectic coughs of consumptives were echoing the robust shouts and yells of the surging crowd in William Street. Glittering coupés drove up to the doors of the great banking and brokerage houses, with fair dames veiled and loaded with jewels, who leaned back upon the satin-covered cushions and waited to learn the prices of stocks.

Three weeks after we had started on our balloon excursion, we pulled the valve and let out a little gas, in other words, we realized a part of our profits by selling everything except our interest in Fort Wayne and in our individual pools. The Fort Wayne we had decided, must be held for 150, and as for the pool interests, they could not be sold, because we had, on the blind confidence principle, surrendered the control of them to the rings which managed the different stocks which they undertook to hoist. L——, who was the boldest of the quartette, had realized $89,000. E—— $27,000, and W. B. C—— $22,000; while my net profits in hand, since the 9th of December, were $42,000.

Then we said we would go up town, and rest for a week. But we could not sever ourselves long from stocks. Our vacation was only for a day. We all met in the street the next morning, which was Monday. We only came in to take a look at the market.

We did not "mean business." L—— went into Morse's office, came out smiling, and said he had a point. Fort Wayne was to be jumped in a day or two!

By eleven A. M., we held two thousand shares apiece, which cost us from 116 to 118. The next day, just as twelve o'clock was hammered from the belfry of Old Trinity, I had sold all my Fort Wayne, at a profit of $57,000!

"This is the end. No more speculation for me, *except now and then a little flyer.*" Such was my mental resolution, as I deposited $100,000 in my bank, intending to use that sum for permanent investments. I still had $20,000 in my broker's hands. This sum was to furnish me my diversion, which was to consist in *taking flyers.* How many men can trace their ruin to that first or last flyer! There is nothing delusive and dangerous, to which they may not be likened. That flyer, in the shape of one hundred shares of stock, is the maggot in the brain; the springe set for the woodcock; the gilded butterfly, which leads its pursuer over the precipice; the bladders on which "little wanton boys" swim over the treacherous depths of a pool; the rainbow which hangs over the roar of the cataract.

The same afternoon that the little fortune had been snugly laid away in the burglar proof vaults of the —— Bank, L—— brought me another "point" out of Morse's office. *A great many Ohio and Mississippi certificates had lately been going into that office.* The par value of an Ohio and Mississippi certificate was $1,000. Ten of them were equal to one hundred shares of stock. I bought ten Ohio and Mississippi certificates at 49. They rose to 50; I bought fifty more. They rose to 53; I bought one hundred and forty more. Then I gave my broker orders to "sell them at 65—order good till countermanded." Thereupon I went into the country to buy a span of horses. Not that I had a passion for horses. On the contrary, I considered them very perishable property; delicate in health, and like a lady of fashionable circles, rather ornamental than useful. I had sold my horses the preceding fall, and was glad to dispose of them at forty per cent. below what they cost me. Still it is the thing for successful Wall Street men to own horses with ranging necks and long stride, Hambletonian trotters descended from the Godolphin Arabian, or connected by some dark affinity of lineage with Bucephalus or Pegasus. Brown, and other Wall Street men had horses, and why shouldn't I.

That trip to the country was not an agreeable one. My heart was not "in the Highlands;" it was in Wall Street. At the first railroad station I came to, on my way home, with my span of equine elephants, I bought a newspaper, and saw Ohio and Mississippi certificates 69! I telegraphed to my brokers and received answer: "Your certificates sold at 67!" My profits on this *flyer* were $29,100, less interest and brokerage.

The five hundred shares in the Canton pool, had always seemed a mere trifle. I paid very little attention to it, except to buy the stock outside the pool, and make fifteen or twenty thousand dollars. The party that held Canton under their control was not a strong one. There were three rings in it in 1864. The first ring was formed on the basis of 32–33. In February, a new ring was formed on the basis of 38.

This was the ring in which I had an interest. As I had only ten per cent. margin, *i. e.* five thousand dollars, I was perfectly willing to let the brokers, O——, S——, G—— & Co., take the entire control of the matter. But now that it had risen to 60, it began to look enticing, and I commenced to take fly-ers freely in it, especially when one of the daily papers had stated that the property of the company was marked down on its books as being worth par, and the manipulators of the stocks asked me what I thought of 150 as the future price. When Canton reached 66, a third ring was formed. This was to be a sweetener. The heavy capitalists were going into it now, and the price was to be carried up to par. "Would I go into it, and take a thousand shares? No additional margin would be required. I had a large profit on their books now." "Yes, I would." This thousand shares of Canton would give me di-version, something to think about and talk about. I was member of the new pool to the extent of one thousand shares.

Canton is one of the few stocks on the list, which has a history of thirty years. It was based upon property in Baltimore; lands, wharves, warehouses, etc., etc. To be sure, it was not dividend paying. That circumstance was of little weight, however. Erie had just paid a dividend, and why not Canton? The suggestion that it might be used as a government navy-yard, was a good one; so was the idea that Baltimore was a growing city, and that a railroad ran through the property. In 1835 this stock sold for three hundred. This was a pleasing fact to remember. F. B——, a wealthy merchant, had loaned the ring a large sum, not to be called for in several months, the interest on which was payable in gold; the shorts were in it heavily. I bought one thousand shares at 65. The price dropped back to 60, then rose to 70. E—— and I thought we would go in now and buy five thousand shares of this stock. But before doing so, we took a trip to Baltimore for the purpose of examining the Canton property, which as we held an undivided interest of three-twentieths, we thought ourselves justified in calling *our* property. We stopped at East Baltimore, and after making the proper inquiries, succeeded in *locating* the property in question. E—— took his position on a pile of rubbish, and waving his hand to southward and westward over a dreary waste of vacant lots, thinly besprinkled with mouldy looking brick and wooden buildings, delivered a brief oration as if he were addressing the entire executive committee of the Canton Company. He commenced by alluding to the fact that appearances were deceitful, that this celebrated property—our property—had a great future before it; that at some time, it might be only a few years, and it would certainly be within the next century, this property was destined to have value. He pointed to the various heaps of rubbish in evidence of the activity of business thereupon, alluded to the memories of Canton, and closed by inviting the committee to his hotel (a small shanty), in the city of Canton, where they might refresh themselves after their arduous labors, with the wine of hops and malt, otherwise lager beer.

It need hardly be stated that when we got back to New York *we sold our* outside interest in the Canton

Company, and I wished I had never gone into the last ring at 66.

And now, while in search of "flyers," in which to employ profitably my loose cash, and of investments for my $100,000, I found something which seemed, at once a most tempting flyer and a most permanent investment.

CHAPTER XVIII.

BUBBLE COMPANIES.

Ripples, Oscillations and Tide Waves in Speculation—New Enterprises on the Crest of the Wave—Wall Street Men Become Miners and Mineralogists — Mining-patter and Wealth Going a Begging — How They Blow the Bubbles—"A Limited Number of Shares" Offered to the Public—The Bubble Full Blown; it Glitters Like the Rainbow—Ropers-in Pulling in Victims—The Corpulent Gentleman in Gold-bowed Spectacles—What's in a Name?—Very Much in the Case of a Mining Company—We Go In on the " Hard-pan " Basis— Chasing Bubbles Through the Market—We Catch Them Without Difficulty—Fighting for Subscriptions—" Gregory Consolidated," and " Gunnell Gold " Books Open—A General Bursting.

LL former speculations in Wall Street had been merely ripples, or at most, waves of oscillation on the ocean of finance. This was a great tide wave, let us say rather an earthquake wave of the tropics, embracing in its huge semicircle, every form of hazardous venture. Its crest was already whitening with foam, but few, very few, caught the low, dull roar, which was soon to swell into thunder, as it broke on the beach—Ruin.

" The earth hath bubbles, as the water has."

These bubbles are stock companies, formed on the basis of property, the value of which, sometimes, bears to the nominal capital of the company, no more than the ratio of 1 to 1,000. The actual cost of the property of the Titan Ledge, and Back Mountain

Gold, Silver and Copper Company, for example, was $1,000. Its actual paid in capital, was $1,000,000. The Grand Junction Gold Mining Company's property cost $40,000. The subscribers to this stock, had to pay only $30 per share, and as there were 60,000 shares, they paid $1,800,000 for their interest. This was generous on the part of the projectors of the enterprise. They only made $1,760,000, when they might have made $3,000,000.

The flood of paper money poured from the steam presses, working day and night, sufficed now to float all kinds of speculative enterprises.

March, and the first days of April, 1864, were palmy days for the bubble blowers of Wall Street. Having inflated railroad-stocks to a profitable altitude, they proceeded to organize companies in all manner of those useful, costly, and beautiful things, which bountiful mother earth pours out of her lap in the rough. Samples of these things could be seen in Wall Street; brokers and bankers appeared to have been suddenly smitten with a passion for mineralogy. Their offices were transformed into cabinets of minerals, containing very fine specimens of sulphuret of lead, carbonate of copper, and oxide of iron, besides blocks of quartz bespangled with virgin gold, and lumps of coal which burned like a candle. Their talk was in mining slang, and "pockets," "fissure veins," "faults," "spurs," "lodes," "pyrites," "chimneys," ran all through their vocabulary. They had a deal to say about "Comstock Ledge," producing at that time, $1,000,000 per month, not to particularize respecting "Gould & Curry," "Ophir," "Yellow Jacket," "Crown Point," and a host of other successful claims.

They appeared to have transferred their speculative affections from Rock Island, Fort Wayne, and the railways generally, to "The Alligator Bayou Salt Company," "The Big Mountain Iron Company," "The Black Valley Coal Company," and "The Angels' Rest Quicksilver Company."

The press teemed with advertisements of these various enterprises, and some of the daily journals devoted columns to the record of what had been done, was doing, or was about to be done, in this new field of speculation. There were unsuspected gulches, where the precious metals were a drug. There were mountains of silver and copper, where junks could be had as a gift. Gold ready to be torn from the loose embrace of the maternal quartz. In fine, far off in the wilderness, as well as close to the fringes of civilization, there were hidden treasures without number, materials for wealth without stint, ungarnered, unminted, unmoulded, almost unwatched. These companies were organized in the following manner:

Mr. A——, a gentleman having some connection with the mining interests of the country, and owning a claim which had been staked out on some auriferous ledge in Colorado, being naturally desirous of disposing of his property to advantage, would go to some prominent banker, for the purpose of negotiating a sale. But prominent bankers are not in the habit of paying cash for property two thousand miles away. Accordingly, this particular banker would propose that the claim be made the basis of a stock company, and that the owner convey his property in it to the company, and receive therefor a certain sum

in cash, say $10,000, to be paid out of the first sub-
scriptions, and also a certain number of shares of the
stock. The nominal capital of the company to be,
say $2,000,000, represented by forty thousand shares
of $50 each, and the subscription price at which it
was to be offered to the public to be $25 per share.
This proposition being acceded to, specimens of the
gold ore perhaps in the form of sulphurets would
be submitted to some well-known chemist and min-
eralogist, who subjected them to an *assay*, and in due
time gave his certificate that these specimens furnish
by assay, $1,000 in gold to the ton of ore. (The
amount of gold extracted by an *assay* is, be it remembered, vastly greater than what is actually taken out
in the practical working of a mine.) The banker
would then approach some wealthy merchant and
hold out an inducement for him to lend his name as
one of the directors of the company. This inducement might be the gift of one or two thousand shares,
or the subscription price might be lowered from $25
to $12.50 in some cases, for the merchant, of course,
would wish to "go in" on "hard-pan," as it is called,
i. e., the lowest subscription price. The merchant's
name having been secured, it was an easy matter to
get other names which would add strength to the
company in the public estimation, among which generally were, a well known retired capitalist, a heavy
manufacturer, and perhaps a philanthropist, who desire to have the riches of the country developed.

Thereupon the company would be duly organized
under the general mining and manufacturing law of
the State of New York. A president, secretary and
treasurer would be chosen, the last of which offices

would be filled by the banker aforesaid. A name would then be selected which would be likely to strike the eye of the public. This name might be suggestive of what is at once rich, barbaric and inaccessible. Something lone, far off and guarded like the diamond of the desert, *e. g.*, the "Arizona Metaliferous and Scalping Ledge Gold and Silver Mining Company," or the "Mount St. Elias Silver Lode and Gold Vein Mining Company." Perhaps it might suggest birds, beasts or fishes of prey, *e. g.*, "The Vulture's Nest, or the Wolf's Peak, or the Pickerel Lake Nugget and Virgin Gold Pocket Company." All this gave play to the fancy of the future subscribers.

Then came the flaming prospectus, setting forth all the richness, activity and certain success of the enterprise, got up in the greatest splendor of typographical art, and worded cunningly with a view to any possible future legal liability of the projectors. The advertisement in the daily journals, set forth that the subscription books were open for a *limited number* of shares of the company (no personal liability of the stock-holders), at the office of the banker aforesaid, at the low price of $25 per share.

"Don't all speak at once, gentlemen! The shares are going off very rapidly; only one thousand are left, but we have reserved a few shares of treasury stock for our friends, which can be had by *immediately* applying to the office of ——, the banker, as the books are to be closed irrevocably on the 10th instant."

Somehow there always is a large reserve of treasury stock for the friends of the projectors in all these cases.

On the first of April, the whole market hummed

and rang again, with the most tempting solicitations to subscribe and make a fortune. The bubbles swelled, and shone with all the colors of the rainbow, while each investor gazed upon them through the prism of hope and fancy, which lent new glories to the iridescent, but, alas! unsubstantial orbs.

Bubble companies have their scouts and whippers-in. Outside machinery. These gentry are on the look-out for one hundred thousand dollar men. They scrutinize the bank accounts of operators, and track their profits. They point their detecting fingers at columns of figures, and then make the acquaintance of the man who piles up the money represented by the figures, to the ultimate end of making themselves familiar even to the handling of the piler's money.

The scout who tracked the profits of the quartette, named in our last chapter, was a corpulent gentleman, who wore gold-bowed spectacles. E—— tells me, that ever since March, 1864, he can never see a pair of gold-bowed spectacles, without a sense of goneness in the region of his pantaloon right pocket. He was presented to us, by his request, one day just after dinner. He saw us go into Delmonico's, and waited for us to come out. A kitten might play with a Wall Street financier, after a dinner at Delmonico's, particularly when he had that day bagged a profit of $29,000 on Ohio and Mississippi certificates. He invited us to his office, which was round the corner, on the first floor. The bubble-blower's office is often on the first floor, for he knows that the successful operator dislikes to exercise his gastrocuemius by climbing stairs.

In a twinkling we found ourselves in the spider's

19

parlor. It was a complete curiosity-shop. Models of petroleum barrels, made by a new machine, which took a log of wood into its jaws, chewed it for five minutes, and then threw it out again, a perfect barrel, statuettes of nymphs, made out of cannel-coal, small hydrostatic presses, etc. The walls of the parlor were papered with prospectuses of companies. The mantle-piece and tables spread with specimens of ore. Specks of gold winked out of masses of quartz. Crystals of lead, shone like candelabra. Virgin copper blushed by the side of its green-eyed sister, the carbonate of the same metal. On the wall, above the chimney-piece, was a section of a quartz ledge in profile, which resembled a rocky giant, with his face carved as if into a fixed chuckle, over the nuggets buried in his capacious pockets. The corpulent gentleman produced a box of Partaga firsts, out of a drawer in his desk, and furtively drew forth from the recesses of a cupboard, a bottle which looked as though it might have been recently dusted, to give it the appearance of age. The sherry from this bottle, tasted of alum, burnt sugar, and bitter almonds, but the partagas were unimpeachable.

Then came business. Our host rattled away gaily, and at length remarked (quite incidentally) that he never speculated in railway-stocks. He thought that he was the true benefactor of the human race, who succeeded in developing the internal resources of his country. Then he took high patriotic grounds, and waxed eloquent. It was the bounden duty of every capitalist to take a pecuniary interest in the great work of bringing out the riches of that magnificent wilderness, stretching out from where the mighty

THE END OF A GREAT SPECULATOR.

KINGDON & BOYD S.

father of waters rolled his torrent, to the shores of the Pacific, etc. At the conclusion of his oration, he exhibited his specimens. First, lead. We looked rather coldly on the fine crystals of this metal, as he turned them around and made them sparkle, for at that very moment, at least two of us had, folded up in very small compass in our pocket-books, several hundred shares of Buck's Lead Company, which the year before we had bought at the highest market price, and which was then selling at one dollar a share. He seemed quickly to discover the secret of our coldness on the subject of lead, and judiciously changed the subject, dropping his lead, and sounding us on the subject of gold. His free gold specimens were really splendid, but his sulphurets were his pride. They had been found to produce from five to twenty thousand dollars to the ton, by *assay*, and he showed us certificates of eminent chemists to that effect.

"Were these picked or only average specimens?"

"They were," he replied, "only average specimens, the run of the mine."

Next, he mentioned the names of leading public men associated with him in these laudable enterprises, and showed us their autographs on his books; and having at length exhausted his theme, concluded with a brief peroration, in which he did not fail delicately to hint at the immorality of stock-jobbing in Wall Street, and broadly express his conviction that every capitalist would do well to "salt down" a large proportion of his profits derived from stock-speculation, into something like a permanent investment in these mining enterprises, which could not fail to pay him a large return. He would only add, "that the demand for these shares was very great, and he could not say how long the opportunity would be open to subscribe for them." We had been inoculated and the virus worked.

In five days we were striking a bargain with the corpulent gentleman in gold-bowed spectacles, on the subscription price to four different gold mining companies, viz.: the Woolah-Woolah Gulch Gold Mining and Stamping Company. Capital, $3,000,000; shares numbering thirty thousand; par value, $100; subscription price, $60 per share. The Gulliver Canon Gold and Silver-Lead Mining and Water Sluice Company. Capital, $8,000,000; shares numbering one hundred and sixty thousand; par value, (we should not forget the par value,) $50; subscription price, $25 per share. The Federal Republic Gold Dust and Silver Dirt Mining Company. Capital, $2,500,000; shares numbering five hundred thousand; par value, $5; subscription price, $3 per share. (This was the biggest swindle of all). And, lastly, The Dry Digging and Gold Washing Company. Capital, $800,000; shares numbering twenty thousand; par value, $40; subscription price, $15 per share.

We objected to these subscription prices. We demanded to be let in, if at all, on the "hard-pan" price, and at length we thought we had carried our point, when twenty per cent. was knocked off from the subscription price, as a special favor, which fact, of course, we were never to mention to a living soul.

The mining-bubble fever rose higher as March rolled away. We began to look for other invest-

ments on the "hard-pan" basis. It was not difficult
to find them. Opportunities presented themselves
on the first story; and above us, on the second and
third stories, below us in the basement, as well as in
windows and hallways. The Newspapers teemed
with them. Little boys stood on the corners and
handed elegant prospectuses to the passers-by. Mineralogists and geologists were in clover.

We had commenced with gold and we ran down
the scale according to value, through silver, copper,
lead and graduated into iron. Then we commenced
over again with the rocks, starting with marble, and
ending in trap and sandstone. After that we got into
fluids. This move carried us into petroleum, of which,
more hereafter. E. O—— (a deacon) introduced us
to iron and coal. The projector in this enterprise was
another professional bubble-blower, who had an office
not a thousand miles from Pine Street. He was a tall
man, with a hang-dog look, a fringe of gray whiskers
and a baritone voice, who delivered orations on the
importance of getting ready to supply the South with
iron and coal, as soon as the war was over. We took
a few hundred shares of the Fallset Iron and Coal
Company, against the happening of that much wished
for and long expected event.

Late in March, the fever had risen to its height.
One day about this time, E—— and I saw L——
issue from the swinging doors of Delmonico, looking
very red and smiling. He hailed us beamingly, and
announced to us the interesting fact, that on the morrow the books of the "Gregory Consolidated" would
be opened at the office of J. R—— & Co. He had
just spoken (he said) to three capitalists, who had

told him (in confidence) that here was a great chance. " Don't fail to be on hand to-morrow," said he, " there is *only a limited* number of the shares to be had, and there will be a great rush to subscribe." Then jocularly bidding us to charge the next morning, where we saw his purple necktie wave, he disappeared through the door of the banking house of Morse & Co.

The next day, the 31st of March, was fine. The golden sun threw its golden rays on the curtains and carpets of our eastward-facing chamber, as E—— and I, rose bright and early, and throwing open the casement, like Parsees, paid it our adorations, as the tutelar genius, and fit symbol of Gregory Consolidated Gold Mining Company!

A crowd of expectant subscribers, were hovering about the office of J—— R—— & Co., at an early hour. Few of them were recognized as regular operators in the street. Most of them were outsiders who had come prepared to invest in something that *would pay*. One man, the proprietor of a millinery store, up town, pulled off his glove, and showed me four one thousand dollar bills, which he was about to cash down, in return for one hundred shares of G. C. Co. Another was a clergyman, from one of the river counties, who had taken the early train down to the city that morning, in order to secure fifty shares of the stock. Lawyers, doctors, mechanics, and retired capitalists were also fully represented As soon as the books were opened, L—— who was the tallest, and most robust of the quartette, succeeded in establishing himself in the line which extended from the counter, where the subscription book lay, to the street, not however without a brief, but severe struggle with a short resolute-looking countryman, who, after he had yielded his position, was heard stoutly affirming his right of precedence.

The capital stock of Gregory Consolidated was $5,000,000. Its shares numbered fifty thousand, at the par value of $100 each, and the subscription price was $40 per share. In one hour from the time when the books opened, the whole amount, $2,000,000, was subscribed!

A few tardy individuals now made their appearance, eager to subscribe, but too late. They bid two per cent. premium for four thousand shares, but in vain; the holders of the stock could not be induced to part with their precious investment. L—— divided his subscription of one thousand shares equally among the quartette. Then he led the way to the office of Morse & Co. We followed him, and here another scene took place. This time it was in Gunnell Gold Company, the subscription books of which were open at that office. The subscribers to this stock actually fought to get their subscriptions recorded. After a short struggle the whole capital was subscribed for, and $100,000 more. The subscribers to the overplus begged and importuned the projectors of the company to surrender to them the individual interest they had reserved for themselves. Their prayers were answered; the projectors generously waived their private interests and gave up their reserved stock to their petitioners.

During the six weeks which intervened between March 1st and April 10th, 1864, the nominal capital of the joint stock companies presented to the public in Wall Street, has been estimated at $300,000,000, and the amount of cash embarked in these different enterprises, is said to have aggregated over $60,000,000.

It would be injustice to say that all of these were bubbles, and incorrect to say that all of them were ultimately failures. But the large majority belonged to that class of enterprises of which we can only say

"They rise, they shine, evaporate and fall."

Let the history of the Mining Board which was subsequently formed, tell the fate of these companies. Let those glossy dividendless certificates be brought forth from the unopened drawers of many a safe, bureau, and closet; then let them be framed and hanged over the doors of investors as a warning against Bubble-companies.

CHAPTER XIX.

PANIC — FALL OF A. W. MORSE — CLEARING AWAY THE WRECK.

Going In for *Just One More Operation*—Standing on the Apex of a Fortune—The Bull-leader in His Glory—Helping the Unlucky Ones— Daniel Drew Selling Erie—A Constitutional Bull—The Last Spirt in Stocks—Signs and Auguries of the Disaster—Morse Trying to Sell Fort Wayne—Planning the Last Stroke—The Market Trembles, Totters and Falls—Panic All Day and All Night—The Evening Exchange Pandemonium—" 'Tis Done ; but Yesterday a King, and Now He is a Nameless Thing, so Abject yet Alive "—Morse After His Ruin—The Last Scene of all that " Strange Eventful Story "— The Fortunes of The Quartette—Meeting a Prophet of Evil—A Black Sunday and a Blue Monday—Bubble Company Stocks at a Discount.

E may assert with confidence, that, granting these three things, viz.: that a man has become habituated to speculation in stocks; that he has $100,000 in the bank, and that he daily visits the stock-market; then, and in that case, he will be sure to make *just one more venture.*

The experience of hundreds and thousands of operators, will attest the truth of this proposition. Speculation, at first a sentiment, or if you please, a taste, passes next into a habit, then it grows into a passion, a master passion, which like Aaron's serpent, swallows up and strengthens itself with other passions. It becomes at last more fierce than anger, more gnawing than jealousy, more greedy than avarice, more absorbing than love. The stock-market may be likened to a withered old harridan, enameled, painted, and decked in the latest mode, which leers on the speculator, and points to golden prizes, that like the desert mirage, fades away and leaves him to his ruin. The chronicles of speculation are little else than a list of tornadoes and wrecks.

On the 10th of April I stood $160,000 ahead of the market, without counting the profits on Canton. One hundred thousand dollars of this amount was cash in bank, forty thousand was invested snugly and permanently in various enterprises, looking to the "development of the internal resources of the country," and twenty thousand was in the hands of brokers. Included in this amount, was the five thousand dollars margin on five hundred shares of Canton at 38. This was the apex of my fortunes, to which I had climbed, with the ladder of the five hundred dollars planted on Old Southern in 1857.

"*Facilis descensus Averni.*"

On the 1st of April, the bull-leader, Morse, was at the height of his glory. Every stock that he touched had turned into gold for the fortunate buyers. Rock Island, Erie, Fort Wayne, Pittsburg, Ohio and Mississippi certificates responded in succession to the wand of the great enchanter. Great fortunes had dropped from his hands into the pockets of his followers. Not content with making the rich richer, he had lifted many an unfortunate out of the slough of Wall Street poverty—the worse species of poverty —into affluence. One of these unfortunates was L. H——, who had lost everything—money, credit and friends. He went to Morse in the form of a mendicant, disclosing his forlorn condition and begging that he would assist him. Morse took him by the hand and told him to buy two hundred shares of Fort Wayne, and send it in to his (Morse's) office for his account. L. H——, instead of buying two hundred shares, bought seven hundred shares. Morse thought this a little cheeky, but took charge of the stock, and in six weeks, by this and other successful operations, under the wing of his generous banker, L. H—— made $50,000. Many such deeds as this marked the career of the great speculator, and should help to cover his after pecuniary short-comings.

During that brief, but brilliant campaign, he had fought the bears as one would his natural enemies, and now throughout the whole market, it was in vain to search for any of that tribe. Yes, there was one— an old veteran who did not fear to sell stocks. It could be no other than Daniel Drew. While Erie was selling from 128–130, every day a nimble young broker could have been seen reporting to him the price of Erie, whereat he would chuckle and give orders to sell by the thousand shares. He was converting his bonds into stock and delivering it to fill his contracts. He also obtained authority from the Legislature to increase the capital stock of Erie, and used ten thousand shares of the new stock to load up the bulls at these inflation prices.

Early in the month last named, there came a lull in the market. Then a sudden leap upwards, and the fire burned more fiercely than ever. It was like a tongue of flame, shooting from a palace, just before it falls in ruins; the funeral pyre of a thousand speculators. This spirt in the market, took place at the

Evening Exchange. It deceived many, and among them the writer of this narrative. Three times had the market been lulled into dullness, and each time the lull had been followed by a new burst upward. Then came regrets that I had ever sold out, and calculations of how much I would have made by holding my stocks.

W. B. C—— was a bull, from the crown of his head, to the sole of his foot. In all his veins there was never a drop of ursine blood. Consequently, he had not yet sold his stocks, which, for a man who started six months before, with only $6,000, showed him an enormous profit. "Let your profits run," was his constant cry. For two weeks he had fairly bristled with information, (commonly called "points,") respecting certain roads, especially Reading, Fort Wayne, and Galena. These stocks had hardly yet begun to rise. The names of the manipulators were a tower of strength. Money was so easy, and the bull-element was so powerful. The earnings of the roads, too, justified a further rise. Consolidation, Morse, W. B. Ogden, etc.,—these were the themes of his taurine dissertations.

On the morning after the last upward leap of stocks, I drew out sixty thousand dollars, distributed it among three different brokers and bought three thousand two hundred shares of railroad stocks of which one thousand was Galena, at 142; one thousand Fort Wayne, at 145; nine hundred (full shares) Reading, at 163, and three hundred Old Southern, at 117. Before night the market sagged and my stocks could not have been sold without a considerable loss. I was like a wild thing caught in a trap, not daring to break away with the loss of a limb, and waiting in terror the coming of the cruel hunter.

Miserable days passed away in agonies of doubt. There are seasons when Wall Street men are agitated by

" More pangs and fears than wars or women have."

when after fortune has smiled upon him, he suddenly sees her beginning to frown. He has incurred a small loss which he dares not accept, but fears every day a greater loss. If there is then any handwriting on the wall of the speculator's banqueting hall, he sees it, aye, and interprets it, perchance; and yet, though " the joints of his loins are loosed, and his knees smite one against another," he keeps his seat and flies not from the enemy as terrible to him as the Medes and Persians were to the king of Babylon.

Signs and portents of coming disaster multiplied, as that weary week drew to its close. Wise financial prophets like Jay Cooke, had been heard to predict an approaching evil. The Secretary of the Treasury had been selling millions of gold, and locking the proceeds in greenbacks, in the sub-treasury. Money was palpably tightening. Conservative banking-houses, such as Lockwood & Co., refused any longer to *buy* stocks on margins, or, except for cash; but offered to sell stocks short for their customers, on ten per cent. margins. Wild rumors were afloat, of how Morse had gone down on his knees to certain bank cashiers, and begged for a million dollars on Fort Wayne, as collateral, but without avail. At the Evening Exchange on Friday, the 15th of April, he mounted the rostrum beside the president, while one of his lieutenants stood beside him. In a husky voice, and with a feeble smile upon his haggard face, he offered to *sell* ten or twenty thousand shares of Fort Wayne. A shiver went through the hushed crowd, and low, ominous whispers were heard, "The bull leader isn't quite himself to-night." "What's the matter with Morse?" "Is he in liquor?" But all these signs of disaster failed to open the eyes of the deluded multitude, who still clung to their treacherous favorites.

Speculative fevers must run their course, before they turn the sharp corner which leads into the great darkness. Stocks had now reached this corner. Men's nerves are not of steel. Julius Cæsar had his Brutus, Anthony W. Morse had his Secretary Chase. The causes which were to precipitate ruin had been silently gathering force. The chain had been heated and welded, and rove into the huge block, which had been hoisted and suspended aloft. Its fall was to crush and pulverize the fabric of a thousand stately fortunes, and now the chain was to be severed by the hand of panic.

On Saturday the 16th, and Sunday the 17th, Morse took a survey of the market. He had six weeks before, pledged himself to a crowd of capitalists, who ranged under his banner, to lead them to victory and wealth. Now they crowded around him, and begged him to redeem his pledge. His resolution was soon taken. Like a commander-in-chief hard pressed by the enemy, he determined to abandon all his other fortresses, and concentrate his forces in one stronghold. Early on Monday morning he decided to sell all the other stocks he had, and then hold up Fort Wayne against all odds.

The 18th of April fell on Monday. The interval of Holy-day, had only strengthened the downward tendency. When he entered the regular board that morning, he found nearly every broker eager to sell at heavy concessions, before the call of stocks opened, and the feeling in the street was still worse. He turned and left the room. At half-past eleven o'clock, a broker rose in his seat, and announced the failure of Morse & Co. An appalling stillness, like that which precedes a tornado, followed the words, then the storm burst. The board-room seemed suddenly transformed into a Cyclopean work-shop, where a hundred great trip-hammers were being plied. Pillar after pillar toppled over, till the dome fell. The palace of enchantment, builded by a strong and cunning magician of so many golden hopes, passed away like a cloud-pageant.

A three months mad revelry of speculation, in which were concentrated all the emotions, all the incidents of a century of sober, legitimate traffic—then the dark dawn of another melancholy awakening!

All day long the panic raged, without pause or hindrance. The Evening Exchange was a Pandemonium. A crowd of ruined operators reeled and surged up to the rostrum, half crazed by their losses, and stupefied or maddened by drink, while the whole room rang with yells and curses. The space outside the railing was jammed with weary faces, on which was written only the word—ruin! Close to the door stood a figure in widow's weeds, wild eyed and shrinking. She had risked her last dollar on Fort Wayne, which was selling for 90. She stood there only for a moment, and then passed out into the damp, chilly night forever.

Above all the chorus of execrations was heard the word "Morse." Human nature now showed its basest side. No epithet too vile with which to couple the name of the prostrate financier. He had fallen like Lucifer in one day, from the zenith of his fame. The men who, but yesterday, extolled him to the skies, now vied with each other in cursing him. His failure was irreparable. He owed millions to his brother brokers, and to depositors, who had trusted him. The lion of the hour had become a dead jackass. The king of the market was a lurking fugitive. Men calling themselves gentlemen, met him in the street, and showered abuse upon him. Shoulder-hitters, who had lost some of their ill-gotten gains by his fall, sought him out, and struck him like a dog.

This was outrageous. Let us give Anthony W. Morse his due. He *was* a great arithmetician, a shrewd, far-seeing, bold financier. The subsequent history of some of the stocks in which he dealt with such recklessness, has justified his then apparently wild predictions. Fort Wayne, Rock Island, and Pittsburg have proved a mine of wealth to those who bought them in December, 1864, and have held them to the present day. He was a free-hearted generous man, and would if he could, have nullified the decrees of fate, and made the fortunes of his followers. But like most great speculators he got at last to believe in his star. Then he attempted impossibilities. A longer and more cautious training in the school of finance, and it might have been different. But it was not so ordained. The example of A. W. Morse, only serves as a moral to close the lesson taught by Wall Street speculation.

His end speaks to all like a warning voice. He departed from the arena, a stripped, penniless, heart-stricken man. Out of the troops of wealthy friends which but lately clustered about him, only one or two still clung to him. He had now only the shadow of a great name. He was pointed out in the streets as the man who had once set the market in a blaze, but capitalists shrunk from him as if he had the leprosy. His attenuated face now and then flitted past the streaming throng in Broadway. One day, more than a year after his failure, he was seen on the street, and Fort Wayne *rose five per cent.* His name still spread alarm among the bears, and inspired the bulls with new courage, like Ziska's drum beaten at the front of the battallions of the departed king. Then came disease gnawing at his nerves and heart-strings. He became a changed man. No longer blithe and gay of mien, but morose and irritable. The vast burden of his debts and losses wore upon him. He sought relief in gambling, his old excitement, but under a new form. A gentleman who had lost by Morse's failure, one evening visited, out of curiosity, a notorious gambling hell in Twenty-fourth Street. Sitting near the dealer was one whom he remembered having seen in happier days. A gaunt, pallid face, the features sharpened by the fell disease under which he was suffering, and wearing those death-like lines with which consumption marks its prey. Alas! how changed from that Morse, who but the year before, had led his dashing ranks to the summits of the market. A few months more and he lay upon his death-bed in a second-class boarding-house, and without means to pay for the common necessities of life.

20

Even when he died, his landlady held his body for the trifling debt which he owed her. It was only when some friend stepped forward and paid the sum, that the funeral rites could be performed over all that remained of what was once a king of Wall Street.

The feeling and condition of the stock-men, after the panic of April 18th, 1864, had subsided, can never be forgotten by the actors in those scenes. Wall Street was like a city of the dead, a kind of Pompeii or Herculaneum, when the volcanic fires were still seething, and the lava still hardly cooled, which had buried, in the course of one brief sun, the high raised hopes, the garnered fortunes, and the financial identity of thousands. Men hardly dared inquire what might be the status of their debtors, for fear they should know too clearly, the certainty and irreparableness of their own losses.

In the midst of this universal distrust, unfounded rumors were bruited abroad, concerning the solvency of wealthy houses. One report said that Lockwood & Co. had failed. Another, that D. Groesbeck & Co. had succumbed, but this latter story was promptly squelched, by the card of that firm, published in the daily journals, showing the snug amount of $1,300,-000 to their credit in bank, and offering to carry stocks on a reasonable margin, and at six per cent. interest.

But how stood the quartette after the storm? During the week preceding the panic, we were engaged in bolstering each other up, not by money, for we thought ourselves impregnable in that respect, but with arguments in favor of another rise. We knew we were wrong, but tried to convince ovrselves that we were right. On Saturday, the pressure of our internal convictions became too strong to withstand. We decided to unload. And now we made the same mistake, made by so many others. We limited our brokers in the price at which they were to sell. I succeeded in getting rid of three hundred shares of Old Southern, at a loss of $2,800. The afternoon found me with two thousand nine hundred shares still on hand, on which there was by this time a heavy loss, of which I was reminded, in a disagreeable way, by a call from various brokers, *for more margin.* L—— thought there was a "better feeling," towards night. E—— said that he had resolved to hold his stocks through everything, and W. B. C—— said there would be a reaction next week, and hummed "rally round the flag boys, rally round the flag;" but this patriotic pæan sounded like a dirge, as he hummed it.

We started to go home early in the afternoon. At the corner of William Street and Exchange Place, we met S——. He was once a man of wealth, but he had left it all in that same unfathomable abyss on the brink of which we were just then standing. He was a harmless but very disagreeable lunatic, a Cassandra, who predicted nothing but evil. A horrible man to look upon. The skin on his face was like yellow wrinkled parchment, his mouth a chasm, his eyes a glassy blue, over all of which a ghastly smile constantly played. He had for six weeks been uttering his doleful prophecies. When he caught sight of us, he began to throw up his hands and give vent to hollow laughs, which grated very disagreeably on our keyed-up nerves. "I told you so! I told you so! Ha, ha, ha!" We tried to shake him off, but he stuck to us like a leech, hovered about us like an owl, and chuckled when he had wrenched out of us the reluctant acknowledgment that we had not yet sold our stocks. This conversation was unpleasant to men who had lost altogether during the past four days, one hundred thousand dollars. At last he left us, shaking his skinny fingers in our faces, and telling us to "look sharp at stocks on Monday, and see how we came out." S—— was only one of the prophets of evil who seemed to dog our steps during the next thirty-six hours. We met them at the Evening Exchange, in the Fifth Avenue Reading Room, on the street, everywhere. Just as E—— and I were doffing our unmentionables preparatory to seeking our couches in that room, which three weeks before had been illuminated by the sun of "Gregory Consolidated," but which now was barely lighted from the single gas jet, which burned blue on that moist spring evening, L—— made his appearance and said he had just heard P——, a wealthy operator offer a heavy bet that Morse would break before the next week was past.

The Sunday's rest and quiet weighed upon us like an incubus. On Monday, we screwed our courage to the sticking point, and gave the order to sell every thing at the market price. But this order was not given till after the failure of Morse had been announced. The quartette stood by the door of the Regular Board for one hour. E—— was looking pale, L—— scowling; W. B. C—— strove to look cheerful, and failed.

In three hours we knew the very worst. Out of

$120,000 cash in hand the week before, only about $20,000 was left to me. The Canton profits and margin were swept away, and I held only my mining stocks as the memento of my forty thousand loose cash. These stocks were neither saleable nor negotiable, of which fact I was disagreeably reminded by the sardonic smile of my bank cashier, when I applied to him the day after the panic, for a small loan of $1,000 on what had cost me $40,000.

CHAPTER XX.

MARGINS, POOLS, CORNERS, POINTS, AND OF HOW BROKERS MAKE THEIR MONEY.

Philosophy of Rises and Panics in Wall Street—Margins Before and Since 1862—Effect of Doing Business on Margins—Different Kinds of Pools—Percentages Paid by Bears for the Privilege of Selling Stocks—Do Pools Pay?—Instances of Unsuccessful or Successful Pools—Why They are Generally Unsuccessful—Trying to Unload Upon the Shoulders of the Outsiders—Points! What are They?— Engineering a Short Interest—How Brokers Make Money in Pools —The Time to Buy, and the Time to Sell Stocks—They Sell or Buy in the Stocks of their Customers—The Percentage Paid for Carrying and Turning Stocks—Jolly Old Boys Keeping Their Dimes Busy.

HE first thing a man does after he has recovered from the shock of a great and mysterious disaster, is to philosophize about the causes of that disaster in particular, and other disasters of a similar nature.

When do great rises and great panics in stocks take place? Rises take place when the majority of operators *desire* to buy and buy. Panics, when the majority of operators *desire* to sell and sell. By the term *majority* I mean the greater number of persons, and the larger amount of *money*.

This brings us to the matter of *margins*, a word which we have already defined. This word *margins* contains the *essence of stock-speculation*. Great fortunes are made and lost by speculating on margins.

It is the facility with which large amount of stocks can be bought with a small amount of money-margin, that stimulates great rises, and it is the facility with which those same money-margins are wiped out when stocks fall, that creates the fear which precipitates a panic.

As already described, the amount of the margin depends on circumstances. Before the late war, stocks could be bought generally on five per cent. of the par value of the stock; e. g., a hundred shares of New York Central of the par value of $10,000 (market value 70) called for five hundred dollars margin.

But the heavy fluctuations in prices produced by the greenback inflation which commenced in 1862, rendered larger margins necessary to guard the broker against loss. Ten per cent., and by conservative brokerage houses, twenty per cent. was then generally exacted from their customers. But many of the new tribe of brokers who did business on the curb-stone or in the Public Board, were still willing to buy stocks on five and even three per cent, margin, protecting themselves against loss by continually watching the market and selling their customers' stocks on the least alarm.

It will be readily seen that as the fear of loss is stronger when a man has bought stocks on a small margin, he will be more likely to sell frequently and change his position continually, very much, of course, to the advantage of his broker. One brokerage firm, doing business on small margins, has derived an immense income in commissions from their customers in this way. When everything is bright and stocks are advancing, brokers are often very lib-

eral in allowing their customers to buy, but when a
panic comes, accompanied by a scarcity of money,
they will refuse to carry stocks on any amount of
margin. Their customer must then either pay for
his stocks in cash, or *sell them.* The latter is generally the only practicable course The stocks are accordingly slaughtered, *i. e.*, sold out at low figures
with loss, and even ruin to the customer. This was
the case in the panic of April, 1864. Man, everywhere a gregarious animal, is never more so than
when in Wall Street. A flock of sheep following the
bell wether trotting up hill,—this is a picture of the
stock market, during a rise. Now supposing that
same flock sees, on the top of the hill, a scare-crow;
it wheels about and rushes down hill twice as fast as it
goes up. Lambkins are trampled under the feet of
their maternal ewes, and the bell wether tumbles
head over heels. When the flock reaches the bottom
of the hill, it turns about and stares with innocent
wonder, at the scare-crow on the top of the hill. This
is a picture of the stock-market in a panic. Everybody seems crazy to sell. The customers dog their broker's footsteps, begging them, as a personal favor, to
sell their stocks at any price, only to sell immediately.
The brokers are apparently as eager to sell as their
customers. Capitalists who might keep their stock,
catch the infection and sell. To crown all, the bears
emerge from their dens, swell the panic-chorus, and
sell everything in expectation of lining their pockets
by the decline.

Such are some of the beauties of the margin system. In fact a margin may be called a device con-
trived to create rises and panics, and to keep the

market in a ferment, so that brokers may make, and their customers lose, money.

As for pools, cliques and rings; terms which are used synonymously in these pages, these combinations are traps in more senses than one, for they not only serve to ensnare the bears by cornering them, but generally to result in loss to the members of the combinations themselves.

Pools are of different kinds.

First, there is the secret pool, the operations whereof are carried on in darkness, until some fine day the bears find themselves unexpectedly in a tight place.

Second, the open and above-board pool, into which the bears walk, because the very frankness with which the combination talk of their plan, leads the bears to suppose that there is nothing in it, for who would suspect a poolist of frankness. This species of combination is of rare occurrence.

Third, the moderate pool, which is satisfied with five or ten per cent. advance in the stock under manipulation. Daniel Drew has often worked Erie on this plan, taking in as his associates, only one or two members, and holding only five, ten or twenty thousand shares of the floating stock in some favorable conjuncture of the market.

Fourth, the grasping and voracious pool, which aims at the entire control of a certain stock and the extermination of outside sellers.

Fifth, the vindictive pool, which aims to punish its opposers. Vanderbilt and Drew have both tried their hands at this game.

Pools may be also classified into two other forms.

First, those having for their object the raising of

stocks, artificially, irrespective of their intrinsic values. The more worthless the stock, the more men will go short of it. This better enables the combination to manipulate the stock, and finally to compel the short sellers to settle up on the terms which they may dictate, the Cumberland pool of 1866 and 1867, when that worthless fancy was raised from 35 to 90 is an example.

Second, those having for their object, the control of stocks possessing a high intrinsic value. The New York Central pool of recent fame, is an instance of this second species.

By far the larger portion of the short sales now made in Wall Street, are transacted by selling the stock, and then borrowing it for delivery. Suppose B—— desires to go short of Erie, when all the floating stock is in the hands of a pool. B—— has no Erie stock, remember, but sells, that is agrees to deliver, one hundred Erie at 30, to C——. He then borrows the one hundred shares of the pool, and delivers it to C——, who pays for it by a certified check for $3,000. This certified check B—— passes over to the pool, and then owes it (the pool) one hundred shares of Erie, which is payable on demand. On returning them one hundred shares of Erie, the pool pays B—— his $3,000. If the stock should go up to 40, B—— in that case, if called upon for the stock, is obliged to go into the market and pay $4,000 for his Erie, thus losing $1,000 by the operation, which sum is presumed to go into the pockets of the combination. In some cases, when the pool has control of all, or nearly all the floating stock, they compel B—— to pay them a fixed sum, instead of calling upon him to return the stock. When a pool holds most of the floating stock of a railroad or other company, they are in a position to play the lock-up game, in other words to make the corner. They call upon the bears to whom they have loaned stock, to return it, and if they fail to do so, they buy them in under the rule as already described, or allow them to keep their contracts open by paying a fixed sum daily, for that privilege. As high as one per cent. per day, *i. e.*, one hundred dollars for each hundred shares of the stock due, has been sometimes exacted. The bear, it will be remembered, gets interest generally on his contract, but in this case, he is paying interest at the ruinous rate of over three hundred per cent. per annum, and may be in addition finally compelled to buy in his stock at a heavy loss.

The difference in price between *cash stock* which is deliverable and payable the same day it is bought, and regular stock which is deliverable and payable the next day, has occasionally run as high as five per cent., and in the case of stock sold, seller three, as high as ten per cent., and of a stock sold, seller thirty, as high as thirty per cent. Difference has been paid between the seller's option price and the cash price. But this occurs rarely, except when a general locking-up of the stock by a pool takes place, and is invariably when the pool is trying to unload, or to compel the bears to cover.

How many of these combinations make money out of their operations? Very few. A large number actually lose money. A bare list of those which have proved disastrous to their projectors, would fill the rest of this chapter. Among them, we may note the

Morris Canal and Banking Pool, of some thirty years since. In this case, the bears refused to settle their contracts, and the matter was left to the arbitration of the Board of Brokers, who decided that it was a conspiracy, and accordingly released the bears from their contracts. In the Norwich and Worcester Pool, Jacob Little lost $1,000,000, as related in our fourth chapter.

Within the past ten years, the successful pools may be almost numbered on one's fingers, while the names of those unsuccessful, are legion. The Hudson combination, which carried that stock to 180, in the summer of 1863, is said to have divided 12 per cent. among its members.

Of all the pools formed during the great rise of 1864, there was scarcely one, if any, that did not finally end in heavy loss to its members. The Morse Rock Island pool of December, 1863, and January, 1864, is said to have netted a profit of only 4½ per cent. But all the members of this combination, we believe, without exception, allowed their profits to remain in the hands of the bull-leader, until the panic of April following, swept them away. The great Pacific Mail pool, already mentioned, and more fully to be described hereafter, could however, hardly have failed to show a handsome profit to each of its members. The Vanderbilt pools have been thoroughly successful, because they have continued to hold and control the stocks of the Harlem, Hudson, and New York Central. But, the pool in Erie which lasted a year from April, 1865, to the same month in 1866, under the direction of Daniel Drew, is said to have netted a heavy loss to all its members except the old man and one or two of his friends. The same is true of the Erie pool, which lasted five or six months, during the summer and fall of 1866, and these are only a few out of a hundred similar cases.

The general result of these combinations, is to inflict great damage, first on the bears, who lose their money by selling the pool stocks short, and finally, on the bulls who have inflated the prices. The bears might appropriately say, under such circumstances, in the language of the great dramatist, slightly altered: "He that robs us (by a cornering operation,) doth not enrich himself, but makes us poor, indeed."

It will not be difficult to explain why it is that pools are so generally unsuccessful. They are treading on dangerous ground always. Even the deer will turn and stand at bay when hard pressed by the hunter, and how much more the veteran, resolute bear in Wall Street. Sometimes a powerful combination will be formed by those who are short of the market, to lock up money and thus break down their rivals by compelling them to sell out their stocks. Sometimes the directors of a railroad, the stock of which is under manipulation, will secretly issue a large amount of fresh stock, sell it to the pool at high prices, and then proclaim the fact of the new issue. This is sure to produce a panic in the stock and the pool is broken up. These tactics were resorted to, not only in the Old Southern A. G. Jerome pool, but in the more recent cases of Erie and Rock Island.

One of the greatest obstacles to the success of a pool, is the treachery of its members who, knowing when the summit price is reached, sell out their interest and perhaps go short of the stock besides. In this way, the pool find themselves saddled with a large amount of stock at high prices, since they are obliged to buy all the stock offered in the market, in order to keep up the price. Thereupon, after shouldering the weary weight for a season, they are forced at last to let it drop amid a hail-storm of anathemas from the poolists against their treacherous associates.. Again, supposing a pool has raised the price of the stock thirty per cent. above its original value, it does not follow from that circumstance that a profit of thirty per cent. will accrue. The cost of the stock bought at different prices, may average within ten per cent. of the inflated price, and after the short contracts have all been closed, the pool may find itself unable to sell at even an average of twenty per cent. below the ruling price.

All sorts of inventions are resorted to in that case. Sometimes a new pool is organized on the basis of the then market price, golden hopes are held out of putting the stock very much higher; new members are brought in and urged to take a large interest, so that the old members may slip out. If this plan is not feasible, various influences are brought to bear on the outside buyers, to induce them to come in and take the load. In some cases, the stock is allowed to drop heavily, and a new crop of bear contracts are garnered up; then the price is run up again, and the bears cover their contracts at a loss to themselves and at a profit to the ring. This process is repeated several times, the price going lower at each successive drop, until the ring, or pool, can show a net profit, or what is more probable, a net loss, on all their operations.

Pools and points, the two P's of Wall Street, are inseparably connected. A "point," as the reader is doubtless well aware, is a piece of information furnished by one operator to another, respecting the upward or downward course of a stock. The operator who gives the point, is presumed to know what he is talking about. He may have intimate relations with the director of some railroad company, the stock of which is actively dealt in, or he may himself be a director. Perhaps he is known to do his business in the office of a prominent brokerage-house, where pools are organized, or, which is more probable, he may be a member of a pool.

No one who has speculated in stocks, will have failed to notice how eagerly information is sought for, by parties interested in stocks. When a man is writhing under the sense of expected loss, or wildly eager to grasp a profit, his mind is like a photographer's negative plate, ready to receive the subtlest impressions. The first question which an operator asks his fellow, on meeting him in the morning, or in fact at any time during the day, is, "What do you think?" If he is a German, he says, "Vot you dinks?" If a Frenchman, "Vich is dat of vich you teenks?" He wishes to get an opinion respecting stocks, and this question often leads him to "points." These points are often given as merely rumors floating in the market, which the informant does not vouch for; he merely gives them as he has heard them. Sometimes, they are breathed into the ear of the operator, as facts not generally known, but which are now communicated to him alone, under the pledge of the strictest secrecy. The susceptible mind of the recipient of the rumors or facts, promptly makes its decision, and then acts on it, buying or selling, as the case may be. Thereafter he imparts the "point" to his nearest friend, who does not fail to spread the information for the benefit of *his* nearest friend.

In this manner, pools are enabled to engineer a short interest in a stock, and when they are ready to unload, they also make free use of points, in order to get the public to take their stock off from their hands.

Short sales are indispensable to a pool. A large part of the stock which they buy, is not actual stock, but contracts for the future delivery of stock, *i. e.*, short sales. These short sales benefit them in several ways, especially by enabling them to *carry* the stock by lending it to the short sellers. When a stock is heavily oversold at a low price, it is almost certain to go up, just as when the majority of operators are long of stocks at a high price it is as certain to fall.

Various methods are adopted to entice operators to sell short the stock which a pool have under their manipulation. Sometimes the price is made to simulate a weakness which deceives the street by producing the false impression that the price will soon be lower. This is the partridge trick. That game bird, it will be remembered, flutters as if wounded, in order to draw the hunter away from her young. As soon as the price of a stock looks "weak," it becomes the mark for short sales. The bears rush in and sell it under the expectation of a further decline. After a sufficient number of the contracts of these gentlemen have been taken by the pool, the price is lifted again, and the short sellers find themselves in the trap. This in the slang of the street is known as the "scoop game."

Instances are not unfrequent where members of the pool are paid by their leaders to solicit and procure short sales. One quarter per cent. has been occasionally paid on the short sales influenced and procured in this way.

B——, a member of the pool goes to a friend or acquaintance and gives him a "point." The pool, he may say is short of money, and is paying heavy rates to have their stock carried, or he may simply decry the market value of the stock. If, on the faith of what he says, his friend should sell one hundred shares, the operator receives twenty-five dollars for his wages. This amounts to robbery, for it is nothing else than hiring a man to put his hand into his friend's pocket and taking one, two or three thousand dollars therefrom, and delivering it to the pool, since the short sale thus induced, is quite certain to be covered at a loss.

We have stated that scarcely any one ever makes any money in these stock pools. We should except from this statement the brokers, who, whether the pool ever divides a profit or not, are sure to receive their profit. If they are members of the pool, they know exactly when to slip out. If they are merely the manipulators of the stock, they know just when to buy and just when to realize their profit outside of the combination. Their surest source of profit, however, is from the enormous brokerages resulting from the purchases and sales which they make for the pool's account. During the three, six or nine months

21

that the operations of one of these operators may continue, the whole capital stock of a railroad amounting, perhaps, to six or eight millions, may be bought and sold by the brokers of the combination, four or five times over, and the brokerage on these transactions often amounts to more than $50,000. Besides this brokerage, there are multitudes of pickings in the way of interest and profitable turns, which help out the sum total.

In general speculation, everything seems to work for the benefit of the broker. One of his principal sources of revenue which we have already alluded to, is the use he makes of his customer's stocks.

It is an adage in the stock-market, that the outside public, as it is called, buys stocks when they are high, and sells them when they are low. When a dull season has been succeeded by an active market, and stocks have risen very high, the entire speculative community seems to have emptied itself into the purlieus of the stock-market. From many a lonely hamlet, from many an inland city, as well as from the brown-stone fronts, and marble hotels of the great metropolis itself, they pour amain into Wall Street, to *buy high-priced stocks.* A few weeks before, the same stocks at a price twenty per cent. lower, failed to tempt them, but now, stocks have become suddenly valuable. "Points" are communicated on every side, with the greatest freedom. The prevailing feeling says *buy.* The broker says *buy.* The pools say *buy,* for this rampant market is their harvest time, in which they shuffle off their loads upon the shoulders of the new gangs of buyers.

The hour and the men for the brokers have now both

come. The public give orders to buy these high priced stocks. The brokers execute their orders, and buy. But speedily a cracking sound is heard. The market prices begin to break. The broker quietly throws his customer's stocks on the market. This helps on the decline. The customer, in sad unconsciousness that his stocks have been sold, clings to his supposed loss. Then he is called upon for more margin, but when stocks have fallen ten or fifteen per cent. from where he has bought, they no longer seem valuable, and at last he gives the order to sell, as eagerly as but lately he gave the order to buy. His margin has been transferred to the broker's pocket. This having been accomplished, the customer begins to regret that instead of buying, he did not sell short, and thus profit by the decline. Whereupon he studies the market. It has gone down, (reasons he) to be sure, but not so low as it might go. It is quoted now as "weak," and "heavy." The "points" now are in favor of selling. He sells short at the low price, but scarcely has he done so when the market suddenly stiffens, and he finds that he has made another mistake. Still he clings to his loss. The broker, on his part, seeing the market advancing, promptly buys in the stock of which his customer is short, and when the market has risen nearly to the limit of the customer's margin, he notifies him of this fact, and asks what shall be done. Ten chances to one that the customer thereupon orders him to buy in and cover the short contract, not knowing that it has been already covered at a much lower figure. Thus the broker makes another profit out of his customer. This process is kept up, the customer buying at high, and selling at low prices, till his money and patience alike are exhausted, and he retires from the scene of his labors, to renew his strength, and after a time returns refreshed and replenished, to repeat the same old moves, buying when everything is selling at summit prices, and selling when the market is depressed and weak.

This use of his customer's stock is, however, made at the risk of the broker. For, if the market should rise after the customer's stocks are sold by the broker, as before described, and thereupon the order is given to realize, of course the broker has to pay the customer's profit out of his own pocket. But generally, the broker protects himself, by being in the market constantly, and guiding himself accordingly.

Another way in which the broker makes his money, is to sell out for cash, the stocks which he holds, and to buy them back, seller ten or thirty, at a difference of several per cent. Here again, he is exposed to the possibility of loss. For if the party who sells him the stock on the seller's option, should be unable to deliver, in consequence of a great advance in the price, he, the seller of the cash stock, would suffer the loss. But this contingency may be guarded against, by calling on the seller of the option for margin, to be deposited in some Trust Company, to abide the event. This mode of turning stocks, may be better explained by the following account, viz:

A——, a broker, having one hundred shares of cash Erie stock, sells it to be B——, another broker, at 40, ... $4,000
And buys of D—— one hundred shares Erie, seller 30, at 36,   3,600

A—— makes 4 per cent., or, ... $400
That is, if the seller's option is delivered according to contract. But supposing Erie rise to 50 and the seller's

option at 36 can not be delivered on account of the failure
of D——, the party who contracts to deliver it upon his
option at 36, obviously B—— loses the difference between

one hundred shares at 50, ... $5,000
And one hundred shares at 40, ... 4,000
                                                  _____
B—— is out $1,000

But, as already stated, he may protect himself
against this liability by calling upon D—— for margin as the stock rises.

The wealthier members of the brokers' board use
their money very profitably in "carrying" stocks for
their associates, whose means are more limited. The
rate at which stocks are carried, varies according to
the condition of the money market. When money
is scarce, or in Wall Street parlance, *tight*, the rate
has sometimes been as high as one per cent. a day.
But this is a very unusual interest. From one-quarter
of one per cent. to one per cent. a month, and seven
per cent. per annum in addition, is the common rate
when money is tight. This is usurious and illegal.
But the law against taking more than seven per cent.
is evaded by selling for cash, the stock to be carried,
and buying it back regular at a small difference, which
is paid by the person who desires to have his stock "carried." In times of money stringency, the wealthier
class of brokers derive a great revenue from these
differences, which are paid them by their brethren,
whose waists, pecuniarily speaking, are more slender.

These "common carriers" on the Wall Street road,
are, many of them, capitalists who have retired from
the active business of buying and selling, and are
content to earn twenty or thirty per cent. on their
money by carrying stocks. Sleek old boys, with blush-

ing autumnal faces, surrounded by snowy December locks and beard, they keep their nimble sixpences always busy, and like the ivy-green which "creeps o'er ruins old," they fatten and flourish in times of panic, or when the interest rate is cent per cent.

Douglas Jerrold wittily defined marriage as the result of an insane desire on the part of a young man to pay a young woman's board. Speculation may be in like manner defined as an insane desire on the part of a stock operator to pay the board and make the fortune of a broker.

CHAPTER XXI.

THE SECOND HARLEM CORNER.

More Figuring on Balances—Gathering Up the Fragments—A Flyer on Five Hundred Fort Wayne for Cash—What Can I Sell Short?— One Solitary Column Standing Erect Among a Heap of Ruins—The Commodore Holds up Harlem and Waits for His Revenge—" Sell Harlem at 190, and now You're Right "—History and Causes of the Second Harlem Rise—The Plot to Break Harlem—The Counterplot —The Stock on the Rampage—The Biters Bit—The Greatest of All the Bears in the Trap—Daniel Drew Selling Calls—A Lobby-engineer with a Broken Wing—Bears Dancing on Red-hot Plates—The Commodore says, " Put Up the Price to One Thousand "—The *Coup de Grace* to All the Bears—How I Came Out on Selling Harlem Short—A Cotton Operation.

N the Arabian Nights' Entertainments there is a story of an honest butcher, who sold meat to a magician, and received his pay in what he thought was money, which he carefully laid away, but when he went to count his hoard, he found instead of gold coin, nothing but withered leaves. This tale exactly illustrates the condition of stock-speculators, after the panic of April 18th, 1864. Instead of golden profits, they had only a beggarly account of minus balances. Many of them had simply lost their all. Others were largely indebted to their brokers. The sole assets of some, were debts due from their brokers, who had failed flat. He might be accounted fortunate, who had a few thousands left, with which to begin over again.

The quartette met by appointment, at the office

of L——, at eleven A. M., April 19th. Four weary leaden-eyed men, breathless and scathed, after a three months' storm, ending in thunder, lightning, and wreck. A dead silence, and then W. B. C—— took out his pencil gloomily, and commenced figuring on a sheet of paper. Poor fellow! He had been hit hard. His two brokers had failed, and out of what was worth $78,000 one short week before, he had only $500 in cash left. The rest of his assets were what his brokers owed him, (about $15,000,) the certificates of those confounded mining companies, and a *call* for two hundred shares of Harlem, at 175. E—— could muster only $8,000 in cash, and *his* mining company certificates. L——, out of $190,000, had $28,000 in cash, and *his* certificates.

I turned my pockets inside out, and took a new inventory of assets. Result: $20,000 cash, the bubble certificates of course, and a small paper, three inches by four, which declared me entitled to call on a well-known operator, for two hundred shares of Harlem at 200, any time within sixty days, from the fifth day of April.

By Plutus! Wait a bit! What is this? A memorandum of $175,000 at par in 7 3-10 bonds, with a margin of $8,000 and accumulated profits of at least twice as much more! I had forgotten all about this transaction during the fierce campaign just over. The bonds had all this time been snugly lying in the vaults of different savings banks, drawing interest, while I was sleeping or trying to "work the oracle" on 'Change. Then I commenced figuring in hot haste.

Ten months interest in gold on $175,000, 7 $\frac{3}{10}$, . . . $10,645 80
Premium on gold at 170—70, ... 7,452 06
                                            —————
                                            $18,097 86

The interest charged by the savings banks of 5½–6 per cent. in currency, had been paid for six months in advance, in January. The bonds were selling, even in that panicky season, at 109. This swelled my profits $8,000 more, for the bonds had only cost me 104–105. I had $46,000 to start the ball rolling once more. After our figuring had been thus completed, we held a council of war, and decided upon the following policy, viz: First, to buy only as much stock as we could pay for. Second, to look about, and see if there was any high-priced stock, which it would answer to sell short, for the late panic had taught us the bear-lesson, that money could be made by selling stocks at a high price.

I now leave L——, E—— and W. B. C——, to shift for themselves, for a season, and give my individual experience while endeavoring to construct a new edifice out of the debris of my late high-piled fortunes.

What could be bought for cash which would pay best? On taking a survey, I pitched upon Fort Wayne, my old favorite. It had fallen from 153 to 90. But after every severe panic there is always a sharp recovery of prices, or as it called, "the reaction." This is often produced by the fact that the bears sell largely of stocks which they do not actually hold, and when prices have reached the bottom of the hill, they rush in to cover their shorts by buying. Fort Wayne had already begun to feel this reaction, and was now selling for 101. I asked one of my brokers—the least shaky of them—if he would buy five hundred Fort Wayne, if I would give him $20,000 in cash and orders on three savings banks for $175,000, 7 3-10 bonds, which he might sell on the first of May, the margin and accumulations being $26,000. He hummed and hawed, looked distrustful (for money was five per cent. a month, and the whole street was ringing with reports of failures), and finally inquired if everything was right and regular about the bonds.

"Send your boy up and get the orders accepted, if you are not satisfied with what I tell you."

"All right, I'll take your word for it. You must excuse my suspicions, but the whole street just now is rotten, you know."

The five hundred Fort Wayne was bought at 102. This purchase was made in fear and trembling. We were not yet out of the jaws of the panic.

If we could judge from the doleful looks of bank cashiers and money-lenders, everything said *sell!* The whole street was in ruins. Of all the stately columns, one only, still stood erect. It was Harlem, which now loomed up like Pompey's pillar under a desert sky. It had reeled and quivered during the storm, but stood bravely at the height of 190. Beside this solitary column, like Marius among the ruins of Carthage, sat a grim old man, brooding over his wrongs, and preparing to revenge them. Our Marius was none other than Cornelius Vanderbilt. For thirty days his masons had been at work rearing the column of Harlem, while the Commodore propped and buttressed it with four millions of hard cash. It was to be the engine with which he would accomplish his revenge. To sell Harlem short at that time, would seem in the light of what afterwards happened, to be little less than madness.

But Harlem, selling at 190, nearly everybody said was more than one hundred per cent. higher than its true value. It was held up by artificial means. It would break down heavily at sometime, and if a man would sell it for future delivery, and *stay short of it,* he would make a great profit. So said they who understood not the true significance of the Harlem movement. My broker evidently thought it a great piece of folly to buy Fort Wayne at par, as I had done an hour before, but when I spoke of going short of Harlem at 190, his face lighted up as if he would say "Now you're right."

The order was given, "Sell two hundred Harlem at 190–195." In three minutes a tall, slender individual (one of the Commodore's men) had gobbled my two hundred shares, with an air and look that reminded us of young Oliver asking for more. I was short of Harlem at 190, and long of Fort Wayne at 101. My position was apparently in strict accordance with that great maxim, *sell stocks when they are high, and buy them when they are low.* This maxim was verified by the rapid upward movement in Fort Wayne. During the next four days it rose to 129. Profits on this operation, $12,000. The maxim, however, was utterly falsified by the rise of Harlem during the same period, to 230. When it reached 200, I sold two hundred shares more at that price, and gave my broker orders to sell two hundred shares more, when the price reached 210. It touched 210 almost as soon as I had given the order. My broker had just time to sell two hundred Harlem at 210, and then up it bounded to 220.

My profits on Fort Wayne were being swallowed up in the Harlem shorts. It was a race between a bull and a bear, between buying stocks for a rise and selling them for a fall. I bought Canton at 35, and sold it at 40, with a profit of $3,000, but my short Harlem eat up that profit, and stood me still $1,500 out of pocket. I bought other stocks and made profits every time on my purchases, but Harlem kept relentlessly moving up and the profits I made on my purchases were not sufficient to cancel the fresh losses which accrued from Harlem as it rose.

But before giving the result of this race, it may not be uninteresting to the reader to go back and give a brief history of the Harlem rise, with the causes which produced it.

As we remarked in a preceding chapter, the primary object which Vanderbilt had in view in buying so largely of Harlem in 1862 and 1863, was the investment of some of his spare millions, in order to make him snug and comfortable in his old age, for already he clearly foresaw that Harlem, under proper management, would soon pay dividends. When he found himself opposed and thwarted by his enemies, in the courts of law, in the Common Council and elsewhere, he turned upon and twisted Harlem up to 180, and in this way punished his enemies, who had sold it short in expectation that the measures they had taken would depress the stock to a very low point.

After that and in the fall of 1863, the price had fallen back to 75–90. The matter of the franchise grant now rested with the Legislature, and the new campaign in Harlem was to be fought in Albany. Soon after the opening of the session, a bill was reported favorable to the grant. In expectation of this move, many members of the Legislature and the lobby, and their friends, as well as the adherents and coadjutors of Vanderbilt, had bought the stock freely from 90 to 105.

When the favorable report was known to the general public, they rushed in and loaded themselves up with the stock, which now rose rapidly to 150. One of Vanderbilt's confidential agents at Albany, telegraphed repeatedly that the bill would surely pass. The Commodore and his associates largely increased their line of stock, and as high a figure as 200 was confidently predicted.

But while everything promised well, and already in imagination, the advocates of a Broadway railroad, saw that renowned thoroughfare lined with street cars under the management of the Harlem board, a sly game had been playing at Albany. The members of the Legislature, seeing the facility with which the price had been raised from par to 150, by a favorably reported bill, rightly concluded that an adverse report would depress the value of the stock to par. They accordingly sold to the Commodore's friends, at from 140 to 150, the stock which had cost them somewhere in the neighborhood of par, and then went heavily short of the stock. On the 25th of March, the conspirators sprung the trap on the unsuspecting old sea-faring man and his mates. The price fell in two days, amid the greatest excitement, to 101.

The short gentlemen thought they had feathered their nests nicely, beside giving the Commodore a bloody coxcomb in return for what he had given them, by twisting Harlem to 181 in the summer of 1863. They fluttered about the market uttering loud clucks of exultation.

One of these individuals was Y——s, a plump little man with an eye like a startled cock-partridge. He had affiliations with the lobby and also with the Common Council, and having been caught in the first Harlem corner, he looked upon that stock as something which owed him money, not to say revenge. Having been so fortunate as to put out shorts at 140, he might have been seen on that loud Saturday when Harlem sold down to 101, hovering about the market, beaming with smiles and hob-nobbing with his numerous bear friends. Of course he did not take his profit (bears often seem very reluctant to do this) for he thought Harlem would drop to 75. Towards night he became less gushing in his manifestations of delight, for Harlem had mysteriously risen to 110. In a few days he subsided into that state of financial incubation called "sitting on his shorts." When Harlem had risen to 190 he still sat there as "patient as the mourning dove." A week after he suddenly took flight with a brokers billet under his wing, showing him stripped of plumage and financial eggs broken to the amount of $40,000.

But let us return to the thread of our narrative. How happened it that the Harlem Broadway Franchise Bill was killed, when, as the Commodore supposed, a majority of both houses were pledged to its support?

Treachery in the camp! The Commodore's agent had deceived him. His friends in the Legislature had betrayed him, and were now adding injury and insult to their treachery.

That very day, while the whole market was a playground for the merry and exultant bears in Harlem, in the recesses of a mind capacious of such things,

Commodore Vanderbilt organized a scheme of revenge so "wide and ample" that it would embrace in one fall and tremendous circle, faithless adherents, enemies, both secret and open, as well as all others whom he regarded as hostile to his schemes, in consequence of their selling short his pet stock. Summoning around him his trusty lieutenants, he issued his orders that they should buy every share of the stock that might be offered whether on sellers' or buyers' options, or for cash or "regular."

The bears fortified with a margin of thirty or forty per cent. profit, were not displeased with the opportunity to put out more shorts at a higher price than 101, and the contest commenced. As the price rose, each party waxed furious.

Every day, at the Public Board or in the street, John M. Tobin could have been seen bidding for and buying thousands of shares, his face pale with excitement and his opalescent eyes blazing like a basilisk's. He grabbed at the stock with fury, for he had suffered by the decline.

"No feeling, John!" vociferated the crowd, as the stock rose with wild leaps to 127.

"I'll make you feel," retorted he.

In ten days, the stock, in the face of enormous sales, had risen to 150—the highest price at which the legislative bears had lately commenced their short sales. A week later and the price rose to 185, and then for ten days dully vibrated between 175 and 200. When the movement had carried the stock to 140, the bears, remembering the terrible trouncing they had received eight months before, and remembering also how sweet was revenge to their powerful and inflexible antagonist, began to reflect and inquire whether it might not be advisable to close up their contracts and pocket their loss. But while they were in this dubious state, a circumstance occurred which served to fortify them in their course, and thus to lead them to their destruction.

The hundreds of bears who had been already caught in the death-trap, Harlem, now saw approach the biggest, merriest, most cunning of all their tribe. He nosed the trap, then put his forepaws upon it, and finally put his whole body into it.

It was Uncle Daniel!

Who would suppose that *he* could have been deceived? But so it was. He had sold (rumor said) thirty thousand shares, one-third of the capital stock, in the form of " calls." He who sells calls in a stock, acts upon the supposition that the price will not rise higher than the price named in the calls; he is a bear, and the party who buys and holds the calls, is a bull in the stock. A call sold by an operator who is known to be wealthy and able to respond when called upon for the stock described in the call, is often as already mentioned, used as a margin by the holder to *sell short* that particular stock. Suppose, for example, that Daniel Drew sell to John Smith, in consideration of one hundred dollars, the privilege of calling on him, Daniel Drew, for two hundred shares of Harlem at 145 at any time within thirty days. John Smith takes this contract to his own broker and orders him to sell short, two hundred shares of Harlem, at 145. If the price of the stock goes down, John Smith buys it at the *reduced price*, delivers it to the party to whom he has contracted to deliver it at 145, and makes, as his profit, the difference. But if the price rises and shows

John Smith a loss, he then calls upon Daniel Drew to deliver the stock at 145. This keeps John Smith whole in the transaction.

By selling thirty thousand shares in the form of calls, Daniel Drew had really loaned his credit to the amount of millions to the call-holders, to be used in the form of margins on which to sell Harlem, short. In this way, for the trifling consideration of $15,000, paid to him by the call-holders, he helped to forge the very chains in which he was soon to be led captive at the chariot wheels of the triumphant Harlem ring.

When it became noised abroad that Uncle Daniel stood ready to sell calls on Harlem, running for thirty or sixty days, the bears knew that a powerful and crafty ally had joined them. The calls were eagerly snatched by those who wished to hold them for a rise, as well as by those who used them as a margin to sell short. Members of the ring snapped them up greedily. L. W. Jerome and John M. Tobin, personally held calls, which a few weeks after showed Drew indebted to them $138,000.

The speculative public were selling Harlem all through the street. Conservative brokerage houses sold it slyly. The whilom bull, A. G. Jerome, although his brother Leonard was heavily embarked in the upward movement, was a large seller of the stock. Any broker who had Harlem in his office could lend it any moment of the day, to those who were selling short. One of the customers of L.—— & Co., had six hundred shares of the stock. These certificates were loaned to another customer, who sold it *short* to the ring, who then, after taking the num-

bers on the certificates, loaned it to another bear who
sold it again, in open market, *to the ring*. This operation was repeated six times, by as many different
men, who all went short of Harlem, using these identical certificates for that purpose.

As the price approached 200, through all the darkness which hung over the short sellers, only one ray
of hope gleamed. They saw something drawing
near ; itself a gloomy and terrible shape, to them it
had rather a semblance of brightness and deliverance.
It was *Panic*, to which they looked for relief ! Panic,
which would be ruin to a thousand others, would be
salvation to them, for it would throw Harlem down
in its sweep, and help them to fill their contracts.

That panic was not wholly due to the action of
Secretary Chase in selling gold and locking up greenbacks; it was heightened, beyond doubt, by firms
who were short of Harlem, and were willing that the
public should suffer frightful losses, provided only
Harlem could be broken down, so that they could
extricate themselves from their unfortunate position
as short sellers.

The 18th of April came, but it brought no deliverance for them. In vain they strove to make money
still tighter, and filled the whole market with their dismal auguries, though stocks were falling on every side,
and the hammer blows rained on Harlem, it stood
like a rock. Now that the panic was past, they
could only stand and gaze stupidly at their enemy,
and still hope for that which was never to come, a
break in the corner.

The agony was soon to be over. One day in May,
when Harlem was selling for upwards of 200, the

manipulators of the stock called on the Commodore, and told him that they held stock, or contracts for stock, to the amount of twenty-seven thousand more shares, than the whole capital of the company, which was $4,500,000. Then, said Vanderbilt, put the price up to 1,000. The manipulators, including John Morrissey, demurred to this, on the plea that this proceeding would break every house in the street. Accordingly, it was decided that 300, or thereabouts, would be a more judicious figure. Straightway Harlem rose, in long leaps, until it reached 285. At that point it was firmly held. The very day it reached this price, contracts matured for the delivery of more than fifteen thousand shares of the stock. These were closed at a loss of over one million dollars to the short sellers.

The Commodore was taking his revenge. Five hundred strong men, hard of head and deep of coffer, lay at his mercy. Never telling their losses, one by one as "mute as fox mong'st mangling hounds," they walked up to the offices of the brokers of that terrible old man, and settled their differences. Each morning new wrinkles seemed to have been graven, and old lines hardened, in their faces. As for the smaller tribe of the entrapped ones, they were caught up and whirled away like chaff, never to show their faces in the street again. No one but they and their payers will ever know the amount paid by all these men who were short of Harlem, but the aggregate would foot up something frightful.

But how did the greatest bear of all, to wit, Uncle Daniel, succeed in extricating himself from the trap in which he found himself fast caught? His losses on Harlem at 285, would, it was said, amount to $1,-700,000. This would take a large slice out of his late profits on Erie. His first movement was to throw himself on the tender mercies of the Commodore, and plead old friendship, etc. Vain appeal! The bosom of the ancient steamboat mariner and railroad king was steeled against the entreaties of the old bear, and he very pertinently inquired whether, if Harlem had fallen to 75, instead of rising to 285, he would in that case, have paid any portion of his (Vanderbilt's) losses. Failing in this appeal, his next movement was to set up the plea of conspiracy, and that he had been entrapped by false representations, etc.; "besides," said he, "these contracts merely say that you may *call* upon me for so much stock; they say nothing about my *delivering* the stock. *Call* then, and keep *calling*, I am not obliged to *deliver* any stock." So he stood at bay, telling his opponent to seek redress in the courts of law.

But as Wall Street abhors litigation, a compromise was at last talked of. Tobin and L. W. Jerome were now nearly every day closeted with him, in his den at No. 15 William Street, and a settlement was at last effected for about one million.

After the price of Harlem had been kept in the neighborhood of 280 long enough to close all the short contracts held by the ring, it fell like lead to 115, and not a single bear could be found with hardihood enough to sell it for future delivery during its downward course.

This Harlem rise is said to have crippled or ruined more men than any similar movement in the annals of Wall Street, while it enriched and gave new prestige to Vanderbilt, who in connection with his associates in the movement, is said to have netted money enough to buy the whole capital stock.

I now return to the story of the six hundred shares of Harlem, of which I was short, at an average of 200. Of course, as the price rose, I "sat on my shorts," clinging manfully to my loss after the most approved Wall Street plan.   At 280 I had to close like my ursine brothers, and found my loss $24,000.   I had hoped, however, that this would be diminished to the amount of $8,000, since the two hundred shares sold at 200 was secured by the call before mentioned, which a wealthy (?) operator had sold me a few weeks before for the trifling sum of $12.50.   This occurred in a moment of badinage at Delmonico's, when the wealthy (?) operator (while Harlem was selling at 130), offered me the privilege of calling on him at any time within sixty days, for two hundred shares at 200, in consideration of the trifling sum last named.

But an operator, wealthy on the first of April, is not necessarily so on the twenty-fifth of May following, at least in Wall Street.   The operator in question had been laid low in the Morse panic, and when I *called* for two hundred shares at 200, the response was anything but satisfactory, in fact to the extent of $8,000 out of my little surplus.

As for W. B. C——, he kept his call, and when the price was 275, *he called* and was answered.   He made exactly $10,000 out of what cost him only $50.

It was while smarting under the Harlem flagellation that I made my first operation in cotton, buying one hundred bales of that useful staple at 87½ cents per pound.   The history and result of this speculative purchase will be given hereafter, under another head.

CHAPTER XXII.

IN SEARCH OF A BROKER—THE GOLD-BURST UP-WARDS—DULL TIMES.

The Three Brokers; a Vulture, a Sparrow, and a Jolly Boy—Brokers' Safes are Like the Lion's Den—Lunching in the Office of N—— & Co.—We Find What We are Looking For, and Put Our Margins in the Lunch-Room—A Jag of $50,000 Gold and What Came of It —Beautiful June and Halcyon Days for the Quartette—A Financial Dissertation at an Inn on the Road—The Military Outlook—Grant's Hand on the Throat of the Rebellion—Congressional Folly and Its Consequences—The Gold Bill—We Take a Trip to Rockaway—Telegraphing in Cipher—Wherein of a Telegraphic Puzzle—The Gold Burst—A Mistake Which Gave Me a Profit of $85,000—Buying 50 Gold Instead of Selling 50.

HE customer, after every severe loss, is apt to cherish towards his natural enemy, the broker, a feeling of dissatisfaction, not to say mild indignation. Thereupon he casts about him for another broker, some paragon who may do his little business for him, and render him happy with a continuous series of the plumpest and most delicious of profits, over which the shadow of a loss may never come. He must be young and jolly, and honest of course. He must be ready to communicate the most reliable points, he must never be obstreperous on the subject of margins, and above all he must always, and under all circumstances, be buoyant.

L—— enjoyed an extensive acquaintance among those gentry who are popularly supposed to do a "strictly commission business in buying and selling stocks." On learning that I was in search of something new and improved in that line, he kindly offered to show me what I wanted, viz., a broker who was an "entire and perfect chrysolite." "The first man I shall introduce you to," remarked L—— after we had set out on our search for this paragon broker, "may not be a very prepossessing man at first sight, but I can indorse him as in every respect, the man for your money. I've just made ten thousand in his office!" This little profit had prejudiced L——, I think; for a moment after, on entering the office of the individual referred to, I saw a tall, heavily-beaked man, who was craning over a couple of customers with bony knees and wearing a flaccid drained look, and apparently impressing on them the necessity of handing over more margin, or of being sold out incontinently. Physiognomy has certainly something to do with the selection of an agent to buy and sell stocks, though it does not always follow that a man may not smile, and smile, and yet be a broker. As soon as introduced, I began to study the face of the tall man. The ruling expression suggested only one trait, and that conspicuously—cruelty—which wandered through and lurked in every line of his face, but took up its permanent abode in his eye—that cruel eye. The bony knees of the flaccid-looking customers and that cruel eye were enough. We hastened away to continue our search for the paragon aforesaid.

The next office we entered was that of W——, quite a different kind of man. If the tall, heavily beaked man from whom we had just parted brought

to my mind the solitary vulture, W—— as strongly
reminded me of a chirping sparrow constantly in pursuit of worms. He was a short man, with a magnificent chest and slender legs, dressed in a style of
sombre gorgeousness. He never was quiet an instant.
Now dancing up and down the street; now taking
short flights to the Board; then back again, perching
for a moment in his office and off once more. He
seemed to be constantly in pursuit of worms—I mean
orders. He had little time to talk English. His
language was the Wall Street patter, clipping syllables audaciously. Commission, which seemed to
be the most frequent word in his vocabulary, he called
" commish," " Pittsburg," " Pitts," and so on.

Action is the essential of oratory, first, last, and
always, said Demosthenes. Activity is the essential
of the brokerage business. Activity means orders to
buy and sell. Activity means commissions for the
broker. But I had discovered some time before this,
that activity on the part of the broker was productive
of large brokerage bills, which his customer would
have to pay. W—— was a trifle too active in the
line of commissions, and so we looked farther.

" Now," said L—— " I've thought of *the* man to
take care of your margins."

And while he was speaking, he opened the door
which conducted into the banking and brokerage
house of N—— & Co. The first feature that struck
the eye, on entering this office, was the safes. In
one corner stood a large salamander safe; sunk in
the wall there was a burglar proof safe; under the
cashier's desk, there was a small safe, which looked
like a lineal descendant of the salamander, before

named. All this conveyed the idea of security, at least, for the banking and brokerage firm. Experience has certainly taught us, at this date, however, that brokers' safes are like the lion's den, the tracks of the gentler beasts all lead in, and none lead out from it. A constant stream of checks pass away from the relaxed fingers of the customers, and flow into those chilled iron doors; but never again do they flow out to gladden *his* heart, or to be crumpled up in his "itching palm."

From the private office of this house, came a sound of mirth and revelry, mingled with the clinking of glasses and the clattering of knives and forks. A slim clerk, dressed in the height of the fashion, nodded gaily as we entered, and then jumped off the high stool, on which he was sitting before a desk, protected by a lofty barrier of black walnut, and walking rapidly to the private office, threw open the door, disclosing thereby a banqueting scene. Several men were sitting around a table loaded with the delicacies of the season, and surmounted with tall, slender flasks, bearing such labels as *haut sauterne*, *amontillado*, etc. Beside each chair was a champagne cooler, from out of which protruded the neck of a bottle swathed in ice. We thought at first sight that we had made a mistake, and were in a restaurant, where some board of a mining company was celebrating the anniversary of subscription day. But we were quickly undeceived, by the appearance of the senior member of the house, wiping a bit of lobster salad from his exuberant beard. He was a stout, well-fed man, with a dome of brow fit for the intellectual habitation of some illustrious statesman, and thinly adorned with blonde curls. After introductions had been exchanged, he led us, nothing loth, to two vacant seats, which, as he remarked, seemed to have been providentially reserved for us. As "swift as dreams," we found our plates heaped with good things, then was heard a gurgling sound, as of a hidden brook, and a moment after, healths all round were drunk in champagne frappé, out of the most delicately-moulded, wide-brimmed French glass beakers.

N—— sat at the head of the table, uttering in a barytone voice between mouthfuls of salad, the most daring financial paradoxes interspersed with amusing anecdotes, in which he dwelt with much humor upon the singular facility with which the margins of speculators were disposed of. Then he passed into the prophetic vein and predicted future rises to empyrean heights. Gold and its future course seemed to be his pet theme. It was to rise to 300 within six months, and on this assertion he booked a little bet with a sallow complexioned gentleman on the opposite side of the table.

The genial glow diffused by the lunch, and the barytone buoyant predictions as to the course of gold, had their due effect. In fifteen minutes after the company rose from the table, I had deposited all my cash with N—— & Co., who then bought for me $50,000 in gold, which cost 179. Then I introduced E—— and W. B. C—— to the convivial man with the fine dome of brow and keen financial apprehension. They also took flyers in gold, and on the strength of this thought themselves entitled to the privileges of lunch which was spread every day in the most sumptuous style. It may be here related that E—— informed me several months after, that these lunches had cost him an average of $200 dollars each, a fact that he was reminded of on contemplating the last account which N—— & Co. had rendered him, on taking leave of their eminent banking and brokerage house.

After that we spent two or three weeks very pleasantly, exercising our steeds and airing our light wagons and phaetons in the park, breakfasting out on the road, dining at Delmonico's, and, of course, lunching at our broker's, where we "lay off" on ample sofas and dabbled in stocks, losing more than we made, but caring little for this, so long as gold kept us more than whole by rising to 198.

Beautiful June, queen of the months, was come. Perfect days, and nights more beloved than the days. South-west winds at evening, and bespangled skies of unfathomable blue.

It was on one of those matchless nights that we sat on the piazza of a suburban hotel, on the High Bridge road. We heeded not the "unutterable glory of the stars," nor the breath of "the sweet south," but were deep in the discussion of gold, its future course, etc., all the while sipping our Cliquot and puffing furiously at the finest regalias.

From August 1863, gold had been steadily rising from 122, the point it reached after a series of Union successes. This rise seemed to depend little upon those temporary and artificial causes which make stocks go up. The laws of commerce and of money were at work, steadily depreciating the value of paper currency, and so affecting the market price of the precious metal. *This* rise was founded on reason.

The amount of paper currency was already more than five times greater than before the war. That gold should have ever risen above 200, is not wonderful. The wonder is that it never rose to 500. The fact that it did not so rise, proves the confidence of the great body of the American people in the resources of their country and in the ultimate success of the Union army.

The tremendous panic of April 18th, produced little effect upon the price of gold. There was no combination in it like those which sent stocks so wildly upwards, nor did its movements depend upon the scarcity or abundance of money to be loaned in the market place. Upon the results of the summer campaign on the Potomac, depended its future course. Victory would bring down the price; defeat and even a doubtful issue would cut the cord, and away the price would fly into the clouds.

Twelve myriads—one hundred and twenty thousand good men and true, horse, foot, and artillery—were lying on their arms north of the Rapidan, waiting for the two words of command. One bright May morning those words passed through the ranks— "forward! march!" Corps after corps, division after division, brigade after brigade, regiment behind regiment, they swept across the stream, soon to be reddened with their blood; on, threading the death-labyrinths of the wilderness, piling great mounds of shroudless graves around Spotsylvania and Cold Harbor, and gathering at last in dusky circles about Richmond and Petersburg.

Of all the millions of eyes that watched the onward march of the Grand Army of the Potomac, none

were riveted upon it so closely as the gold speculators.   Every source of early information from
the front was explored.   It was not enough to scrutinize the columns of the daily press for every scrap
of army news; the telegraph operators were subsidized, government officials were tampered with, and
a more perfect system of couriers and messages
adopted, in order to advise the speculators as to the
exact condition of matters on the Rapidan, the Pa-
munkey, and the James River.   If a great army
movement was about to take place, the gold speculator in Wall Street would receive a message from his
coadjutor at Washington, or at the front, something
like this, "John is still here."   If an engagement,
disastrous to the Federal army, had taken place,
word would come "Henry is worse."   This meant,
"buy gold."   Or if a victory had been won, "John
is sitting up to-day."   This meant, "sell gold."

It would be safe to assert that there were only two
classes of persons who always knew the exact status
of the campaign.   First, the government; second,
the gold operators, for both these classes obtained
the earliest information, not only from the Union, but
from the Rebel army.

When, after a series of bloody battles and flanking
movements, Grant was preparing to draw his lines
around Richmond, it might have been expected that
the price of gold would have declined.   But these
successes were interpreted by financiers, to be of a
character not sufficiently decisive to affect the price,
which stood firmly at 198.

Something new now entered into the calculations
of the gold dealers.   Congress had just passed a bill

affixing severe penalties to the practice of dealing in gold by contract for future purchases and delivery, and that bill only lacked the President's signature to become a law. How would this affect the price of gold? The act intended to repress speculation in the metal, passed March, 1863, had been used as an argument to throw gold down from 172 to 156. This was the problem which puzzled us, as we discussed matters on that pleasant June evening. On the whole, we were inclined to sell, but came to no decision then, though we had dwelt upon the subject till the last light wagon had bowled past us in the direction of the city. Then we whistled for our team. It was sharp twelve, before we reined in our dapple grays in front of their stable door, and betook ourselves to our several hotels.

When we met the next morning, two things were settled upon. First, we would sell our gold at the market price. Second, we would unite in a trip to the sea-side. L—— was the arithmetician and telegraph operator of the party, and so to him was delegated the matter of giving the order to sell, which we were to send down to the office of N—— & Co. by the city telegraph.

Previously to this we had agreed with N—— & Co., upon a telegraphic cipher, as follows, viz.: "Ben" meant sell, "jag" meant our gold, "whirl" meant at the market price, and "Bob" meant buy. Our telegram read thus: "Ben, jag, whirl, answer to us at Rockaway, *signed*, etc., etc., etc."

In three hours after, we stood on the smooth, firm beach at Rockaway, listening to the breakers' roar. It was not till the next day, that we received from our buoyant and festive broker, the following telegram: "*Got*, jag, Wiggins, whirl, Morrissey, everything lovely, signed, etc., N—— & Co." Which being translated, signified: "Got your gold at 199⅓, market price strong and higher. Everything lovely."

This telegram bothered us. Instead of saying Benny, which meant sold, our broker had written *got*. On this fine old Anglo-Saxon word *got* we held a philological discussion. It seemed here to signify *bought*. But our order was to *sell*. L—— having sent the telegram giving the order to sell, defended the answer vigorously, and asserted that *got* was here applied to the *getting* of our profit, or it might mean a joke on the part of N—— to inform us that we were "got" by selling out just before the price rose. But what logical connection in that case between the fact that the price had risen after we had sold and the expression "everything is lovely?" The discussion was brought to an end, however, as soon as we recollected that *our* telegram was certainly correct; and if N—— & Co. had made a mistake we could hold them responsible for any consequences disastrous to ourselves arising therefrom.

The stock operator is rarely much of a society-man. It is never written on his tombstone, "sociability was his pride." At the watering-places, instead of passing his time with that portion of the fair sex, who there resort, forming what is usually known as society, he withdraws to quiet corners, calls around him his little clan of fellow-operators, and occupies and diverts himself with exchanging views, conning telegrams, rummaging in the money articles of New York dailies, and chewing the sweet and bitter cud of prospective profit and loss. While thus engaged for ten days, our coterie became, from time to time, apprised of the flutterings of the Volscians at Corioli, otherwise, the gold dealers of New York.

Great doings on 'Change!

The law of Congress, forbidding all time contracts in gold, under penalty of heavy fine and imprisonment, first took effect on the 21st of June.

This piece of legislative fatuity, was promptly interpreted by the financiers, as a confession of weakness on the part of the government, and of its conviction that the war was to be a protracted one. Its first effect was to compel all who were short of gold, to cover their contracts. The demand thus suddenly created, drove up the price in one day to 225. Its second effect was to throw out of gearing, the entire machinery of the banking, and of the importing mercantile business; for time contracts in gold, ever since 1862, have been employed in legitimate trade, as well as in speculation.

When an importer wishes to pay duties on his goods, or remit exchange to Europe, he borrows gold of his bank at the market price, provided he thinks gold is going down, and buys gold in the market for the same purpose, whenever he thinks that gold is going up. If gold should go down in the former case, then he repays the gold borrowed of the bank, buying it in the market at the lower price to which it may have fallen, thus making his profit; and if gold goes up in the latter case, his imported goods will feel the effect of the rise, and in this way he also makes a profit.

On the 23d of June, gold sold for 245, and during the week which ensued, it vibrated twenty and thirty

THE DREAM OF A SPECULATOR.

per cent. a day, throwing the commercial community into the greatest confusion. The price soon reached the highest point known during the war.

Meetings in the Chamber of Commerce were held, and petitions forwarded to Washington, praying for the repeal of the law. But though the repeal took place shortly after, it did not undo the mischief which had been wrought. Gold did not, for many months, fall back to 185, the point from which it started upwards, when the gold bill was first agitated in Congress.

We set out for New York, on the first of July, in consequence of receiving another mysterious telegram from our broker. This message read as follows, viz.: "Hannah is jumping now, what shall I do?" "Hannah" was gold. What did N—— & Co. mean? They seemed to be soliciting orders very strangely. The last train down from Jamaica, was delayed by an accident. We reached the Fifth Avenue Hotel just after the Evening Exchange had adjourned. As we entered the hall, a short, rubicund gentleman, whom we recognized as one of the customers of N—— & Co., hailed us as if we were so many rising suns, and grasping our several hands with fervor, congratulated us on our good luck.

"Good luck? Oh, in gold. Yes, we have done pretty well, about $10,000 apiece," was the response,

"About $10,000! Why, the book-keeper of N—— & Co. told me to-day that you could sell out for sixty-five thousand dollars apiece. Gold sold for 55 to-day, (i. e. 255,) you know."

A light broke in upon us at these words. The mysterious telegrams were now as clear as noon-day.

23

N—— & Co., instead of selling our gold at 199⅛, must have bought as much more. We exchanged significant glances, and received the congratulations of the rubicund gentleman quite as a matter of course. Just at this juncture, entered N——, looking, if that were possible, more exuberant than when I first saw him dispensing the favors of his lunch table. He also congratulated us on our good fortune. On the last lot of fifty gold, which cost 199⅛, there was a profit of about $28,000, and on the first lot of fifty, which cost me 179, there was a profit of $37,500, as N—— rapidly showed me by figures in his memorandum book. This profit was on the basis of gold at 255. "What would I do; sell out on the spot?" "No, wait till to-morrow." I waited, and sold out at 275 the next day, which was the 2d of July, when as every one will remember, gold sold up to 285. My profits were $85,000 net. It appears that N—— & Co. had made a mistake in reading L——'s telegram, instructing them to sell our gold, and had read "Ben," i. e. sell, as "Bob," i. e. buy, and so bought another lot at 199⅛, instead of selling what we had.

It would fill a volume to give an account of the fortunes made and lost during the eleven days from June 22d to July 2d. One bold broker, doing business on a capital of $9,000 bought $250,000 of gold at about 200 at the Evening Exchange on the 21st of June, and by a series of lucky operations, selling at higher rates and buying back at lower rates, as the price oscillated, found himself in forty-eight hours $140,000 richer. Another man who had on the 20th of June been obliged to cover his shorts with the loss of everything that could possibly be used as a margin, excepting three diamond studs, pawned these for $200, and in a week had made from this little capital, over $12,000.

Our quartette drew out all our profits from N—— & Co., got our several checks certified at the bank, and having carried them in our pocket for two days, then went back and deposited them with N—— & Co. as margin for a new campaign. L——, however, bought a brown stone front with part of his profits, and there every evening we held a council of four, deliberating how we might increase our file.

CHAPTER XXIII.

DULL TIMES—AVERAGING ON "POINTS."

A Retrospect of the Situation—An Army Without Leaders—Description of a Dull Market—"Playing With Stocks" to the Tune of $22,000 —Buying on "Points"—A Disagreeable Looking Millionaire—A Wall Street Pointer; His Picture, Antecedents and Mystery—His Geese Always Lay Golden Eggs—We Buy Five Hundred Cumberland Joint Account on a "Point"—Averaging a Loss—How Men Save Themselves by Averaging—Advice Given to an Operator in a Tight Place—"Cumberland not Worth Ten Cents on the Dollar," and I am Long of it at 80—A Bad Show for a Profit—Keep up Your Averaging, My Dear Boy.

HE two great features of the market in Wall Street in the summer of 1864, were Harlem and gold, both of which, by a singular coincidence, rose to 285. The general stock market was lifeless, at least compared to the preceding spring and to the summer of 1863. The situation in respect to the conflicting parties, stood thus.

The bears, owing to their heavy losses during the Morse campaign and the Harlem rise, were too demoralized and impecunious to become the assailants and take advantage of the causes which tended to produce lower prices.

The panic of April 18th had given them moral encouragement, though they had derived little or no pecuniary advantage from it. But as they were gathering together their shattered forces, the gold-burst came and once more disconcerted them.

The bulls, on the other hand, who had been severely crippled by the same panic, had their courage and money forces bolstered up by Harlem and the gold rise. And yet they still lacked something always essential to an upward movement, viz.: bull-leaders. Their army had no general. A. G. Jerome had retired after the defeat which he suffered in August, 1863, on Old Southern, at the hands of Henry Keep. A. W. Morse had been blown skywards as he was scaling the ramparts of Fort Wayne. The Commodore was engaged in nursing his investments. Tobin was resting on his Harlem laurels. Of the other chieftains, not one advanced to cheer on their ranks to victory.

The strong upward movement which followed the April panic was the natural rebound after so heavy a fall, rather than any concerted scheme on the part of the bulls. In May, June and July, various stocks had been taken hold of in succession and lifted by main strength several per cent.; but somehow in all these cases, just as the lifters were preparing to reap the reward of their exertions, stocks would suddenly be depressed as if by some unseen power, and then all the bears would join hands and execute a *pas de fascination* around the venerable form of Uncle Daniel, who, as the master of the ballet, would thereupon gaze with an approving smile upon his nimble pupils.

The tendency of stocks was downward.

Sultry August brought with it the reign of *dullness*, that condition of things in the stock-market forcible but somewhat inelegantly styled the "dry rot," to which, allusion has been made in Chapter VII.

Imagine five hundred men all standing before the pendulum of a gigantic clock, and ejaculating with every tick, "Here she goes, and there she goes." This is the likeness of Wall Street in a dull season. Stocks move up one per cent., then down one per cent., and so on day after day, and week after week. No orders to buy or sell are given by the heavy operators; the outsiders stand listlessly by and wait for the moving of the waters. In the Board, feeble attempts are made to create an excitement in some old favorite stock, which responds lazily to sharp bidding and moves up a notch; but as soon as the bidding ceases, down it plumps again to the figure from which it started. Little knots of speculators are made in the street, to talk stocks and book small bets on the course of the market. The song of the curbstone broker becomes still and small. Ever and anon some spruce and agile clerk of one of the prominent commission houses worms his way into these street knots and bids for one or two hundred shares, when deep voices immediately take up the note like the boom of the bittern in some lonely swamp. Then the throng of buyers and sellers roar out a stave of some patriotic song, such as "Rally round the flag," or "In the prison cell I sit," some one cries out, "Shoo fly, don't bodder me," and the song ceases as suddenly as it began. "The boys" often amuse themselves by playing pranks. A newly arrived gentleman from the rural districts, who is a looker-on on the scene, finds his hat suddenly tipped over his eyes, or his shoulder smartly tapped by one of the habitues, who immediately mingles with the crowd, while the butt of these little practical jokes is looking vigilantly on every side for his tormentor. A dignified old veteran stalks about with a placard, *"For sale at auction,"* which some mischievous broker has fastened to his coat-tail.

In dull seasons, the only thing left to operators is, "playing with stocks." This, it need not be remarked, is very much like playing with fire, for the operator is almost sure to get burnt. However, as this is the sole remedy for that restlessness, which dogs and urges the speculator on from behind, like the iron goad of destiny, he gladly avails himself of it, even though he knows it may cost him a pretty penny in the way of losses.

In the course of this diversion, it would be hard to mention the name of a stock to which we did not pay our respects, as "the Cynthia of the minute." After fifty or sixty different operations, in which I had jumped in, and then jumped out again, I found my losses in these transitory enterprises, had amounted to $22,000.

Then we (the quartette aforesaid,) joined forces, and gave four separate orders to as many different brokers in the Public Board, to buy one thousand shares of North-western Preferred, at the market price. The stock rose three per cent. under our joint purchase of four thousand shares. Naturally it was very gratifying for us to know that we had sufficient influence to make North-west rise three per cent., but this feeling of gratification was somewhat marred, when the price fell back again, entailing upon us a loss of four hundred dollars apiece.

Then we tried our hands at making those "quick

turns," which brokers so delight in. "Quick turns" are buying or selling for a profit of a quarter per cent. or more. No returns were rendered to us on these operations, though our broker reaped a harvest of commissions.

All our little operations for two months during the summer were based upon the most reliable "points," which we gathered from every conceivable source, with the greatest assiduity. As the market was generally a declining one during this period, we had barely saved ourselves from being thoroughly impaled on these points, by "cutting short our losses," in every case, excepting one, and that was my private and individual case, as will be seen by the following statement.

While perambulating in Broad Street, in search of points, I met J——, a stock-market acquaintance. He had a most unprepossessing countenance, in fact quite disagreeable. Some would have called it sinister in its expression, but he was worth $500,000, and consequently Wall Street voted him as good looking and agreeable. In society he was set down as fascinating.

"Did he know of any stock to make a turn in? Just a flyer of a thousand shares, good for one or two per cent, enough to pay for a trip to Niagara?" I asked.

"Well, no! I'm only this morning in from the country, and a'nt posted; but here comes G——, he can tell you something worth knowing, I'll wager."

So saying, he introduced me to G——, and passed on. I had often seen G——, who haunted the market, and had wondered who he was. *He* also had a very unpleasing face, which always wore a fixed Mephisto-phelian smile, commonly known as the clam-shell smile. He vainly endeavored to hide the ravages in-flicted by twenty-five years of a speculator's life, by dyeing his full beard a dead black. I had understood that he had affiliations with several leading railroad directors. A second cousin of his was said to be connected with the Erie direction, and his wife's brother had relations to the coal interests. His uncle was a permanent investor in New York Cen-tral. Then there was his grandfather, a venerable stock operator, who could have been seen toddling down two or three times a year, wearing the family smile. G—— was the image of his grandfather, only more so.

As he had dropped three or more fortunes in differ-ent convenient places around the street, he was, and had been for several months, living on very short commons, so much so that his most intimate acquaint-ances alleged that he never at this time was in the habit of taking more than one square meal in a day. As to costume, however, he could not be impeached, for he "traveled on his style," and always found it pay to dress. His toilet was an important part of his capital in the trade, which he worked at. *This trade was selling points.* Here was unfolded the mystery of his existence. He sold information; he jobbed off secrets; he dealt in "points" warranted not to cut in the eye, and thus extracted sustenance for himself and the young buzzards which fluttered in his domestic nest. He would put in his "point" against the capital of some wealthy friend, who, on the information thus furnished, would buy or sell one or more hundred shares of stock, G—— having a certain interest in the operation. If there was a profit growing out of it, G—— had a part of it, allotted to him as a remuneration for his point. If a loss occurred, G—— would give his note for his proportion, but owing to G——'s impecuniosity these notes, of course, were never paid.

It will be readily seen that G——'s geese generally laid golden eggs.

In some cases he was known to give contradictory points to different operators. He would tell one operator, for example, that Erie was about to be put up; on this point two hundred shares of Erie would be bought. Then he would go to another operator and inform him that Erie was about to be dropped; and on this point, two hundred shares of Erie would be sold short. Then G—— "had a sure thing;" out of one of these transactions a profit would certainly accrue.

G—— looked me steadily in the face as if he would take the latitude and longitude of my bank account. Then he seemed suddenly to grow to me like a limpet to a rock. He hooked his arm in mine, jerked his head in a southerly direction, and walking rapidly round the corner of Exchange Place, passed through several winding passages into the tunnel leading to the Regular Board, then halted to breathe something in a husky whisper into the ear of a small, but very well-groomed broker, passed down stairs into Beaver Street, stalked into Delmonico's and sat down opposite to me at a little table. Then calling for some rare, delicious beverage, such as can be got only at that temple of Bacchus, he gazed at me, trying very hard to infuse into his smile, something at once plaintive and affectionate.

Mysterious silence! G—— was evidently pregnant and laboring with some momentous secret. Suddenly his left eyelid drooped, then closed very tight; he bent over and whispered in my ear:

"Do you want to make some money? Of course you do. I'll put up a job for you, if you say so."

"Yes. What's your job?" replied I.

"Buy five hundred shares of——. I'll tell you the stock if you say you'll do it. Joint account, profit and loss, you and I."

"All right! What's the stock?" rejoined I.

Thereupon he delivered a brief and impressive dissertation on the value of coal-stocks in general, and of this stock in particular; and, looking all around him, to assure himself that no listener was near, he pronounced the word "Cumberland!" Having paused for a moment, to see the effect produced by this communication, he winked again very hard and continued: "Saw a director this morning. Slope mine; sale soon to be consummated. Cash dividend, ten per cent. Bet you twenty-five dollars (taking out a very lean pocket-book as if he was eager to plank down his money) that Cumberland sells at par in thirty days. Don't wait, buy five hundred right away."

In fifteen minutes after this interview, five hundred shares of Cumberland were registered on the stock-book of N—— & Co., as held for the joint account of G—— and myself. It cost about 80. In the course of the next week it had fallen five per cent. The loss on it was twenty-five hundred dollars. The next best thing to cutting short a loss, is "averaging" it by buying more stock at a lower price.

G——, who turned up when Cumberland was selling at 74, reported that the sale of the Slope mine had been delayed, and that the stock had been dropped for the purpose of "Scooping a few more shorts." He advised that we keep our position, and "average," by buying more stock at the decline. We *averaged*, by buying five hundred more Cumberland at about 74.

This averaging or buying separate lots successively as the price declines, when an operator is saddled with stock at a high price, is all very well if stocks soon recover themselves, or if the buyer's margins are sufficiently ample to enable him to keep buying until the tide turns. Should the stock, however, fall fifty per cent., the operator who starts by buying five hundred shares, and repeats the purchase at every five per cent. decline, will find himself at last loaded with five thousand five hundred shares, at an average loss of twenty-five per cent., or about $125,000, rather a heavy burden for any one but a millionaire. Still, very many of the Wall Street men follow this plan with great success so long as they gauge it according to their means.

M——, a noted Wall Street man, has been heard to boast that he never sold a stock at a loss during the past ten years. He bought one hundred shares of Erie at 128, during the Morse rise, and bought another hundred at 95, and after that at every ten per cent. decline, repeated his purchase till April, 1865, when Erie after touching 42, rose again to 98.

His average was 79, and after nearly eighteen months, his stubbornness was rewarded with a profit. The same individual, in 1868, bought one hundred Erie at 80, and now holds five hundred shares which averages him 55. He has waited two years for the tide to turn, and we venture to predict that he will yet sell his Erie at a handsome profit.

To resume our story. Cumberland continued falling, and we (G—— and I,) continued averaging. G—— always had some plausible story to tell about the occasion of each five per cent. decline. When Cumberland reached 56, we held two thousand shares which brought us in for a loss of more than $30,000. By this time G——'s point had vanished, without leaving a residuum, and he about the same time was missed from Wall Street. Nothing was left to his partner but to keep averaging, or sell out, and pocket his loss.

When a man is in danger of heavy loss upon a purchase, it is remarkable how lavish his friends are of advice and information of a disagreeable nature. So it happened during the Cumberland drop to 56. One of the first men I met was a prominent broker of the "party," for there was a "party" in the stock. That mysterious word, "party." Somehow there always seems to be a "party" in every stock on the list. "Don't hold a share of it," said he, "the party are getting out of it as fast as they can, and in six weeks the whole capital stock will be knocking around the street dear at 40."

The next man I met was an old capitalist, who had been a dealer for twenty years in Cumberland. When I said "Cumberland" to him, he pranced and curvetted, metaphorically speaking, like an aged war-horse at the sound of a trumpet.

" Cumberland ?" cried he.

" How much is it worth ?" inquired I.

" Well, about ten cents on the dollar. Dividends! it never has and never will pay a dividend. We made up a party and bought nearly all of it at five cents on the dollar, five or six years ago, and then subscribed five per cent. as a working capital. We tried to work the mines, but it was no go. We lost the whole of our working capital, $250,000, and then sold out our stock at five, the price we paid for it."

The advice given by the prominent broker, and the information elicited from the capitalist, were not calculated to give nerve to a man who held Cumberland at 80.

And yet I stood up and prepared myself to continue my programme.

Dull seasons in the stock-market are always the precursors of some marked change one way or the other. If stocks have unduly risen, a dull time precedes a fall; if they have been unduly depressed, it precedes a rise. And so it fell out. As August drew near its close, there were signs and omens of approaching change.

Before telling how I came out of Cumberland, it will be proper here to switch off our stock train into the track of gold. As I have before mentioned, it was not till August, 1864, that a separate place was assigned to the dealings in this commodity.

Soon after the repressive Congressional act was repealed, Gilpin's reading room, on the corner of William Street and Exchange Place, was the place of meeting first selected by the gold crowd. Here commenced an era of speculation in the precious metal, which was to last six months, and was marked by greater vicissitudes in fortune, than even the stock speculation, which was its forerunner.

It should be noticed here, that enormous transactions were privately made every day, during the operation of the act against dealing in gold on contracts, proving how little power legal enactments have over a trade which promises great profits.

CHAPTER XXIV.

THE BREAK IN GOLD—PANIC-BIRDS.

The Gold Fire-balloon—Vibrations from the Cannon's Roar—The Gathering of the Clans in the Gold-room—Desperate Speculators at the Front—Portraits of Operators—N—— Bulls Gold, and We Bull It—A Loss, first on the Long and then on the Short Side—A Call for More Margin, and an Examination of our Bubble-company Assets—A Visit to the Den of the Bloated Spider—The Clergyman and Farmer Looking After Their Investment—They Find the House " Swept and Garnished "—We Meet the " Corpulent Gentleman " in a Picture Gallery—The Interview and its Result—The Fall of Atlanta, and Gold on the Rampage Downwards—Panic-birds at Their Feast—A Portrait of the " Stormy Petrels "—Buy Cumberland—I " Average " out of My Loss.

ROM July 2d till August 30th, 1864, gold hung from 250 to 280, like a monstrous fire-balloon by the side of a thunder-cloud. Not a few daring aeronauts sailed over the massed blackness, which darkened the financial sky, as if they would garner its thunder-bolts in sheaves.

Low mutterings already foreboded a storm which would either drive gold before it to 500 and depress greenbacks to twenty cents on the dollar, staggering if not prostrating the shaky system of Government credit, or which should hurl gold down to the neighborhood of par amid the ruin of American commerce and all its dependencies.

On the James River two hosts lay watching each other sullenly through the embrasures of mighty liam Street and Exchange Place, was the place of meeting first selected by the gold crowd. Here commenced an era of speculation in the precious metal, which was to last six months, and was marked by greater vicissitudes in fortune, than even the stock speculation, which was its forerunner.

It should be noticed here, that enormous transactions were privately made every day, during the operation of the act against dealing in gold on contracts, proving how little power legal enactments have over a trade which promises great profits.

earth-moles, or behind sand bags, or couched in trenches through many a circling league; Sheridan and Early were playing a bloody game of tag, up and down the Shenandoah, while every one was listening to catch the sound of the cannon of the army of the Tennessee,.as it swept up to the gates of the confederacy. Ever and anon the deep booming of the guns of Sherman as his long deep columns rolled past the blood-stained heights of Kenesaw, on! on! across the Chattahoochie, awoke dismal echoes in the hearts of the gold-bulls. And now Atlanta was beleaguered.

The dull season was over at last, and the carnival of speculation had commenced. Even on tame days the price vibrated two or three per cent. in an hour, and there were not many tame days. Here was the swiftest chance to make or lose a fortune in a day. Stocks were nothing to it. The wildest and most desperate speculators from every side flocked into the new gold room, a motley multitude of well dressed barbarians with seamed faces and cavernous eyes, screaming and brandishing their arms from morning till night. Their voices were like that of Stentor, their lungs like iron, their fingers seemed fairly electrified with charges from the ticking telegraph.

Many of the operators in the crowd went in for short turns, buying and selling millions in a day. Among these was a short thick-set Missourian, named C——. He stood on a chair in one corner, registering his purchases and sales in a little book which he constantly held in his hands. The heavy break three weeks after, clipped his audacious wings, and he disappeared from the scene. High above the din occasionally could be heard the hollow bull-bison roar of

24

D. H——, whose face wedged between the shoulders of the crowd, resembled that of a blonde and apoplectic bull-dog.

Another man who operated on short turns for enormous amounts, was S——, who might have been a member of the Lydia Thompson troupe, with his hair of pale tow, and his eyes of the hue and sharpness of a newly polished axe.

Later in the day, a conspicuously tall and ugly man might have been seen, generally holding in his hand a crumpled paper, containing the latest news from the Southern Confederacy. It was C——, and when he bid for $100,000 gold, the price always stiffened. Then the crowd would be crazy to buy. Lockwood's man would sell them half a million or so, and the excitement would subside.

Fresh news from the front. "Johnston driven back by Sherman." Now, everybody wanted to sell, and gold would drop off two or three per cent. These scenes were renewed at the Evening Exchange, and in the bar-room of the Fifth Avenue Hotel; telegrams flew around like snow-flakes, while gold changed hands by the million.

Late in August the bankers held gold in a firm grip at 260. Large sums had been locked up, and as enormous short sales had been made by the bears on the faith of better military prospects, gold could be readily carried by loaning it to the short sellers. A serious disaster to any one of the Union armies would have driven the price up to 300. And in the absence of any news, the fears of the bears would have induced them to bid it up to 275.

N——, our buoyant broker, had never abated one

jot of his confidence of the ultimate rise of gold to 300. He talked it up at lunch-time; he bought it in magnificent lots in the gold room, in fact he bulled it always and everywhere. Hence it was that in company with L—— I made a venture at that perilous height. I bought $100,000 at 260; in two days I cut short my loss by selling at 250. Ten thousand out on this flyer. The price stayed not long at 250. Suddenly on the last day of August, the grasp of the gold bulls was paralyzed, and the price fell with a dull thud to 233.

What was the matter?

Trouble in the secession camp. The underground telegraph kept up a constant click. Little groups of rebel sympathizers, scowling and glum, stood on the side-walk, while the looks of those who were long of gold disclosed their secret consternation.

If Sherman took Atlanta, gold would fall fifty per cent. L—— and myself reversed our engines and sold $100,000 gold at 235. This time we clung to our loss till the price had risen to 250. Then we covered. Twenty-five thousand dollars gone in two weeks! Besides these losses on gold, I stood minus $17,000 on Hudson and North-west Preferred, and $30,000 on Cumberland!

N——'s dome-like brow was over-clouded. He called us into his private office, and told us that we must margin up on our stocks, twenty per cent.

Things began to have a mixed look. We must examine our assets.

Most of our assets, outside of margins in our broker's hands, were in the compact and permanent shape of certificates of mining companies. What could they be sold for? We threw them upon the market. For Gregory Consolidated, we had never a bid. Gunnel Gold, we sold, wonderful to relate, for forty per cent. less than we had given for it.

As for " The Alligator Bayou Salt Company," "The Big Mountain Iron Company," " The Black Valley Coal Company," and " The Angels' Rest Quicksilver Company," there were no quotations.

We next sought out the corpulent gentleman, with gold-bowed spectacles, who had succeeded in placing our money, at least $25,000 of it, in the securities last named. His office was near by, just round the corner from the Regular Board of Brokers. As L—— and myself approached it, we saw a couple of countrymen deeply engaged in deciphering two placards, one of which hung in the window, and announced that these offices were *To Let!* The other placard informed anxious inquirers that the office of various mining companies, therein named, was removed to —— William Street, Room No. 28. A look of quizzical wonder sat on the faces of the two men, who were studying the placards. They had come to the city to see how their investments were doing, and to inquire for dividends. The taller of the two was evidently a clergyman. He seemed to take in the situation with remarkable rapidity, and after staring into the windows meekly, for a moment, turned up the street, and walked away as if he were shaking the dust off his feet. The other, who was apparently an agriculturist, had a weather-beaten face, a country made coat, and a blue cotton umbrella. After reading the placard on the door, he aired his eye at the keyhole, then went into the street, and gazed into the window, saw that the office was swept and garnished, cast a searching glance about him, as if he were hunting for specimens of gold quartz, and then, giving a prolonged whistle, ejaculated, "Sloped, by gosh!"

We left the rustic ruminating upon the uncertainty of mining investments, and wended our way to —— William Street, Room No. 28, fourth floor. We found this apartment locked and cob-webs over the key-hole. By removing these obstructions, and looking through the aperture, we could only discover a pile of dusty stock certificate books and a small heap of stones on the floor, which we recognized with some difficulty, as being those remarkably rich samples and specimens of quartz, sulphurets, etc.

We shed no tears, yet we had " thoughts too deep for tears," as we walked homeward that night. Nothing was left to us except to find the corpulent gentleman with gold-bowed spectacles, and see if he would take our certificates off our hands, even at ten cents on the dollar; " failing in that," remarked L—— " we can resort to arms and punch the head of the author of our woes."

On the way home, we happened to step into a picture sales-room on Broadway. The paintings in this establishment were advertised to be the collection of a gentleman just about to start for Europe, and some of his pictures were fondly supposed to be works of the old masters. They embraced the usual themes to which artists are prone to devote themselves, viz., a certain number of cherubs rather beef-faced, and run to fat; several portraits of women with very high color, staring eyes and Roman noses; two or three nude figures after Greuze, a historical picture, the battle of Brandywine, besides landscapes, etc., etc., all newly varnished and in bright gilt frames, made to order.

While contemplating the beauties, and endeavoring to penetrate the "clear obscurity" of these works of art, we became conscious that some one else had joined us, and on casting our eyes around, saw the very man we were in search of, breathing asthmatically, and standing like some gigantic owl directly in front of a very stout Magdalen, and feasting his eyes upon it.

Two hands clapped upon his fat shoulders and two pair of wrathful eyes startled him nearly out of his artistic trance. He stepped back an instant, then recovering himself, grasped our hands affectionately and inquired after our healths with truly paternal solicitude.

"A soft answer turneth away wrath." We were taken aback by so much courtesy, but regained ourselves and cross-examined him on the subject of our investments, and begged to know if he would take them off our hands at a discount.

"Well! no!" replied he, "I am not buying now."

"What's the matter with the securities?" inquired we.

"Antimony is the matter; sulphur is the matter," was his reply. "You see that our gold ores are very rich, but the gold is mixed up with antimony and sulphur, and it can't be extracted so as to pay. But this problem of separating the gold from the antimony and sulphur will be solved before long, then you'll wake up and find yourselves rich, etc., etc."

Although we thought it extremely improbable

that this problem would be solved in our day, yet the corpulent gentleman was so exquisitely bland, and ready with his explanations, that from indignation, we relapsed into uncomplaining sorrow, which in turn passed into forgetfulness, and in three days we had ceased to call to mind how much money we had sunk in bubble-companies.

It is a remarkable trait in human nature, this facility with which the outside public forget how they have been bamboozled by these bogus companies. Perhaps they do not really forget, but they certainly seem to forget how much money they have thrown away in these investments. It may be, that their vanity keeps them from disclosing how they have been taken in.

Meanwhile gold had risen to 254, and was scarce for delivery. It was the news that General Hood was sending his advance guard to Columbus, which had thrown gold to 233; it was the absence of any news, which had driven the price back to 254.

One hot afternoon, at four o'clock, early in September, the gold dealers emerged from their den, and stood on the sidewalk, in a compact and almost silent group. Something hung over the market. The operators stood staring at each other; not a bid or an offer was made. All at once a burly man appeared on the edge of the crowd, and bid for fifty thousand gold, in a loud voice. The price grew firmer when two or three men were observed selling quietly large amounts, and then the price sagged to 250.

There was news in the market! It must be from Atlanta!

That evening every gold-man was at his post, long

before the appointed hour. The bulls were prepared to bolster up the tottering column; and the bears, to make up some of their losses incurred during the past summer; for late that afternoon, the news had been flashed over the wires that Atlanta had fallen.

The Evening Exchange now was like a blacksmith's shop. Gold fell to 243, under the hammers of fifty operators, all striking at once. But just as this anvil chorus was swelling into the roar of a panic, the heavy holders of gold girded up their loins, and arrested, by sharp bids, the downward movement. Their only course now was to let the market down as easily as possible, and stave off a panic until they could unload.

This course they followed for two weeks, selling all they could secretly, and bidding up the market openly. Once or twice the price broke away from them, when gold would fall in a semi-panic, fifteen or twenty per cent. in an hour; but each time that it did so, they stepped into the gap, and ran up the price again, "scooping" many a bear just as he was stretching his paws for the profit, which he thought he had in his grasp. When at last they had sold out, though at a heavy loss, they let the price go, and down it dropped, amid the wildest excitement, to 187.

Our profits in the great gold break will be recounted in the following chapter.

We now return to our "averaged Cumberland."

While gold was flying wildly about, oscillating in long arcs towards 200, Cumberland all at once sprang in a day back to 68, and a great mass of stock was hurled upon the market. The ring had during the dull season taken a great number of short contracts

and then twisted them by bidding up the stock.
But the fifteen thousand shares which they sold upon
the rise, soon carried the price back to 60. Here it
stuck for two weeks. Stocks which had been tending
downwards for five months had received a fresh im-
petus in the same direction, from gold as it fell.

The 6th of October following came a panic which
carried Cumberland to 41. On that day I made the
acquaintance of one of that class of stock-operators
whom we shall designate as *panic-birds*. These men
are the stormy petrels of Wall Street. They are
never seen in the market when everything is bright
and buoyant, but let a tempest breed there and when
stocks are going down by the run, they flock to the
scene of disaster, prepared to take advantage of it by
buying stocks at low prices. Any one who has passed
through panics will remember those strange faces
standing near where the contest is raging, and quietly
giving their orders.

Who are they, and where do they come from?
All of them are veterans of the market, who have
learned by sad experience, that the only way to make
money in stocks is to buy when everybody else is
selling, that is during panics. Some come from the
country, stay over one train and then depart, loaded
with securities bought at a low price, and all of them
take their flight the moment stocks turn and react
upwards. One of these veterans has seen twenty
panics with his own eyes, and boasts that he has
made his fortune of $200,000 by never buying except
in those seasons.

F. S—— was a type of this class. I saw him for
the first time, during the October panic of 1857.

Then he disappeared from view for more than three years, turning up again in April, 1861, after the bombardment of Fort Sumter. In July, 1862, in May and September, 1863, on April 18th, 1864, in the gold panic just described, and finally on October 6th, following, he was always on the spot, not one minute too late to see prices reach the bottom of the grade.

A singular looking man. His mould was of the herculean pattern, and he turned the scale at sixteen stone two pounds. His face was like a tame eagle's, carved out of red oak; his hair was cut fighting fashion, as if he wished to keep himself in constant training, to cope with the bruisers of the stock-market, and while brokers were shrieking as the prices fell, he would stand very firm on his legs with his square solid set head cocked on one side, puffing firmly at a regalia as long as a small bowsprit.

I stood beside him on a mound of dust in Broad Street, and being in a fever of anxiety, such as is usually brought on by staring at a loss which threatens to fall on one, sought to relieve myself by asking his opinion about the market. He said nothing for a moment, then turning his head put his fat hand to his mouth and gurgled into my ear: "Buy Cumberland." Our account stood us out something over eighty thousand dollars, and now it was "play or pay."

Thanks to my short gold operations, to be hereafter described, I could buy one thousand Cumberland for cash, at from 42 to 45, and two thousand shares more on a margin at 46–47. In three days it rose to 59, and I was enabled to unload for a trifling loss.

A new campaign was now opening in gold, but before pursuing that jagged, serrated line of financial history, by which may be traced as on a many colored chart of alternate mountain peaks and lowland flats, the rising and sinking fortunes of the gold men, let us turn aside for a chapter to notice the speculation in something more substantial and staple than stocks; a speculation which sympathized with that in gold, moving up and down in lines parallel to it.

CHAPTER XXV.

PIGS OF GOLD IN A CORNER.

The Rise in New Mess—The Pork Trade—Its Magnitude and Seat—A Village Built of Hogs—The Movements of the Article—Cornering the Packed Pigs—I Make $10,000 in Cotton and then Slip into Pork Barrels—An Evening Lecture on Provisions, etc., at the Fifth Avenue Hotel—The Pork Corner of July 1864—Who Made It?—My First Visit to the Corn Exchange, and What I Saw There—A Crowd of Porkists—The Retired Pirate Buys a Thousand Barrels at 47—Panic on the Produce Exchange—I Sell a Call, Buy a Call, and Make $59,000 on One, and Lose $6,000 on the Other—Multiplying $500 by $100.

NO one connected with the agricultural interests, more especially with that branch which is concerned in the raising and fattening of swine, will fail to remember the great rise in pork which took place in 1864. This article in the provision line, so useful in regulating our foreign exchanges, and so sweet to the palate of those who delight in the dish popularly known as pork and beans, had risen from nine dollars per barrel in 1861, to fifty-three dollars per barrel in July 1864. If the deliciousness of a viand is proportioned to its price, then, indeed, was pork a delicious viand. Had one of the old Roman epicures survived till 1864, he would doubtless have mingled pork with the peacocks' brains, and ostriches' tongues, which gave zest to his banquets.

Few, who have not visited the Western States, will be able to estimate the extent of the business done in this commodity.

"This is a great country," remarked H——, a New York merchant, one day as we were traveling together with our faces turned towards the setting sun.

The place where this trite observation was made, was a small town on the western bank of the Mississippi; the time was the dead of winter in 1863, and the occasion of it was simply pork, or as it is called among the killers and packers, *hog*. We walked up to the village hotel between *hog*, we stepped over *hog*. Hecatombs of hog were piled up on every side, in stacks, in pyramids, in mountains. It met us at breakfast, dinner and tea, fried, baked, boiled and stewed. From our chamber window we overlooked a wide expanse of country, dotted with droves of hogs, and in great pens in the village, thousands of hogs were squealing, grunting, piling on, and suffocating each other in search of warmth (for the mercury stood five degrees below zero) of which last fact, (the piling,) we were notified by a hoarse voice calling out in the hall of the floor where we were sleeping that night: "John Hackerberry, your hog are piling! Turn out and look arter 'em!"

In this way we got our first ideas respecting the magnitude of the pork trade.

The harvest of the pork-raiser is in the winter. From December till April the carcasses are forwarded to the cities of Chicago, Cincinnati and New York etc., to be packed in barrels. The packed pork continues to come to New York from the West till July, after which there are small arrivals till the ensuing winter.

After July the regular cornering season commences, for corners are engineered in pork as well as in stocks. The number of barrels of pork on store in New York is accurately known. This is an important fact entering into the calculations of ambitious provision dealers, when they plan a corner in the article, since a new issue of pork cannot be made by those who are seeking to break down the corner, by throwing a fresh supply upon the market, as bearish railroad directors are wont to do in stocks, when they find themselves cornered.

A corner in pork is just as close, and the cornerers themselves just as remorseless, as those in stocks.

This was how I came to be caught short in one of these same corners. The five hundred bales of cotton bought in May, netted me $10,000, the price having risen, in ten days, no less than forty cents a pound.

This lucky operation at once brought me into the speculative mercantile circle. I began to take an interest in the price of produce and provisions, and to learn the A B C of operations in tobacco, sugar, grain, and PORK.

The Fifth Avenue Hotel has long been the financial up-town evening center, and in 1864, all who were interested in the rise and fall of merchandise, etc., as well as stocks and gold, flocked thither like boys round an emptied sugar cask.

One evening, early in July, a few days after the gold-burst upwards, six men sat in a circle within the reading room of that huge marble tavern, exchanging views upon a great variety of subjects. Two of these men, L—— and myself, were stock operators, one was a noted gold broker, and the other three were in the dry goods and raw cotton line. What we didn't say on the subjects of stocks and general merchandise, would hardly be worth telling, for our session was a protracted one, and one or the other of us had taken flyers in almost every speculative direction. First it was stocks and gold, then cotton, iron, petroleum, turpentine, wheat, tea, molasses, butter, cheese, etc., etc., through the whole scale.

At length some one said "Pork!" and now all our tongues wagged merrily. "Pork was the thing to go into now, on the short side." Four of our circle had bought it a few weeks before, and sold out at a profit of ten dollars a barrel, and seemed thoroughly booked in the business; while L—— and myself had taken notes on it, for a month previous, and were watching the article in question, as it slipped upwards on its greasy trail.

Enter J. L—— at this moment.

He was a partner in the house of R——, H——, B—— & Co. He stared round the room, quickly espied our circle, and steered towards it, discharging volumes of cigar smoke as he drew near. He was an authority on the subject of pork, for his firm was in the provision business.

"How is pork?" chorused all.

"Strong! Fifty-three dollars bid for August deliveries," was the reply.

After that he gave us an account of the "corner," which had been engineered in the pork market.

The leader in the movement was C——, a wealthy packer, and storage man. With him were joined a number of other firms who had bought pork at various prices, from thirty dollars upwards. Three circumstances had assisted them in their scheme, viz., the great ease in money which had ruled in June at five or six per cent., the rise in gold with which pork as well as other exportable commodities sympathized, and the enormous short interest in pork. The more conservative firms, in consideration of its rise of four or five hundred per cent., had been selling it for future delivery, and the cornerers had taken their contracts for July and August. If money continued easy, and gold kept up for six weeks longer, pork would rise to seventy dollars per barrel, but if not, then it would drop back to thirty or forty dollars, and the corner would be broken up.

These were the questions to be answered.

But whereas after so protracted a season of easy money, it was likely to grow tight, and gold, after a rise of one hundred per cent., might naturally fall fifty per cent., (so we all reasoned,) pork was a better sale than purchase. We would sell short to-morrow. This was the decision of L—— and myself, when we parted that night.

The next morning we went to the office of R——, H——, B—— & Co., in Water Street. The senior member of this firm, a stout, cheery, wholesome looking gentleman, intimated that we were on the right track if we sold pork; "in fact," said he, "I should take a chance at it myself if I hadn't been heated up and cooled down so often;" meaning thereby that he was now on the shady side of fifty.

So we accompanied J. L—— to the *Corn Exchange,* or, as it is sometimes called, the Produce Exchange. This is one of the institutions of New York. A huge brick building on the corner of Whitehall and Pearl Streets, only the upper part of which however is used by the association of merchants who meet there from twelve to two o'clock daily. The hall in which they meet, occupies the whole of the second floor of the building. The clock struck twelve as we entered this room, which was already crowded with dealers. They were a very different looking set of men from those who congregate in and about the Stock Exchange. There was about them an air of solidity and of legitimate trade. As the hour flew by we waited for business to commence, but nothing seemed to be doing. There was no noise, and all the conversation was carried on in a low tone. They seemed to be waiting for something which never came, and reminded us very much of the visitors inspecting an agricultural fair. Some of them gathered round little pans of flour, and took pinches between their fingers and moistened them in saucers, as if they were making paste samples; others poked their fingers into lard tubs, or punched out small pieces of cheese, or spooned up little lumps of butter and tasted them, smacking their lips and holding their heads on one side, with the most knowing of looks upon their faces. One old gentleman in a black coat, black stock, and a wig of the jettiest hue, was peering into a barrel of beans, like a magpie squinting into a marrow-bone. The majority of the crowd, however, seemed to be engaged in pleasant, social conversation.

In the north-east corner of the room, stood a cluster of twenty or thirty men who were apparently more busy. Those of low stature were in the center, and the tall ones looked over their shoulders. They

25

talked almost in a whisper and in a very few words, handling their memorandum books briskly and jotting down as they talked. What could they be doing? Buying and selling pork! We joined this coterie, and J. L—— informed us that if we wished to sell, he could dispose of two thousand barrels of new mess, deliverable in July or August, at forty-seven dollars per barrel, and ten dollars a barrel margin to be put up by both parties. We gave the order. Our two thousand barrels were immediately snapped up by a sallow little man in a green vest, yellow pants, red neck-tie, covered with a profusion of jewelry, and looking very much like a successful and retired pirate, who was hovering about the skirts of the crowd.

My proportion of this short sale was one thousand barrels. For the next two weeks we sought the fellowship of the pork men. Pork on the brain. We thought pork, talked pork, handled pork, dreamed of pork, and did everything with it except eat it, because it cost too much. The pork men are very much after the pattern of the Wall Street men. Jolly boys, astonished at nothing, much given to the eating and drinking of good things, fond of jokes which border on the broad, and always on the lookout for commissions, with a sharp eye to the margins of their customers.

Everything now "went merry as a marriage bell," for pork was falling, and we were preparing to put money in our purses. It was also gratifying to our vanity, when we reflected that we were right in the financial reasonings on which our sales of pork had been based. Money, we said, would tighten, and gold fall. Sure enough, gold did drop to 244, and as

for money, it became suddenly as scarce as roses in
December. This pressure, the pork men said, was a
"squealer." There were palpitations and flutterings
at the Corn Exchange that morning, and the stalwart cornerers shook in their well greased boots, for
was not new mess pork down to thirty-eight dollars?

I could cover my short sale at $9,000 profit, not
reckoning in the commission due to R——, H——,
B—— & Co., which was two and one-half per cent.
on $47,000, the contract price at which the pork was
sold. But who ever heard of a man covering a short
sale in a panic? Prices looked then as if they would
never recover themselves. So it was now, instead of
taking my profit I sold another thousand barrels at
37. In one week pork had risen to 42. Then I
covered, and found, instead of a nice little profit, I
had a nice little commission bill of $2,000, to pay
R——, H——, B—— & Co. In fact, I found that
pork owed me money, and was uneasy till pork paid
me that money, or—owed me more. That money
must be recovered. How could it be done? I dared
not sell, for I was in the position of the burnt child,
who dreads the fire. Ha! a thought! I would sell
a call on favorable terms.

Calls and puts are sold in pork, just as they are in
stocks.

I sold a call for one thousand barrels of pork, that
very night at the Fifth Avenue Hotel, or rather J.
L—— sold it for me. I thus became responsible to
deliver to —— ——, any time within sixty days, at
forty-three dollars and fifty cents per barrel, one
thousand barrels of new mess, and in consideration thereof, I received one thousand dollars. This

partly wiped out my loss, but there was the call still hanging over me.

"These calls are nasty things," observed Uncle Daniel, after his Harlem fight.

"So say we all of us." Especially a sixty day call.

If pork should go to seventy dollars, I should stand out fifteen thousand besides commissions, which should never be forgotten in these little operations.

This was late in August, gold was tottering, but sixty days is a long time. There was one way in which I could save myself; I could hedge by buying a call for the same amount; let the one call offset the other.

I bought my call. Pork rose, and in two weeks it showed me a net profit of five hundred dollars. Atlanta had just fallen, and gold was on the down grade, but all my spare cash was locked up in margins. I yearned to sell, but could not.

But while dwelling on my uncomfortable position, I remembered the profit on my call. I took the contract to my broker, but he refused to accept it as a margin. As I was going out of the office, I met the Lobster, so called from his very red face and bulging eyes. He had recently gone into the business of buying and selling on commission, and so was willing to make concessions for the purpose of getting business. His eyes bulged still more, and his face grew a shade redder, as he listened to my proposals, then thrusting my call into his pocket, he rushed into the gold room, and in the twinkling of a star rushed out again and announced that he had sold ten thousand gold at 243. In twenty-four hours gold struck 230, but the Lobster had been meanwhile kept diligently at work selling for my behoof, and already I had $6,000 profits. In two weeks after, when gold reached 214, my profits had run up to $19,000. Now gold flew up to 228, and if my transactions had been closed at that figure, I should have stood just where I started. But the upward spasm soon passed, and gold resumed its downward course. When it touched 190 I gave the order to cover my shorts. This was done at a profit of $39,000. Then reversing my engine, I bought $200,000; when the price shot to 200 the next day, I sold and raked in $20,000. In one month I had made $59,000 out of a pitiful $500 on a pork call.

Now that pork owed me nothing, I closed my pork call without either profit or loss. Still there remained the thousand barrels, which I had agreed to deliver at forty-three fifty, with pork rising every day. It touched 43, and I bought one thousand barrels to hold ready for delivery, when a little speck appeared in the western sky, in the shape of a provision and produce panic, in Chicago and other western cities. Money grew tight, and the pork and grain men were in distress. They had stood up firmly under their loads, but contemplating the fall of gold, and its reduced price for ten days, was too much for their nerves, and they weakened.

The 7th of October was a lively day among the pork men of the New York Corn Exchange, as I afterwards learned from L——, (who had an interest of five hundred barrels in the pork market, and to whom I had delegated the task of looking after my thousand barrels that day, inasmuch as I was then busily engaged in taking care of Cumberland.) The first thing which caught his eye, on approaching the pork crowd, was the retired pirate to whom I had sold my first thousand barrels, flying about as if he were busily engaged in scuttling some merchant vessel. He came up to L——, and recognized him at once, as his legitimate prey. Unfortunately, our broker was late that day, and the pirate ascertaining that fact, from L——, promptly volunteered his services, which L—— as promptly accepted, for pork was dropping one dollar per barrel, every five minutes.

"Sell fifteen hundred barrels at 42," said L——.

"All right!" said the pirate, and he shuffled off to execute the commission; poking his head under the coat-tails of a tall, weary looking porkist, he came back speedily, and reported the best price as 41½.

"Then sell at 41½," said L——.

Again his volunteer agent insinuated himself into the crowd, and *stayed there*. The crowd kept up a perpetual whispering. L—— was in dismay, for pork was now reported as offered at 41, and weak at that; he poked his long arm between two heads, touched the pirate on the shoulder and nodded very hard to him to sell; he nodded back, and kept his place in the crowd.

L—— then made a feeble offer of fifteen hundred barrels of new mess, at 41. Several turned round and stared at him, and then resumed their whispering. L—— said he felt very bad.

The pirate here made his appearance, and taking L—— affectionately by the arm, led him aside, and informed him in confidence, that he knew a party, a friend of his, who would take that fifteen hundred barrels at 40¼. That was about the market price.

tered ourselves that we had helped to puncture the caseous balloon, and contributed to the collapse of the aeronaut who had inflated it, to the sorrow of all lunchers and sandwich-eaters.

Finding, that after a campaign of three months on the Corn Exchange, we had come out nearly even, we bid adieu forever to pork, corn, wheat, butter, and cheese, except in a dietetic way, and in the future, concentrated ourselves upon gold and stocks, having discovered that we knew more about our own special trade than about cut meats and cereals.

CHAPTER XXVI.

THE WORSHIPERS OF THE GOLDEN CALF.

THE gold men moved into their new room on the corner of William and Beaver Streets, late in September.

The downward course of gold after the fall of Atlanta, seemed so reasonable, that a new element entered into the speculation, consisting of cooler and more cautious men. As the current rolled down from the mountain height of 254, they put their arms up to the elbows in the golden gravel, and in ten days became as mad as the maddest of the throng.

The gold room was like a cavern, full of dank and noisome vapors, and the deadly carbonic acid was blended with the fumes of stale smoke and vinous breaths. But the stifling gases engendered in that low-browed cave of evil enchanters, never seemed to depress the energies of the gold-dealers; from "morn to dewy eve" the drooping ceiling and bistre-colored walls reëchoed with the sounds of all kinds of voices, from the shrill, piping treble of the call boys, to the deep bass of R. H——, J. R——, L. J——, etc., etc., while an upreared forest of arms was swayed furiously by the storms of a swiftly rising and falling market.

When we consider the number of operators, the amount of capital employed, and the volume of business transacted, the wide and rapid fluctuations, and the frequency with which operations were repeated, it will be no exaggeration to say, that in that room from September, 1864, till July, 1865, more fortunes were made and lost, than in any space of the same size before or since. Here occurred most of the Atlanta tumble, the rocket-like movement from 187 to 260, the swift and countless vibrations between 260 and 200, the flying gallop, which carried the price from 200 to 128, and finally, the hoist to 146, all in the course of nine short months.

The story of great fortunes made in a day, drew thousands from all parts of the Republic. Solid men of Boston; spare men from Connecticut, whose sharpness, as regards money, might have enabled them to beguile St. Peter to swap his golden keys; logy men, with bovine eyes, from the state of Maine, stalwart Westerners, familiar with the game of bluff from their earliest boyhood; besides that numerous army of speculators from south of Mason and Dixon's line, already mentioned. These were only a squadron of the host.

Each broker and commission house seemed to have

been transformed into a human magnet, attracting to itself all the old and young "files" who thought their teeth sharp enough to bite into the golden pasty; while the wealthy banking houses, by their very name and reputed solvency, received by mail, by hand, and even by telegraph, in the form of credits, vast amounts to be used as margins, and passed them rapidly out of sight forever of the hopeful depositors. Those men who had money, and were known to be of a speculative turn of mind, were approached directly, by the nimble mercurial tribe of younger brokers, who solicited their business, painting in glowing hues the prospect of making speedy fortunes.

After gold dropped to 187, on the 26th of September, it reacted to 200, then fell back to 190–191, where it remained for ten days.

There were now, as there always are, in the stock market, two sets of opinions. One of these was loud-mouthed in the expression of the belief that gold was on the way to 150. The other as strongly held to the belief in another great rise. But this latter opinion was scarcely expressed. The party which looked for a further decline, was the more numerous and the more clamorous, besides being strengthened by the large profits on their short sales during the recent fall. The party which looked for another rise was by far the more wealthy, and numbered in its ranks most of the great banking houses. It was observed that they were continually crying down the price of gold and as continually buying it. The short sales were immense, and were as usual, quietly taken by the bull party. For a few days the market was in suspense.

One morning the roar of cannon was heard in the bay, and a report ran through the street, that Richmond had been captured. The bear cohort rushed in a body to the gold room and sold millions in expectation of a fresh break. The price never yielded under this tremendous pressure, and in twenty-four hours, gold was 203. The bear cohort never flinched, but kept selling. In three days, gold was 216. The faces of the short sellers here became elongated, when news came of cavalry Sheridan's victory, after his swift gallop up the valley of the Shenandoah, and down fell gold to 208. Now the bears commenced again their furious hammering, but only succeeded in knocking the price down one-half per cent., when whisk! it jumped to 220.

The crew of short sellers now sat like shipwrecked mariners upon a coral reef in mid ocean, watching with wild eyes for a sail, which was never to appear, while night and storm closes above them.

The tide rose rapidly, and the agony of the shipwrecked ones was soon over.

Gold, in ten days, was 246, then surging back to 230, it gathered itself, and poured in one great wave up to 260. The same men who had sold it at 190, and predicted its fall to 150, now bought it, and laid bets that it would be at 300 inside of thirty days. Frailty, thy name is the Wall Street bear!

Of all the exultant crowd, who bathed in Pactolian waters, and upon whom the golden rain had fallen in showers, six weeks before, who was the richer now? They had prayed for riches, " Let the stream of wealth be swift and violent." The golden torrent had come in answer to their prayers. On September 26th, they laved in it, rolled in and drank of it to intoxication. On November 9th, they woke as from a dream, and found, instead of a golden torrent, nothing but a bed of stones and sand. They who had engineered this enormous rise, and had wrought the ruin of so many, were blown up with wealth, and with the self-confidence that was, in four short months, to lead some of them to their ruin. But now they were triumphant, counting their gains, and planning new stratagems.

After every great rise and fall in stocks and gold, there comes the gazette, in which the names of the losers, and of the financially dead, are recorded. This gazette is not like that which follows a battle, published and spread abroad, but circulates only in the stock-market, or among the friends of the losing individuals.

Men drop out of the ranks, and their forms are seen, and their voices heard no more on 'Change. The word goes round, "Brown has gone up!" the next day he is forgotten. The rise of gold to 260 broke up our quartette. W. B. C—— left the street in despair at his losses, and never returned to it again. E——, my *alter ego*, lost all of his fortune except $5,000.

The writer was fortunate enough to receive a lesson early in the campaign, which taught him to stand clear of short sales.

It happened thus:

One day in October, just after gold had fallen to 208, on the news of the Sheridan victories, I met, in the doorway of the gold room, one L. O——, a German Jew, who strikingly resembled, in his personal appearance, a huge wharf rat, smoothly shaved and dressed in the garb of a broker. Hailing me, he spoke, breaking English into the following pieces:

"Hein! Mishter——, a vort mit you. Vy you not do your bishness mit me? I do your bishness sheap. I sharge you only dree per shent. marchin, dree tousand dollars on von hoondert tousand gold, and you bay me dree dollars and von shilling comeeshion, den I garry it eider way, long or short. Shell a hoondert dish minoot, you mak blanty moonish."

The bargain was clinched on the spot by my handing him a check for three thousand dollars, and ordering him to sell one hundred thousand gold at the market price. Whereupon he dove into the bowels of the crowd, waved his hand and screamed out something that sounded like von hoondert, and returned to me, reporting that he had sold $100,000 at 208½, though I am confident now, that the rascal never sold a dollar. Then he vanished up the street.

I thought that gold seemed a little stiffer that morning, and on coming back to the gold-room, after two hours' absence, gold stood at 210½.

L. O—— soon made his appearance with a woebegone look on his face, and asked me what he should do. While I was deliberating, he broke in upon me.

"Oh! Mishter ——, tish all right. You geep your poseetion; but I musht have more marchin; gif me dree tousand dollars more and I geep you short of gold, den you mak monish."

A second check for three thousand dollars was drawn and duly consigned to the pocket of L. O——, who just then seemed to recollect some important business which required his presence elsewhere, and vanished as before.

It need hardly be told that I kept my position in accordance with the advice of L. O——.

In forty-eight hours, gold was 215.

"Shoost von leetle sheck more for dree tousand dollars," said my Teuton.

He received it and vanished as usual.

It was growing interesting. Gold kept rising, and when it reached 217, "von leetle sheck more" was handed over.

On visiting the Evening Exchange that day, I learned from one of the door-keepers that some one had been bawling out my name a moment before, and on entering, I saw L. O—— jumping about like a chittagong rooster which had been feasting upon brandy-cherries, and bidding "two hoondert and seventy-one for von hoondert tousand gold." The moment he caught sight of his luckless customer, he ran towards him, vociferating, "von leetle sheck more for dree tousand dollars, or I buy in your gold. Tish shtrong, tish dretful shtrong;" (meaning the market was rampant and rising.)

He was quieted down by receiving his "last leetle sheck," together with an order to buy in my hundred thousand, short.

This transaction taught me at an expense of $12,500, not to go short of gold on *that* twist.

But L——, whom we called the richest, wisest and strongest of our quartette, was not so fortunate.

Poor L——, what fortunes and what a fate was his!

One evening in the month of August, while sitting on a balcony of his brown stone front, in ——— Street, he told us the story of his Wall Street life.

He came into the market in 1862, with $10,000,

and in less than a year had $250,000 to his credit at his brokers. He resolved to retire when he had made $500,000, but having been caught short of Pacific Mail, found himself in four months, poorer by $100,000. Five months after this, his "pile" showed him $200,000; in two months it was only $50,000. The Morse rise had put $100,000 into his pocket, and the panic which followed it, had taken $90,000 out of his pocket.

In August, and while telling us his story, he had still $80,000 lying in a very exposed situation, being deposited as a margin at his broker's, besides owning the brown stone front house, in which we were then sitting, which had cost him $40,000.

"I am going to make it up to $150,000," said he, "and then, good-bye Wall Street."

The Atlanta tumble took place, but L—— did not profit by it.

When gold rose to 200, he sold $200,000 short, and made $20,000. Then he made a lucky turn on the short side, in Erie, when it dropped to 85 in the panic of October 6th. He lacked now, only $500 of the $150,000, on which he purposed to retire. Gold had soon after risen again to 200, and L—— sold $100,000 at that price, giving his broker orders to cover at 199⅜. This would have exactly made the $150,000, and L—— would have reached the golden climacteric of fortune and repose.

But alas! this was not to be.

Gold rose in less than a week to 210. L—— commenced "averaging."

He sold another $100,000 at that price. It rose to 216, and then gave him the shadow of a hope, by falling back to 207, which was quickly dispelled by its rise to 220. Again he sold $100,000. The price mounted to 230. Once more he sold the same amount, and repeated the sale at 240. He stood a loser in twenty-four hours, in the sum of $130,000. Still he kept his position manfully, strained his credit, borrowed $20,000 fresh margin, and sold another lot at 250. Three hours later, and his broker called for more margin, and L—— failing to respond, bought in, at 251, the whole $600,000 of which his unfortunate customer was short. L—— had lost everything, cash, margin, brown stone front, horses and furniture, and owed more than $30,000 borrowed money. But this was not his worst loss. He lost the one thing that sustains the ruined operator—Hope.

Three weeks he lingered, hopeless and haggard, on the fringes of the market, and then disappeared. After two days had gone by, and we had not seen him, I called with E—— at his boarding-house. He was no longer there, nor could the landlady give us a hint as to where he might be found. We saw him no more for six weeks.

Meanwhile the gold carnival was at its height. Each day the crowd grew denser, it packed the gold-room with fervid masses, it formed in a three-quarter segment of a circle at the corner of William and Beaver Streets, buried ankle deep in the muddy slush, watching the indicator, which recorded their gains and losses. The whole strength of the speculation was here. While stocks were halting and bobbing up and down in minute arcs of a circle, gold rose and fell in huge parabolic curves.

The stock-dealers poured into the crowd. They
26

who had got their hand in by dealing in New York
Central, which moved in a stately promenade, generally closed up the ball by a frenzied galopade or a
daring swing on the flying trapeze in the gold-room.
As the winter wore away, the fun "grew fast and furious." No hour without some change in the scenes,
fortunes vanished in a day, or rose like exhalations
in a night. Fresh bands of revelers rushed in as the
weary ones departed, and margins with long trains
and ciphers, danced about and then disappeared, like
Tam O'Shanter's witches. In the pauses between the
mad cotillons, the well-known Wall Street game of
"beggar your neighbor" was industriously played.
Then suddenly would be heard the roar of the Union
and rebel guns at the front, calling off new figures in
the dance, when the bulls and bears grinning at each
other, *vis-a-vis*, started once more up and down, cross
over, *dos-a-dos*, cutting all manner of capers, and
each one "holding out to dance the other down."

From 9 A. M. till 12 P. M., fifteen hours every day,
speculation knew no pause. All day long champagne spouted in foam-fountains at Delmonico's and
Shedler's, and more fiery potations stimulated the
jaded speculators in the evening, at the Fifth Avenue
Hotel.

Winter was rolling away, and the sun was climbing the sky towards Cancer. Night fell on one dark,
stormy day in January. The "street" had been agitated by a thousand rumors of battles, and disasters
to the Union armies. Gold was flying upwards. The
crowd at the hotel was never madder than upon that
evening. The market was riotous. We stood, wedged
in the center of the circle, watching the fate of the

$100,000 we had just staked, when a face peered over the shoulders of the outside ring, and a long arm thrust a letter before our eyes. It was directed to B——, or to me. Opening it we read: "L—— is dangerously ill. He wishes to see you immediately. Come to —— —— Street." The letter was dated the evening before, and should have reached us that morning. We forced our way through the press, and hurried to the place indicated.

The storm had broken away; it was a wholesome night. The air was pure and still; the moon, in her first quarter, was sailing down the sky like a great birch bark canoe. Whether it was from distempered fancy, or the reflection of the rifted storm-clouds, we know not, but it looked as though it were made of gold. Hastening on through glimmer and gloom, in the direction indicated by the letter, we soon reached our destination. It was a miserable tenement house, only six blocks due east from the palaces of fashion. We climbed five flights of stairs, and found ourselves in a low attic, apparently untenanted. As we stood in the hall, our ears caught the sound of stifled sobs, which proceeded from a door which was half-way open. We approached, and gazed into the chamber. The dim light from a tallow candle would have failed to show us the interior, but the yellow moon-light, streaming through the attic window, fell upon a truckle-bed, where knelt the sobbing wife, and lit up the ghastly features of a dead man. We stepped softly in, and gazed upon all that remained of L——, our old friend, and late comrade in the battle of speculation. His losses had killed him. * * * * *

The clocks from a hundred belfries slowly ham-

mered out twelve as we turned again into Fifth
Avenue. The long lines of gas-lights winked at us
like so many flaming cressets, all converging in the
baleful focus of the Evening Exchange, and seeming
to beacon us away. The moon was set, and the
great constellations were marching up and down the
sky. But the crowd of sodden-faced men who poured
out from the front of the hotel, as we passed on our
way, took no heed of Arcturus beaming in the
northern sky, nor of the stars blazing in the belt
of Orion. Their eyes were bent on each other in
ravenous greed, or cast down upon the muddy pavement, while they marred the beauty of the night
with their hoarsely screamed bids and offers.

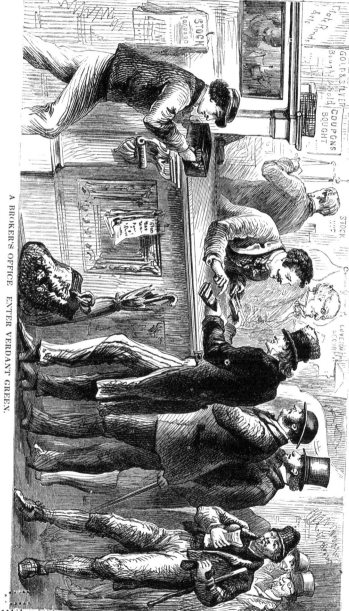

A BROKER'S OFFICE ENTER VERDANT GREEN.

CHAPTER XXVII.

ASTRAND AND AFLOAT AGAIN.

The Gap Closes Up, and the Column Moves on as Before—Loss on Loss—Tobin Comes to the Front—Fifty Millions of Gold Sold—E——makes a Little Mistake—A Dinner at Delmonico's—A Philharmonic Concert—Lengthened " Sweetness Long Drawn Out "—Golden Dreams—A Slight Misunderstanding Cleared Up in a very Disagreeable Manner—$45,000 Loss by a Slip of the Pen—Sunlight Again—The Bears Putting In Their Sickles to Reap a Harvest—Who Went Short of Gold?—A Bold Stroke for Fortune—On the Rack Once More—E—— and Myself Stand Guard Over $2,000,000—A Speculator's Dream—The Fatal Order Given and We are Astrand—The Final Break-up—Floating Away on a Pot of Money.

E have said that a man without money was nothing in the calculations of the stock-market. Let us add that a man's *life* counts for little there. The beggared operator buffets the waves unregarded, and when he throws up his arms and sinks below the surface of the stormy sea, by which he has so long been tossed, not even a ripple marks the place where he went down. Even his friends, the companions of his voyage, soon forget his loss amid the din and whirl and absorbing anxieties of their daily life.

We had to fight the battle alone now—E—— and I. On the 15th of January our positions were reversed—E—— had made fifty thousand, and I had lost the same amount. Standing up, like a pugilist under punishment at the hands of some strong opponent, for five weeks, I had received more blows than I had given. Holding gold at 230, the victory of Nashville had shaken $10,000 worth of it out of my grasp. The capture of Savannah had torn away $20,000. The surrender of Fort Fisher had cost me $20,000 more.

These blows came heavy and fast. Gold dropped to 200, when nearly the whole force of the market seemed suddenly to change front. The great banking-houses who had been buying gold, now commenced selling it for a further decline. Vast sales were made between 200 and 205. When the price touched 198, it stood firm for two hours in spite of the most terrific hammering.

Some power behind the scenes was holding it up! It mounted to 201. Then the hidden cause revealed itself. During the preceding two months, John M. Tobin had been persistently selling gold short, at high prices, predicting that he would "take it in" at 200. His predictions proved true. He had "taken in" his short gold at 200, and then bought heavily for a rise. At four o'clock, P. M., he made his appearance on the street, just as the board adjourned, and commenced bidding for lots of from $100,000 to $1,000,000, while a little black-eyed Jew broker stood by his side and recorded his purchases. The price rose rapidly to 205. The bears, supposing he was making bluff bids for the purpose of selling through other brokers, at first sold him all he bid for, but at length they saw he was an actual buyer, and paused. The amount of short sales made in the course of the forty-eight hours previous, was estimated to have been fifty millions.   There was not this amount of gold in New York.   The market was "oversold."   The short sellers at once saw their situation.

The crowd began to lift up their voices in supplication and astonishment.   "Oh, let me off from that last half million I sold you, John!"

"What's your game, Tobin?"

"Boys, you've been selling more gold than you can deliver, and I've been buying some of it," replied Tobin.

Although many of the smaller and more timorous of the bear tribe, now covered their shorts, the stronger and thicker-waisted ones still kept their position, judging that Tobin would fail in carrying up the price, in the face of Union victories.

E—— and myself were each short of $50,000 gold, at 200¼.   When it rose to 206, under Tobin's bids, our mood of mind became highly reflective.   The pressure at last became too great, when we remembered how neatly we had been caught in the October rise. We decided to cover our shorts, and buy for a rise; E—— filled out a joint order, by which the "Lobster" who was now our sole broker, was empowered to buy in, at the market price, the $100,000 of which we were short, and also buy another lot of $100,000 for the rise which seemed about to take place.

Without waiting to see at what price our gold was bought at, we took a hack and went up town to Delmonico's, where we partook of a sumptuous repast, with the concomitants; in fact, a dinner such as deserved that name. Our bill of fare read as follows, viz. :

Soup—Julien.	*Petit Pois—Pommes a la Lyonnaise.*
Poisson—Filet de Sole.	
Vin—Haut Sauterne.	*Vin — Veuve Cliquot.*
Bifteak—Au naturel.	*Omelette Soufflé.*
Gibier—Perdrix roti avec Truffes.	*Glaces—Café noir.*

Eau de vie—Partagas.

After that we dressed and went to the Philharmonic. The music there, of course, was very classical, and we tried to enjoy it; but at the conclusion of each piece we devoutly hoped that the musicians could not be prevailed upon to repeat the performance, for our thoughts were roving away from the concert hall to that garden of Gul(l), the Gold Exchange, where we had "garnered up our heart." At last, overhearing a gentleman, who had just come in as the last piece but one was being worked through slowly on the violoncellos, whisper to a friend that gold was 208½ at the Fifth Avenue, we broke away from the musical treat we were trying to enjoy, and hurried thither. The Lobster had gone home, but R. H—— reported to us that gold was "strong at 208⅜, with a mounting tendency." We were on the right track now. That night we dreamed that it rained double eagles and a variety of other golden coins. The next morning the idea struck us of remaining up town and operating by telegraph. We did so. At eleven, A. M., we telegraphed as follows, under a new system of cipher which we had lately agreed upon : "To —————— —————— (the Lobster), —— Exchange Place. "How is Joker?" (Joker meant gold.) Signed, etc."

The answer received at three P. M., read thus: "Joker Sampson whacker, axed, signed, etc.," which was, being interpreted, "Gold very strong at 215, what shall we do?"

Our reply went back on the wings of the lightning thus: "Swallow Plum," (*i. e.* Sell $100,000.)

Then we went to a dinner, very much on the sample of the evening before, and after that strolled into the Fifth Avenue Hotel, prepared to receive the congratulations of our broker, on having bagged that day, a profit of between $8,000 and $9,000 apiece.

The first man we saw was the "Lobster," his face a shade less glowing than usual. He came towards us on the double quick, and stretched out his claws, as if he wanted something. This something was more margin.

"More margin!" cried E—— and I, in consternation, "how so?"

"Why, you're short $400,000, and your loss, with gold at 218, the price it has just sold for, is $45,000. You must give me more margin, or I shall have to buy it in and charge you with the difference."

"But, my dear fellow, didn't we give you an order to buy in our $100,000 short at 206, and buy one hundred thousand more for a rise?"

"Not a bit of it. Here is your order to *sell* 100,000 at the market price, and I sold it at 206¼. Then you telegraphed down to sell 100,000 more at 115, and I executed your order."

There was our order sure enough, in letters that seemed to our distorted optics, two feet long. Sell $200,000 at market price, (206.) E—— had written by mistake *sell* instead of *buy*.

We margined up, and waited in trepidation the result of the Tobin movement. Gold jumped to 221, and nine thousand more of our margin was gone.

And now, the nervy fingers of the arch-cornerer were extended to pluck the fruits of his venturesome enterprise, when the price collapsed to 218. The market was shuddering under the first breath of astounding news. The telegraph had just flashed over the wires, that the commissioners of the Southern Confederacy were treating for peace, with President Lincoln on board a gunboat on the James River, and once more gold dropped to 205.

Tobin's losses in this attempted corner were rumored to have been $1,500,000.

E—— and myself, instead of losing $45,000 now bagged a profit of $6,000 on the whole of our joint sales.

Sherman and Grant, that modern Thor, meanwhile, were raining blows with their ponderous hammers upon the shell of the Confederacy, which now showed to the whole country a yawning lateral fissure. A fierce and bitter contest was going on between those who still dared to hold gold for a rise and those who sold it for a fall. Every speculator from Maine to Minnesota, who knew what selling short signified, felt that this was the time to do it. The ranks of the bears were swelled by fresh accessions, daily. Telegrams kept flying in, "Sheridan has cleaned out Early;" "Sherman has sacked Columbia and is sweeping through the Carolinas;" "Grant has advanced his parallels and is shelling Petersburg;" yet still gold stood like a rock, near 200, in the strong grasp of Tobin and many other bull operators. E—— and myself, after a series of petty losses, still stood $40,000 ahead. Now we made a bold stroke for fortune by selling $1,000,000 apiece at 200. We were led to do this by joining the *Hotel Brigade.*

Among the thousands of mysterious indviduals with which the great metropolis abounds, there is a certain class which we cannot describe better than by calling them hotel men. They dress in "purple and fine linen, and fare sumptuously every day," but how they get their living is a problem to the casual observer. They may be seen loitering in the reading-rooms and halls of the different hotels throughout the day, and are always in their seats when the dinner hour comes. The problem of their existence is solved when we state that they almost invariably have small capitals of from $5,000 to $20,000, which they employ in Wall Street, when the market is in a favorable condition, buying after a panic or selling short when the market is higher than is reasonable. On every such occasion, these men who are generally stout, rubicund fellows, may be seen wending their way to Wall Street, as fast as their corpulency will permit, and walking from the same cause, somewhat wide between the legs, "as though they had gyves on." Their shrewdness and good judgment in stock operations is quite remarkable. Hence it was that E—— and myself joined this coterie, when they marched down in one solid column, to sell gold short in February, 1865.

We had now placed ourselves on the rack. Our margin of four per cent. was liable to be used up any hour. The "Lobster" had consented to keep us short till the price rose to 203; provided we would, for his protection, watch gold every moment from early morning till twelve o'clock, P. M. Then the torture commenced. The price rose to 202½. Only one-half per cent. more and we should be shut down upon with a loss of thirty thousand apiece, when we were relieved by the price falling to 201.

We stood guard thus for four days, now wrenched with agony by a slight rise, and now cheered up by as slight a decline. Sleepless nights and days of pain. To me sleep came at length; but such a sleep. It was after a day of more than usual suspense that I returned home at seven in the evening, leaving E—— to stand sentry, and, if necessary, give the order that sealed our fate, for gold stood again at 202½.

Dropping on a lounge in my chamber, I was in an instant lost in sleep, heavy and dreamless, as if struck by some unseen hand. It was four hours before the *brain awoke* and showed me dreams. I was wandering through splendid halls, listening to music; banquets and garlands were spread upon tables, around which forms flitted and faces lightened. Then the scene shifted to a wilderness of beauty, moonlit and lonely. Suddenly a sound of roaring waters broke in upon me, and looking up I saw the face of L—— stretched cold and stark in his miserable attic, far above me as if miles away; while a terrible figure stretched down its hands filled with treasure, just beyond my reach, and beckoned me to follow it. Then a bell tolled slowly, and finally rang quick peals. I awoke and saw E—— standing at the door.

The agony was over.

At eleven o'clock gold had risen to 203, and E——

LOCKING UP GREENBACKS.

had given the fatal order to cover. The Lobster wedged his way into the crowd, and bid 203 for fifty thousand, and bought it at that price. While he was bidding for $100,000 more, a well-known operator rushed in from the telegraph room, and bid 203¼ for five hundred thousand. In thirty seconds gold was 204. Our $1,950,000 was bought in at an average price of 203¾.

Out of forty thousand dollars, I had five hundred only remaining; exactly the amount which I had deposited eight years before, in the hands of O——, as a margin for my first venture in Old Southern.

Naturally enough, E—— fell sick on this result, and for four months the stock-market never saw his face. I was now alone.

If there is a blissful feeling, it is that experienced by the weary operator, when, after a long campaign, in which fortune has run against him, he rests from his toils, with the consciousness that all is not lost, so long as hope and a small margin still remain.

After such a rest for two weeks, I rejoined the ranks.

Meanwhile, the sword of Sherman, which scarred the fair bosom of the Carolinas, was cutting great slits in the balloon of the gold speculation, which was fast collapsing. Gold had broken to 87, and then, on the news of the repulse at Fayetteville, North Carolina, ran up to 194. That news came one morning at the Exchange, and I sold $5,000, on the pledge of my now modest margin of $500.

It has been already stated in these pages, that the amount of gold and silver in the United States, in 1863, was estimated at $250,000,000. But the amount floating about, outside of the banks, the sub-treasury, and the private hoardings, was comparatively small, and grew still smaller in the summer of 1864.

In February, 1865, immense sums in gold coin, which had been locked up, were suddenly brought out and thrown on the market, in view of the speedy termination of the war. Some of the New York banks sold all the gold they held. The merchants, also, wishing to hedge against the prospective loss on the large amounts of imported goods they held, and which they had paid for when gold was high, now borrowed large sums in coin from the banks, and sold it, expecting to repay it by buying gold at a much lower price, within sixty days.

The burden became too great for the gold bulls. They fought stubbornly against the decline, but all in vain. One after one relaxed their hold, and let their precious nuggets drop on the market. But some of the largest holders still kept their position, hoping that something would happen to turn the tide in their favor. Gold fell to 175. Then they became desperate. Something must be done to stem the downward current.

Which of these men it was who played the game I cannot say; but one evening, at the up-town exchange, a speculative broker of small means entered the crowd and bid for gold by the million. In a few minutes he had bought three millions. The next morning the price, instead of rising on these heavy purchases, fell three per cent. The failure of the buyer was announced; and though he claimed that the purchases were for his own account, it was understood by the street that it was an arranged plan between him and certain leading gold bulls for the purpose of arresting the decline; but finding this move failed to accomplish the object, they made their broker the scapegoat. This was the last card played by the desperate holders of high-priced gold.

Nothing was left for them now but to slide out as well as they could. The immense number of short sales which had been made during the preceding six weeks created a constant demand for gold, and helped the heavy holders to dispose of the vast amounts they held. But many a million, won upon the great upward movement, was swallowed up as gold fell with sharp spasms down, down, to 128.

When it reached 140 I figured up my profits. Fifteen thousand dollars, all made in four weeks out of $500 by putting out a series of short contracts as the price dropped. I had snatched treasure out of the wreck, and was now ready for a new voyage on the sea of speculation.

CHAPTER XXVIII.

DREW PLAYS ON HIS ONE-STRINGED LYRE—ERIE.

Uncle Daniel in Clover—His Views Respecting " Them Erye Sheers "
He Plays on His Musical Instrument, Erie—Buy! Oh, Buy! Sell!
Oh, Sell!—He Pays Off Some of His Old Harlem Scores—He Slides
Down Hill with no Erie in His Hand, Then Picks Up Erie and
Travels Up Hill—D—— and S—— Form a Partnership—Setting
and Baiting Traps for Shorts—Springing the Traps and Bagging the
Game—The Old Man Soliloquizes—My Fortunes During the Erie
Rise—A "Point," and Advice from R——, the Railroad Director—
The Trick My Broker Played on Me—The Final Twist—A Big Gold
Trade—The Ketchum Forgeries and Their Effect on the Stock-Mar-
ket—The First Move for Another Corner.

ALL STREET, April 3d, 1865. The bears
were on a "bender," that day; the market
was full of honey-combs, on which they
were feasting, for Erie had been hurled down from
90 to 42.

Then was Daniel Drew's hour of triumph. For
nine months stocks had been on the downward track,
and he had predicted it. In the summer of 1864, he
showed by an ingenious argument, that Erie was selling too high; stated in his homely vernacular, it was
as follows, viz.:

"Them Erye sheers are a sellin' naow for a leetle
more'n they're wuth. It costs a heap naow to pay
runnin' expenses. The Erye Railroad Company has
to pay up'ards of $20,000 for an ingyne what cost

only $10,000 afore the war. Coal and iron has riz, so has men. Whar are dividends a comin' from? You, boys, better not be too fond of your sheers."

The "old man" was right. Erie at par, was a capital short sale.

In the fall of 1864, he commenced a campaign in that stock, which was to last four years, a campaign in which he took revenge on old enemies, wiped out old losses, filled his treasury with plunder, until 1868, when he retired from the field a heavy loser, by the closing battle. During three years of that time, Erie was like a one-stringed Chinese lyre in his hands, on which he played two tunes; when its price was high, he sung "who'll buy my Erye? who'll buy my valuable Erye? buy it, oh buy!"

When it was low, he sung "who'll sell me Erye, who'll sell me worthless Erye? sell me Erye, sell, sell!"

And the "street" listening entranced to his mellifluous voice, bought it of him at a very high price, and sold it to him at a very low price. Every night Uncle Daniel dreamed of money-bags, and every day his dream turned out true. He coined money out of his musical performances on his one-stringed Chinese lyre—Erie.

In October, 1864, Erie fell with a crash to 85. This fall tempted two prominent members of the Harlem Combination, L. W. J——, and J. M. T——, to take up Erie and corner it. No corner could be engineered without the concurrence of the leading director, who was, of course, none other than Daniel Drew. Accordingly the would-be cornerers broached the matter to him. Nothing could have suited him

27

better, for now he saw an opportunity offered to pay off old scores in Harlem. He loaned them a very large sum, and made an agreement with them not to sell any Erie above a certain price. The cornerers thereupon bought an immense block of Erie above 90. The price quickly rose to 105, and everything looked rose-colored, not only to them, but to Uncle Daniel. "Love laughs at locksmiths;" Daniel Drew laughs at contracts, for he generally finds a gap in them, through which, though it may not be "as wide as a church door," he manages to slip, when it is for his interest to do so. The cornerers found themselves loaded with fresh stock at summit prices, and began to sag under their burden.

December passed into January, and Erie broke down to 80, then lurched heavily upward to 87.

Now was the hour for the "old man" to act. He arose and saddled his coal-black steed, named Panic, and descended like Thalaba the destroyer into the Dom-Daniel caverns to evoke to his aid the spirits of financial fear and distrust. He sold a large amount of Erie, and thereupon made ready to depress the price. Having conveyed to one of his minions $20,-000 worth of convertible bonds, he instigated the procuring of an injunction forbidding the payment of any dividends by the Erie company.

Then he constricted the money market, and called upon L. W. J—— and J. M. T—— for the money which he had loaned them. This demand compelled them to throw overboard their stock. The price fell twenty per cent. The would-be-cornerers had lost a million, and the Harlem "calls" were partially avenged.

Now Uncle Daniel prepared to reap a more substantial harvest. When Erie had reached the neighborhood of 50, he covered his shorts at an enormous profit.

Grant and Sheridan were pounding at the gates of Richmond, and another great stampede now took place. Wall Street then might have been taken for Landseer's picture of Highland bulls in a storm. They who had bought Erie at 80, and thought it cheap at that, now sold it at 45, and said it was not worth 20. It was offered and sold in blocks of five thousand and ten thousand shares. As fast as it reared itself upwards, fresh blows threw it back lower than before. It touched bottom at 42.

The two leading bears, Uncle Daniel and Dr. S——, (whom we have before described,) now became metamorphosed into bulls, and formed an alliance to lift Erie out of the slough into which it had fallen. Having bought all the stock they could buy under cover, when concealment was no longer possible they bought openly immense amounts. A rumor went through the street that all this stock, which daily was sent into G——, their broker, was merely to cover their shorts.

The fever for selling hardly flagged as Erie rose to 49, at which price E. B. K——, whose forgeries soon after startled the street, sold D—— & S—— ten thousand shares, seller 60. In three days the price of Erie was 63, when it broke and fell back to 54. Again the cry went up, "Sell! Sell!" on every side. The conspirators gathered from this a fresh supply of shorts. Then Erie rose to 65.

D—— and S—— were still gluttonous for shorts.

The whole street was full of traps, baited to catch short sales. All these traps were connected with the great slaughter-trap set by D—— & S——. The bears furnished their own bait, as follows: The price of Erie ought to go lower. First, because it has to borrow the money for its dividends. Second, because it has risen twenty-three per cent. in two weeks. Third, because it is not intrinsically worth 20. Fourth, because ten thousand shares are coming from Europe, etc., etc.

These baits were quickly swallowed, and in thirty days the traps were full of game—shorts.

All this time Erie had been rising with the usual downward spasms for the purpose of encouraging the ensnared ones. As it rose, D—— & S—— bagged the game, in other words, compelled the bears to cover. It touched 85 and the shorts were all taken in; then broke in a panic to 68. Tobin here stepped forward and arrested the fall by taking ten thousand shares on his sinewy shoulders. Dr. S—— now retired from the field with a profit of several hundred thousands, and Uncle Daniel "went it alone" on a new twist.

Once more the traps were set and baited as before. Once more the bears seeing the mistake they had made by closing their contracts, swallowed the bait in crowds. Erie, early in July, rose to 82, then dropped back to 76, and looked very weak. The bears were again jubilant. For three weeks, Erie vibrated dully between 76 and 80. Like some huge monster of the deep, its torpidity was feigned, for it was only waiting for more shorts. Many of the short sellers were pupils and imitators of Uncle Daniel in his old bearish policy, and they could hardly persuade themselves now, that the "old man" was not on their side instead of working against them.

He stood one day on the steps of his broker's office, and soliloquized thus, as he looked on the noisy crowd, where "his young barbarians were all at play," selling Erie:

"Happy creeturs! how merry they be. Wal, wal, I guess I must pinch 'em."

He did "pinch 'em." That very day Erie rose to 85. The market fairly smoked with excitement. There was no pause in the upward movement during the next forty-eight hours.

The 31st day of July was a scorcher. From the blistering pavements of Broad Street, wave after wave of heat rose and vibrated in mid-air, while the merciless sun kept radiating new volumes.

W. R. T——, wiping his flaming forehead with the finest of cambric, was overheard to whisper to a brother broker in his peculiar stutter, "B–B–Big th–th–thing in Erie."

The price rose to 92, fell back to 87, mounted to 95, fell back to 94, then galloped to 98⅞.

All the time from March till the middle of June, I had been patronizing the "Lobster" with orders on the most liberal scale, buying or selling on an average, two or three thousand shares per day. Twice my margin had been swelled to thirty thousand, and twice it had shrunk back to its original amount, fifteen thousand. I had paid my active broker nearly fifteen thousand dollars commissions by these quick turns.

Now this helping to support brokers is a weary business, unless one can make a little money by it.

It was this conviction that led me to sell two hundred Erie short at 76, with the intention of staying short, whatever might betide.

When Erie rose to 80, I also "averaged" by selling a second lot of two hundred shares. But when it jumped to 85, under the nipping fingers of Uncle Daniel, I thought the matter should be inquired into, and accordingly proceeded to consult R——. Some men are born poets, others are born railroad directors. R—— belonged to the latter class. For aught that may be said to the contrary, a railroad stock-certificate may have been the ominous plaything of his childhood, and he may have organized mimic boards of directors among his school-fellows. At all events, he was now a railroad director, and although we do not assert that he belonged to the Erie Direction, he was always presumed to know a thing or two about Erie. R——, it should be remembered, was the lucky speculator mentioned in our third chapter; but in 1865 he was very much changed from the slender youth of 1857. He was thick-set now, with jowls which hung down like the dewlaps of a prize ox. As for the color of his face, to say that it was red would feebly express it. It was not suffused by "the patriot's shame," nor by the celestial roseate tinge, which has been, with doubtful truth, at least in this age of brass, called "love's proper hue." It fairly glowed and blazed, on the morning when I consulted him. He lay in bed in his chamber, and the very sheets borrowed a ruddy tint from that burning, blood-red face.

He was a man of few words. Men of his kidney always are. But the substance of what he said was, "Keep your position, and let Daniel squeeze you."

Not doubting that this advice was given in good faith, I kept my position.

When Erie reached 94, it grew scarce for delivery. In fact my broker told me it could not be borrowed either for love or money, and that unless I could deliver it in fifteen minutes, he should be under the painful necessity of buying it in, and closing me out, with a loss of $6,400. In fifteen minutes the stock was bought in, and in an unguarded moment my broker entrusted me with the duty of reporting it at his office, whereby a very large cat jumped out of the bag. It appears that the faithless Lobster, not satisfied with the commissions to the amount of $15,000, which he had already extracted out of his customer, desired to make an additional sum by speculating on my margins. When I reported the four hundred shares of Erie to the Lobster's book-keeper, "This," said he, consulting his books, "makes you long of Erie, at 94."

"How so," replied I.

"Four hundred shares of Erie, bought at 81, appears on my books to your credit. That closed up your shorts. This last lot makes you long four hundred, at 94."

Sure enough, my shorts had been bought in without my knowledge, and the Lobster expected to put the difference between 81 and 94, or $5,200, into his own pocket. The ingenuousness of his book-keeper saved me this amount, and in one hour I made $800 on my four hundred shares by selling it at 96.

I need not add that my account was removed from the office of the Lobster as soon as his treachery had been discovered.

"New brooms sweep clean." At least I thought so, two hours later, when I raked in three thousand by selling Erie at 98½ and taking it in at 92¼, in the office of my new broker. Suddenly Erie sprang up again to 96. Groesbeck, Drew's broker, had called upon the "short" gentlemen aforesaid, for thirty thousand shares. Then Uncle Daniel began to twang his Chinese lyre, "Buy my Erie, buy, oh buy!"

Never did the market so bristle with "points" as at four o'clock on the afternoon of that day. Fifty men could have been seen whispering in the ears of fifty other men, or grasping them affectionately by the arm and leading them apart from the roaring crowd, to tell them that Erie was the thing to buy. The jackals who hunt in the track of the lions of the market, were all 'loping about to induce the outsiders to relieve plethoric gentlemen of their heavy loads of stock.

At this juncture, R——, the railroad director, drew me aside and imparted "*his point.*" "Daniel Drew is going to put Erie up to 110 in less than twenty-four hours. Buy all you can swing." R——'s advice, respecting my short Erie, had somewhat impaired my confidence in his judgment, and yet still I believed him honest. I bought eight hundred shares at 97. That evening Erie broke, and the next day sold at 90, lessening my margin by $5,600. During the entire three months' campaign which we have been describing, something was going on below the surface which was shortly to disclose itself and rock Wall Street to its foundations.

One night in June, about eleven o'clock, after the crowd of operators had thinned out, a bloated inebriate stood in the bar-room of the Fifth Avenue Hotel. He had recently won a hundred thousand dollars in gold, and now "flown with insolence and wine," was "bluffing" the little knot of operators who surrounded him, by bidding 146 for one million of gold or any part of it. No one dared to sell it. A tall, slender man, named W. H——, at last approached him, and waited quietly until he renewed his bid.

"I'll sell you that million," murmured the tall broker.

"I'll take another million," said the inebriate.

"Sold," said the tall man, who then offered to sell one million more, but the inebriate was full enough now.

The next morning, gold fell seven per cent., and the rash buyer was ruined, while the seller had made more than $100,000.

The person who sold that gold through the tall broker, was E. B. Ketchum.

This operator, afterwards so notorious, had been speculating for more than a year, to an enormous amount. In 1864, he was reported to have made $1,500,000. The gold break in March, had made him the loser of millions. When Erie was hoisted by Uncle Daniel, he covered at 76, one lot of ten thousand shares, which he had sold for delivery, at 49. This transaction cost him $270,000, and was only one in a series of losses, which footed up an aggregate that made even the thorough-paced Wall Street man stand aghast.

For months the fatal drain had been going on. He lost money by selling short, and then he lost money by buying stocks. The capital of the banking-house to which he belonged was four millions, and still a large sum of money was lacking to meet his engagements. In an evil hour he forged gold certificates, to how large an amount will never be exactly known, for some of those who advanced money upon them refused to tell their losses; but these forgeries are known to have run up to several millions.

On the 15th of August, something was plainly brooding over the market. Mysterious whispers were afloat. That evening the same tall broker above-mentioned sold out for the account of E. B. K—— forty thousand shares of stock. The secret was known. K—— was a fugitive. Stocks fell in a fierce panic.

The next day Erie was driven back to 76. Uncle Daniel bought twelve thousand shares of the Ketchum Erie, and laid his plans for another corner.

CHAPTER XXIX.

FEMALE SPECULATORS.

DO Women speculate in stocks? This question is readily answered in the affirmative. More than this, they are not only frequent, but daring speculators. They encounter risks that would appall the stoutest Wall Street veteran, and rush boldly into places, where even a Vanderbilt would fear to tread. The female character is, in many respects, suited to a life of speculation. Speculation is founded on hope, and women are generally remarkably prone to hope. Speculation requires patience and fortitude, which are, or should be, both womanly virtues. Speculation derives its food from excitement, and women often feed on excitement. Speculation comes from fancy, and women are much given to fancy. Women of a certain type, are naturally, or by education, inclined to speculate in stocks. Perhaps they may catch the infection from their brothers, or uncles, who talk stocks while bolting their meals in haste, so that they may hurry down town, and buy a little more Central, or cover their short gold. Wealthy ladies, who are their own mistresses, and have plenty of leisure time, might be expected, as they sit embroidering golden bees and butterflies, on black velvet, to have their thoughts turned upon stock-flyers, and to dream of new equipages, jewels, and silks, won out of stocks or gold. From whatever cause it may arise, there are no more eager and venturesome gamblers at Baden Baden, in Germany, than women, and there are no more eager and venturesome speculators in stocks, than women.

On almost any bright day, when stocks are rising, a dozen or more showy carriages may be seen drawn up in front of the offices of prominent brokerage houses, waiting for the gorgeous dames who ride in them to come out, when they have transacted their business with their brokers. Most of these speculative ladies are dowagers with large bank accounts, for which they, perhaps, thank their departed husbands, or fathers, or uncles, and which they are now using as margins in stock-speculation, almost always for a rise, for it seems to them an incomprehensible thing that any money can be made by a fall in stocks. Like so many Magdalens, they roll their fine eyes, not repentantly, but avariciously upwards, towards the towering heights of Rock Island, or New York Central, where they hope to make their profits.

Besides these middle-aged matrons, there are not

a few misses in their teens, whose faces are turned Wall Street-wards.

Imagine these sylph-like creatures ogling the elephantine bulk of Erie as it paces up with a dignified stride, or casting sheep's eyes at Pittsburg as it dances on the tight-rope held by the hands of a clique.

One fair young creature, with wealth of blonde hair, leans pensively on her hand, and indulges in pleasant thoughts of Reading, or in her sleep has sweet dreams of Old Southern. Another quick brunette opens with palpitating bosom a billet-doux from her broker, informing her of the closing prices, and enclosing a balance of profits which she devours with her eyes; or perhaps it is a more unpleasant missive, by which she learns that Erie, her first love, has proved treacherous, or gold has ceased to respond to her vows.

At Saratoga, in July, 1863, three young ladies, possessed of a will and several thousand dollars of their own, made up a "pool" in Harlem on their individual account, and bought two thousand shares in the neighborhood of 100. Within four weeks the rise to 181 showed them to be winners to the amount of $75,000. This seemed to justify them in going into the wardrobe line. Consequently, they might have been seen every day sitting on cushioned stools at Stewart's and Arnold, Constable & Co.'s palaces, and making heavy investments in moire antique, Mechlin lace, and India shawls. But alas for the vanity of human expectations; they did not sell their Harlem, and six or eight weeks from that time they received, not a billet-doux, but a call for more margin, for Harlem had sold down to 75, and instead of making $75,000, they would, if they sold, now lose $25,000.

Fortunately all of these young ladies belonged to the heroic mould, and instead of going into hysterics or sitting down and having a good cry, they went manfully, or rather womanfully, to work and raised money, furnished the necessary margin to their broker and vowed by Nemesis that they would hold their Harlem till they could make their $75,000 once more.

Brave girls! Their heroism in six months was rewarded, for in the latter part of April, 1864, while the Commodore was hoisting Harlem, they drew $80,000 out of their broker's hands.

One of the notable female speculators in Wall Street is a maiden lady, who counts her property by the million. She is never seen there, however, except when stocks are falling, and properly belongs to the class of panic-birds before described. In these seasons she may be seen in her "customary suit of solemn black," tripping down to her broker's office, prepared to buy at the lowest prices, and when stocks go up she always sends word to her broker to sell out. Her profits from these investments have sometimes risen to more than one hundred thousand per annum.

The most remarkable case of all, is that of a lady whom we will call Miss M——. She belongs to the class of the strong-minded ones. Her face is that of a goshawk, and the white dove which she wears sometimes upon her jockey hat, seems constantly in the act of playfully swooping down upon the less amiable bird beneath. In her views on financial questions, she has always taken high moral ground, discountenancing all attempts to raise the price of gold. During her ten years' experience she has made and lost a fortune every year. In the great rise of 1864, she stood one hundred and thirty thousand dollars better than she was in 1863. Then, woman-like, her hopes rose to the ambitious height of half a million, which seems to be the goal which most speculators propose to themselves. But

> "When lovely woman stoops to folly,
> And finds, too late, that stocks betray,"

and brokers beguile! She awoke from her dream of fortune on the 18th of April, 1864, when panic was raging, with the residue of her fortune, about $4,000, fast locked up in the hands of her broker, who had failed, and was unable even to pay her this small balance.

But brokers are the most elastic of mortals, commercially speaking; their failures are generally only temporary, and in three weeks our heroine received from her supposed insolvent agent, $2,000 of her balance. With this she commenced to operate on the short side, for her losses in the panic had, as is usual in such cases, converted her into a bear—a she-bear, now mourning for her whelps, and on the third of April, 1865, she had recovered forty thousand dollars of her losses. What little bird now whispered in her ear, "buy Erie," cannot be told, but she bought it at 45, and flew up with it to 90, like a witch astride of a broomstick. Once more she had built up her fortune, but she did not snatch it out of the jaws of the market, always open and ravenous. The vision of a half million still haunted her. She caressed several of her stock-favorites. Pittsburg, Old Southern, Fort Wayne, etc., etc., all of which conduct cost her dear. Her margin was rapidly diminishing. In May, 1866, she ceased to buy stocks, and commenced to operate for a fall.

Gold had dropped to 126. Everybody said gold would go down to 110. Her broker told her that Government was selling, and so she staked her remaining $60,000 on a short sale of $200,000 gold, at 130.

The gold-bulls celebrated their carnival, in May, 1866. When the price fell to 126, in April, nearly every banker, broker, and operator in the street stood short of it, for future delivery. This time the bears thought they were right. Some said the price would go to par, others to 110, but all concurred in believing that gold would never go up again. Three times more gold had been sold than could be borrowed for delivery.

A sound from across the Atlantic, like "a fire-bell in the night," awoke them suddenly from their dreams of fortune. A panic in London!

But how should a panic in London make gold go up in New York?

Let us explain.

All commercial transactions, it should be remembered, are conducted, in England, on a gold basis. When money is easy, and the Bank of England has a low rate of discount, an active business is often done in American securities, particularly in railway-bonds, and Governments. It is estimated by Commissioner Wells, that one thousand millions of the latter are held in Europe. When the rate of discount by the Bank of England is raised, and money becomes tight, many of these securities are sent to the United States to be sold, and the proceeds of these sales, in gold, is remitted to England, diminishing in this proportion, the amount of gold in this country.

Gold had risen to 130, and rumors of commercial distress in London were already forewarning the bears of their dangerous position, from which they saw only one means of relief, viz.: the *sales of gold by the Government.* These sales in a few days ran up to $30,000,000. The Government agent was beset by those who were short of gold. He was waited for, button-holed, and his coat-tails were almost torn off, by the eager buyers, when he entered the gold room.

Still the price stood firm.

Late in May the storm broke. The arrival of the Cuba brought the news of the greatest financial panic which had ever occurred in England. The Government stopped selling, and gold jumped to 40. Erie certificates and Government bonds came pouring in by every steamer, and every outgoing steamer carried millions of gold. In six weeks, more than $40,000,000 had been sent out of the country.

On the 9th of June the price stood at 169. One of the largest holders of gold at 130 was the firm of M—— & D——, and this house was almost the only prominent one which bulled gold heavily. Their profits there, after the arrival of the Cuba could be counted by the million.

Many a shrewd merchant and operator found himself during the rise bound hand and foot.

J. M. T——, the great speculator, was caught short of a million or so, which he bought in at something over 150. This same individual then bought largely, and sold $700,000 of his purchases to the noted merchant, H. B. C——, at 169. As for the smaller tribe of operators, the field was strown with their financial corpses.

This "spirt" in gold, it should be noted, arose purely from commercial causes.

How fared it with our heroine meanwhile?

She "sat like patience on a monument" of short gold. When it touched 150, she descended from her pedestal, and gazing with tearless eyes upon her losses, ($50,000,) then proceeded coolly to gather up the wreck, and reconstruct her edifice.

Who will say, after hearing the story of Miss M——, that women cannot speculate? ·

A large number of the stock accounts, standing in the name of women, on the books of brokers, represent the wives of stock-operators, who have had settled upon them by their husbands after some lucky hit, a large sum against the wet and dark day, which is almost sure to come in the career of a speculator. As already noted, the wife of the heavy stock-operator is quite certain to be provided for, and when her husband loses his all, he can fall back on his wife's money, and renew his fortune. Most of the women who speculate in stocks, conduct their speculations in the names of male friends and relatives. Hence it comes that they very often make money, for what broker would be so ungallant, (and all brokers are gallant to the fair sex,) as to suffer a lady to lose money in his office. Sometimes the broker, or operator, in whose name these accounts stands, puts his shoulder under the load, when a panic occurs, and saves his lady-customer at all hazards. Sometimes he introduces her to a magic ring, and she speedily becomes the bride of fortune. When her margin is exhausted, she may be said to travel on a margin of beauty, grace, and smiles, which, with a skillful tear now and then dropped, quickly subdue the hyenas of the street, and supply her with the sinews of war on 'Change.

A few days since, two fair young girls, evidently from some inland, city, accompanied by an elderly gentleman, stood gazing into the back windows of the Long Room, upon the dark, turbulent crowd within— cherubs gazing on Pandemonium. Ten, twenty, thirty minutes they stood there, as if fascinated by the strange scene.

"I don't see why you won't buy some Rock Island for me, papa. James said I could make some money if you only would," remarked the elder of the two, as they walked away.

Thus the sympathetic female nature catches the contagion of speculation.

It is well, however, that women rarely come in person into the stock-market to look after their interests. One can easily imagine the effect produced by several hundred women interested in stocks, being present at a panic and giving way with feminine impulsiveness to the feelings of the hour. We might then expect some new and strange appearances in these disasters. A bevy of dames dissolved in tears, with hair disheveled, and giving way to hysterics, or screaming like "Pythoness possessed," and slaughtering stocks as eagerly as the veteran stock-butchers.

We have answered the inquiry, "do women speculate?" and now we ask, could or would or should a woman be a broker? Could, or would, or should she line her delicate throat with bell metal, put triple brass upon her face, change her tender heart into stone, crush out her human sympathies with the unfortunate and the distressed, and see men reduced from affluence to beggary, and profit by it as a broker?

This profession of a stock broker would seem to be almost the last one that woman would aspire to fill, and yet already two ambitious ladies have entered the ranks of that profession within the past two months. We disclaim here and now distinctly, any intention to advertise brokers in this volume; but we cannot refrain from giving these two ladies' names in full, viz.: Mrs. Victoria C. Woodhull and Mrs. Tennie C. Claflin, who compose the new firm of Woodhull, Claflin & Co., doing business at No. 44 Broad Street. Let us wish that their courage may win success in this unwonted field of feminine enterprise.

PLOTTING THE GREAT GOLD RING OF '69.

CHAPTER XXX.

THE FORTUNES OF A COUNTRYMAN.

A Scene in a Broker's Office—B——t Has the Petroleum Fever—Blowing Bubbles in Oil—A Masterpiece of the Engraver's Art—Ravages of the Petroleum Epidemic—The Mining Board and How They Make Corners There—The Bubble Breaks, and the "Lobster" is Busted—We Take a Nervine—B——t Buys a Call in "Prairie Dog"—H. G. Stimpson and Billy Marston Carry the Bears Up in a Balloon—Prairie du Chien in the Clouds—What Came out of B——t's Call—$20,000 Made from $200 in Forty-eight Hours—"Calls and Puts" on the Brain—Henry Keep Nursing His Pet Stock—"Buying In Under the Rule"—Uncle Daniel Says "We Must Ingine 'em"—The Story of Pacific Mail—L. W. Jerome Unloading His One Hundred Thousand Shares—B——t's Luck in Pacific Mail—He Takes a Flyer in Atlantic Mail and then Buys One Hundred Erie of *White* for Cash.

HE first scene in this chapter, is laid in the office of the "Lobster." The time is in January, 1865, while we, (E—— and I,) were sweating under heavy burdens of gold. We are sitting in the private office of the broker aforesaid, which we made our head-quarters, engaged in our usual occupation of figuring, and perusing the literature of the stock-market, *i. e.* quotations.

Enter a rustic, cut out on the usual stage pattern, viz.: tall, gawkey, and eccentric-looking.

"Ah!" quoth E——, "here comes more tribute to the Moloch of Wall Street."

As he approached us, smelling strongly of the pine

woods, a shade, either of surprise or regret, passed over the expressive features of E——, who recognized the rustic as one of his country relations. He rejoiced in the euphonious surname of B——. After the customary salutations had been exchanged, the countryman produced a portly wallet from his breast pocket, and proceeded to rummage in its recesses for certain documents. The first paper he produced was a certificate of good, moral character, from his school-master. The second was a certificate of the deposit of $2,300 in the bank of his native village. It need scarcely be remarked, that he found the latter certificate much more potent in Wall Street than the former. Then he produced half a column cut out of a newspaper, unfolded it, and spread it before our eyes. It was headed thus, in very large letters, PETROLEUM! and set forth substantially, that the books of the Sixtieth National Petroleum Company were still open for subscription. Capital, one million dollars, one hundred thousand shares at ten dollars par; that the company had (magnanimously) allowed the public to take an interest in the shares, by paying $3.00 per share; that the property consisted of thirty acres in fee simple, in the very center of the oil region, and only ten miles from the celebrated Buchanan Farm; that three wells were already sunk, and ready for tubing, another down below the first sandstone; room for more wells; every indication of oil. A dividend of two per cent. a month *guaranteed*. Books to be closed positively and irrevocably on the 21st instant. Then followed the names of the directors, all well known men of business.

"Them air Petrollum shares is what I've come for.

Two per cent. a month dividends is enough for me," remarked the rustic.

The glittering bubble of Petroleum Stock Companies had caught the eye of B——.

E—— and I had long prior to this time pricked our own bubbles, and thereafter had resolved ourselves into a vigilance committee of bubble-prickers for the benefit of other people.

But here was a very obstinate case. B—— had resolved *to invest*, and in that particular company. It was only after long argument, and by quoting to him the familiar agricultural proverb, "Never put your eggs all in one basket," that we prevailed upon him to invest only $1,300 in this company, and keep $1,000 for some of the other tempting opportunities which then abounded in the market. Then all three of us went to the office of the company, No. —— Broadway, where B—— paid out his $1,300, and received in return certificates of four hundred and thirty-three shares. B—— thought the engraving on these certificates was really beautiful, and so it was. In the foreground was a flowing well, sending an oleaginous jet one hundred feet or so into the air, and falling in a graceful parabolic curve into a huge tank inscribed with the name of the company, near which was a pile of barrels apparently as large as the pyramid of Cheops. In the background were several vessels and railroad trains being loaded with petroleum. B—— feasted his eyes upon this work of the graver's art, and looked hopefully forward to his guaranteed dividend.

The Petroleum Stock Company fever raged for nine months, and culminated in February, 1865.

Companies with a nominal capital of $300,000,000, were organized during that period. All that has been said in our chapter on bubble-companies, applies with equal force to Petroleum. A volume might be written to describe how the English language was twisted and turned, to paint the prospect of fortunes and avoid the legal liabilities incident to false representations; how the bubbles shone as if colored with every brilliant dye that could be extracted out of Petroleum; what engines were set at work to bring in the public; what stool-pigeons were called from the solid and respectable circles, from the halls of legislation, from the learned professions, and from the church, to entice dupes, and feather the nests of needy adventurers; how the owners of lands that smelt of oil, the mineralogists, the geologists, and chemists were in clover, and then to tell how one by one the phantom-flowing wells dried up, the magnificent oil territory became abandoned to its original desolation, watched over only by skeleton derricks, while the thousands of victims came dropping in, file after file, to draw their dividends, as the bubbles were bursting. It would form a chapter in the history of speculation, at once interesting, instructive, amusing and sad.

The Petroleum fever gave rise in February, 1865, to the organization known as the Petroleum Stock Exchange, which however, died in a few months with the fever which produced it, and its remains were incorporated with what is now known as the Mining Stock Board, another fragment hurled off from the meteoric speculation, in the unsubstantial properties incorporated in joint stock companies.

This institution is a miniature of the Stock Exchange, and numbers now upwards of seventy-six members. Here, on a smaller scale, corners are engineered, and close pools organized, which make many an outsider weep tears of gold. Two circumstances conspire to make these pools highly successful. First, the general worthlessness of the stocks bought and sold there, which tempts in short sellers. Second, the ease with which stocks are manipulated owing to the small amount of money required to carry them, and the fact that they are generally held in a few hands after the original subscribers have sold out in disgust, over long delayed dividends. When three or four men hold all the stock of one of these companies, they can very readily "milk the street" by simulating a great activity in that particular stock. This is done by what is known as "wash sales," *i. e.*, sales in which no stock is actually delivered. A. pretending to sell, and B. pretending to buy, in the open market under a secret agreement. In this way a price is made, and often numerous transactions are reported which are never really carried out. Of course these fictitious sales are forbidden under penalty of expulsion, but are continually made without any fear of detection. As soon as a stock is thus made to assume an activity, the outside public pricks up its huge ears and listens to the disinterested suggestions of the whole tribe of " pointers," " singed cats," and " ropers-in," who ply their vocation in the stock-market. If inclined to buy, they take "jags" of the stock in question, whereupon the price suddenly breaks from under them and they " cut short " their losses by selling in pursuance often of the same disinterested suggestions. Or perhaps in view of the worthlessness of the stock, they make short sales, when up the price jumps and they have to "cover" at a heavy loss. A certain stock, the intrinsic value of which was less than twenty-five cents a share, was in 1867, washed up to twenty-five dollars per share, catching a wealthy customer of a prominent banking house to the amount of forty thousand dollars. This movement was made purely on the strength of this one short sale which had been made when the stock was selling at 5, twenty times more than its true value.

But to return to the fortunes of B——. His individual bubble, collapsed in less than five months, when he shook off the odor of petroleum from his skirts, by selling his stock for ten cents a share. Meanwhile, he had not lain upon his oars. His first operation was in gold, which he had sold short, or as he called it "bought short," and made $5,000. Then he mounted on the wave of Erie, which washed five thousand dollars more into his capacious wallet, when it broke at the height of 98. We tried to release him from the claws of the "Lobster," when we discovered his treachery, in buying in our shorts, but unfortunately B—— had bought Erie at 96, and now that it had fallen back to 90, he preferred keeping his position on the "Lobster's" books.

We lost sight of him for three months, until one day in November, when he rushed into our new headquarters, crying out, "The Lobster has busted, and I'm busted."

He had just $200 remaining out of his $11,000. It was a vile day in November, 1865. The air was chill and muggy, the pavement had broken out into a cold perspiration, and the buildings were covered with damp blotches. Everybody looked blue, and B——'s face was the longest and bluest of all. He looked as if a little stimulus would help him.

"Come and get a nervine, B——!"

"A nervine! what's a nervine?" said B——.

"Come and see."

We went to the neighboring chateau of Lorenzo Delmonico, sat down at one of the tables, hailed a sombre-looking Ganymede, who looked as if he might be the grandson of some old French soldier, who went through Napoleon's Russian campaign, and had his nose frozen therein, and requested him to bring three nervines. This singular beverage is, by a pleasing fiction, made out to be compounded of decoctions of roots and herbs, gathered by Indian squaws, in the vicinity of Baffin's Bay, when the moon is at the full, and blended "judgmatically" with the fluid known to chemists as $C^4 H^6 O^2$, but more generally recognized under the name of alcohol. During the percolations and genial glow diffused by this beverage, B—— opened his stiffly starched shirt-bosom, and showed us the fox gnawing at his financial entrails.

B—— *had borrowed money* from friends in his native village in order to meet the demands of the rapacious Lobster for more margin. This obligation weighed heavily upon his spirits, for he had not yet learned the Wall Street art of bearing with an air of graceful unconsciousness a vast burden of debt. While he was bewailing his sad condition, C——, a well-known operator, joined us in the most joyous of moods, inasmuch as he had made that morning $5,000 on Prairie du Chien, which, after rising to par, had fallen back to 91. C—— was a bear in Prairie du Chien. He predicted that it would sell at 50 inside of a week, and volunteered to sell calls in it at 110, and which should run deliverable at any time within thirty days.

B——'s face brightened. He plucked C—— by the sleeve, and told him he would give him two hundred dollars for a call of two hundred shares. C—— filled one out, signed it, sent it in to his broker, who guaranteed it, and handed it to B——, who completely emptied his pockets by giving C—— the $200 agreed upon. The precious little memorandum was folded by B—— into a wad small enough to be enclosed in a filbert and hidden in the most secret compartment of his wallet. Then he retired to his boarding-house to " recooperate," as he expressed it.

November, 1865, was made memorable in the history of Wall Street, as all my readers· will recollect, by the Prairie du Chien combination. The leader in this enterprise was H. G. Stimpson, a tall, taciturn man, with a face as if cut out of yellow sandstone, and seeming to wear a look which says, " I am never to be bluffed." His lieutenant was William H. Marston, commonly known in the market as Billy Marston, a portly gentleman, with a twinkling eye and great fondness for bidding up stocks five per cent. at a leap.

These were the two conspirators, who in the summer and autumn of 1865, did with pecuniary intent, and contrary to the peace of Wall Street, and all the bears therein and thereunto appertaining, buy and take unto themselves, all, or nearly all, that certain stock, known as Prairie du Chien, otherwise Prairie Dog.

It was not a heavy burden, for there were only twenty-nine thousand and some odd shares of the stock to be handled. During the Ketchum break in August, its price was 33. Within less than three months, and on that Saturday, when B—— bought a call, it had risen to par. On the following Monday it sold from 125 to 250, in twenty minutes, amid the fiercest excitement ever known before in the Brokers' Board. On that day could have been seen, the singular spectacle of brokers shedding tears over their own losses, and strange to say, over those of their customers. Here, too, should be recorded, an instance of generosity on the part of Stimpson, the pool-leader. He gave to his customers who had been unfortunate in previous operations, an interest in the pool, and enabled them, in this way, to recover their losses. This is a bright example, shining out of that dreary waste of selfishness—Wall Street.

B——, worn out by his labors and losses, slept late on that black-bear Monday, and when he reached the lobby of the Brokers' Board, Prairie du Chien had just struck 200.

His face grew white with joy. With hands that trembled with eagerness, he fumbled once more in his wallet, brought forth his precious "call," sent it into the board to his broker, and in three minutes he had sold the two hundred shares at 210. In ten minutes more he "called" upon C——, who bought the stock at 225 and delivered to the party to whom B——'s two hundred shares had been sold.

B——'s $200 had in forty-eight hours, swelled to $20,000.

It was natural after this happy event, that "calls

and puts" should run like a silver thread through the
tangled skein of B——'s existence. He wound his
way through the mazes of the "street," hunting for
them as if they were so much game, until one fine
day in February he heard that Henry Keep, sur-
named the "Silent," was selling calls in Old Southern
on the most favorable terms. Our hero snatched at
this opportunity as a pike bites at a shiner. In due
time he had hidden in his wallet, calls for five hundred
Old Southern, duly signed by Henry Keep.

This celebrated stock magnate had taken hold of
his pet stock in January, and was brewing a cup of
"cold poison" to put to the lips of the bears who
were then dancing Juba in their Wall Street garden,
for stocks were tumbling on every side.

When these ursine individuals heard that Keep was
selling calls in Old Southern at a price slightly above
the market, they reasoned that Keep was not such a
fool as to sell calls on Old Southern, if it were going
to rise. They accordingly bought the calls and used
them as a margin to sell short. This was exactly
what Keep desired, and he succeeded thus in pro-
curing a large short interest in the market, while Old
Southern danced swiftly upwards.

After a time and when the price had risen sufficiently, it was announced that Keep was selling
"puts," also on the most favorable terms. Then the
bulls bought these puts and used them as margins
to buy Old Southern. In this way he stiffened the
price in a double ratio, first, by inducing short sales
at a low price, and second by inducing purchases at
a high price.

Then he put on the screws. Two hatchet-faced

brokers in the regular board, and two bullet-headed
brokers in the open board, to whom the task had
been delegated, stood by the levers, turned the screws,
and squeezed the bears as in a hydrostatic press.
"Their silver skins were laced with their golden
blood," while their growlings shook the massive walls
of the new Stock Exchange. When they were obstinate, the order went forth to "buy them in under
the rule." Whereupon the stentorian voice of the
vice-president was heard proclaiming that he had
been directed by the brokers of Keep to buy in for
the account of John Doe, Richard Roe, etc., etc., so
many shares of Old Southern to complete their contracts." "What is it offered at, gentlemen? I will
give 98 for one thousand shares, 99, 100, 101," at
which last named price he bought the stock, and
thus compelled the recusant bears to cover their contracts. While the stock was thus selling for 101
cash, it was offered at 94 regular, i. e., deliverable
next day, and at 86, seller three, i. e., deliverable at
the option of the seller within three days. Such
is the magic worked by rings.

Among the herd so neatly caught that day, there
was no one who roared so loudly with pain as Uncle
Daniel. He had agreed to deliver two thousand
three hundred shares, at a price twenty-five per cent.
lower than the then price, and now thought $50,000
"a good deal of money" to pay for the amusement
of selling short. His broker, D. G—— came to inform him that the stock would be bought in, unless
he "came to time." The old man sat in his easy
chair, with a most lugubrious face. After ruminating upon the situation for a moment, he replied,

"we must ingine 'em, we must ingine 'em." (Ingine,
Drew-anglice injoin.)   He did ingine 'em.   A temporary injunction was granted by a justice of the
Supreme Court, forbidding the president of the Board
of Brokers from buying in two thousand three hundred shares of Old Southern, for S——, C—— & Co.,
the brokers from whom it had been borrowed.   But
this did not save Uncle Daniel, for his own broker
took the responsibility of buying in, and delivering
the stock, very much to the disgust of the old man.

"We must ingine 'em," has ever since been one
of the jokes of the street.   It was Uncle Daniel
who inaugurated that system of injunctions, which
has played so important a part in the tactics of the
stock-market, for the past four years.   As our hero
had not yet learned the art of selling stock on calls,
as a margin, he simply held his call for five hundred
shares, and when it touched 98, he *called*, received
the stock, sold it for cash at 100, and made a profit of
$12,000.

"Bless thee, Bottom! thou art translated."

For the first time since his entrance into the stock-
market, he burst through his outer integuments, shone
forth in all the glory of the tailor's art, and sought the
fellowship of capitalists.   Good clothes, and $30,000
were all the passports needed, and he soon made the
acquaintance of H——, who told him the wondrous
story of Pacific Mail.   Pacific Mail has been by turns,
the great yellow Chinese dragon of the stock-market;
now flying, with its courageous riders, to the highest
peaks of fortune, and now, like the bears of the
Himmalaya Mountains, rolling down from crag to
crag, amid the consternation of its holders.

For fourteen years, from 1850 to 1864, it had been twisting and twirling, shooting upwards and flying downwards, dizzying the brain, piling up, or scattering riches, and driving to suicide the men who dealt in it. Then for two years it moved upwards, with periodic and tremendous strides. In 1865, its capital was increased from four to ten millions, and still the price stood at 240. In 1866, the capital was further increased to $20,000,000, an assessment of $3,000,000 was levied on the stock-holders, and dividends made in full paid scrip to the amount of $7,000,000. Even then, the price stood at 180, while the assets of the company were reported at $34,000,000. He who had bought at par in 1862, and had held his stock till the autumn of 1866, would have made, by selling his stock, including the regular yearly dividends of twenty per cent., a profit of over nine hundred per cent.

Brown Brothers & Co., the trustees of the pool described in our ninth chapter, held, in the autumn of 1866, one hundred and thirty thousand shares for the benefit of the combination.

L. W. Jerome, the "superb," now made one of his great operations. He contracted with the pool for the sale to him of one hundred thousand shares, at about twenty per cent. below the market price. This huge block amounting in its market value to nearly $20,000,000, Jerome proceeded to unload upon the shoulders of the "street," by selling it in the form of sellers' options, or borrowing other stock for delivery, in this way creating the impression that he was a short seller. The sharp ones thought they had

29

caught him this time, and snapped greedily at the supposed short sales.

Now, in order to clear himself, Jerome would have to sell his stock at about 145. A large portion of it he actually succeeded in working off at higher figures. But the autumn report of the company marked down their assets to $22,000,000. This showed the intrinsic value of the stock to be 110.

The buyers of the Jerome stock at 170 now began to open their eyes. Just after this came the great depression of the winter of 1867, resulting from the contraction of the legal-tender currency to the extent of $28,000,000. The irrevocable stock-power held by Brown Bros. was released, and Pacific Mail stock came on the market in a deluge. The price fell in a few days from 163 to 115. Jerome's losses were estimated at $800,000. Subsequently, the pool released him from his contract to the extent of forty thousand shares, and once more he " came up to scratch smiling," as they would say in the language of the prize ring.

The same blow which felled Jerome, the financial giant, also struck hard upon B——, our bucolic pigmy.

Attracted by H——'s brilliant story of the fortunes won in Pacific Mail, he took four hundred shares at 175, and put up 60 per cent. margin. This time, as he expressed it, he had " a dead open and shut thing." "Sixty per cent.," said he, " is certainly a judicious and ample margin." And so it would have been on every stock *except* Pacific Mail.

In thirty days, B——'s "judicious and ample margin" was wiped out, and in order to prevent any further loss, he sold, at the suggestion of his panic-smitten broker, at the lowest cash price, his four hundred shares, with a loss of $24,000.

Why didn't B—— draw out his $30,000, invest it in Five-twenties, and retire to his native village content with his competency?

Operators never do draw out their money, at least novices do not, so far as we have heard. They come into the street with the intention of making five or ten or twenty thousand dollars, which having been done, they say they will draw out their profits and retire. But they don't. Their broker blandly hovers over and guards their precious little piles *for himself.* He inquires in an insinuating voice, just as he is going to the board, whether his customer "has anything to say." The customer generally has something to say in the shape of an order to buy or sell, and then in five minutes or thereabouts, he finds his pile is locked fast as a margin in the fond embrace of his broker, who sits over it and feeds upon it till what with interest, commissions, turns, losses, etc., the precious little pile dwindles, and finally either disappears into the broker's till, or is sprinkled upon the tails of innumerable "kites" and flyers.

B—— for a month was lost amid the "awful solitude" of his native forest, and then returned scintillating with speculative enthusiasm. *His* pile was only $5,000 now, but by a series of lucky turns, he had in eight months swelled it to $13,000. It was upon the very day that his broker's account-books disclosed to him this pleasing fact, that he run across H—— the veracious historian of Pacific Mail, who gave him a "point" smoking hot, from the forge of a ring. *This* "point" was respecting Atlantic Mail, another famous steamship stock. As its price had fallen twenty per cent., and now stood at 93, it looked to B—— reasonable to operate in it for a rise. He bought a hundred shares, and as he remarked at the time, "Success in Wall Street, is purely a question of stamps," he deposited seventy per cent. margin, *i. e.* $7,000 on this purchase.

But as ill-luck would have it, Atlantic Mail began to drop that very day; it hung at 87 for a few more days, and then broke in one hour sixty-four per cent. downwards till it struck 23. Of course B—— now sold his stock at the lowest price. Men always do under such circumstances.

After these unfortunate trials of the merits of the margin system, B—— resolved to buy nothing except what he could pay for in cash. For five months this worked well, and B——'s small balance was climbing up towards $8,000, when he met one fine day, early in August, WHITE. White was a man who rolled a vile eye in his wicked head, and did business, under the familiar firm name of White & Co., in a den in New Street, just below the gold room.

White was just at that time playing a "little game," in a way so highly illegitimate that shortly after, when it became known, a considerable portion of the Wall Street crowd waxed indignant and sorrowful by turns.

Stock certificates endorsed by some member of the Stock Exchange, be it remembered, fly about from hand to hand in the street, just as if they were so much money or negotiable paper, no one stopping to inquire whether or not they are properly in circulation. Such is the looseness with which business is done in the stock-mart.

Now White's "little game" was this. He would buy ten share lots of Erie, New York Central, and other stocks, erase, by the means of acids and other appliances best known to himself, the word *ten*, and write in the place of it, the words *one hundred*, and dispose of the altered shares at the highest market price, or procure loans upon them. One day he turned up missing, and banks, brokers, and operators inquired vainly for White. He took several hundred thousands away with him, as the profits of his nefarious transactions, and it must be here added, that just prior to his stampede he succeeded in foisting one hundred shares of bogus Erie on our unfortunate hero, who thereupon retired forever from the field of stock-speculation, with $2,500, just $200 more than he had brought down in his original certificate of deposit.

CHAPTER XXXI.

WOODWARD, FISK Jr, GOULD.

The New Race of Financiers—W. S. Woodward—His Portrait, Character and Fortunes—The Ulysses of the Stock-market—His Wealth —James Fisk, Jr.—A Theatrical Character—His History and Antecedents—His First Appearance in the Street—A Funny Man— Anecdotes—Scenes in His Life—Jay Gould's Portrait—Erie Under the Care of Drew—The Marston Pool—Uncle Daniel Cornered— He Makes Terms and Revenges Himself on the Cornerers—New Chapters of Erie—The Market Crowded with Losers—Drew and Vanderbilt Take all Their Money—An Original Opinion Respecting Vanderbilt and Drew—Drew Throws Dirt—Fortunes of M——.

ROM 1862 till 1866, the ground shook with the tread of the new race of financiers who came filing into the stock-market. As the foremost retired with the spoils of their campaigns, or routed and disheartened to sleep the last long sleep after their "life's fitful fever," fresh men stepped in and filled or more than filled their places.

W. S. Woodward is the purest type of the class stock-speculators now extant in Wall Street. Always in the market, he may be said to have bought and sold more stocks on his own account during the past five years than any other man in the street. It would be hard to mention a leading railroad stock that has not felt the effect of his strong manipulations. Erie, Pittsburg, Reading, New York Central, Old Southern, and more lately Rock Island, have been favorites in the repertoire of this noted operator, and an account of the cliques and corners he has organized would fill a volume, which could with truth be entitled "The Speculator." A short, quiet-looking gentleman, with an assiduous air, a dark eye, a face moulded into a fixed expression of solicitude, the deep brown stubble of his beard closely mown, he hardly looks the daring and incessant speculator that he is. His reputation and credit as a business man, stand high on the books of the stock mart.

His career has been, speaking commercially, a most chequered one. If any man deserve the epithet of the Ulysses—the much enduring man of Wall Street, it is Woodward. He has wandered about that treacherous sea for many years, been shipwrecked on its desert islands, threaded the narrow channel between Scylla (panics) and Charybdis (corners), visited the cave of the Cyclops (Polyphemus Vanderbilt), heard the Sirens sing (Uncle Daniel and his Chinese lyre), sojourned among the Lotus Eaters (in a dull market), and feasted in the gardens of Alcinous (Rock Island). Like the Homeric hero, however, he always comes out right. Drew has hammered him upon his anvil, and the Commodore has hoisted him skywards with most Olympian kicks, but he seems to have as many lives as a cat. When short of stocks, he has been twisted by the bulls up long spiral shafts, and flattened like a pancake against the iron dome of a rampant market; when long of stocks, he has (speaking in the same figurative manner), time and again been thrown by the bears out of six-story garret windows, with nothing to break his fall but an India rubber credit, but like his feline prototype, he has always alighted on his legs and "sailed in" once more, as if nothing killing had happened.

In the summer of 1863, his contract was said, in the street, not to be worth fifty dollars. In 1870, his exchequer is rated at from two to four millions. As we pen these words, he might exclaim, as he emerges victorious from his last Rock Island campaign, "Our castle's strength will laugh a siege to scorn;" but whether this boast can be made hereafter, depends upon circumstances, over which the richest and shrewdest operators have little control.

"Look here upon this picture and on this."

What portraits could be more unlike than that of the dark, still, care-laden Woodward, and the blonde, bustling and rollicking James Fisk, Jr., who in 1865, came bounding into the Wall Street circus, like a star-acrobat, fresh, exuberant, glittering with spangles, and turning double summersets, apparently as much for his own amusement, as for that of a large circle of spectators. He is first, last, and always a man of theatrical effects, of grand transformations, and blue fire. All the world is to him literally a stage, and he the best fellow who can shift the scenes the fastest, dance the longest, jump the highest, and rake up the biggest pile.

His whole business career has been a series of scenic hits and stage metamorphoses. His first appearance was as the Prince of Peddlers in New England. His wagon was magnificent; his four horses sleek and mettlesome. At different points in his triumphal progress through the rural districts, he was met by a train of his subalterns, who filled the sheds of the country inns with their wagons, held audience with their chief, and obeyed his orders. His next appearance was as a dry goods merchant, a member of the well-known house of Jordan, Marsh & Co. Then quickly the scene changes once more, and he looms up as a stock-broker in New York, with a capital of $64,000, the profits of his season at merchandise. His office in Broad Street was a banqueting hall, in which he presided over tables which groaned daily with the most sumptuous lunches.

From this point of time (1865) there has always been in the turbulent stream of Erie an undercurrent and an upper whirl of James Fisk, Jr. Uncle Daniel welcomed him, (or perhaps we should say his bank account,) patted him upon the back, indoctrinated him into the mysteries of pools, (of course always in Erie,) gave him a paternal hug, during which James saw his pile growing small by degrees and beautifully less; and early in 1868, as he told a friend, he was not worth a dollar in the world.

Six months after this the scene changed again, with much rumbling and the shifting of blazing and many-colored lights, and he stands forth with a million dollars at his bankers, the high comptroller of Erie, a general theatrical manager, a steamboat potentate; in fact, Prince Erie James Jubilee Admiral James Fisk, Jr. Now the scenes shift swiftly—the eye can hardly follow them—first to Wall Street, where, to use his own words, "he made Rome howl" in the Erie ring of November, 1868; then to the courts; then to the office of the Union Pacific Railroad Company, amid the hammering in of great salamander safes with ponderous sledges; then back to Wall Street, amid the growlings of a thousand bears and the bellowings of as many bulls, in the great gold ring of September, 1869; then in the courts once more, tampering with the commodore's iron chest, all the while the voices of his enemies raining odium and curses upon him, which fall off like water from a duck's back as he drives on his dozen teams, railroads, steamboats, theaters, pools, contracts, political combinations, etc., etc., as imperturbable as a faro-croupier, and as "cool as a couple of summer mornings."

Boldness! boldness! twice, thrice, and four times. Impudence! cheek! brass! unparalleled, unapproachable, sublime!

Perhaps the strong point of this man is his physique, so robust, so hale, so free from the shadow of every peptic derangement. His boldness, *nerve*, and business capacity are supplied by this physique, which also supplies him with animal spirits beyond measure. He is continually boiling over with jokes, good, bad and indifferent.

Once when he and his father were peddling goods in New Hampshire, an old woman charged Fisk Senior with having deceived her as to the value of a piece of calico worth twelve and one-half cents.

"Well, now," said Fisk, Jr., "I don't think father would tell a lie for twelve and one-half cents, though he might tell eight of 'em for a dollar."

He always seems to look upon his operations in Wall Street, no matter how large they may have been, as a gigantic side-splitting farce. After the great gold break of September, 1869, one B——, a broker, called upon him at the Erie railroad office, for the purpose of tendering to him $500,000 gold, which he claimed to have sold him. Now, as this amount of gold would weigh something like a ton, Fisk was well aware that B—— had not brought it with him, and therefore, the tender could not be legal. So as soon as B—— stated what he came for, Fisk promptly replied, "Certainly, Mr. B——, we will take that gold. Here, John, (calling to an attendant,) go down and help Mr. B—— to bring up his gold." Poor Mr. B——, not having brought his ton of gold with him, could only look sheepish and retire.

Jay Gould, is the complement—the foil of James Fisk, Jr. He is a short, slight man, with a sable beard, a small, bright, introverted eye, and a cool, clear head. His forte is planning, and he represents the man of thought, as Fisk does the man of action, in the firm of Fisk & Gould. He is the engineer, with his hand on the engine-lever, while Fisk is the roar of the wheels, the volume of smoke from the stack, the glare of the head-light, and the screaming whistle of the locomotive. But let us return to the stock-market in 1866 and 1867.

The block of twelve thousand shares of Erie, which Daniel Drew took off the hands of the luckless Ketchum, from 76 to 80, served partly to replace what he had sold at higher figures, when the price culminated in July 31, 1865, and again he proceeded to play his new role of bull, by hoisting Erie to 96, again he tortured the bears and bled them one per cent. a day for the use of Erie stock to complete their contracts. But it is one thing to bid up Erie to 96, and quite another to sell it at that price. The "street" would not buy it, the public would not buy it, and Drew and his associates held nearly all of the stock.

> " Ye know not of the ways I have,
>   I turn, and pass, and come again."

This was his old song, and he sang it now in an under-tone, when he recommended a friend, Captain H——, to buy a few thousand shares of Erie on the point that the "pool" would put it higher. Captain H—— bought ten thousand shares, but discovered accidentally, that this lot of stock came from Drew's brokers, in fact, the old man was selling the very stock that he had recommended Captain H—— to buy. The victim stopped the payment of the check, kept the stock and compelled Drew to cancel the bargain. Uncle Daniel thus thwarted, gradually relaxed his hold on Erie, and it dropped to 56 with great loss to the pool, assisted in its downward course by the short sales made by D. D——, who once more resumed his old character of a bear.

It was in the spring of 1866, while the market was shuddering with the great London panic, the sound of which came rumbling along under the waters of the Atlantic, into Wall Street, that a new party took hold of Erie, the same that had so successfully cornered Prairie du Chien, in the preceding November. William H. Marston was the leader of this new ring. The enormous short sales of Daniel Drew, and those who sold under his inspiration, between 56 and 65, enabled Marston and his associates to obtain complete control of Erie, which by the middle of July, they had raised to 75, and once again Drew found himself cornered quite to his astonishment, since he thought himself thoroughly master of the situation in view of a little stroke of financiering, which he had plied with the Erie Railroad Company a short time before. The corporation being in urgent need of money, had borrowed of him $3,500,000, giving him twenty-eight thousand shares of new stock, and $3,000,000 in bonds convertible into stock, as collateral for the loan. A part of this collateral had been already disposed of at lower prices, when he found himself cornered as above mentioned. He now foresaw a way by which he could revenge himself on those who had conspired against him, and make up his losses. The first step to this way was through diplomacy. He made terms with the ring, and having compromised his back contracts, struck hands with them secretly in their scheme for putting Erie up. That same day the price was allowed to drop ten per cent., converting by these means hosts of jubilant bulls into bears; thereafter for two months the price was manipulated to work in a large short interest; then it was jumped in swift leaps to 97.

September was a halcyon month for all the bulls, great and small. Marston, the bull-leader, was a veritable tycoon for a few weeks. The crowd of those who had suffered in the spring tumble and during the summer, had haunted the purlieus of the Long Room in a variety of doubtful costumes, or "boozed" in the neighboring gin-mills, now skipped gleefully through the halls of the Fifth Avenue Hotel in gay attire, or sipped their champagne at Delmonico's. Erie had shot up, and stood towering like some monarch of the forest; Billy Marston was seated in a crotch of the trunk, his eyes twinkling with delight, the bright plumaged broker-birds twittered on its branches, and many a hungry operator was plucking of its fruit.

And now the "old man" came in the darkness and cut down the tree, sent Billy Marston sprawling, and put to flight every bird and beast which sat on its limbs, then staggered away under the burden of his harvest. To return to the language of the matter of fact, Daniel Drew had sold twenty thousand shares, or thereabouts, at summit prices, and thus took his revenge by breaking the ring, besides pocketing $1,000,000 by the operation. Erie kept falling till it reached 52. This was in the spring of '67. Then commenced a new chapter in speculation, and covering thirty months of time, and marked by more singular events, perhaps, than ever occurred before in the financial history of this or any other country. Battles between the money kings; the Courts of Law and Legislatures of States ranging themselves for or against the rival factions; swift rises, ruinous panics, all ending in the aggrandizement of the few and the impoverishment of the many.

Daniel Drew, Cornelius Vanderbilt, and the other stock potentates, stood all the time in the market like so many mountains of magnet which drew to themselves all the metal out of the pockets of thousands of lesser operators. In 1868 and 1869 the street swarmed with men who came, staked their money, lost, and then vanished, or still haunted the vestibules of the Stock Exchange, possessed by the illusive hope of retrieving their fortunes. The tales that could be told of some of these unfortunates would be as marvelous, doleful and moving as any romance. How they enlisted in the ranks of the speculators, ran down through the whole sounding scale of wealth, joy, splendor, doubt, disaster, penury, misery, then up again, and so on to the end of their career. Such stories as these often contain dark secrets, and belong to the unwritten lives of those men, only to be told by their close-mouthed brokers and those mysterious stock-ledgers, which, like dead men, tell no tales of the customer, either how he made and lost, or from whence he obtained his fresh supplies of cash margin, whether from robbing banks or using the funds of widows and orphans.

It will be noticed by any one who visits the market how greatly the unhappy losers there are given to gossip, in which respect no tea-party of old women in a country village can surpass them. They collect in knots of three or more on the sidewalk and pick financial characters to pieces. They ventilate discreditable stories affecting the credit of noted operators; in fact they convert the stock-mart into a school for scandal.

Naturally the money kings come in for their full share of abusive gossip from these individuals. Vanderbilt, they call a brigand. Drew, a sneak. Fisk, a cut-throat, etc., etc.

In the summer of 1869, while E—— and I were standing in New Street, near the entrance to the Long Room, our attention was attracted by two singular looking men who belonged to the class above described, and were conversing in a style which drew about them a small group of amused listeners. They were giving their opinions respecting the Commodore and Uncle Daniel with more freedom than elegance.

One of them after asserting that it was easier to make money in every business than in stock-speculation, followed up this proposition by announcing his belief that the only way to win a fortune in stocks, was to tickle Vanderbilt and Drew, meaning thereby to make ones self agreeable or useful to the great bull and bear. The idea of Cornelius Vanderbilt and Daniel Drew writhing with inextinguishable laughter under the seedy operator's fingers, as they were poked in among the small ribs, was followed by a burst of merriment from the little audience who seemed to thoroughly appreciate the truth as well as the ludicrousness of the remark. No doubt any one who could tickle Vanderbilt and Drew could make a fortune by it, just as one can catch a bird if he can put salt on his tail.

The other of the two was a man, in whose face the comic and the sad were strangely mingled, though on the whole the comic predominated. He gave his views of Daniel Drew thus:

"You see, boys, that Uncle Daniel, as you call him, (I wish he *was* my uncle,) is a dirt thrower. He spoils every stock he touches."

"How so?" inquired his auditors.

"Why! he started in life as a cattle drover, and when his cattle didn't drive to suit him, he used to pick up mud and throw at 'em until he'd plastered 'em all over, and so when he brought 'em to market they were just one mass of mud and filth. Now he treats stocks just as he used to treat cattle, he pens 'em, drives 'em up and down the market, corners 'em; in fact, Daniel Drew calls stocks his critters and abuses 'em accordingly. He waters 'em and plasters 'em all over with dirt till they are not worth shucks."

This original illustration of Drew's policy in depressing stocks, led me to inquire the name of this eccentric-looking individual.

"I know him," replied E——, "it is M——, one of that numerous class who have a regular business out of which they make a small fortune every year, and then lose it in stocks."

"He is a liquor dealer," continued E——. "I became acquainted with him in 1860. His store, or, as he was pleased to call it, his office, was in —— street, close by the Stock Exchange. It consisted of two floors; the ground-floor was his sample-room, lined with bottles, having on them the newest possible of labels, bearing such nectareous inscriptions as "London Cordial," "Otard, 1816," "Mountain Dew," "Royal Lach-na-gar Whiskey," "Milk of Kentucky." The cases of claret on the floor, always looked as though they were fresh from the plane of some carpenter in Greenwich Street, or Manhattan Alley, and the corpulent casks ranged in dignified rows along the rear wall, reminded one of the Benzine Barrel Company, rather than of the French coopers of Bordeaux.

The other floor was the basement, and about this apartment always hung the odor of mystery, and of a druggist's shop, until one day, paying M—— a visit, and not finding him in the sample-room, I penetrated to the subterranean regions. There I found M——, as busy as a bee, distilling honey out of poisonous flowers. He wore a white apron, which bore a great variety of suspicious stains, and was engaged in fill-

30

ing bottles from a large tank. He hurried with me up stairs, as soon as he could doff his apron and wash his hands, but in the brief survey I took of his laboratory, I noticed several vials of oil of cognac for manufacturing brandy out of proof spirits, together with various other flavoring essences; a large bottle that looked like tincture of logwood; jars of alum, and sugar of lead; others which looked as if they might contain chrystallized strychnine; and still another labeled hydrocyan—which I interpreted to be prussic acid.

A flood of light suddenly burst upon me. I had often remarked diagnostically, singularly disagreeable sensations, not only in the head, but also in the stomach, in the morning after imbibing at M——'s sample-room. I now smelt the rat, I might almost say the ratsbane. M—— was a compounder as well as a seller of liquors. In the basement of his store, he mixed and manufactured cordials, and various other beverages, to suit the palate of his customers. As he informed me in a moment of confidence, "what people wanted was fuddle, and he accordingly mixed his beverages with a sharp eye on fuddle."

By diligence in business, and by the suavity with which he commended his doses to a bibulous and too confiding public, he succeeded in amassing about $20,000. This was in 1863. Then he looked about him for some judicious investment or other means for swelling the dimensions of his little pile. He did not have far or long to look. Money could be made (or lost) with wonderful speed in the neighboring stock-market. The speculative movements in Wall Street had long attracted his notice, which was kept alive by the numerous brokers and operators who took their arid lunch of crackers and cheese at noon-day in his sample-room. Some of them had been customers for years, and had doubtless consumed whole hogsheads of "Mountain Dew," "Milk of Kentucky," etc., and thus created a great activity in the trade of poisonous drugs used in the adulteration of liquors, besides paying M—— a pretty penny, to say nothing of doctors' bills. The talk of M——'s customers was of margins, profits, commissions, "puts and calls." As for the word "profits," they tossed it about in their conversation with the most enchanting freedom. Fifty thousand dollars was but a drop in the bucket, and their marginal notes and references put all the laws of legitimate profits at defiance. Five thousand could be made in an hour by one lucky turn, and a hundred thousand in a short campaign.

Is it any wonder that M—— should have caught the infection, or that the *feu de joie* fired daily in his presence should have "put his soul in arms and eager for the fray?" And so it did; for one fatal day he found the little fortune of $20,000, which he had scraped together, was too hot to hold in his pocket. A poetic and unconscious revenge was about to be taken on M—— by P——, a broker and his oldest customer, in return for the stupefying and stomach-deranging draughts which he had so often imbibed at M——'s sample-room.

The $20,000 was deposited in P——'s hands.

A few weeks passed in see-sawing up and down the market; then a bold dash at Harlem on the short side, accompanied with a little coquetting with gold, and M—— found his fortune had dwindled to $500.

P—— and his brother brokers, the customers of M——, had unconsciously taken a terrible revenge on the unfortunate sample-room proprietor, who thereupon returned immediately to his unhealthy laboratory, plied his trade with new vigor, and drew to his sample-room large accessions from his new acquaintances of the Stock Exchange. He talked glibly in the street, his nectar-fluids flowed in cataracts, his office clinked with glasses as of a chime of bells, and a perpetual shower of fractional currency and greenbacks, made his counters verdant as the herbage after a rain.

Time rolled on, and in twelve months he found himself in possession of $15,000. This pleasing fact came under his notice, when he was taking account of stock, April 1st, 1864, just when the bulls were enjoying their spring carnival, led gaily on by their dashing leader, A. W. Morse. He drew out all his money from his bank, emptied his till of its loose change, and in an hour was in the office of P——. M——'s customers welcomed him back to the market, and speedily stuck him so full of "points," that his head fairly bristled with them.

What it was that finished him this time, whether it was that treacherous lake, Erie, the tumbling ramparts of Fort Wayne, or the precipices and toppling crags of Galena, I cannot say, but on the 19th of April, the day after the great panic, he was seen scudding under bare poles, in the direction of his chemical haven. Five times has he repeated this experience. Five times has this poetic revenge been wreaked upon M—— by his thirsty and unconscious customers. Five times, with a resolution worthy of some moral (or perhaps I should say immoral) hero, beaten but not subdued, has M—— returned to his regular, though (to others) "unwholesome business."

"His present status in the stock-market," added E——, "rests upon a slender margin of four hundred dollars, no thanks to Erie, or Daniel Drew."

CHAPTER XXXII.

THE BATTLES OF THE GIANTS.

HE wealth of the richest valley shone upon by the sun—the valley of the Mississippi and its tributaries—is poured into the lap of the Queen City of America, through three grand trunk railways—the Pennsylvania Central, the Erie, and the New York Central. The first of these lines long since passed under the control of a combination of wealthy capitalists. The second had been for ten years previous to 1867 a kind of stock ten-pin, set up and bowled down in Wall Street by Daniel Drew and his associates; while the third had for many years, prior to the year 1865, been supposed to be under the control of the Albany Regency as a part of their political machinery.

Cornelius Vanderbilt, in 1864, took possession of the Harlem & Hudson lines, two mouths of one of these trunks. The next step in his programme was to secure the control of the trunk fed by these mouths, viz.: the New York Central. But this could not be done without a struggle. His earliest attempt to obtain his object was a failure. Henry Keep, his antagonist in the first onset, triumphed, and in 1866 was chosen president of the company. But Henry Keep had merely certain ends of his own to subserve in becoming president of the New York Central; and when these ends had been subserved, he retired from the position. The way was then open for a new campaign, which Vanderbilt speedily undertook, and in 1867 he had secured the prize. He was master now of Hudson, Harlem and Central.

The next move was upon the works of Erie, the only other competing line which it was possible for him to obtain control of. In the summer of 1867, Vanderbilt and his friends had secured a majority of the Erie stock, and were about to elect a new board of directors, in which *Daniel Drew's name was not to appear*.

To throw Daniel Drew out of the Erie board would be like skinning the bear, or plucking the plumage from the peacock; it would strip the "old man" of his prestige, deprive him of his bread and butter, and send him forth to wander in desolation through the stock-market.

Daniel Drew felt the iron enter his soul at this prospect, and threw himself in supplication at the feet of Cornelius Vanderbilt, who was moved by the spectacle, and comforted the old bear. A compromise was made, and early in the fall of 1867, Daniel Drew was allowed to come into the combination as a director, and the treasurer of the Erie Railroad Company. Daniel Drew could no more refrain from playing his old games in Erie, than the veteran gamester can withold his hand from cards and dice. It was play to him, but death to others. He intrigued to enlist in his schemes, the most active and able of the board of directors, and in January, 1868, they were with him in furthering these schemes.

A pool in the Vanderbilt interest was then engaged in engineering a rise in Erie, and the street was full of rumors of something which was to carry Erie to par. It reached 79, when suddenly it fell back heavily to 71, to the astonishment of the bull faction. A great mass of stock had been quietly shuffled off by Daniel Drew, on the shoulders of the pool.

On the evening when Erie stood at 71, the whole strength of Wall Street seemed to have poured into the halls of the Fifth Avenue Hotel. Daniel Drew, with his face pucked into an expression more than usually sombre and solicitous, stood near the grand stairway, watching the writhings of his victims, the late exultant bulls. A prominent broker accosted him as follows, "Well, Mr. Drew, is Erie going down?"

"Other folks think it is," replied Daniel Drew, with an ill-suppressed chuckle, "though I can't give you any pynts in it."

"Other folks is fond of cats," remarked Mr. Brooks, the pieman in the Pickwick papers, when Samuel Weller of famous memory, observed the great number of those useful domestic animals frisking about the pie-shop.

The hollow truce patched up in the preceding summer, had been broken. Daniel Drew, true to his bitter instincts, had been undermining the Com-

modore and his friends who composed the pool be-
before named, and now the Commodore fired the first
gun which was to usher in the battle. This gun
roared out on the 17th of February, in the form of
an injunction obtained from the Supreme Court, forbidding Drew and his brother directors from the payment of the interest and principal of the $3,500,000
borrowed of Drew in 1866. This was followed up
by another action petitioning for the removal from
office of Mr. Treasurer Drew. On the 3d of March,
another injunction was issued forbidding the Erie
Board to issue any more new stock, by the conver-
sion of bonds or otherwise, in addition to the two
hundred and fifty-one thousand and fifty-eight shares
appearing in the last report of the company.

Prior to this, and on the 19th of February, by a vote
of the Erie Board, the stock of the road was increased
to four hundred and fifty thousand shares ($45,000,-
000 at par.) Five millions of convertible bonds were
forthwith sold to Daniel Drew, who promptly converted them into stock, and on or about the 29th of
February, those shares were disposed of in the market, carrying down the price of Erie to 65, to the delight of Drew, and the entire bear brigade, which
fought under his banner. But just as these triumphant mercenaries were counting the hours when Erie
should plunge down among the fifties, it wheeled and
rose like lightning to seventy-three, under the enormous purchases of the Commodore, fortified as he now
was, by the injunction forbidding the issue of any
more stock. The smaller bear tribe were scooped up
as in a net by the dozen, but the leaders in the downward movement preserved their serenity in the face

of this sudden blow. Drew chuckled a little more often. Fisk, in his cataract of shirt-front, and enveloped in an atmosphere of patchouli, attended his Nourmahal to the opera as usual, and Gould glided with a sinuous grace, through the conclave of directors, who met just at this time, with remarkable frequency, at the office of the Erie Railroad Company.

The secret of this serenity was soon disclosed. The Erie conspirators prepared five thousand convertible bonds, and promptly converted them into fifty thousand shares of stock. Then they addressed themselves to strike the blow. They had been ordered to stand still, by the last Vanderbilt injunction granted by one judge, and now they applied for and obtained, an injunction in the name of a third party, from another judge, forbidding them to stand still.

The plot was ripe. It only remained to select the broker who should strike the blow. The broker selected was William Heath, the head of the prominent and favorably known firm of William Heath & Co. He was a Boston boy, and his career as a buyer and seller of stocks on commission, dates back only to the year 1864, when his fortune was swallowed up by the Morse failure, and he was thrown back on his oars to start life again as a broker. But in that brief period, by main strength exerted in the exercise of an unwearied industry, and by the display of fine business qualities, he built up an enormous business, and won for himself a worthy name and high credit on 'Change. He is said to have earned in five years the gross sum of nearly one million dollars in commissions; and when it is remembered that a large portion of this sum was from buying and selling on a commission of one thirty-second, *i. e.*, three dollars and twelve cents on each hundred shares bought or sold, the extent of his business can be better appreciated.

A tall, lithe man, with a trustworthy face, depressed by no vices, controlled by one idea—the buying and selling of stocks—no one who has visited Wall Street will have failed to notice him as he goes swinging on, plying his trade like some automatic and powerful machine. It should be here remarked that he has never had an interest in any of those combinations which have so often employed him to buy or sell their stocks, but has acted for them merely in the capacity of a broker.

On the 29th of February, Uncle Daniel might have been seen scuttling into the office of William Heath & Co., No. 19 Broad Street. A few moments later, that office was resonant with the rustling of fifty thousand shares of fresh, crisp, Erie certificates, like the chirping of locusts at noontide in July. On the 10th of March again, in the same office, was heard the rustling of fifty thousand fresh shares, as they dropped from the plump jeweled fingers of James Fisk, Jr.

The open board met as usual at ten o'clock in the morning. Erie stood firm as a pillar of granite at 79. The Vanderbilt cohort sat with grim smiles upon their faces; their glances and voices were level with assured triumph. The nods, becks, winks, and odd smiles exchanged between them, seemed to tell their adversaries that, struggle as they might, it was all in vain; that they would have to settle up, or pay the piper a swinging rate.

Most of the bear brigade who dared still to keep short of Erie, unconscious of the measures taken for their speedy release, were a pallid group endeavoring to hide their agony by looking straight before them, or conversing in short jerky whispers with those who sat next to them, or lolling back in their chairs, feigning indifference, with their eyes fixed upon the adipose cherubs frescoed upon the ceiling.

The whole market hung on one word—Erie. The strident voice of George Henriques, the Vice President of the Open Board, was heard calling off in quick succession, Government Bonds, State Bonds, Pacific Mail, New York Central, then a pause, a shadow rippled across his face and a shiver ran through the hall as he ejaculated in a tone still more strident—Erie! For ten minutes bedlam seemed to have broken loose. Every operator and broker was on his feet in an instant, screaming and gesticulating. The different Vanderbilt brokers stood each in the center of a circle, wheeling as on a pivot from right to left, brandishing their arms and snatching at all the stock offered them. As the presiding officer's hammer fell and his hoarse voice thundered out, "That will do, gentlemen, I shall fine any other offer," Erie stood at 80. The crowd leaving the other stocks not yet called, poured into the street, where nothing was heard but Erie. Vanderbilt's brokers had orders to buy every share offered, and under their enormous purchases the price rose, by twelve o'clock, to 83.

Meanwhile, William Heath had not been idle. The fifty thousand shares of stock which had been given him to sell, had been distributed in lots of five and ten thousand shares to his sub-agents, and by half-past one, they had all been disposed of.

In the very height of this battle between giant avarice, fighting like a demon with his fellow over the grave of all the passions, a whisper was heard which sent an electric thrill through the whole market. This whisper, breathed thus, was "thousands of shares of fresh certificates, dated three days back, and in the name of James Fisk, Jr., are on the street." The price dropped like lead to 71.

Vanderbilt had lost the day. The news of this disaster was carried to him by a friend, who asked if he would now sell his Erie? He roared a thundering No! His situation was indeed critical, loaded as he was with ten millions of fresh Erie stock, which marked down the intrinsic value of the stock to 50, to say nothing of the huge blocks of Central, Hudson, and Harlem, which he was carrying on his aged shoulders. Any lack of nerve would have produced a financial collapse, which would have involved himself and thousands of others in frightful loss, and perhaps ruin. But he never flinched.

His first move was to punish his adversaries, by bringing them under the process of the court, whose injunction they had disregarded.

The executive committee of the Erie Board were holding high festival over their triumph, at the offices of the company, at the foot of Duane Street, on the morning of the 11th of March. Uncle Daniel's corrugated visage was set into a chronic chuckle. Jay Gould's financial eye beamed and glittered, and the blonde bulk of James Fisk, Jr. was unctuous with jokes, when a messenger arrived, conveying to them the intelligence that process of the court had been issued, to punish them for contempt of its mandates, and would soon be placed for service in the hands of the high sheriff's spongy officers.

Then there were hurryings to and fro in the Erie Railroad Office. A few moments later, and the policeman on that beat observed a squad of respectably dressed, but terrified looking men, loaded down with packages of greenbacks, account books, bundles of papers tied up with red tape, emerge in haste and disorder from the Erie building. Thinking perhaps that something illicit had been taking place, and these individuals might be plunderers playing a bold game in open daylight, he approached them, but he soon found out his mistake, they were only the executive committee of the Erie Company, flying the wrath of the Commodore, and laden with the spoils of their recent campaign.

By three o'clock that afternoon the fugitives had established their headquarters at Taylor's Hotel, in Jersey City, and were sheltered from the process of the New York Courts under the broad ægis of the free and sovereign State of New Jersey. They were provided with ammunition in the shape of from six to ten millions of money, principally the proceeds from the sale of one hundred thousand shares of new Erie stock, which they had saddled upon Vanderbilt, and now were ready to open fire all around, though at long range.

The old proverb, that laws are cobwebs which catch only small flies, while the large flies break through and escape, was now fully illustrated.

The litigation which followed, was a carnival for

the legal fraternity. The fees of one of the lawyers amounted to $150,000. This was only one item in a bill of costs payable to an army of attorneys and counselors. The files of the courts were stacked with affidavits and counter affidavits, complaints, answers, replies, demurrers and orders. The Supreme Court rang with the criminations and recriminations of the rival factions, while reluctant witnesses were stretched upon the rack and badgered and threatened in order to elicit from them the dark secrets of the stock-trade. The gravest insinuations were made against the purity of the judicial ermine.

Outside the courts of law, the battle was renewed in other fields. The press, siding with one party or the other, teemed with articles and affidavits affecting the combatants by forestalling public opinion. In the Legislature of New Jersey, an act was passed making the Erie Railway Company a corporation of that State. In the Legislature of New York, a bill was introduced for the purpose of legalizing the new issue of Erie stock, providing for a broad gauge connection between New York and Chicago, and forbidding the consolidation of Erie with Central. The securing of the passage of this bill was entrusted to Jay Gould, a master of diplomacy, who, braving the process for contempt which was out against him, succeeded in establishing himself in Albany, fortified with a trunk full of greenbacks, and proceeded to lobby for its passage. The Erie Company leveled another blow at Vanderbilt, by lowering the tariff of freights and passengers on their road, to a ruinous rate.

Meanwhile the withdrawal of the vast sum carried

away by the conspirators into New Jersey, had created a stringency in the money market, and stocks
declined in a semi-panic. New York Central fell
from 132 to 108¾. The market was full of rumors
affecting the solvency of Vanderbilt. He had declared his intention to hold up Erie, if he had to
mortgage every dollar of property he possessed. But
could he do it? He was exposed to fresh issues of
Erie stock, which it was reported his opponents had
threatened to make. Some of his associates, terrified at the prospect, threw their New York Central
stock upon the market. Heavy bets were made, that
the bill legalizing the new issue of Erie stock would
pass the Legislature, and that New York Central
would go down to par.

The whole street seemed to be selling Central.
When it reached 108¾, it wheeled and shot back to
111, amid the consternation of the bears, who still
persisted in selling.

Monday, April 20th, was a dark, cloudy day. The
effect of the weather upon stocks is very apparent.
That strange, and many-chorded instrument, the
human nerve, is nowhere more delicately strung, or
more responsive to the subtlest influences, than in
the orchestra of stock-speculation. Eye, ear, touch,
and all the ganglia, are morbidly alive. Sometimes
a harmless piece of tissue-paper, thrown by one operator to another, or a half-uttered confidence, would
seem to be enough to start a panic, or send the market "kiting" up among the tall figures. The outside
atmosphere is one of these influences. Hence it is
that the barometer of finance seems to respond to the
atmospherical barometer, the nerve fluid seeming to

be as susceptible as the mercury in the bulb. When cliques have control of a stock, they rarely select a wet, unpleasant day in which to run up the price.

But this rule did not hold good in the case of New York Central. On the Monday before mentioned, at twelve o'clock, meridian, the news reached the Long Room, that the Erie bill had passed by a large majority. The bears (who generally sympathized with the Erie faction), now sold Central short on every side. The skies grew black, and a pouring shower followed, amid which the strong hand of the Commodore, regardless of the elements which were against him, hoisted the enormous bulk of Central to 120.

How did it happen, that he had thus resumed his grip on Central? Had a settlement been made by the litigants?

Vanderbilt understood the character of Drew. He knew, and said that he had "no backbone," and would be inclined to compromise. The event proved that he knew his man. Hardly had the Erie confederates been installed in Taylor's Hotel, when his younger, and more robust associates, noticed the workings of his timid, vacillating nature. He had been borne along by their stronger wills, and now felt painfully his trying position. He missed his pleasant fireside, where had so often toasted his aged limbs, and dreamed of panics.

One evening he was missed from the conclave; where could he be? His associates distrusted him, and put detectives on his track. He was followed to Weehawken ferry, and it was ascertained, that he was making secret visits to New York. From that

31

time, he was never free from the surveillance of detectives. He drew out the money, which had been brought over at the time of his flight, and carried it to New York. James Fisk, Jr., attached his securities in Jersey City, and compelled him to restore it.

Under the process of the court, Daniel Drew was liable to be immured in Ludlow Street jail. But Sunday brings, besides its other blessings, immunity from arrest. One Sunday in April saw the "old man" at the house of the Commodore. Once more he shed salt tears and supplicated for mercy. "The gentle dew of mercy" was dropped upon him, and a few days after that he was seen in Broad Street, on a week day. Rumors began to spread, but nothing definite was known for some weeks. The rise in Central, however, told the story to those who chose to put two and two together.

The terms of this settlement have lately been made public in the most thorough manner, in the great suit of the Erie Railway Company *vs.* Cornelius Vanderbilt.

He was relieved of fifty thousand shares of Erie stock, and received therefor, $2,500,000 in cash, and $1,250,000 in bonds of the Boston, Hartford and Erie Company, at 80. He also received the further sum of $1,000,000 for the privilege given the Erie Company thus purchased, of calling upon him for his remaining fifty thousand shares at 70, any time within four months. This settlement was effected late in April. The day after it took place, Fisk, Jr. could have been seen on the street in a nobby velvet coat, whispering into the ears of his old comrades, "Erie is going down."

The next thing to be done was to sell the one hundred thousand shares of Erie. How could it be effected? for one hundred thousand shares is no flea bite. Very easily, thus: Orders were given every day to sell a certain amount of the stock and to hold the market steady meantime. The stock thus sold, was borrowed of different parties for delivery, and in this way the impression was created among those not in the secret, that a large short interest was being made; this induced the belief that Drew and Vanderbilt were working together to raise the price so as to sell their stock. In a few weeks, one hundred thousand shares were sold. Then the parties from whom the stock had been borrowed, were repaid with the hundred thousand shares held jointly by the Erie Company and by Vanderbilt.

Three months of comparative dullness in Erie passed away, and then Uncle Daniel took down his rusty and cobwebbed armor, donned his bear-skin cap, and prepared to enter a new campaign against all the bulls. Erie was to be depressed. The first step towards this depression had been already taken. The Erie Company was now under the control of Jay Gould, who had been chosen president, and James Fisk, Jr., who had been chosen comptroller of the company. The leaders of the Tammany ring, Peter B. Sweeney, and William M. Tweed, were added to the Board of Directors. During the four months prior to the 24th of October, 1868, fresh issues of Erie stock, had been forced upon the market. The capital stock had been increased by two hundred and thirty-five thousand shares, and now stood at $57,766,300. The stock-price ran down to 44.

The next step was to lock up greenbacks, and thus produce an artificial stringency in the money market.

It has been stated in these pages, that money in the fall season, flows westward and southward, away from New York. The money system is like the circulatory system in the human body. The sub-treasury in New York, is the financial heart of the nation. The money which flows in and out of that great depository, is the blood of commerce running through great arteries.

It was now proposed, that this circulatory system should be constricted, so that money could flow with less freedom, and stocks be depressed.

Three doctors, Daniel Drew, Jay Gould and James Fisk, Jr., now put their fingers on the financial pulse and then constricted the money arteries by *locking up greenbacks*. This is a device of comparatively recent invention. It is accomplished in this way. Checks for a large amount are drawn on various banks by some of the heavy depositors. Then these checks are certified as good by the banks, and greenbacks are borrowed upon them as collateral and locked up. A scarcity of money ensues and stocks fall.

The Erie conspirators had in their possession many millions, the proceeds from the sales of the new stock. Drew added four millions to the combination. Thereupon, $14,000,000 was withdrawn from the circulation. The money rate tightened fearfully, and the large holders of stocks saw ruin impending. Among the number was Henry Keep. He was loaded down enormously with North-west stock, and would break unless he could secure $2,000,000. In his extremity he

VAULTS OF THE STOCK EXCHANGE.

applied to his old associate Drew, who saved him by loaning him the required sum.

Drew now retired from the "locking up" combination. This excited their ire. The old man was short of 70 thousand shares of Erie, and his associates resolved to punish his treachery. They bought an immense amount of Erie at low prices, and then "unlocking greenbacks," money became easy again. Erie was hoisted to 61. Drew was cornered, and tried to compromise his contracts, but his old associates refused to "let him up." He had to buy in his shorts with the loss of a million and a half of dollars.

CHAPTER XXXIII.

THE GREAT GOLD CONSPIRACY OF 1869.

How Gold was Put Up and Down since 1865—Gold Looks Downwards in 1869, and Why—Jay Gould Organizes a Scheme—Amount of Gold to be Handled—The Complicity of Government Sought to be Obtained—Influences Brought to Bear—The Leaders of the Conspiracy —Everybody Selling Gold Short—The Vast Sums Bought by the Clique—Jay Gould on the Rack—Fisk Comes to the Front—A New Programme—The Conspiracy Draws to a Head—Dawning of Black Friday—Strategy Adopted—Actresses Gazing on the Drama—The Battle in the Gold-Room—Rout of the Conspirators—Speyers Bidding Up Gold—The Bears Triumph—Scenes in Broad Street—The Stock Panic.

N the corner of Twenty-third Street and Eighth Avenue stands a white marble palace, adorned on the exterior with statues and elaborate cornices, and hollowed in the interior into a sumptous opera hall, surrounded by spacious and richly furnished rooms—at once a fortress and a temple. Here have been planned the fiercest campaigns in the stock market, and here, too, have been exhibited the most gorgeous scenes of the spectacular drama. Pike's Opera House, since 1868, has been known as Erie Castle.

This now famous block of buildings passed, two years since, into the hands of the stock and theatrical impressario, James Fisk, Jr., by whom it was leased to the Erie Railway Company as their principal office.

Here, sitting at their ease, surrounded by luxury, in a magnificent apartment, with shrewd lawyers at their elbow, two confederates plotted the great gold conspiracy of 1869, and coolly organized the ruin of thousands.

From April, 1865, to September, 1869, a period of more than four years, the movements of gold had been brought about by artificial means, in conjunction with commercial causes, or rather pretexts. The price of Government Bonds abroad, wars or rumors of wars in Europe, disturbances of trade, the shipments of the precious metal in payment of our imports, sales of gold by our government; these and a thousand other strings were harped upon by the gold gamblers to produce those singular upward and downward oscillations in the price, which enriched the members of the Gold Board, while they disturbed the peace of commerce and beggared a host of infatuated outside dealers.

Wall Street, like history, repeats itself. Every summer, since 1865, there had been a rise in gold. In March, 1869, gold fell to 131. The astute intellect of Jay Gould now foresaw another opportunity to push up the price of gold, and having purchased $7,000,000 of it, by playing on the strings of the Cuban insurrection, the Alabama difficulties, the prospect of a war between France and Prussia, etc., terrified the bears and rushed up the price to 145. Emboldened by the success of this move, he formed a new and daring scheme.

We call it a daring scheme, for outside influences to help it there were none.

At home, the Republic was at peace; barns bursting with a garnered harvest, cattle on a thousand hills, cotton whitening innumerable fields. The government rapidly diminishing the debt, gave assurance of the speedy resumption of specie payments. The balance of trade necessitating the shipment of coin to foreign countries, was but slightly against the United States.

Abroad, the cloud of war between France and Prussia had faded to a mere speck. England was looking with equanimity upon the Alabama claims. The policy of our government toward Cuba was that of non-intervention.

It was to be a dead lift. Nothing but the shorts would help it. It could only be successful by a judicious application of the great law of supply and demand. The demand must be created, and then the supply must be shut down upon.

Jay Gould, the arch conspirator, calmly surveying the situation, and undeterred by the difficulties it presented, proceeded to organize in the most secret forges of Wall Street, a band of Vulcans, who should weld and rivet the chains by which all the bears on 'Change should be bound and made to dance as if on red-hot plates; first to slow, and then to quick music.

To accomplish the ends proposed, both the actual and the possible supply of gold in the city of New York must be provided for.

Gold coin in the city of New York is found under three conditions. In the first place, there is the floating gold, which is used by the speculators to make their deliveries, and for other commercial purposes. In August, 1869, the amount of this floating gold was estimated at from $15,000,000 to $20,000,000.

This was but a bagatelle for a ring to buy up. In the second place, there is the gold held by the banks, a part of which is loaned to the importing merchants, for the payment of duties to the Government. But little of this gold, held by the banks, comes upon the street. In the third place, there was the gold in the sub-treasury of the United States, amounting to a daily average of $80,000,000. The Government, in the summer of 1869, was selling one million of this amount every alternate week.

The pivot upon which the whole scheme would turn, was the policy of the Government in their sales of gold. The coin in the sub-treasury hung like an avalanche over any combination which should undertake to raise the price. The complicity of high officials would have to be secured, in order to keep down the sales to a limited amount.

As far back as June, an unsuccessful effort was made to secure the appointment of a sub-treasurer in the interest of the ring.

The President of the United States was then approached directly, for the purpose of ascertaining what the future financial policy of the Government might be with respect to sales of gold, but without eliciting any information from our reticent chief magistrate.

A plausible theory respecting the necessity to commercial interests of high-priced gold, was suggested by James McHenry, a prominent English financier, and was ventilated freely by Jay Gould for the purpose of forestalling official action.

The medium selected by the conspirators for securing the complicity of the high officers of the

Government, was the now notorious Abel R. Corbin, who, by virtue of a marriage connection, claimed to be able to influence the chief executive of the nation in the matter of gold sales. Upon the promises and representations of this man, hung the whole success of the plot. The planners relied sufficiently upon him to proceed to organize their forces and enter upon the prosecution of their scheme.

The nucleus of the combination consisted of Jay Gould, James Fisk, Jr., W. S. Woodward, the veteran speculator, and Arthur Kimber, the youthful agent of a wealthy London banking house. Around this nucleus revolved a number of rich bankers, sly politicians, officials, and corporations made compact by the potentiality of a wealth beyond the dreams of avarice, and cohesive with the hope of plunder.

When gold fell, in August, to 131, it looked as if the finger of a child could have rolled it down to 120. Nearly everbody thought, and said, that the price was doomed to fall lower than at any time since 1862. All the world, in a commercial sense, stood ready to profit by the fall. The importing merchants borrowed it, and sold it, by the million. The foreign bankers sold it by the car load. The brokers sold it all around the board; the bond-holders, the administration politicians, and the outside public, all sold it for future delivery. They "stood on their shorts," or rather, sat incubating on them, as if they were golden eggs. The clique bought this gold.

About the middle of September, Woodward bought nine millions, at $133\frac{1}{2}$ to 134, for the account of himself, Kimber and Gould. Prior to this, large amounts of gold had been bought.

The price rose heavily to 138, at which price Woodward and Kimber are said to have sold their interest, and retired from the combination. Their associates enlisted new coadjutors and still persisted in their scheme.

On the morning of Wednesday, the 22d of September, the conspirators held several millions more gold than was in the city of New York, outside of the sub-treasury, and yet the price had risen, in the face of these purchases, only to 141.

The price would soon have to be bid up to 150, at least, but the buying of high-priced gold in the form of contracts from those who were selling it for future delivery, is quite a different thing from buying the actual coin, which the Government might sell and deliver.

It was natural, in contemplation of the difficulty with which the price was raised, that Jay Gould should feel anxiety as to the ultimate success of the movement. He knew thoroughly well how much depended on the influence of Corbin, in retarding official sales, and already he more than distrusted him, with how much reason the event has shown. He well knew that if his suspicions were correct, and official sales of Government gold should not be withheld through Corbin's influence, the only thing to be relied upon, was a bold game, to terrify the shorts and compel them to cover their contracts at a high figure. The personal magnetism and brute pluck of James Fisk, Jr., were now brought to the front. Let this individual tell the story in his own characteristic manner.

"When Gould found himself loaded down to the gunnels and likely to go under, the cussed fellow

never said a word—he's too proud for that—but I
saw him tearing up bits of paper. When Gould
snips off corners of newspapers and tears 'em up in
bits, I know that there's trouble. Then I come in to
help—he knows I'd go my bottom dollar on him,—and
said to him, 'Look here, old fellow, when I was a boy,
on a farm in Vermont, I've seen the old man go out to
yoke up Buck and Brindle; he'd lift the heavy yoke
on to Brindle's neck, key the bow, and then, holding
up the other end, motion to old Buck to come under,
and old Buck would back off and off, and sometimes,
before he could persuade him under, the yoke would
get too heavy for dad. And, Gould, old fellow, Wall
Street won't be persuaded, and the yoke is getting
damned heavy—and here I am to give you a lift.'"

The time was rapidly approaching when the decisive blow must be struck. The vaults of every bank
in the Union, in Montreal and the Bank of England
had been called upon to disgorge, and the gates of
the national treasury had been stormed with prayers
to let loose the coin and save the country, or at least
the bears.

On the evening of the 23d of September, the
clique rushed in and took possession of the private
office of William Heath & Co., after the firm had left
for the day. A sumptuous banquet and wine were
ordered in from a neighboring restaurant. Nothing
definite seems to have been resolved on at this meeting, except that the bears must, within a day or two,
be compelled to fulfill their contracts. It was at sometime on the same day, however, that a new programme
was determined upon, for which purpose William
Belden, a former partner of Fisk, was brought ac-

tively into the combination. He proceeded to buy
that day not less than $8,000,000 for the account of
the clique, and thus appeared prominently as their
agent.

The question always to be asked in buying stocks,
is for whom they are to be bought, who is responsible
for them. By the rule of law, every agent dealing
for an unknown principal, is personally liable for all
the contracts he makes. The new programme decided upon, was the making of William Belden, a
man of little means, the principal in immense contracts for purchases of high-priced gold, which were
to be made through Fisk, who was to act merely as
an agent, and would thus avoid all personal liability.
A paper was given by Belden to Fisk, granting him
unlimited power to buy gold for his (Belden's) account. The brokers employed by Fisk would buy on
his orders, supposing that he was the principal.
Belden was in this way to be the scape-goat on whose
shoulders an immense burden of liability for purchases of high-priced gold would ultimately fall.

On Thursday, the 23d, Fisk made his personal magnetism felt by visiting the gold-room, where he struck
terror into the hearts of the bears, by offering a bet
of any part of $50,000, that gold would sell at 200.
Wherever he went that day he bulled gold, predicted
an enormous rise, and openly boasted of the complicity of the Government in the schemes of the conspirators. He proposed to his associates that a complete list of two hundred and fifty firms, known to
be short of gold, should be published in the daily
papers of the next day, stating the amount that each
firm was short of; declaring how much gold the

clique held; and informing the victims that if they did not settle at 145, by three o'clock, a higher rate would be demanded. But this proposition was rejected upon the advice of counsel.

The extent of the operations of the clique can be best understood by a few figures. The calls or options for the delivery of gold by other parties, and the cash gold which they held, was stated to be from $80,000,000 to $110,000,000. The amount of short interest is said to have been $250,000,000, the larger portion of which had been made under 144.

The plot was ripe on the evening of the 23d, when the conspirators held a meeting as already described. The cash gold bought had been loaned by the ring to the bears, who, to fulfill their contracts, were in this way carrying it for the clique in the manner described in our preceding chapters. This fact dispensed with the necessity, on the part of the clique, for any very large amount of money. One prominent brokerage firm held $10,000,000 and upwards, which had cost them an average of 138, and on which they had received no margin from the clique. They carried it by loaning it, and fortified by a rise of four or five per cent. advance in the price. Belden is said to have received no margin, and, having little money himself, provided in the same way for the cash gold which he bought.

Here it should be noticed that the Gold Bank affords the greatest facilities for speculation by the system it has adopted for paying differences, which dispenses with the cumbrous machinery of deliveries, and enables men with a few thousand dollars capital to do a daily business of millions.

The problem now was how to compel the bears to

cover, for they were obstinate and refused to believe in the upward movement.

Beneath the Stock Exchange there are dungeons for the confinement, not of men, but of money. The resources of art have been exhausted to make these dungeons secure. Hundreds of safes, built of huge granite blocks, lined with chilled iron and tempered steel, closed with treble patent locks, are ranged in long rows in the dim gas-light, and guarded day and night by trusty watchmen sitting behind grated bars. Here is more wealth laid away than in any other depository on the hemisphere. In these vaults it was proposed that on the morning of the 24th, the gold that had been loaned should be called for, locked up, and then that the bears should be forced to settle by buying them in under the rule or otherwise.

To this end the Tenth National Bank, where the principal members of the clique owned a controlling interest, was instructed to certify the checks of their brokers to any amount which might be called for. This precaution was taken to provide for the large sums necessary in shifting the gold from the bears, who had borrowed it, and locking it up in the vaults of the Stock Exchange.

But this plan was disconcerted in the following manner. Some of the bears, noticing the extent to which checks were certified for the account of the clique, made representations at Washington to the effect that the bank was overstepping its legal powers. Accordingly, on the morning of the 24th, the bank examiners made their appearance for the purpose of investigating the books of the Tenth National Bank. Although the bank passed through the ordeal unscathed, there is no doubt that the operations of the clique were greatly hampered by this move.

The programme now was to put up gold swiftly, and terrify the bears into settlements. Albert Speyers, a wealthy German, who, after a life of chequered experience, had settled down into a gold-broker, was the agent selected to accomplish this, under the orders of Fisk and Gould. Speyers is a true type of the gold-dealer class. A slender, wiry man, with inflammable eyes, a face criss-crossed with wrinkles, and an impulsive, dashing style in making purchases and. sales, he was a supple tool in the hands of his principals. The private office of William Heath & Co. was chosen as the head-quarters of the clique. The services of other brokers were retained to negotiate settlements with the bears. A brigade of other agents and sub-agents was marshalled, to help on the movement as they best might. Everything was now ready for the blow to be struck.

The sun rose up lightly and brightly on the morning of that black-Friday, September 24th, 1869, as though the day were to be a jocund one. To-day the play was to be played out; so it had been announced by the theatrical manager. The audience assembled early; every window on the west side of New Street had its spectators, the walks and roadway were jammed, the gold-room was packed to suffocation. A carriage wheeled into the street. On the back seat sat the actresses, Miss L. W——, and Miss P. M——, the latter the queen of the blonde troupe.

> "Her lips were red, her looks were free,
> Her locks were as yellow as gold."

A thick-set, blue-eyed man, dressed in magnificent

costume, and perfumed like a milliner, descended from the carriage, and entered the office of William Heath & Co. It was James Fisk, Jr., "the oiled and curled Assyrian Bull" of Wall Street. He came prepared to play a part, but in no mimic drama. The curtain rose with gold at 143½. Fifty men, the agents of the conspirators, put their shoulders under it, and held it like a rock, while a hundred bear-hammers rained blows upon it as if it were an anvil. The price rose swiftly, 145, 146, 147, 148, 149, and at eleven, gold stood at 150. The duo, James Fisk, Jr. and Jay Gould, sat in their head-quarters. The business of the former was to hold up the price on his broad back. The latter sat cool and silent, watching the battle, preparing new moves, and whispering low his orders to his lieutenant, the irrepressible Fisk.

Meanwhile the other agents were busily at work frightening the bears into settlements. The bears hurled defiance in their teeth. "Up she goes, then," cried Fisk, and in five minutes gold was selling for 160. Albert Speyers bought during the morning, $26,000,000.

William Heath, on the order of the duo, wedged his way through the throng and bid 160 for $1,000,000. The bid was followed by an appalling silence. The crowd saw Heath, the cautious, steady broker, rarely seen personally in the gold-room, now standing in the thickest of the throng, and heard him bidding for a million. No one was bold enough to meet the bid. He stood only for an instant, with his finger poised high in the air, and then, as if with some presentiment of the coming panic, he wheeled and fled from the room. 32

Many of the bears, terrified at last, were now pouring into the office of Smith, Gould, Martin & Co., of which firm Jay Gould is a partner, and were settling up their contracts to the amount of millions. But the heavy foreign bankers still stood firm under the standard of Brown Bros., Duncan, Sherman & Co., Seligman, and others.

"Settle up!" shrieked the cornerers.

"Never! do your worst," was the retort.

Up it went, then, to 162½, while Speyers bid for any number of millions. The bear leaders wiped their brows, and prayed that Boutwell or night would come. High noon was "clashed and clamored from a hundred towers."

While Speyers was bidding furiously for gold at 160, Gould was selling all the gold he could through a dozen different brokers, at 135 to 140, and still Speyers, his black eye flaming, and his wrinkled face purple with excitement, kept up his bids, "160 for a million, 160 for any part of a million." He bought seven millions in two lots, when a shiver ran through the crowd as some one cried out, "the Government is selling." How much? "Thirteen millions!" rang out the voice of some bold bear. Down, down fell the price, twenty-five per cent. in two minutes, and then up again to 160, like a gigantic shuttlecock, as some one cried out, "the Government will only sell four millions." Speyers brandished his arms and shrieked only seven words, "160 for a million." Winged missiles, bids and offers hurtled through the dense air for an instant, and then the bear-hammers seemed to have been all welded into one great sledge, which fell upon the price like a forty-ton boulder, and smashed it down to 135, while Speyers fell back into the crowd, quivering like an aspen. Lights seemed to dance before the eyes of the multitude, and then go out in darkness, as they rushed tumultuously into Broad Street.

From Wall Street to Exchange Place there was a sea of bewildered, pallid faces. The wildest rumors were afloat, but none worse than the ruinous facts which stared all in the face. Frenzied operators hurled curses at the clique leaders, and battered at the offices of Smith, Gould, Martin & Co., which were closed and barred, while hard-featured men, deputy-sheriffs and shoulder-hitters, guarded the avenues which led to the head-quarters of the conspirators.

A. Speyers, looking like a goblin rather than a man, with dim eyes and face as pale as ashes, was vibrating between the offices of Smith, Gould, Martin & Co. and William Heath & Co. His limbs moved automatically. His fortune of one million dollars had been swept away in five minutes. In the Gold Bank, on Thursday, the 23d, $239,000,000 of clearances had dizzied the arithmetic of a hundred pallid accountants. On Friday, the 24th, $500,000,000 more paralyzed them. The Gold Bank tottered; its assets had been loaned to shaky firms; and this mighty foster-mother of speculation passed into the hands of a receiver.

The guilty authors of all these calamities had slunk away on the first intelligence of the catastrophe, and were now buried in the recesses of Erie Castle in Twenty-third Street.

But ten days before, and Wall Street had been waving with banners of pride and fortune; on Saturday, the 25th, it was a Golgotha—a place of skulls. The celebrated firm of William Heath & Co., it was claimed, were responsible for millions of gold which Fisk, without any authority from them, had ordered to be delivered to them. In this supreme hour, they had nearly one million dollars locked up in the gold bank until clearances could be made. But the margins on the gold they were carrying, had been wiped out in an instant, and the clique owed them an immense sum. Thus, although they had no interest in the conspiracy, they were made to suffer by it. The situation of a firm standing so high, added to the general distrust. Fortunately the gold bank soon released the funds so locked up, and enabled the firm to resume payment.

Ten of the other principal gold dealers were known to have failed. Some of the great banking houses were reported as shaky. No one knew in whom to confide. Many whose assets were in the possession of the gold bank, suspended temporarily. Scarcely one was a gainer by the collapse. The street was full of the rueful faces of those who had settled their short contracts with the clique. They who had sold gold to Speyers for account of Belden, were little better off; their profits were in the form of lawsuits. One bold operator had gone short of gold at 160, to the amount of $7,000,000. When gold fell, he covered his contracts at from 135 to 140, but the parties to whom he had sold failed, and he found instead of making a profit of $2,000,000, that he was saddled with $7,000,000 of gold, which was selling five per cent. below the price at which he had bought. His losses were more than $300,000.

There was, however, one operator who brought in "jetsam and flotsam" out of the wreck. He had, on the morning of the 24th, nothing in the shape of property, except his seat in the Gold Board. Having nothing to lose, and everything to gain, he boldly sold half a million at the highest point, and luckily the dealer to whom he sold was able to respond and receive the gold. On the next day the seller took as his profits more than $100,000.

Night fell, but brought no rest. A crowd of well-dressed barbarians thronged the halls of the Fifth Avenue Hotel. Men sat on chairs, speechless and stupefied by their fall in an hour, from affluence to beggary. Others sought to drown recollection in deep drinking. One man stood leaning against a column, feebly gesticulating, and moaning, "Lost, lost!" Still wilder rumors filled the air, while the gossips stood in groups, and discussed the fate of their fellows. The liabilities of the clique were rated at $20,000,000, all incurred in the space of an hour. What their profits might be, was the cloudiest of problems.

Saturday dawned upon a market in ruins. The fires of yesterday, smouldering, showed the full extent of the disaster, to the crowd which once more packed the sidewalks of Broad Street. Half of the firms which did business in the gold-room were reported as having failed, and the rest were suspected. The street was full of lawyers. The gates of the ring in Broad Street and at Erie Castle were still guarded, while a host of creditors pressed forward, and asserted claims for millions against the chief conspirators. Two aged men could have been seen slowly making their way through the throng. They were Cornelius Vanderbilt, who came to lend courage to their stock cliques, by his presence, and Daniel Drew, who surveyed, with strange, puzzled look, the ruin just wrought by some of his youngest pupils.

But the worst was not yet. The darkness which had fallen upon the market about noon on Friday, that day of financial wrath and doom, still brooded over it—thunderings lightnings and thick darkness. Monday brought no relief. Firms failing by the score, wild faces, painted by ruin a dead white, were flitting about the market. Human scorpions seemed to have been bred in an hour, who turned and stung those who but lately were their dearest friends. The engine of the law was set at work. Equity!—Heaven save the mark!—put on the mask of injunctions, and came into court with unclean hands. The Gold Bank, the Gold Room, the Stock Exchange, and a dozen prominent firms were tied up with orders by the court.

And now money tightened, first to 100, then to 300 per cent. per annum; and four per cent. a day was charged for carrying New York Central.

A new disaster was soon to take place. The house of Lockwood & Co. had a capital of $5,000,000, and an unspotted credit of twenty-five years' standing. Who, on the first of September would have dared to predict the failure of this house? Their name was a tower of strength on 'Change. The senior member of the firm had expended nearly $1,000,000 on a private residence in his native village in Connecticut. Everything promised a lengthened career of wonderful prosperity.

But their time was come. They were loaded down with untold amounts of Pacific Mail, Lake Shore, and Chicago and North-western railroad stocks, on which the loss was millions, and with money at from 300 to 1200 per cent. per annum.

The rooted pillars of the temple began to totter, and the Philistines trembled when Sampson bowed himself. (The Commodore is our Sampson.) Rumor said that he had been thwarted in his pet scheme of consolidation by Lockwood & Co. He had fed fat his grudge by loading them down with Lake Shore stock at high prices.

Wednesday, the market rallied, and everything looked bright, when a dreadful whisper was breathed, —"Lockwood & Co. have failed."

It was true. Then stocks came on the market like a landslide from the mountain tops. Down! down! New York Central fell to 145—seventy-three per cent. from the highest point. Sweeping away a hundred great fortunes as it fell, a hundred more rested on the ability of one man to withstand the pressure. The whole market trembled when a report ran through the street that the ring was now depressing stocks, and that Jim Fisk had sworn that he would break Vanderbilt. Vain boast!

Suddenly Lake Shore sprang up like magic. The Commodore raised millions and carried his point. He held the key to the gates of the West. He had Lake Shore in his grip. Then he snatched at Central. If that should break lower, no one could picture the ruin that would follow. He held it and then hoisted it.

The market felt the stimulant. The friends of Vanderbilt came to the rescue. Telegrams from distant cities poured in, offering uncounted sums to the great consolidator. He was saved.

Of all memorable days in the annals of finance, from the palmiest hour of the merchant princes of ancient Tyre to this year of grace, the closing days of September, 1869, were the most memorable. Vast fortunes won and lost in a breath, but many more lost than won; firms overthrown whose names were a tower of strength; houses hitherto bright and stainless, tarnished by foul slanders; misery and penury inflicted on thousands by one calamity, from the effects of which Wall Street has not yet recovered.

CHAPTER XXXIV.

THE FATE OF AN OPERATOR.

The Two Classes of Operators, the Shifting and the Constant—What Becomes of the Former—Going up " Spouts "—What Men Lose in Speculation besides Money—The Kings of the Market—Dangers of Speculation—A Word of Advice in Conclusion.

E have heretofore divided the men who speculate in Wall Street, into two grand classes, viz.: the shifting, changing class, and the constant class.

Here we might ask, what becomes of these men who swell the crowd and fret their lives away in the courts of the Stock Exchange?

As for the former class, which is continually renewing itself and disappearing, like the month of March, they come in like lions and go out like lambs. Their life in this sphere of activity ranges from a week to a year. Nay! some exhale their financial perfume like the night-blooming Cereus, only for a few brief hours. If they are inclined to go long of stocks, they rarely live to be yearlings in the taurine herd. If they yearn to make short sales, they still more rarely become full-grown bears. This only we know, and we speak as one having authority; they break away from us, they elude us, they depart from among us, and we ask in vain where is Jones, the doughty operator of yore; where is Brown, the late enterprising capitalist; where is Robinson, the restless, the incessant, the intrepid speculator, whose hand dropped the fattest of commissions, from whose tongue emanated the most profitable orders, and who literally turned his spacious pockets inside out, in his eagerness to empty them into our fortunate tills? The echoes reverberating from the marble and granite walls of Broad Street and from the lofty ceilings of the Long Room, return the very unsatisfactory answer, " Where ? "

A pawnbroker's office is sometimes called a "spout." A broker's office also deserves this name. Broad Street, Wall Street, New Street, Exchange Place, what are these but conglomerations of spouts, surrounded by the most hideous of gargoyles, and decorated by grinning caryatides ? Every broker's office is a "spout." The first movement of each and every one of these evanescent operators, when he enters the "street," is to insert his head into one of these "spouts;" his body gradually follows his head, his legs follow his body naturally, his boots are last seen protruding, and often kicking vigorously; a powerful suction still draws him upward, his boots disappear, and a feeling akin to pleasure is experienced, when we reflect that he has at last successfully "gone up the spout." He, too, poor fellow, feels doubtless some satisfaction when emerging with lighter pockets, he can exclaim, smiting his breast, "I have learned my lesson, and though X, Y or Z, the spout-holders, have my money, I have been taught that legitimate business is better than feverish speculation." And with golden sheaves of dearly bought experience, they pass away from the scenes of their labors. Some delve in the broad ri-

ries, some plow the main, some go back to their ancestral farms, or their avuncular merchandise.

Years after, they sometimes return, larger in girt, heavier in jowl, sedate of mien, and point the youthful operator to the old battle-fields, where they fought and bled, and gaze upon perhaps the very spout up which they were sucked by some financial whirlwind; and watch, with amused anxiety, a great variety and different make of alien boots disappearing up the identical tube, with precisely the same contortions and under precisely similar circumstances. These returned exiles are generally stern moralists, and dispense "solid chunks of wisdom" to the busy crowd, which never profits by it, however, to the best of our knowledge and belief; for few are disposed to learn from another's experience, and, as Sidney Smith once remarked, every one thinks he can "edit a review, drive a gig, or farm a small property." So every one thinks he can make a little money in Wall Street of his own motion, and never thanks his elders for the advice of which they are generally so lavish. In fact, like the young woman whose mother cautioned her against dancing because she had "seen the folly of it," the inexperienced listen but "desire to see the folly of it" themselves, and are not satisfied until they do.

But we are trifling. Let us speak now in the language of truth and soberness.

The story of the whole shifting tribe of operators is little else than a dreary catalogue of losses—losses, not of money alone, but of health, character, heart and life.

Men come into Wall Street with fortune, credit, reputation, hope, strength unbruised, confidence in their fellow-men unworn, they leave it without money, credit, or reputation; with shattered nerves, a blunted sensibility, a conscience seared, a faith in mankind destroyed, and hopes crushed by a Giant Despair. They lose everywhere, buying stocks, selling stocks; by failures of their brokers, by frauds of their contractors, by panics, by corners, by tricks and stratagems of the market. They use their reason, their reason fails them and they lose. Then they abandon reason, and trusting to luck, plunge blindly into the vortex which swallows them up speedily and beyond rescue. If they emerge at last, it is to wander on with little relish or power for active, honest toil, and haunted still by the phantoms of their old life.

As for that constant class of operators who, having once entered the stock-market, pursue fortune there till death, they may be subdivided into two classes representing the different extremes, the one of penury, the other enormous wealth. The former crowds the market daily with the haggard faces of men lost beyond remedy. A melancholy spectacle! They stand watching for something which never comes, still hoping forever against hope.

But are the great and wealthy operators more happy? They have, by the brute force of their millions, or by legalized fraud, won fortune from the ruin of thousands. They are looked upon with fear and hatred. Sons of Ishmael, their hands are against every man's hand, and every man's hand is against theirs. If they fall, they fall never to rise again. If they hold their gains, they are, it is true, kings; but like the kings of hell, described by Virgil, they sit chained to golden thrones, and clank their golden fetters.

> Sedet, alternumque sedebit,
> Infelix Theseus.

Their doom is like that of Ixion whirling on his wheel, or that of Sysyphus, to roll a huge stone to the summit of the hill, and then to have it turn and thunder down upon them. They are crushed under the burden of their ill-gotten millions.

The field of speculation was never more dangerous than now. The market is full of stocks *watered* to five times the amount represented eight years since. Men in Wall Street are treading upon the hardly cooled lava crust which covers a financial volcano; an eruption may whelm them any day in one common ruin.

The fate of a stock operator, at the best, is to be avoided, and to avoid it is easy.

Other fields besides speculation spread themselves before the eye. Our bountiful Mother America pours out for us, her children, many good things to be gathered and shaped by the hand of steady industry. The rivers roll down richness and the Savannahs teem and heave with harvests almost spontaneous.

Far away from the furnace blast of Wall Street, the air blows fresh and cool over prairie, woodland and hill-top. Here fortunes may be earned, fame won, happiness enjoyed.

The pulpit, the forum, the studio, the school, lie open for worthy careers.

The workshop, the granary, the wharf, are always humming with pleasant music in the ears of the cheerful toiler. Choose, reader! anything but speculation.

Drive the plow and reap the grain, sail over the sea, sweep the streets even, choose any *honest* calling, no matter how arduous, anything but speculation. Even if endowed by nature with gifts and favored by fortune, you rise to be one of the money kings, your name will then only go down among the gigantic but disreputable shadows which flit through the traditionary landscape of Wall Street.

Book Agents Wanted.

The Publishers of TEN YEARS IN WALL STREET particularly invite the attention of old and experienced Agents, retired Clergymen, Professional Men, School Teachers and young men from the country to the great and wide-spread popularity of the above named book. The great success which has attended our Agents thus far, assure us that it is destined to have a sale second to no other book. We want

ACTIVE, ENERGETIC AGENTS,

everywhere to introduce it throughout the length and breadth of the land :—and to persons of the right kind we are prepared to offer the most liberal and encouraging terms, and grant the exclusive sale on territory assigned. We publish only standard books and sell them exclusively by subscription through our duly authorized Agents. In this way we are enabled to reach the whole reading public and to sell our books at a lower price than they can be purchased in any other way.

AGENTS WILL FIND AN

AGREEABLE AND PROFITABLE BUSINESS

IN SELLING OUR PUBLICATIONS.

Selling books by subscription is productive of a vast amount of good. An Agent with good books is a moral colporteur. He goes into the highways and by-ways of the land and circulates knowledge. where it otherwise would not penetrate. His calling is a noble one and when pursued with right principles improving to his character. We extend to all a cordial invitation to come and see us—or if that is impossible— to write us for information, terms, etc. Address,

WORTHINGTON, DUSTIN & CO., PUBLISHERS,

148 ASYLUM ST., HARTFORD, CONN.

Made in the USA